Speech Recognition and Understanding

Speech Recognition and Understanding

Edited by:

Zoran Gacovski

ARCLER
PRESS

www.arclerpress.com

Speech Recognition and Understanding

Zoran Gacovski

Arcler Press
224 Shoreacres Road
Burlington, ON L7L 2H2
Canada
www.arclerpress.com
Email: orders@arclereducation.com

ISBN: 978-1-77469-184-7 (Hardcover)

DECLARATION

Some content or chapters in this book are open access copyright free published research work, which is published under Creative Commons License and are indicated with the citation. We are thankful to the publishers and authors of the content and chapters as without them this book wouldn't have been possible.

ABOUT THE EDITOR

Dr. Zoran Gacovski has earned his PhD degree at Faculty of Electrical engineering, Skopje. His research interests include Intelligent systems and Software engineering, fuzzy systems, graphical models (Petri, Neural and Bayesian networks), and IT security. He has published over 50 journal and conference papers, and he has been reviewer of renowned Journals. Currently, he is a professor in Computer Engineering at European University, Skopje, Macedonia.

TABLE OF CONTENTS

LIST OF CONTRIBUTORS

Takialddin Al Smadi
Department of Communications and Electronics Engineering, College of Engineering, Jerash University, Jerash, Jordan.

Huthaifa A. Al Issa
Department of Electrical and Electronics Engineering, Faculty of Engineering, Al-Balqa Applied University, Al-Huson College University, Al-Huson, Jordan.

Esam Trad
Departments of Communications and Computer Engineering, Jadara University, Irbid, Jordan.

Khalid A. Al Smadi
Jordanian Sudanese Colleges for Science & Technology, Khartoum, Sudan

Ing-Jr Ding
Department of Electrical Engineering, National Formosa University, No. 64, Wunhua Road, Huwei Township, Yunlin County 632, Taiwan

Yen-Ming Hsu
Department of Electrical Engineering, National Formosa University, No. 64, Wunhua Road, Huwei Township, Yunlin County 632, Taiwan

Peng Dai
School of Electrical and Electronic Engineering, Nanyang Technological University, Singapore

Ing Yann Soon
School of Electrical and Electronic Engineering, Nanyang Technological University, Singapore

Rui Tao
School of Electronic and Information Engineering, Beihang University, China

Patcharin Kamsing
Air-Space Control, Optimization and Management Laboratory, Department of Aeronautical Engineering, International Academy of Aviation Industry, King Mongkut's Institute of Technology, Ladkrabang, Bangkok 10520, Thailand

Peerapong Torteeka
National Astronomical Research Institute of Thailand, ChiangMai 50180, Thailand

Wuttichai Boonpook
Department of Geography, Faculty of Social Sciences, Srinakharinwirot University, Bangkok 10110, Thailand

Chunxiang Cao
State Key Laboratory of Remote Sensing Science, Aerospace Information Research Institute, Chinese Academy of Sciences, Beijing 100101, China
University of Chinese Academy of Sciences, Beijing 100094, China

Chenghao Cai
School of Technology, Beijing Forestry University, No. 35 Qinghua Dong Road, Haidian District, Beijing 100083, China

Yanyan Xu
School of Information Science and Technology, Beijing Forestry University, No. 35 Qinghua Dong Road, Haidian District, Beijing 100083, China

Dengfeng Ke
Institute of Automation, Chinese Academy of Sciences, No. 95 Zhongguancun Dong Road, Haidian District, Beijing 100190, China

Kaile Su
Institute for Integrated and Intelligent Systems, Griffith University, 170 Kessels Road, Nathan, Brisbane, QLD 4111, Australia

Gaurav
Indian Institute of Information Technology & Management, Gwalior, India

Devanesamoni Shakina Deiv
Indian Institute of Information Technology & Management, Gwalior, India

Gopal Krishna Sharma
Indian Institute of Information Technology & Management, Gwalior, India

Mahua Bhattacharya
Indian Institute of Information Technology & Management, Gwalior, India

Hui Wang
School of Information Engineering, Minzu University of China, Beijing 100081, China

Fei Gao
School of Information Engineering, Minzu University of China, Beijing 100081, China

Yue Zhao
School of Information Engineering, Minzu University of China, Beijing 100081, China

Li Yang
School of Information Engineering, Minzu University of China, Beijing 100081, China

Jianjian Yue
School of Information Engineering, Minzu University of China, Beijing 100081, China

Huilin Ma
School of Information Engineering, Minzu University of China, Beijing 100081, China

Hussien A. Elharati
Electrical Engineering Department, High Institute of Science and Technology, Sūqal-Jum'a, Tripoli, Libya

Mohamed Alshaari
Electrical & Computer Engineering Department, Florida Institute of Technology, Melbourne, FL, USA

Veton Z. Këpuska
Electrical & Computer Engineering Department, Florida Institute of Technology, Melbourne, FL, USA

Edvin Pakoci
Department for Power, Electronic and Telecommunication Engineering, Faculty of Technical Sciences, University of Novi Sad, 21000 Novi Sad, Serbia
AlfaNum Speech Technologies, 21000 Novi Sad, Serbia

Branislav Popović
Department for Power, Electronic and Telecommunication Engineering, Faculty of Technical Sciences, University of Novi Sad, 21000 Novi Sad, Serbia
Department for Music Production and Sound Design, Academy of Arts, Alfa BK University, 11000 Belgrade, Serbia

Darko Pekar
Department for Power, Electronic and Telecommunication Engineering, Faculty of Technical Sciences, University of Novi Sad, 21000 Novi Sad, Serbia
AlfaNum Speech Technologies, 21000 Novi Sad, Serbia

Hyacinthe Konan
Ecole Supérieure Africaine des Technologies d'Information et de Communication (ESATIC), Abidjan, C?te d'Ivoire.

Etienne Soro
Ecole Supérieure Africaine des Technologies d'Information et de Communication (ESATIC), Abidjan, C?te d'Ivoire.

Olivier Asseu
Ecole Supérieure Africaine des Technologies d'Information et de Communication (ESATIC), Abidjan, C?te d'Ivoire.
Institut National Polytechnique Félix Houphou?t Boigny (INP-HB), Yamoussoukro, C?te d'Ivoire.

Bi Tra Goore
Institut National Polytechnique Félix Houphou?t Boigny (INP-HB), Yamoussoukro, C?te d'Ivoire.

Raymond Gbegbe
Institut National Polytechnique Félix Houphou?t Boigny (INP-HB), Yamoussoukro, C?te d'Ivoire.

Jean-Yves Fourniols
Laboratory for Analysis and Architecture of Systems, LAAS, University of Toulouse, Toulouse, France

Nadim Nasreddine
Laboratory for Analysis and Architecture of Systems, LAAS, University of Toulouse, Toulouse, France

Christophe Escriba
Laboratory for Analysis and Architecture of Systems, LAAS, University of Toulouse, Toulouse, France

Pascal Acco
Laboratory for Analysis and Architecture of Systems, LAAS, University of Toulouse, Toulouse, France

Julien Roux
Laboratory for Analysis and Architecture of Systems, LAAS, University of Toulouse, Toulouse, France

Georges Soto Romero
Laboratory for Analysis and Architecture of Systems, LAAS, University of Toulouse, Toulouse, France

Stefano Gorla
Department of Electronics, Information and Bioengineering of the Politecnico di Milano, Como, Italy

Sara Comai
Department of Electronics, Information and Bioengineering of the Politecnico di Milano, Como, Italy

Andrea Masciadri
Department of Electronics, Information and Bioengineering of the Politecnico di Milano, Como, Italy

Fabio Salice
Department of Electronics, Information and Bioengineering of the Politecnico di Milano, Como, Italy

Ab Rahman Ahmad
Faculty of Computing and Information Technology-Rabigh, King Abdulaziz University, Rabigh, KSA

Sami M. Halawani
Faculty of Computing and Information Technology-Rabigh, King Abdulaziz University, Rabigh, KSA

Samir K. Boucetta
Faculty of Computing and Information Technology-Rabigh, King Abdulaziz University, Rabigh, KSA

Jimmy Rosales-Huamaní
National University of Engineering, Lima, Peru

José Castillo-Sequera
Alcala University, Madrid, Spain

Fabricio Puente-Mansilla
National University of Engineering, Lima, Peru

Gustavo Boza-Quispe
National University of Engineering, Lima, Peru

Xinguang Li
Cisco School of Informatics, Guangdong University of Foreign Studies, Guangzhou, China

Jiahua Chen
Cisco School of Informatics, Guangdong University of Foreign Studies, Guangzhou, China

Zhenjiang Li
School of Business Adminstrtion, South China University of Technology, Guangzhou, China

Lingyi Zhang
Wuxi No. 1 High School, Wuxi, China.

Junhui Gao
American and European International Study Center, Wuxi, China

Deyu Zhou
School of Computer Science and Engineering, Key Laboratory of Computer Network and Information Integration, Ministry of Education, Southeast University, Nanjing 210096, China

Yulan He
School of Engineering and Applied Science, Aston University, Birmingham B4 7ET, UK

Martine Coene
Language and Hearing Center Amsterdam, Free University Amsterdam, Amsterdam, Netherlands
The Eargroup, Antwerp, Belgium

Stefanie Krijger
Department of Otorhinolaryngology, Ghent University, Ghent, Belgium

Matthias Meeuws
The Eargroup, Antwerp, Belgium

Geert De Ceulaer
The Eargroup, Antwerp, Belgium

Paul J. Govaerts
Language and Hearing Center Amsterdam, Free University Amsterdam, Amsterdam, Netherlands
The Eargroup, Antwerp, Belgium
Department of Otorhinolaryngology, Ghent University, Ghent, Belgium

LIST OF ABBREVIATIONS

AM	Acoustic Model
ANN	Artificial Neural Network
ASR	Automatic Speech Recognition
BP	Back Propagation
CD-GMMs	Context Dependent Gaussian Mixture Models
CER	Character Error Rate
CLASSIFIED	Classified Advertisements Data Set
CMVN	Cepstral Mean and Variance Normalization
CNN	Convolutional Neural Network
CRFs	Conditional Random Fields
CTC	Connectionist Temporal Classification
CVCVCV	Consonant-Vowel Consonant-Vowel Consonant-Vowel
DBN	Deep Belief Network
DCT	Discrete Cosine Transform
DFT	Discrete Fourier Transform calculation
DNN	Deep Neural Network
DP	Dynamic Programming
DTW	Dynamic Time Warping
EM	Expectation Maximization
FFT	Fast Fourier Transform
FLMs	Factored Language Models
GIS	Geographical Information System
GMM	Gaussian Mixture Model
GPUs	Graphics Processing Units
HMM	Hidden Markov Model
HM-SVMs	hidden Markov support vector machines
HVS	Hidden Vector State
ICF	International Classification of functionality Disability and Health
ICT	Information and Communication Technology

IDE	Integrated/Interactive Development Environment
IRM	Information Request Module
IT	Information Technology
KRM	Knowledge Representation Module
LDA	Linear Discriminant Analysis
LM	Language Model
LPC	Linear Predictive Coding
LVCSR	Large Vocabulary Continuous Speech Recognition
MFCC	Mel-frequency Cepstral Coefficient
MLLR	Maximum Likelihood Linear Regression
MLLT	maximum likelihood linear transformation
MLPs	Multilayer Perceptrons
MMSE	Minimum Mean Square Error
MS	Minimum Statistics
MSE	Mean Square Error
NCCF	Normalized Cross-Correlation Function
OCNNs	Object-Based Convolutional Neural Networks
OOV	Out-Of-Vocabulary
PBL	Problem-Based Learning
PDF	Probability Distribution Function
POS	Part-Of-Speech
SA	Speaker Adaptation
SGD	Stochastic Gradient Descent
SoC	System-on-Chip
SRM	Speech Recognition Module
SS	Spectral Subtraction
STSA	Short Time Spectral Amplitude
SVD	Singular Value Decomposition
TDD	Time Division Duplex
TTS	Text to Speech
VHRI	Very High-Resolution Imagery
VoWSN	Voice Wireless Sensor Networks
WC	World Wide Web Consortium
WER	Word Error Rate

WSN	Wireless Sensor Network
WSR	Window Speech Recognition
WWW	World Wide Web

PREFACE

Automatic Speech Recognition (ASR) is one of the greatest technical challenges of modern times and has been attracting the attention of researchers around the world for more than half a century. As with all speech technologies, this is a multidisciplinary problem that requires knowledge in many areas, from acoustics, phonetics and linguistics, to mathematics, telecommunications, signal processing and programming. A special problem is the fact that it is a problem that is extremely language-dependent.

The task of automatic speech recognition is to obtain an appropriate textual record based on the input data in the form of a sound recording of a speech unit (word or sentence). In that way, the speech is practically converted into a text, that is, it is "recognized" what a certain speaker said.

We distinguish ASR systems that recognize isolated words from systems that can also recognize related spoken words. ASR systems can also be sorted by dictionary size (number of words they can recognize), by whether they recognize only fixed, predefined words or are phonetic (practically recognize individual voices), as well as by whether they are dependent or independent from the speaker.

The applications of the ASR system are numerous and depend on its characteristics. In the widest application, ASR systems are speaker-independent. Such systems are used within voice machines, the purpose of which is to automatically provide services to callers (access to information, initiating and controlling transactions, etc.) - with all the flexibility that speech recognition provides. Namely, the caller does not have to move through the complex menu structure using the telephone keypad, but is enabled to immediately say what he wants, which reduces the call time and increases the efficiency of the system - through the number of callers served.

This edition covers different topics from speech recognition and understanding, including: methods and approaches for speech recognition, speech recognition of different languages, applications of speech recognition in different domains, and methods for language understanding.

Section 1 focuses on methods and approaches for speech recognition, describing artificial intelligence for speech recognition based on neural networks; an HMM-like dynamic time warping scheme for automatic speech recognition; direct recovery of clean speech using a hybrid noise suppression algorithm for robust speech recognition system; deep neural learning adaptive sequential Monte Carlo for automatic image and speech recognition; and fast learning method for multilayer perceptrons in automatic speech recognition systems.

Section 2 focuses on speech recognition of different languages, describing development of application specific continuous speech recognition system in Hindi, multitask learning with local attention for Tibetan speech recognition, Arabic speech recognition system based on MFCC and HMMs, using morphological data in language modeling for Serbian large vocabulary speech recognition, and phoneme sequence modeling in the context of speech signal recognition in language Baoule.

Section 3 focuses on applications of speech recognition in different domains, describing an overview of basics speech recognition and autonomous approach for smart home IOT low power devices, BigEar: ubiquitous wireless low-budget speech capturing interface, using speech recognition in learning primary school mathematics via explain, instruct and facilitate techniques, and prototype of a semantic platform with a speech recognition system for visual impaired people.

Section 4 focuses on methods for language understanding, describing English sentence recognition based on HMM and clustering, a comparative study to understanding about poetics based on natural language processing, semi-supervised learning of statistical models for natural language understanding, and linguistic factors influencing speech audiometric assessment.

SECTION 1:
METHODS AND APPROACHES FOR SPEECH RECOGNITION

CHAPTER 1

Artificial Intelligence for Speech Recognition Based on Neural Networks

Takialddin Al Smadi[1], Huthaifa A. Al Issa[2], Esam Trad[3], Khalid A. Al Smadi[4]

[1]Department of Communications and Electronics Engineering, College of Engineering, Jerash University, Jerash, Jordan.

[2]Department of Electrical and Electronics Engineering, Faculty of Engineering, Al-Balqa Applied University, Al-Huson College University, Al-Huson, Jordan.

[3]Departments of Communications and Computer Engineering, Jadara University, Irbid, Jordan.

[4]Jordanian Sudanese Colleges for Science & Technology, Khartoum, Sudan.

ABSTRACT

Speech recognition or speech to text includes capturing and digitizing the sound waves, transformation of basic linguistic units or phonemes,

Citation: Smadi, T. , Al Issa, H. , Trad, E. and Smadi, K. (2015), Artificial Intelligence for Speech Recognition Based on Neural Networks. Journal of Signal and Information Processing, 6, 66-72. doi: 10.4236/jsip.2015.62006.

constructing words from phonemes and contextually analyzing the words to ensure the correct spelling of words that sounds the same. Approach: Studying the possibility of designing a software system using one of the techniques of artificial intelligence applications neuron networks where this system is able to distinguish the sound signals and neural networks of irregular users. Fixed weights are trained on those forms first and then the system gives the output match for each of these formats and high speed. The proposed neural network study is based on solutions of speech recognition tasks, detecting signals using angular modulation and detection of modulated techniques.

Keywords: Speech Recognition, Neural Networks, Artificial Networks, Signals Processing

INTRODUCTION

Artificial intelligence applications have proliferated in recent years, especially in the applications of neural networks where they represent an appropriate tool to solve many problems highlighted by distinguished styles and classification.

The year of 1943 is known as the beginning of the evolution of artificial neural systems.

The first formal model of neurons through a computer model that includes all the necessary elements and the completion and implementation of the electronic form of this model is not practical or reasonable in terms of tech during the vacuum tube. It should be noted that this model has been applied extensively to describe computer hardware for the vacuum tube [1] . Initially, planned tutorial to update connections of nerve cells that are referred to the law educational learning rule HYIP has stated that the information can be stored in the links and connections. It is recognized that learning technology has proved its benefits in the future development of this field. Hip education Act initial contribution in neural network theory had been built and tested in the first study of the neurological computer in the 1950s, where the application contacts automatically and during this stage the term preceptor called the unit represented for neural cell to invent the term world and divorced on the neuron, he pioneered the term frank Rosenblatt in 1958. This invention was a viable training machine learning and classification of certain models by modulating communication components first. In this way it has become along with the imagination of engineers and scientists and a background to the calculations of this type of machinery which is still used today.

In the early 1960s, a new created method called Adaptive Linear Combiner developed a very useful law [2] .

PATTERN RECOGNITION

Automatic recognition, description, classification and grouping patterns are important parameters in various engineering and scientific disciplines such as biology, psychology, medicine, marketing, computer vision, artificial intelligence and remote sensing. The template can be fingerprint images, handwritten words cursive, a human face or the voice signal. Given the pattern, its recognition/classification may be one of the following two tasks [3] .

- Under the supervision of a classification, discriminated analysis, in which the input pattern is defined as a member of a predefined class;
- Unsupervised classification, clustering in which is the class template is unknown.

Recognition of the problem here is as a classification or classification problems, where the classes are defined by either the system designer in a controlled classification or learned based on similar models in unsupervised classification.

These applications include data mining the definition of "plan". For example, he correlations or independently in millions of multidimensional models, document classification effectively search text documents, financial, forecasting, organization and retrieval of multimedia databases and biometrics. The rapidly growing and available computing power, enabling faster processing of huge amounts of data, also promoted the use of complex and diverse methods for classification and analysis of data. At the same time, the demand for automatic pattern recognition is growing due to the presence of large databases and strict requirements speed, accuracy and cost. Design of recognition system template essentially consists of the following three aspects:

- Collection and preprocessing, data reporting;
- Decision-making process;
- Scope dictates the choice of pretreatment technique.

Schema view and decision making models It is recognized that the problem of clearly defined and sufficiently limited recognition will lead to the introduction of the compact model and simple decision-making strategy. Learning from a set of examples is an important and necessary attribute of most systems of recognition template.

The most prominent approaches for pattern recognition are:

- Matching pattern;
- Statistical classification;
- Syntactic or structural conformity and neural networks.

NEURAL NETWORKS

Neural networks consist of a set of nodes that a special type of account collectively and that each node is the standard unit of account and the contract could work in parallel depends on the interactions among themselves and how they relate to some of the scholars are defined as:

- Mathematical models simulating characteristics of biological systems that deal with information in parallel composed of relatively simple elements called.
- Is a simple entity class of algorithms that are formulated in charts (graphs grouped these schemes a large number of algorithms and these algorithms provide solutions to a number of complex problems [4] .

To highlight the activity of neural networks is the process of classification and coding and to highlight the properties of neural networks are:

- Resistance to noise;
- Flexibility in dealing with the distorted images;
- Maximum resistance to tag images of dismembered or partially decomposed;
- Combinations of parallel processes with a large number of operating units that stimulate by interdependence of processes in addition to the stock of information distributed in parallel.

With non-linear operations, i.e. their ability to make non-linear relationships include maps of noise that makes them a good source of ratings and attribution (classification predication);

- High capacity to adapt the system of logarithms and powers of education internal allows the use of internal adjustment that lives in the vicinity of lasting change.

Types of Neural Networks

Possible to identify the most common types of neural networks with input types and learn some common uses as in Table 1 shown [5] [6] .

PROCEDURE WORKS

The method consists of iteratively selecting the most distant score with respect to mean. If this score goes beyond a certain threshold, the score is removed and mean and standard deviation estimations are recalculated. When there are only a few utterances to estimate mean and variance, this method leads to a great improvement. Text dependent and text independent experiments have been carried out by using a telephonic multisession database. The paper presents the inter-relationship between algorithmic research system developments based on the experience from the speaker using mini-problems during the system design process, and presents a model of speech recognition based on artificial neural networks [7] . Figure 1 shows the diagram of the processing of speech signals.

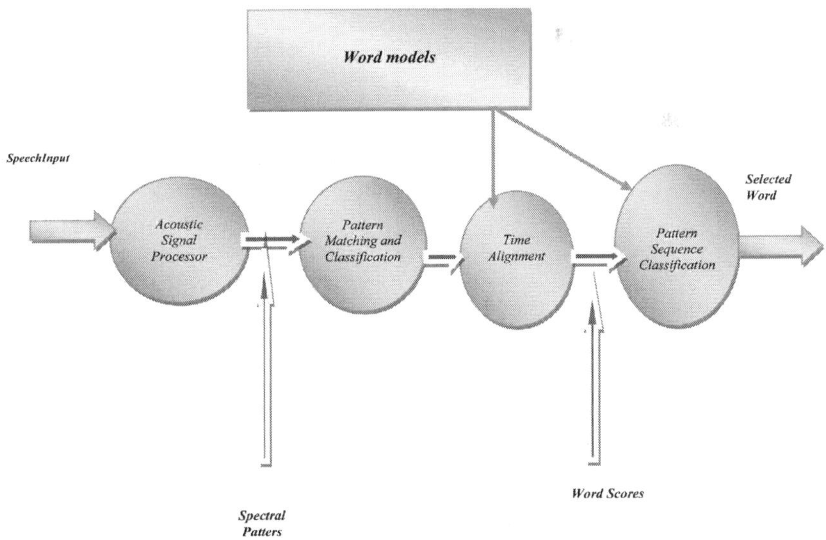

Figure 1. Diagram of the processing of speech signals planning.

Table 1. Types of neural networks and application.

Common uses	Input method	Input type	Types of neural networks
Associated memory to distinguish ASCII characters	Supervised	Binary	Hopfield-Net
Connect with similar dual channel	Supervised	Binary	Hammin_Net
Assembly (adaptive resonance theory)	Supervised	Binary	Carpenter/grassbery classifier
Discrimination and classification of simple shapes	Supervised	Continuous	Perceptron
Featuring complex shapes and classification	Supervised	Continuous	Multi-layer perceptron
Evaluation of vector and speech, and analogy to biological neural networks	Supervised	Continuous	Kohonenself organizing feature map

- Present study of artificial neural networks for speech recognition task. Neural network size influence on the effectiveness of detection of phonemes in words. The research methods of speech signal parameterization. Learn about how to use linear prediction analysis, a temporary way of learning of the neural network for recognition of phonemes. The proposed way of teaching as input requires only the transcription of words from the training set and do not require any manual segmentation of words;
- Development and research of the methods for diagnosing and detecting modulated signals;
- Software implementation and pilot testing on real signals of neural network methods for processing.

Recognition Process Recognition Algorithm

- Input signal into the computer and select word boundaries;
- Allocation of parameters characterizing the signal spectrum;

- The use of artificial neural network to evaluate the degree of proximity of acoustic parameters;
- Comparison with standards in the dictionary [8] .

Voice signal as an input to a neural network, after processing the audio data received an array of segments of the signal. Each segment corresponds to a set of numbers that characterize the amplitude spectra of a signal, to prepare for the calculation for the signal outputs of the neural network to write all the numbers shows in Table 2, where a row which is a set of numbers of each frame.

Where I is the number of values of a set of numbers, N is the number of sets of numbers (frame signal after slicing). The number of input and output neurons is known, each of the input neurons corresponds to one set of numbers, and the output layer only one neuron, which corresponds to the desired value of the signal recognition. Table 3 shows the parameter definition uses in this research as shown in Figure 2.

Equations

To calculate the output of the neural network, it's a must complete the following successive steps [9] :

Step 1: Initiate all contexts of all the neurons in the hidden layer;

Step 2: Apply the first set of numbers to the neural network. Calculate the output of the hidden layer.

$$y_j = f\left(\sum_{i=1}^{1} \omega_{ij} X_{1i} + \beta_i + \omega_j X_j\right) \quad (1)$$

F(x)—non-linear activation function

$$y_j = \frac{1}{1+e^{-\alpha S_j}} \quad (2)$$

for the numbers from 0 to 9.

To recognize the one number you need to build your own neural network it's a must to build 10 of neural networks. Database of over 250 words (numbers from 0 to 9) with different variations of pronunciation, base randomly divided into two equal parts-tutorial and sample tests. When training neural network recognition of one number, for number 5, the desired output of the neural network needs to be unit for the training set with the number 5 and the remainder is zero.

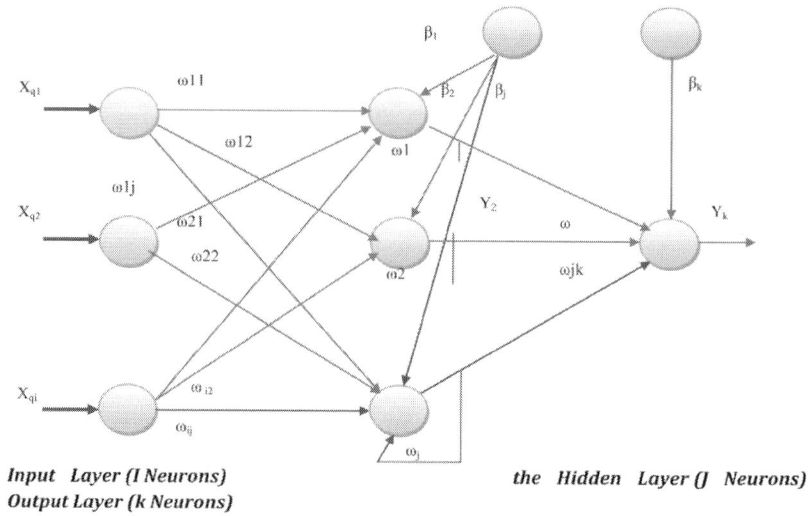

Figure 2. The structure of a neural network with a feedback.

Table 2. Description of a set of speech signal.

Frame	**1-value**	**2-value**	**…**	**I-value**
1-Frame	x_{11}	x_{12}	…	x_{1I}
2-Frame	X_{21}	X_{22}	…	X_{2I}
…	…	…	…	…
N-Frame	X_{N1}	X_{N2}	…	X_{NI}

Table 3. Parameters definition.

Name	**Definition**
x_{qi}	i-th q is the input value to a set of numbers
y_j	Output j-neuron layer
ω_{ij}	The weight of the link connecting the i-th neuron with the j-th neuron
ω_j	weight feedback
β_j	Weight feedback j-th neuron; the offset of the j-the neuron layer

Neural network training is carried out through the consistent presentation of the training set, with simultaneous tuning scales in accordance with a specific procedure, until around the variety of configuration error reaches an acceptable level. Error in the system function will be calculated by the following formula:

$$E = \frac{1}{2N}\sum_{i=1}^{N}\left(y_{ki} - d_i\right)^2 \quad (3)$$

where N is the number of training samples processed by neural network examples the real output of the neural network.

A prototype of a neuron is nerve cell biology. A neuron consists of a cell body, or soma, and two types of external wood-like branches: Axon and dendrites. The cell body contains the nucleus, which holds information on hereditary characteristics and plasma with molecular tools for the production and transmission of elements of the neuron of the necessary materials. A neuron receives signals from other neurons through the dendrites and transmits signals generated by the cells of the body, along the axon, which at the end of branches into the fiber, the endings of synapses [1] [3] .

Mathematical model of a neuron described democratic ratio:

$$y = f\left(s\right), swx_i w_i wb \quad (4)$$

where w_i is the synapse, the weight (b)-offset value, s is the input signal, y-signal output neuron, n is the number of inputs to the neuron, f-function is activated. Technical model of a neuron is represented in Figure 3.

Block diagram of a neuron: $x_1, x_2, \cdots, x_n$ -input neuron; $w_1, w_2, \cdots,$ the W_n-a set of weights; F(S) is a function of activation; y-output signal, neuro control performs simple operations like weighted summation, treating the result of nonlinear threshold conversion. Feature of neural network approach is that the structure of the simple homogeneous elements allows you to meet the challenges of the complex relationships between items. The structure of relations defines the functional properties of the network as a whole.

The functional features of neurons and how they combine into a network structure determines the features of neural networks. To meet the challenges of the most adequate identification and management are multilayer neural networks direct action or layered perceptions. When designing neurons together in layers, each of which handles vector signals from the previous layer. Minimum implementation is smiling two-layer neural network, consisting of the input (switch gear), intermediate (hidden), and the output layer [10] (Figure 4).

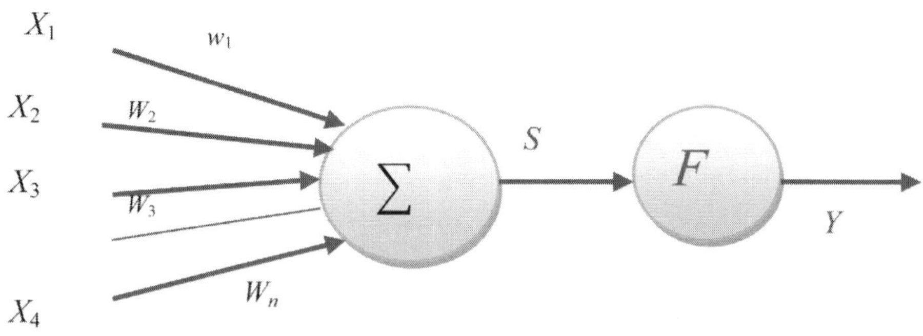

Figure 3. Technical model of a neuron is represented.

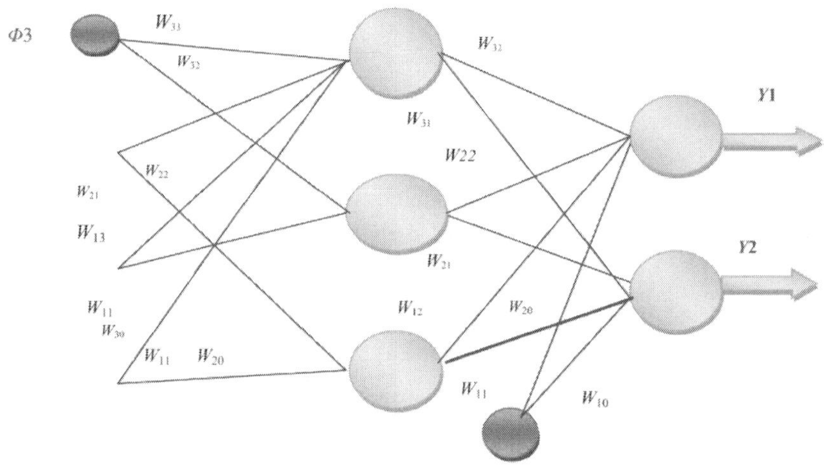

Figure 4. Structural diagram of two-layer neural network.

Implementation of the model of two-layer neural network of direct action has the following mathematical representation:

$$y(\theta) = F_i\left(\sum_{j-1}^{nh} W_{ij} f_i\left(\sum_{j-1}^{nh} w_{ij}\phi_j + w_{jo}\right) + W_{jo}\right) \tag{5}$$

where the dimension of the vector inputs is: nφ φ neural network; nh-the number of neurons in the hidden layer; θ-vector of the configurable parameters of the neural network, which includes weights and neuron-by offset (w_{ji}, W_{ij}); $f_j(x)$-activation function for the hidden layer neurons; $F_i(x)$-activation function neuron in the output layer.

The most important feature of neural network method is the possibility of parallel processing. This feature if there are a large number of international neural connections enables to significantly accelerate the process of signet-data processing [6] . A possibility of processing of speech signals in real time. The neural network has qualities that are inherent in the so-called artificial intelligence [11] .

CONCLUSION

Model of speech recognition was based on artificial neural networks. This was investigated to develop a learning neural network using genetic algorithm. This approach was implemented in the system identification numbers, coming to the realization of the system of recognition of voice commands. A system of automatic recognition of speech keywords that were associated with the processing of telephone calls or a sphere of security was developed. The accuracy level of forecasting on the basis of present data set experience was always better.

REFERENCES

1. Childer, D.G. (2004) The Matlab Speech Processing and Synthesis Toolbox. Photocopy Edition, Tsinghua University Press, Beijing, 45-51.
2. Chien, J.T. (2005) Predictive Hidden Markov Model Selection for Speech Recognition. IEEE Transaction on Speech and Audio Processing, 13.
3. Luger, G. and Stubblefield, W. (2004) Artificial Intelligence: Structures and Strategies for Complex Problem Solving. 5th Edition, The Benjamin/Cummings Publishing Company, Inc. http://www.cs.unm.edu/~luger/ai-final/tocfull.htm
4. Choudhary, A. and Kshirsagar, R. (2012) Process Speech Recognition System Using Artificial Intelligence Technique. International Journal of Soft Computing and Engineering (IJSCE), 2.
5. Ovchinnikov, P.E. (2005) Multilayer Perceptron Training without Word Segmentation for Phoneme Recognition. Optical Memory & Neural Networks (Information Optics), 14, 245-248.
6. Guo, X.Y., Liang, X. and Li, X. (2007) A Stock Pattern Recognition Algorithm Based on Neural Networks. Third International Conference on Natural Computation, 2.
7. Dai, W.J. and Wang, P. (2007) Application of Pattern Recognition and Artificial Neural Network to Load Forecasting in Electric Power System. Third International Conference on Natural Computation, 1.
8. Shahrin, A.N., Omar, N., Jumari, K.F. and Khalid, M. (2007) Face Detecting Using Artificial Neural Networks Approach. First Asia International Conference on Modelling & Simulation.
9. Lin, H., Hou, W.S., Zhen, X.L. and Peng, C.L. (2006) Recognition of ECG Patterns Using Artificial Neural Network. Sixth International Conference on Intelligent Systems Design and Applications, 2.
10. Al Smadi, T.A. (2013) Design and Implementation of Double Base Integer Encoder of Term Metrical to Direct Binary. Journal of Signal and Information Processing, 4, 370.
11. Takialddin Al Smadi Int. An Improved Real-Time Speech Signal in Case of Isolated Word Recognition. Journal of Engineering Research and Applications, 3, 1748-1754.

CHAPTER 2

An HMM-Like Dynamic Time Warping Scheme for Automatic Speech Recognition

Ing-Jr Ding and Yen-Ming Hsu

Department of Electrical Engineering, National Formosa University, No. 64, Wunhua Road, Huwei Township, Yunlin County 632, Taiwan

ABSTRACT

In the past, the kernel of automatic speech recognition (ASR) is dynamic time warping (DTW), which is feature-based template matching and belongs to the category technique of dynamic programming (DP). Although DTW is an early developed ASR technique, DTW has been popular in lots of applications. DTW is playing an important role for the known

Citation: Ing-Jr Ding, Yen-Ming Hsu, "An HMM-Like Dynamic Time Warping Scheme for Automatic Speech Recognition", Mathematical Problems in Engineering, vol. 2014, Article ID 898729, 8 pages, 2014. https://doi.org/10.1155/2014/898729.

Kinect-based gesture recognition application now. This paper proposed an intelligent speech recognition system using an improved DTW approach for multimedia and home automation services. The improved DTW presented in this work, called HMM-like DTW, is essentially a hidden Markov model- (HMM-) like method where the concept of the typical HMM statistical model is brought into the design of DTW. The developed HMM-like DTW method, transforming feature-based DTW recognition into model-based DTW recognition, will be able to behave as the HMM recognition technique and therefore proposed HMM-like DTW with the HMM-like recognition model will have the capability to further perform model adaptation (also known as speaker adaptation). A series of experimental results in home automation-based multimedia access service environments demonstrated the superiority and effectiveness of the developed smart speech recognition system by HMM-like DTW.

INTRODUCTION

Multimedia and home automation services have been popular and necessary techniques in humans' home life. Among multimedia access and home automation applications, automatic speech recognition (ASR) is an important mainstream technique and plays a kernel role for improving the interaction between home members and home devices [1]. The development of speech recognition methods with satisfactory recognition performances in multimedia and home automation applications has been a challengeable issue. This paper will propose an improved dynamic time warping (DTW) speech recognition method, called HMM-like DTW, which brings the statistical model idea of the typical hidden Markov model (HMM) into the design of conventional DTW. The presented HMM-like DTW method demonstrated its superiority in recognition accuracy in the home media access and automation application.

From the viewpoint of application scenarios, ASR techniques can be categorized into two classes, speech understanding and voice command operations. This paper focuses on the aspect of the voice command operation of ASR. Human-machine interactions and media device operations by voice commands are extremely proper in a home environment [2]. For example, voice-command-based recognition operation can increase the convenience of humans' home life in home device control and home media access. Speech recognition using voice commands not only will save a lot of time and manpower but also is helpful for automatic recognition operations without any human operators. However, speech recognition is encountering a lot of challenges due to too many unexpected variables and adverse factors, such as the variety of accents and speech habits on testing speakers [3]. The testing speaker utters the same words for the operated voice command, but these uttered commands will not have exactly the same result so that speech recognition with the correct recognition outcome in each recognition test will be hard to achieve. To overcome this problem, related works on speech recognition enhancements have been quite common in the recent years, and most of those studies aimed at increasing the reliability of the recognition result by improving the recognition system [4] or reducing the mismatch phenomenon between a new speaker and the speech recognition system by performing machine learning schemes [5] or adaptive designs [6] on original speech recognition system.

The current mainstream speech recognition methodologies are hidden Markov models (HMM) [7], artificial neural network (ANN) [8], and DTW [9, 10]. HMM and ANN are categorized into the class of model-based recognition methods, and DTW belongs to the feature-based recognition category technique. Compared with model-based speech recognition, feature-based speech recognition does not involve adopting a statistical model. Training a classification model in advance is not required for feature-based speech recognition and therefore this method is generally considered a conceptually simple and direct recognition technique. DTW, belonging to the dynamic programming (DP) methodology [9], is a type of feature-based speech recognition. Although lots of ASR-related studies focus on HMM and ANN techniques, DTW still has its technical position due to the low complexity recognition calculations and high recognition accuracy, which will be the necessary factor in multimedia and home automation applications [10]. Nowadays, the popular DTW speech recognition has been seen to be largely utilized in the sensing-based applications [11], such as the Microsoft Kinect sensing device.

For model-based HMM or feature-based DTW speech recognition, the most important technical issue is how to effectively increase the recognition rate. In fact, improving the recognition performance of a speech recognition system has been a challenging problem. In HMM speech recognition, speaker adaptation (SA), sometimes also known as HMM model adjustments, has been widely used for overcoming the problem [6]. Speaker adaptation in HMM speech recognition will continually tune the statistical model parameters of HMM such as mean and covariance parameters using the information of the speaker's uttered data, and therefore the recognition system will not be strange to the speaker again after a series of model parameter adjustments [6]. For the feature-based DTW speech recognition technique, however, such speaker adaptation methodology cannot be employed due to the lack of a statistical model. Although related investigations on improving DTW speech recognition have been conducted in recent years [12, 13], most of these DTW-related studies have either developed improved template-matching algorithms [12] or provided modified schemes for a DTW operation optimization framework [13] for increasing the robustness of the recognition system. Speaker adaptation studies on DTW speech recognition are extremely rare.

In the author's previous work [5], speaker learning for DTW speech recognition has been explored where the learning strategy is interpolated into traditional DTW. Under the scheme, the DTW system is additionally equipped with the developed machine learning approaches for modifying the database containing referenced templates of speech patterns [5]. However, the fundamental structure of DTW in [5] is almost still the same as that of conventional DTW except the additionally given machine learning scheme for the database of DTW referenced templates, both of which still belong to feature-based recognition techniques. The DTW system learning performance by the developed work in [5] will still be largely restricted due to the essence of invariable feature-based template matching and the lack of a statistical recognition model when performing recognition. In order to solve the problem, this paper presents an HMM-like DTW approach, which is to thoroughly change the fundamental structure of DTW operations by establishing an HMM-like recognition model. By transforming feature-based into model-based recognition methodologies, the developed HMM-like DTW in this work will behave as the modeling technique of HMM speech recognition and therefore will have all benefits of HMM model-based speech recognition category techniques including the abovementioned speaker adaptation techniques used in model-based speech recognition. Different to the improved DTW approach in [5], the proposed HMM-like DTW in this work is essentially a modeling recognition technique, and the developed HMM-like recognition model for DTW will provide a crucial framework for the development of possible speaker adaptation techniques on DTW speech recognition. The popular HMM speaker adaptation techniques [14, 15] with proper modifications will be able to be extended to the proposed HMM-like DTW herein, which can effectively solve the problem of learning restriction of developed DTW machine learning in [5]. In summary, the proposed

HMM-like DTW approach in this study has several advantages compared with those without

- better performances in recognition accuracy and more flexibility in recognition system alignments,
- a statistical HMM-like classification model with the ability of model adjustments for recognition performance improvements as compared with those enhanced DTW methods that only aim at dynamical programming design of template matching of acoustic features (e.g., [12, 13]),
- more convenience and greater efficiency for further extensions of speaker adaptation, compared with those feature-based DTW system learning methods (e.g., the machine learning method for just the adaptive design of the DTW referenced template database [5]).

The remainder of this paper is organized as follows. Section 2 details the theoretical formulation of DTW speech recognition. Section 3 introduces the concept of hidden Markov model that is employed in the developed HMM-like DTW, followed by the formulation of HMM-like DTW speech recognition, containing model initialization of DTW referenced templates, recursive model training of DTW referenced templates, and recognition estimates of the established HMM-like DTW model in the testing phase. Section 4 presents the experiment results where the effectiveness and performance of presented HMM-like DTW are demonstrated, compared with conventional DTW. Finally, Section 5 provides concluding remarks.

SPEECH RECOGNITION BY DTW

The conventional DTW speech recognition procedure will be illustrated in this section. As mentioned before, DTW is belonging to dynamic programming category techniques. DTW speech recognition combines both time-warping and template-matching calculations for achieving the purpose of speech pattern recognition [9].

The framework of DTW speech recognition is depicted in Figure 1. As shown in Figure 1, DTW speech recognition contains two phases, the training phase and the testing phase. In the training phase of DTW, the main work is to establish the database of reference templates, which could be employed to complete the template matching work in the DTW testing phase. The primary mission of the DTW testing phase is to perform template matching between the testing template and the reference template. When computing the similarity degree between the testing template and the reference template, the low distortion between the two of them suggests a high similarity degree. As could be seen in Figure 1, feature extraction is an important and crucial procedure for such DTW feature-based recognition method. DTW template matching attempts to find an optimal comparison path between the testing template feature vector and the referenced template feature vector. Figure 2 shows the feature extraction procedure indicated in Figure 1. At the end of feature extraction, the input speech signal will be transformed into the parameter of speech features, LPC parameters of the time domain, or linear predicted cepstral coefficient (LPCC) parameters of the frequency domain. This paper adopts the LPCC parameter to be the feature of speech signals in the DTW template matching work.

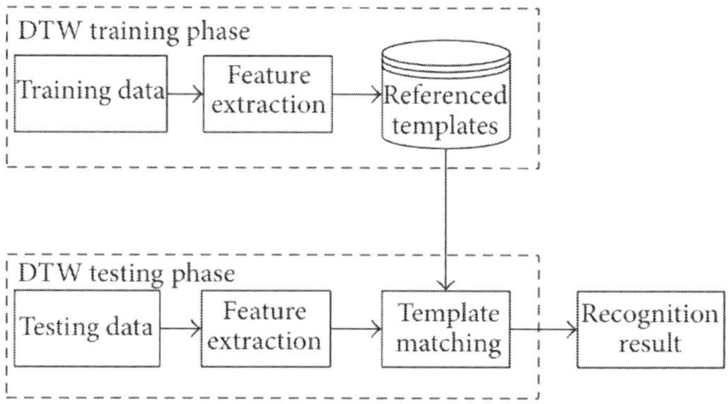

Figure 1: Frameworks of DTW-based speech recognition.

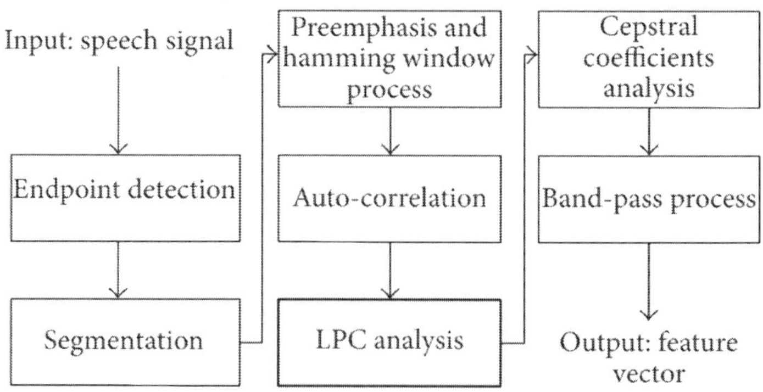

Figure 2: Feature extraction of speech signals.

The DTW template matching operation between the testing LPC feature and the referenced LPC feature is described herein. The testing utterance is composed of T frames and an arbitrary frame (a feature vector), denoted by t. The reference template consists of R frames and the arbitrary frame, indicated as r. The distortion between the T and R frames can be represented as $[T(t), R(r)]$. The starting point and the end point of the comparison path are $((1), R(1)) = (1, 1)$ and $(T(M), R(M)) = (T, R)$, respectively. Based on these DTW operational settings, the DTW distance, d, from the optimal comparison path can be derived using (1). The arbitrary frame t in the testing data is generally not equal to the arbitrary frame r in the indices reference template [9]. Consider

$$D = \min \sum_{m=1}^{M} d\left(T\left(m\right), R\left(m\right)\right). \tag{1}$$

Assuming that the point $((0), R(0)) = (0, 0)$ and $d(0, 0) = 0$, the accumulated distance that selects the optimal source path can be represented as

$$\min D\left(t, r\right) = \min_{(t-1, r-1)} \left\{\min D\left(t-1, r-1\right) + d\left(t, r\right)\right\}, \tag{2}$$

where $\min D(t, r)$ is the shortest distance from the starting position to position (t, r). In the testing recognition of DTW, the recognition outcome is the label of the referenced template with the smallest value of $\min(t, r)$.

Note that, in the previous work on DTW enhancements [5], machine learning schemes to drive the DTW recognition system to be adaptive with a new speaker are to provide proper management on the database of referenced templates (see Figure 1). However, such scheme in [5] will still encounter inefficiency and ineffectiveness on system adaptation due to the lack of a statistical model. A modeling technique for DTW, HMM-like DTW, will be presented in the following section.

THE PROPOSED HMM-LIKE DTW APPROACH FOR SPEECH RECOGNITION

This section describes the proposed improved DTW, HMM-like DTW, for speech recognition. At the beginning of this section, the basic methodology of HMM will be primarily introduced.

Hidden Markov Model (HMM)

HMM is a statistical probability model, which is composed of a series of state transitions. HMM is essentially a hidden Markov chain that could be used to simulate and then model acoustic signals. All frames in the state will have the same characteristics in a Markov chain. In the methodology of HMM, the probability model is employed to describe the pronunciation characteristics of a segment of uttered speech signals. In this uttering process of a speaker, the segment of acoustic signal will be viewed as a continuous state transition in a Markov model. HMM state transition will be the primary work in an HMM-based speech recognition system. Figure 3 illustrates the frequently used left-to-right state transition in HMM speech recognition. As shown in Figure 3, there are *N* states in total in the HMM model; the term a_{ij} denotes the state transition between the state i and the state *j*. Only two ways of state transitions could be done in the HMM model of Figure 3, staying at the same state or going to the next state.

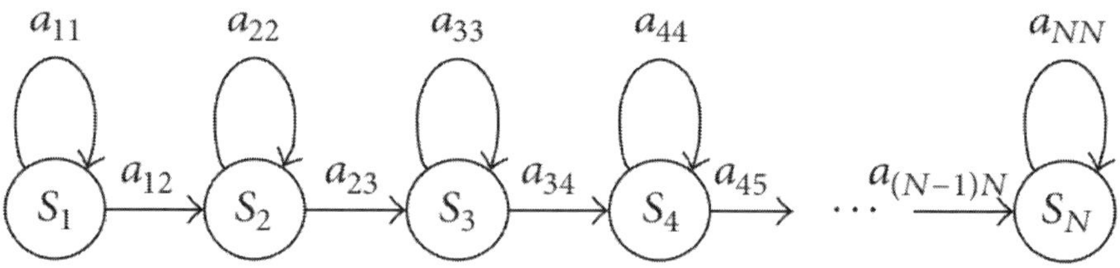

Figure 3: Left-to-right HMM state transition schemes in speech recognition applications.

HMM-based speech recognition is usually used in the keywords-spotting voice command operation applications. As shown in Figure 4, the keywords voice command "“電視”" (pronounced in Mandarin) is modeled as the HMM state sequence composed of 12 states, two 3-state initial parts and one 6-state final part. In Mandarin speech recognition using HMM, the subsyllable method is used to establish the HMM model of each keyword voice command. In general, there are 3 states in the initial part and 6 states in the final part. In this work, the proposed HMM-like DTW approach will establish the acoustic model for each of the DTW referenced template database using HMM-like left-to-right state sequences of the keyword voice command, which will be described in detail in the following section.

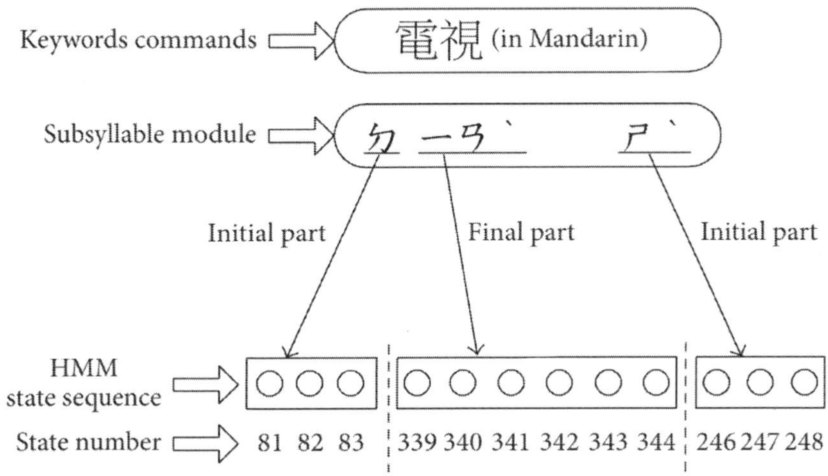

Figure 4: HMM state sequence of the keyword voice command "電視" in Mandarin.

HMM-LIKE DTW

The basic idea of statistical HMM models introduced in the previous section will be incorporated into the design of the HMM-like speech recognition system. Figure 5 depicts the framework of the proposed HMM-like DTW speech recognition, which is different to conventional feature-based DTW and is belonging to a model-based technique. As could be seen in conventional DTW of Figure 1 and in the developed HMM-like DTW of Figure 5, the primary work of HMM-like DTW is to model the DTW system by establishing the HMM-like acoustic model for each of DTW referenced templates of keywords voice commands. HMM-like DTW contains mainly two design phases, the training phase to model DTW referenced templates and the testing phase to use the established acoustic models of TW referenced templates for performing the recognition of the test utterances. The training phase design of HMM-like DTW will be provided in Sections 3.2.1 and 3.2.2, which primarily describe model initialization and recursive model training of DTW keywords referenced templates, respectively. Section 3.2.3 describes how HMM-like DTW with established acoustic models of DTW keywords templates in Sections 3.2.1 and 3.2.2 is used for recognition calculations in the testing phase. As could be seen in Figure 1 and Figure 5, proposed HMM-like DTW changes template matching of conventional DTW as model recognition estimating.

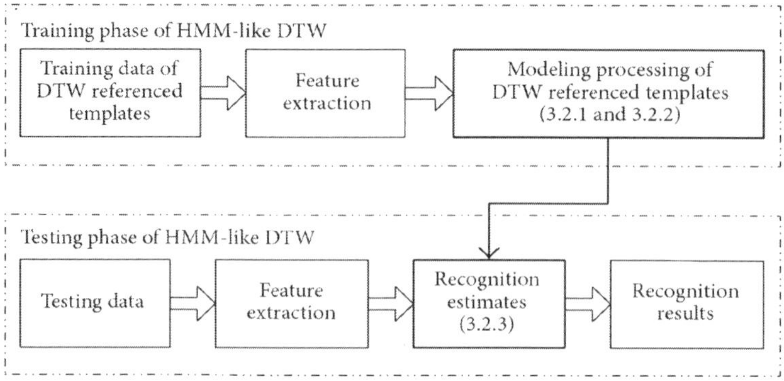

Figure 5: Frameworks of model-based HMM-like DTW speech recognition systems.

Model Initialization of DTW Referenced Templates

The proposed HMM-like DTW will perform the model initialization first in the beginning of the model training phase. Model initialization of DTW referenced templates is to establish the initial model for certain keyword voice command template. The initial model will be represented as the HMM-like state sequence. Figure 6 shows the averaged segmentation procedure for model initialization of certain DTW keywords command template. In the model initialization of the DTW referenced template, averaged segmentation is an important task for establishing the initial state sequence. Averaged segmentation divides each of the training data into a series of acoustic segments with the same numbers of acoustic frames. As shown in Figure 6, *N* states are set for certain keywords voice command "“打開電視,”" pronounced in Mandarin, where the DTW referenced template "打開電 視" is modeled as the state sequence with *N* states. Each of *N* states denotes the characteristics of a series of acoustic frames within certain segment of continuous time and therefore is represented as the corresponding averaged frame segmentation information of the training data. For example, the state S_1 in Figure 6 reveals the statistical information of frames of *N* training data, $Training\text{-}data_1$, $Training\text{-}data_2$,..., and $Training\text{-}data_n$, at the first time interval. The state S_1 is derived using (3) as follows:

$$S_1 = \frac{(f_{11} + f_{12}) + (f_{21} + f_{22} + f_{23}) + \cdots + (f_{n1} + f_{n2})}{2 + 3 + \cdots + 2}. \quad (3)$$

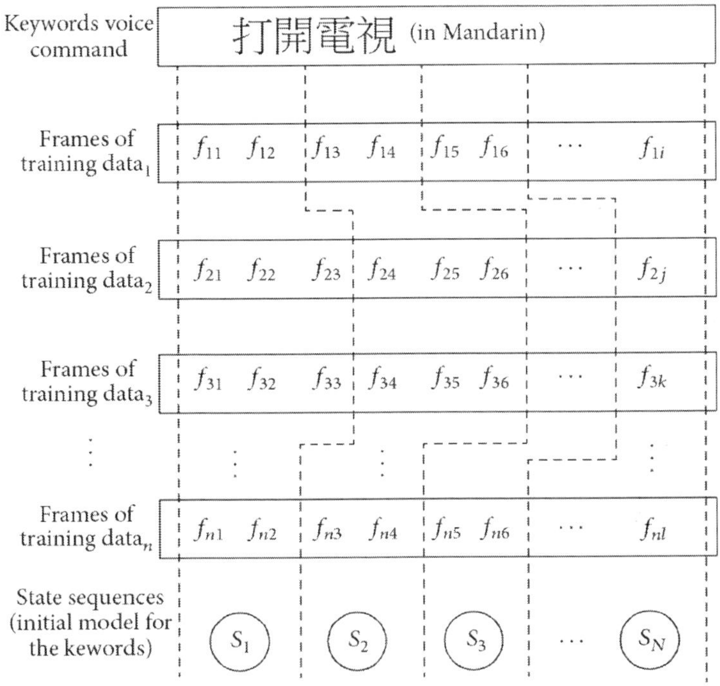

Figure 6: Averaged segmentation for model initialization of certain DTW keywords command template.

The initial model, the state sequence with N states, of certain DTW keywords command referenced template will be further reestimated for achieving the optimal recognition performance using a recursive model training procedure, which will be presented in the following section.

Recursive Model Training of DTW Referenced Templates

Model initialization of DTW referenced templates is to establish the initial model for each of DTW keyword voice command template. These initial models are further tuned for achieving the optimal performance on recognition accuracy. The developed recursive model training procedure in HMM-like DTW is depicted in Figure 7. As could be seen in Figure 7, the Viterbi algorithm is employed to carry out resegmentation of acoustic frames of training data. After doing the Viterbi algorithm, the new model is estimated in the iteration. It is noted that in this training procedure a checking process of the index ξ is performed to verify the performance of the trained state sequence model. The index ξ is the Euclidean distance and is determined using (4) as follows:

$$\xi = \sum_{i=1}^{n} \sqrt{\sum_{j=1}^{k} \left(X_{ij} - \widetilde{X}_{ij}\right)^2}, \tag{4}$$

where ξ is the error value between the current and the last state sequence models; Xij denotes the Gaussian mean value of the jth dimension of the ith state of the current new state sequence model trained in this iteration; X⊠ij is the Gaussian mean value of the jth dimension of the ith state of the past old state sequence model trained in the last iteration. Note that the ideal value of ξ is expected to approach zero in this recursive model training of DTW referenced templates. However, such ideal trained model is hard to be established in the real training situation. The threshold T is set to decide if the value of the calculated ξ is acceptable for model parameter convergence in the recursive model training. When the value of ξ is limited to be smaller than the value of the preset threshold T, the overall recursive training procedure is finished and then the estimated state sequence model of DTW reference templates will have the highest performances in recognition accuracy in the test phase.

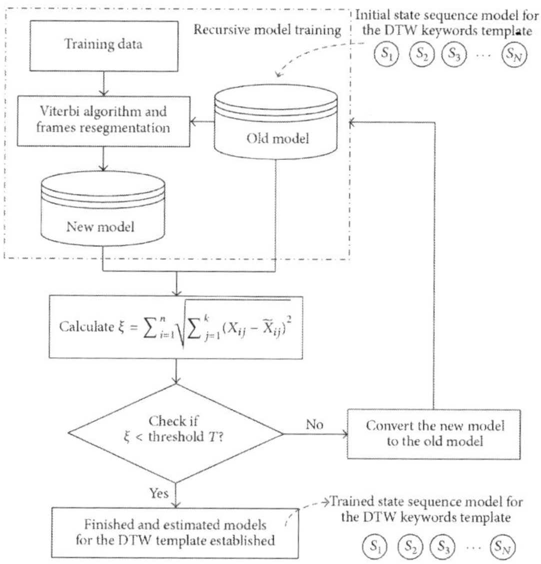

Figure 7: The developed recursive model training procedure in proposed HMM-like DTW.

Recognition Estimates of HMM-Like DTW in the Testing Phase

As mentioned in the previous section, when finishing recursive model training of DTW referenced templates, trained state sequence models for the corresponding DTW keywords templates could be used for online speech recognition in the testing phase. An HMM-like DTW speech recognition system with M keywords command templates in the conventional DTW referenced template dataset will have M trained state sequence models for each of the DTW referenced templates. When performing the recognition estimate of HMM-like DTW in the testing phase, the likelihood degree between each of those M trained state sequence models and the input test utterance of a new test speaker will be calculated. The label of the trained state sequence model with the highest value of the likelihood degree will be the recognition outcome. In this work, a Viterbi-like approach is developed for performing the likelihood degree estimates. Figure 8 depicts the operation of the presented Viterbi-like approach in the HMM-like recognition test phase. Figure 8 depicts the operation of the presented Viterbilike approach in the HMM-like recognition test phase. Viterbi-like approach belongs to the category of dynamical programming in essence, and therefore a global optimization result will be calculated when completing the overall path (P) programming. In this work, the score function $\delta(i)$ is defined as in (5), given the observed set of T speech frames, $O = \{o_1, o_2,...,o_T\}$,

$$\delta_t (i) = \max_{s_1,s_2,...,s_N} P\left(s_1, s_2, \ldots, s_N = S_i, o_1, o_2, \ldots, o_T \mid \lambda\right), \tag{5}$$

where $\delta_t(i)$ has the largest probability at time t and at state S_i; λ is the trained model for each of DTW keywords referenced templates as mentioned in the previous section. $\delta_{t+1}(i)$ is computed as follows using $\delta(i)$ by induction:

$$\delta_{t+1} (j) = \left[\max_i \delta_t (i)\, a_{ij}\right] b_j \left(o_{t+1}\right), \tag{6}$$

where a_{ij} is the state transition probability of going from state S_i to state S_j; $b_j(o_{t+1})$ denotes the Gaussian distribution probability of the observed frame o_{t+1} given the state S_j. The Viterbi-like approach in this study is to solve the iterative procedure of (5) and (6) and the state sequence that has the maximum likelihood will be searched if one keeps tracking of all the states which maximize (5).

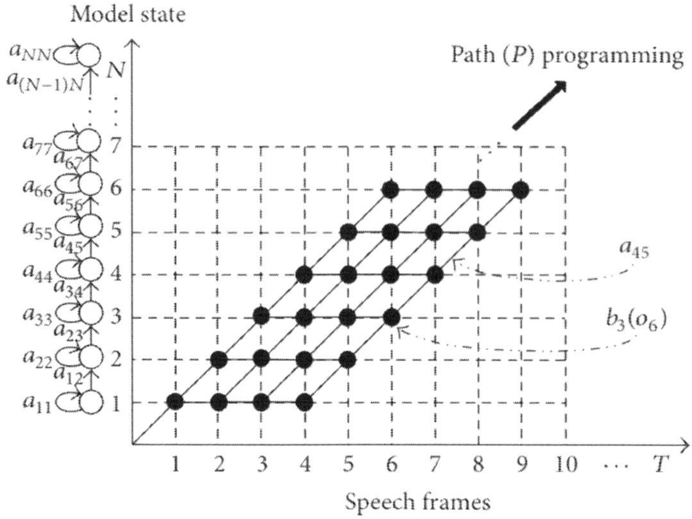

Figure 8: Recognition calculations of HMM-like DTW by the Viterbi-like method in the test phase.

EXPERIMENTS AND RESULTS

The proposed HMM-like DTW speech recognition is performed in the application of multimedia and home automation services. The HMM-like DTW speech recognition system adopts the voice command operation mechanism where a set of DTW keywords referenced template models is established in advance. Table 1 shows the voice command set containing 8 keywords that denote command operations of noticing the strong wing (the index a), opening the light (the index b), showing the temperature (the index c), turning off the air conditioner (the index d), adjusting the temperature (the index e), turning on the TV set (the index f), turning up the volume (the index g), and selecting the TV channel (the index h).

In the HMM-like DTW speech recognition experiments, the sampling rate of speech signals is 44.1 KHz; the resolution of the speech sample is set as 16 bits; the number of channels is one (i.e., mono settings); for each acoustic frame, the frame size is set as 20 ms with a 10 ms frame overlap; the LPCC feature is adopted on feature extraction, and each feature parameter of the acoustic frame is composed of the 10-dimension linear prediction cepstrum parameters. The HMM-like DTW speech recognition experiment is divided into two phases, the training phase that establishes the state sequence model for each of DTW keywords referenced templates and the testing phase to evaluate the recognition performance of proposed HMM-like DTW.

Table 1: The voice command set of keywords in the HMM-like DTW speech recognition system.

Index of keywords	Keywords (in Mandarin)
a	強風
b	請開燈
c	二十度
d	關掉空調
e	調整溫度
f	打開電視
g	放大音量
h	選擇電視頻道

In the training phase, a training dataset for establishing HMM-like DTW models is made. Ten males and 10 females are requested for uttering. Each of the 10 males and 10 females is asked to make 5 utterances for each of the 8 keywords, and therefore there are 800 utterances in total for training these 8 models of keywords, 100 utterances for each of the 8 keywords models. Table 2 shows numbers of states (N) of HMMlike DTW set for each DTW keywords template model and the corresponding recognition performance. Observed from Table 2, when the number of states is set improperly, the recognition rate of HMM-like DTW will be very dissatisfactory. Among all state settings, HMM-like DTW with the state setting $N = 50$ performs best on the recognition accuracy, which achieves 70.6%. HMM-like DTW with $N = 50$ will be chosen to be compared with conventional DTW in the testing phase.

Table 2: Numbers of states of HMM-like DTW for each DTW keywords template model and the corresponding recognition performance in the training phase.

Numbers of states (*N*)	**Recognition rates (%)**
50	**70.6%**
40	67.5%
30	49.4%
20	23.1%
10	25.0%

In the testing phase, the collected 10 males and 10 females are requested again to make the additional utterances for the testing experiments. There are 160 utterances in total for the test experiment, 20 utterances for each of the 8 keywords models. Note that these 160 utterances are completely different from those 800 utterances in the training phase. Table 3 shows the recognition performance comparisons of proposed HMM-like DTW with $N = 50$ and conventional DTW. As could be seen in Table 3, the proposed HMM-like DTW with the developed HMM-like modeling scheme is apparently more competitive than conventional DTW with only simple template matching. HMM-like DTW has a better recognition performance than conventional DTW, which is about 6.8%.

Table 3: Performance comparisons of proposed HMM-like DTW with $N = 50$ and conventional DTW on the recognition accuracy.

Keywords commands	**Recognition rates**	
	HMM-like DTW (N = 50)	Conventional DTW
Index *a*	70%	70%
Index *b*	55%	85%
Index *c*	65%	70%
Index *d*	70%	80%
Index *e*	75%	50%
Index *f*	70%	60%
Index *g*	60%	40%
Index *h*	100%	55%
Average	70.6%	63.8%

CONCLUSIONS

In this paper, the HMM-like DTW method is proposed for speech recognition. Proposed HMM-like DTW provides a statistical model recognition strategy for traditional feature-based DTW template matching using the kernel concept of hidden Markov model. The proposed HMM-like DTW will be able to further carry out model adaptation as HMM. Speech recognition experiments in the application of home automation-based multimedia access services showed that the presented HMM-like DTW with the appropriately designed acoustic model is obviously more competitive than conventional DTW without any statistical models on the recognition accuracy.

REFERENCES

1. L. Ceccaroni and X. Verdaguer, "Agent-oriented, multimedia, interactive services in home automation," in *Proceedings of the 2nd European Workshop on Multi-Agent Systems*, 2004.
2. J. Zhu, X. Gao, Y. Yang, H. Li, Z. Ai, and X. Cui, "Developing a voice control system for ZigBee-based home automation networks," in *Proceedings of the 2nd IEEE International Conference on Network Infrastructure and Digital Content (IC-NIDC '10)*, pp. 737–741, September 2010.
3. V. Young and A. Mihailidis, "Difficulties in automatic speech recognition of dysarthric speakers and implications for speech-based applications used by the elderly: a literature review," *Assistive Technology*, vol. 22, no. 2, pp. 99–112, 2010.
4. I.-J. Ding, "Speech recognition using variable-length frame overlaps by intelligent fuzzy control," *Journal of Intelligent and Fuzzy Systems*, vol. 25, no. 1, pp. 49–56, 2013.
5. I. J. Ding, C. T. Yen, and Y. M. Hsu, "Developments of machine learning schemes for dynamic time-wrapping-based speech recognition," *Mathematical Problems in Engineering*, vol. 2013, Article ID 542680, 10 pages, 2013.
6. K. Shinoda, "Acoustic model adaptation for speech recognition," *IEICE Transactions on Information and Systems*, vol. 93, no. 9, pp. 2348–2362, 2010.
7. L. R. Rabiner, "A tutorial on hidden Markov models and selected applications in speech recognition," *Proceedings of the IEEE*, vol. 77, no. 2, pp. 257–286, 1989.
8. S.-H. Chen and Y.-R. Wang, "Tone recognition of continuous Mandarin speech based on neural networks," *IEEE Transactions on Speech and Audio Processing*, vol. 3, no. 2, pp. 146–150, 1995.
9. H. Sakoe and S. Chiba, "Dynamic programming algorithm optimization for spoken word recognition," *IEEE Transactions on Acoustics, Speech, and Signal Processing*, vol. 26, no. 1, pp. 43–49, 1978.
10. P. G. N. Priyadarshani, N. G. J. Dias, and A. Punchihewa, "Dynamic time warping based speech recognition for isolated Sinhala words," in *Proceedings of the 55th IEEE International Midwest Symposium on Circuits and Systems (MWSCAS '12)*, pp. 892–895, August 2012.

11. J. Wu, J. Konrad, and P. Ishwar, "Dynamic time warping for gesture-based user identification and authentication with Kinect," in *Proceedings of the IEEE International Conference on Acoustics, Speech and Signal Processing*, pp. 2371–2375, 2013.
12. X. Anguera, R. Macrae, and N. Oliver, "Partial sequence matching using an unbounded dynamic timewarping algorithm," in *Proceedings of the IEEE International Conference on Acoustics, Speech, and Signal Processing (ICASSP '10)*, pp. 3582–3585, March 2010.
13. X. Chen, J. Huang, Y. Wang, and C. Tao, "Incremental feedback learning methods for voice recognition based on DTW," in *Proceedings of the International Conference on Modelling, Identification and Control (ICMIC '12)*, pp. 1011–1016, June 2012.
14. I.-J. Ding, "Reinforcement of MLLR speaker adaptation using optimal linear interpolation," *Electronics Letters*, vol. 48, no. 5, pp. 290–292, 2012.
15. B. Das, S. Mandal, P. Mitra, and A. Basu, "Aging speech recognition with speaker adaptation techniques: study on medium vocabulary continuous Bengali speech," *Pattern Recognition Letters*, vol. 34, no. 3, pp. 335–343, 2013.

CHAPTER 3

Direct Recovery of Clean Speech Using a Hybrid Noise Suppression Algorithm for Robust Speech Recognition System

Peng Dai,[1] Ing Yann Soon,[1] and Rui Tao[2]

[1]School of Electrical and Electronic Engineering, Nanyang Technological University, Singapore

[2]School of Electronic and Information Engineering, Beihang University, China

ABSTRACT

A new log-power domain feature enhancement algorithm named NLPS is developed. It consists of two parts, direct solution of nonlinear system model and log-power subtraction. In contrast to other methods, the proposed algorithm does not need prior speech/noise statistical model. Instead, it

Citation: Peng Dai, Ing Yann Soon, Rui Tao, "Direct Recovery of Clean Speech Using a Hybrid Noise Suppression Algorithm for Robust Speech Recognition System", International Scholarly Research Notices, vol. 2012, Article ID 306305, 9 pages, 2012. https://doi.org/10.5402/2012/306305

works by direct solution of the nonlinear function derived from the speech recognition system. Separate steps are utilized to refine the accuracy of estimated cepstrum by log-power subtraction, which is the second part of the proposed algorithm. The proposed algorithm manages to solve the speech probability distribution function (PDF) discontinuity problem caused by traditional spectral subtraction series algorithms. The effectiveness of the proposed filter is extensively compared using the standard database, AURORA2. The results show that significant improvement can be achieved by incorporating the proposed algorithm. The proposed algorithm reaches a recognition rate of over 86% for noisy speech (average from SNR 0 dB to 20 dB), which means a 48% error reduction over the baseline Mel-frequency Cepstral Coefficient (MFCC) system.

INTRODUCTION

The main objective of speech recognition is to get a higher recognition rate. However, lots of factors tend to degrade the performance of automatic speech recognition (ASR) system, such as environmental noise, channel distortion, and speaker variability [1, 2]. Generally, automatic speech recognition system consists of two parts, feature extraction and pattern matching. Therefore, methods which aim to improve the performance of ASR system can be mainly divided into two categories, the "model" approach and the "feature" approach. The "model" approach mainly focuses on improving the speech recognizer, where the speech features are classified into different patterns developed from the statistical properties of speech. As for "feature" approach, emphasis is put on improving the robustness of speech features. The method proposed by this paper belongs to this category.

Noise reduction or clean speech estimation is a straight forward "feature" approach to improve the performance of ASR systems. There are different ways to get the estimation. minimum mean square Error is one of the most important ones. Ephraim derived the short-time spectral amplitude (STSA) estimator using minimum mean square error (MMSE) in 1984 [3], which has become a standard approach for clean speech estimation in speech processing. The advantage of MMSE estimator is very obvious. It is mathematically optimized, which theoretically can get a good estimation of the clean speech. Besides, there is solid derivation making it easier to analyze. Originally, the MMSE-based algorithms were intended to be used for speech enhancement. For speech recognition, several MMSE-based algorithms have been developed. Yu et al. in 2008 developed the MMSE estimator in the log-power domain [4]. The cepstral domain estimator appears also in 2008 [5]. Besides, different distortion models are developed for improving speech recognition system [5, 6]. Recently, some more complicated MMSE-based algorithms which require the so called stereo data input are proposed [7]. Admittedly, MMSE works well for speech enhancement and speech recognition. The main idea of MMSE is to estimate the clean speech from the noisy speech. The success of MMSE in previous implementation reveals that it is one of the means to improve the performance of an automatic speech recognition system (ASR). However, it is not necessarily the only one. Mathematically, the recovery of clean speech from noisy corpus is a problem of solving a nonlinear function. The above mentioned MMSE approach can be treated as a kind of statistical approach to solve the function. However, there are other ways for nonlinear function root finding. In this paper, the iterative root finding approach is incorporated to recover the clean speech.

Unlike many other algorithms, the proposed algorithm does not need stereo data input, which makes it more robust to different conditions. It is because stereo data is impossible to get in practical situations. The novelty of this paper lies in that the two parts of MFCCs (c1~c12, log-power) are processed separately. Direct solution of nonlinear system function is much easier than the statistical approach. Besides, compared with earlier MMSE-based algorithms, the proposed method does not need any additional training. The AURORA2 database is used for verification tests. It is a widely used, standard English database, which contains isolated digits as well as digit serials. Comparison is made against ordinary MFCCs, MMSE-STSA [3], Spectral Subtraction (SS) [8], Cepstral Mean and Variance Normalization (CMVN), the ETSI standard advanced front-end feature extraction algorithm (AFE) [9], and Mean Variance Normalization and ARMA filtering (MVA) [10]. Experimental results show the excellent performance of the proposed method.

The rest of the paper is organized as follows. In Section 2, the system model, nonlinear function, is presented. Section 3 discusses the details of the proposed algorithm, including detailed iteration steps of root finding algorithm, prior estimates for clean speech and noise, and the novel log-power subtraction method. The experimental speech databases, ASR systems and the additional comparison methods are described in Section 4. Conclusions are summarized in Section 5.

SYSTEM MODEL

Following similar derivation procedure from [11], the clean speech waveform is denoted as x_t where t is the time index. It is assumed that x_t is corrupted by the independent additive noise waveform n_t and becomes the noisy speech waveform y_t as shown in

$$y_t = x_t + n_t. \tag{1}$$

The speech signal is cut into frames and transformed into frequency domain using DFT. Then (1) becomes

$$Y_{f,t} = X_{f,t} + N_{f,t}. \tag{2}$$

By assuming the additivity on the powers of the components in the frequency domain [12], the power spectrum of the noisy speech is given by

$$\left|Y_{f,t}\right|^2 = \left|X_{f,t}\right|^2 + \left|N_{f,t}\right|^2. \tag{3}$$

After applying Mel-filterbanks to the power spectra,

$$\sum_f W_f^l \left|Y_{f,t}\right|^2 = \sum_f W_f^l \left|X_{f,t}\right|^2 + \sum_f W_f^l \left|N_{f,t}\right|^2, \tag{4}$$

where W^l_f stands for the transfer function for the lth filter.

Define the log channel energy vectors as:

$$\mathbf{Y} = \begin{bmatrix} \log \sum_f W_f^1 \left|Y_{f,t}\right|^2 \\ \log \sum_f W_f^2 \left|Y_{f,t}\right|^2 \\ \vdots \\ \log \sum_f W_f^L \left|Y_{f,t}\right|^2 \end{bmatrix}, \quad \mathbf{X} = \begin{bmatrix} \log \sum_f W_f^1 \left|X_{f,t}\right|^2 \\ \log \sum_f W_f^2 \left|X_{f,t}\right|^2 \\ \vdots \\ \log \sum_f W_f^L \left|X_{f,t}\right|^2 \end{bmatrix},$$

$$\mathbf{N} = \begin{bmatrix} \log \sum_f W_f^1 \left|N_{f,t}\right|^2 \\ \log \sum_f W_f^2 \left|N_{f,t}\right|^2 \\ \vdots \\ \log \sum_f W_f^L \left|N_{f,t}\right|^2 \end{bmatrix}, \tag{5}$$

where log(·) denotes the natural logarithm

Then (4) becomes

$$e^{\mathbf{Y}} = e^{\mathbf{X}} + e^{\mathbf{N}}. \quad (6)$$

Then changing (6) to the log-power domain,

$$\mathbf{Y} = \log(e^{\mathbf{X}} + e^{\mathbf{N}}), \quad (7)$$

then

$$\mathbf{Y} = \mathbf{X} + \log(\mathbf{1} + e^{\mathbf{N}-\mathbf{X}}), \quad (8)$$

where 1 stands for a vector with all elements equal to one.

Then, the MFCCs can be calculated by

$$\mathbf{C} = \mathrm{DCT}(\mathbf{Y}). \quad (9)$$

ALGORITHM DESCRIPTION

Iterative Root-Finding

Theoretical Analysis

In fact, with no additional constraints, and if $|Y_{f,t}|^2$ and $|N_{f,t}|^2$ are already known, according to (3) the clean speech can be estimated simply by

$$\left|\hat{X}_{f,t}\right|^2 = \left|Y_{f,t}\right|^2 - \left|N_{f,t}\right|^2, \quad (10)$$

where $|\hat{X}_{f,t}|^2$ is the clean speech estimate.

Equation (10) is just the basic idea of Spectral Subtraction (SS) [8]. However, (10) only exists when $|Y_{f,t}|^2 > |N_{f,t}|^2$. If $|Y_{f,t}|^2 \le |N_{f,t}|^2$, then $|Y_{f,t}|^2 - |N_{f,t}|^2 \le 0$. The clean speech estimate becomes zero or negative, which is obviously wrong.

A traditional way to solve the above mentioned problem is to implement a threshold to guarantee the clean speech estimate to be positive:

$$\left|\hat{X}_{f,t}\right|^2 = \max\left(\left|Y_{f,t}\right|^2 - \left|N_{f,t}\right|^2, \varepsilon\right), \quad (11)$$

where the parameter is a small positive constant value.

Equation (11) is a very common way to implement Spectral Subtraction (SS) in speech recognition which will be denoted as SS in later discussion. Admittedly, (11) manages to increase SNR, which in return is a straight forward way to improve the performance of speech recognition systems.

However, there is a very serious problem caused by SS. Because of the threshold, ε, a certain portion of the recovered speech is forced to be corrected to ε. Figure 1 gives an example of the effect of SS on speech spectrogram. The blue area in Figure 1(b) is all equal to ε.

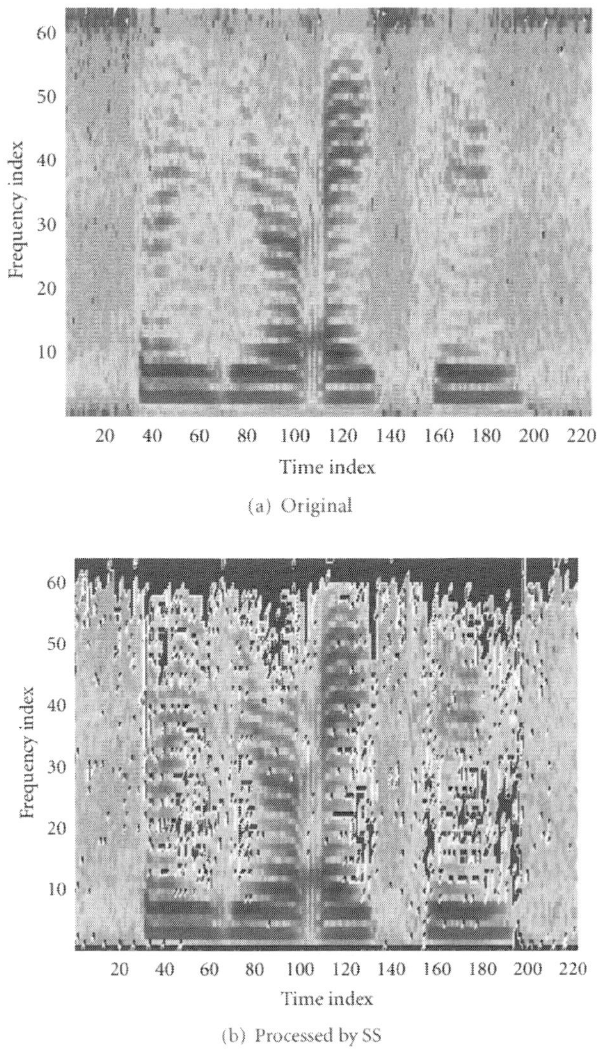

Figure 1: Spectrogram of digital string "3Z82".

After processed by SS or other similar methods, the probability distribution of speech is greatly changed. For example, in Figure 2, it can be easily found out that the probability of speech power equal ε is greatly increased, which makes the pdf of the processed speech discontinuous.

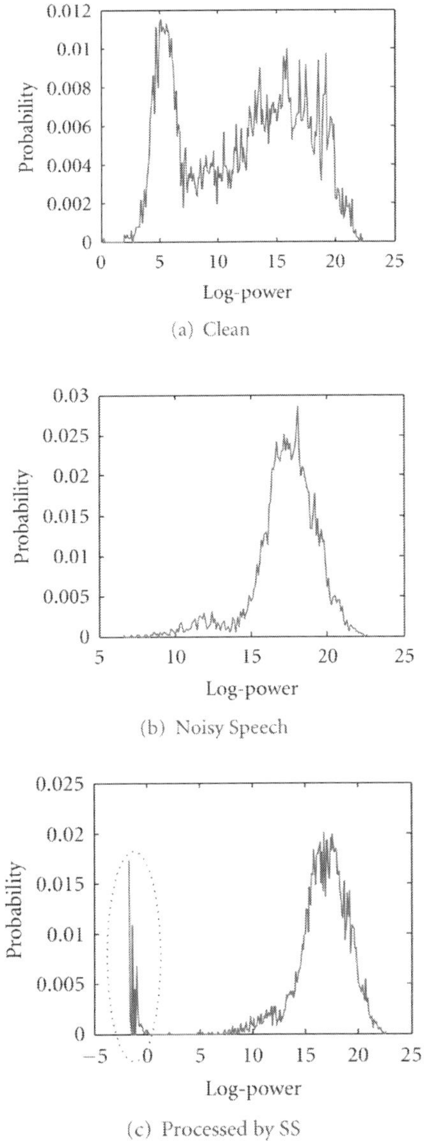

Figure 2: Speech PDF of Mel channel log-power for digital string "3Z82".

Most state of the art ASR systems incorporate statistical methods to perform pattern recognition. HMM is one of the most popular ones. These statistical methods are all developed based on certain statistical model of the speech. In other words, a probability distribution is always assumed as the basis of recognizer derivation. SS like algorithms greatly changes the pdf of speech, which in return causes the performance of ASR systems to drop.

The proposed algorithm intends to achieve the clean speech in an iterative manner, which means the clean speech estimation $|\hat{X}_{f,t}|^2$ slowly converges to a better guess. There would not be a mass force assignment of the negative elements to a certain value. Thus the discontinuity problem is avoided.

Iterative Solution

The novelty of implementing iterative root finding algorithm is that unlike the Spectral Subtraction like approaches it manages to overcome the awkward $|Y_{f,t}|^2 \leq |N_{f,t}|^2$ problem without causing discontinuity in the speech PDF. The statistical approach handles this by applying a series of mathematical operations which are not sensitive to the above mentioned problem. In power domain, the final expression is

$$\left|\hat{X}_{f,t}\right|^2 = G \times \left|Y_{f,t}\right|^2 = \left|Y_{f,t}\right|^2 - (1 - G) \times \left|Y_{f,t}\right|^2 \tag{12}$$

which fundamentally avoids the possibility of $|Y_{f,t}|^2 \leq |N_{f,t}|^2$. It is because the equivalent noise estimate is $(1-G)\times |Y_{f,t}|^2$, which is generated from only the current frame.

As described before, the iterative root finding algorithm can also handle $|Y_{f,t}|^2 \leq |N_{f,t}|^2$ very well. Equation (8) can be reshaped to

$$\mathbf{X} + \log(\mathbf{1} + e^{\mathbf{N}-\mathbf{X}}) - \mathbf{Y} = 0, \tag{13}$$

where Y is the noisy speech vector, X is the parameter that needed to be recovered. If the noise vector N can be reasonably estimated, (13) becomes a nonlinear function about X, which can be solved by iterative root finding algorithms.

Denoting

$$f(\mathbf{X}) = \mathbf{X} + \log(\mathbf{1} + e^{\mathbf{N}-\mathbf{X}}) - \mathbf{Y}, \tag{14}$$

then

$$f'(\mathrm{X}) = \frac{d[f(\mathbf{X})]}{d\mathbf{X}} = \mathbf{1} - \frac{e^{\mathrm{N}-\mathrm{X}}}{1 + e^{\mathrm{N}-\mathrm{X}}}. \tag{15}$$

According to Newton's method, given a function f (X), its derivative f'(X) and a first guess $\hat{X}_0$, the solution to the function can be reached by

$$X_{i+1} = X_i - \frac{f(X_i)}{f'(X_i)}, \tag{16}$$

where i is the iteration index.

For the iterative step

$$X_{i+1} = X_i - \frac{X_i + \log(1 + e^{N-X_i}) - Y}{1 - (e^{N-X_i}/(1 + e^{N-X_i}))} \tag{17}$$

it has to be noted that

$$\lim_{(N-X_i) \to +\infty} 1 - \frac{e^{N-X_i}}{1 + e^{N-X_i}} = 0. \tag{18}$$

Therefore, a threshold β is adopted to guarantee the denominator to be non-zero. Then (17) is modified to

$$X_{i+1} = X_i - \frac{X_i + \log(1 + e^{N-X_i}) - Y}{\max(1 - (e^{N-X_i}/(1 + e^{N-X_i})), \beta)}. \tag{19}$$

With a successful guess of the initial step, clean speech vector $\hat{X}_0$ and noise vector $\hat{N}$, the clean speech estimate $\hat{X}$ can be satisfactorily approximated. Equation (19) can work very well even if $|Y_{f,t}|^2 \leq |N_{f,t}|^2$. About the discontinuity problem, at extreme conditions where the threshold β works, the iteration becomes

$$\begin{aligned} X_{i+1} &= X_i - \frac{X_i + \log(1 + e^{N-X_i}) - Y}{\beta} \\ &= (1 - \beta)X_i - \frac{1}{\beta}\log(1 + e^{N-X_i}) + \frac{1}{\beta}Y. \end{aligned} \tag{20}$$

It can be easily seen that (20) would not cause mass assignment of the same value, which means the discontinuity problem will not appear.

Prior Estimates

In statistics, a minimum mean square error (MMSE) estimator is the approach which minimizes the mean square error (MSE), which is widely used in lots of areas in signal processing. In 1984, Ephraim and Malah derived the short time spectral amplitude (STSA) estimator using MMSE [3]. After that,

MMSE has become a standard approach for enhancing the quality of speech. Therefore, it is chosen to generate the prior estimate of the clean speech. The following equation shows the standard cost function for MMSE approach [3]:

$$\hat{X} = \arg\min_{\hat{X}} E\left[\left(X - \hat{X}\right)^2\right]. \tag{21}$$

By following MMSE-STSA [3] the clean speech estimate can be reached by

$$\begin{aligned}\hat{X}_{f,t} &= \Gamma(1.5)\frac{\sqrt{v_{f,t}}}{\gamma_{f,t}} M\left(-0.5; 1; -v_{f,t}\right) Y_{f,t} \\ &= \Gamma(1.5)\frac{\sqrt{v_{f,t}}}{\gamma_{f,t}} \exp\left(-\frac{v_{f,t}}{2}\right) \\ &\quad \times \left[\left(1 + v_{f,t}\right) I_0\left(\frac{v_{f,t}}{2}\right) + v_{f,t} I_1\left(\frac{v_{f,t}}{2}\right)\right] Y_{f,t},\end{aligned} \tag{22}$$

where $\Gamma(\cdot)$ denotes the gamma function; M(a;c; x) is the confluent hypergeometric function; $I_0(\cdot)$ and I1$(\cdot)$ denote the zero and first order modified Bessel function; $\xi_{f,t}$ and $\gamma_{f,t}$ are the a priori and a posteriori signal-to-noise ratios (SNR), respectively:

$$v_{f,t} = \frac{\xi_{f,t}}{1 + \xi_{f,t}} \gamma_{f,t}. \tag{23}$$

Then the clean amplitude estimate is transferred to log-power domain:

$$\begin{aligned}\hat{X}^l &= \log \sum_f W_f^l \left|\hat{X}_{f,t}\right|^2 \\ &= \log \sum_f W_f^l \left|\Gamma(1.5)\frac{\sqrt{v_{f,t}}}{\gamma_{f,t}} \exp\left(-\frac{v_{f,t}}{2}\right)\right. \\ &\quad \left. \times \left[\left(1 + v_{f,t}\right) I_0\left(\frac{v_{f,t}}{2}\right) + v_{f,t} I_1\left(\frac{v_{f,t}}{2}\right)\right] Y_{f,t}\right|^2.\end{aligned} \tag{24}$$

Equation (24) will serve as the initial guess for the iterative approach.

Log-Power Subtraction (LPS)

Algorithm Description

As is shown in Figure 3, there are mainly four different domains in the MFCC scheme. The proposed algorithm works in the log-power domain.

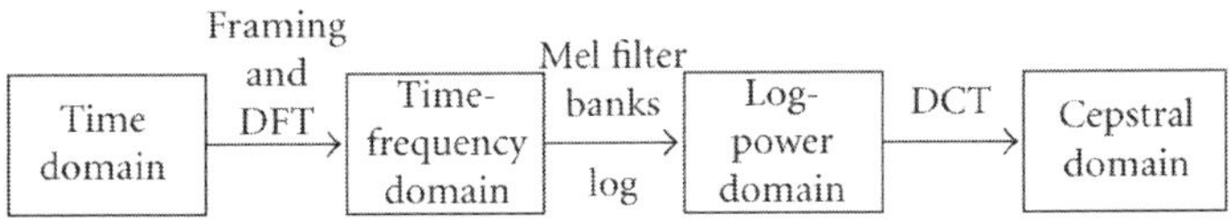

Figure 3: Different domains in MFCC scheme.

The clean speech estimate generated by the proposed algorithm in (19) is actually

$$\mathbf{X} = \begin{bmatrix} \log \sum_f W_f^1 \left| X_{f,t} \right|^2 \\ \log \sum_f W_f^2 \left| X_{f,t} \right|^2 \\ \vdots \\ \log \sum_f W_f^L \left| X_{f,t} \right|^2 \end{bmatrix}. \quad (25)$$

It is the clean speech log-power vector, in the log-power domain as described in Figure 3.

The MFCC static parameters can be divided into two parts, c1~c12 and c0/log-energy. Strictly speaking, the proposed algorithm mainly focuses on c1~c12. For log-energy, traditionally it should be calculated by

$$P_{\log} = \log\left(\sum_f \left| X_{f,t} \right|^2 \right). \quad (26)$$

The clean speech power estimate, $|X_{f,t}|^2$, cannot be perfectly recovered from (25) because of the Mel-filterbanks. Additional distortion will be introduced to the feature vectors. For c_0, although it seems to work smoothly, the recognition results are just about "average". Therefore, a separate noise removing scheme is developed. At the iterative root finding part, an estimate for the noise is reached. The frame clean speech power can be estimated by

$$\hat{P}_c = \sum_f \left(\left| Y_{f,t} \right|^2 - \hat{N}_{f,t} \right). \quad (27)$$

Then the log-energy can be calculated by

$$P_{\log} = \log\left(\hat{P}_c\right) = \log\left[\sum_f \left(\left|Y_{f,t}\right|^2 - \hat{N}_{f,t}\right)\right]. \quad (28)$$

However, problem arises when $\hat{P}_c \leq 0$. Therefore, a weighting parameter is incorporated to reduce the chances of imaginary parts appearing. Then (28) becomes

$$\hat{P}_c = \sum_f \left(\left|Y_{f,t}\right|^2 - \alpha\hat{N}_{f,t}\right). \quad (29)$$

Furthermore, another parameter ε_0 is set the guarantee the log-energy not to be infinity. Therefore, the log-power part becomes

$$P_{\log} = \log\left(\hat{P}_c\right) = \log\left\{\max\left[\sum_f \left(\left|Y_{f,t}\right|^2 - \alpha\hat{N}_{f,t}\right), \varepsilon_0\right]\right\}. \quad (30)$$

Theoretical Analysis

The basic idea of log-power subtraction is similar to the Spectral Subtraction (SS) algorithm developed by Boll in 1979 [8]. Figure 4 shows the diagram of Spectral Subtraction algorithm.

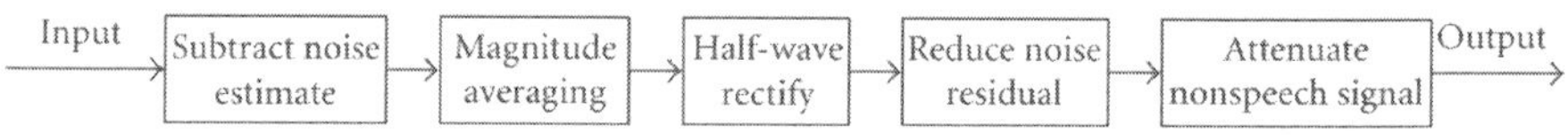

Figure 4: Diagram of spectral subtraction.

Boll defined the SS in the magnitude domain in [8]. When adopted in speech recognition, SS is normally implemented in the power spectral domain.

Most of noise estimation algorithms are developed based on statistical models of clean and noisy speech, which makes the estimation at a specific point, $|N_{f,t}|^2$, more like an expectation or average of noise based on previous frames. Therefore, when used in spectral subtraction, lots of elements will become negative, especially in the non-speech period, which will lead to the problem described in Section 3. However, for the proposed LPS approach the effect of the above mentioned problem is to a certain extent avoided. It is because traditionally the log-power is calculated by (26). It is based on the sum of all the speech power elements in one frame. Mathematically, from (29), the following equation can be derived:

$$\hat{P}_c = \sum_f \left(\left| Y_{f,t} \right|^2 - \alpha \hat{N}_{f,t} \right) = \sum_f \left| Y_{f,t} \right|^2 - \alpha \sum_f \hat{N}_{f,t}$$

$$= F \times \left(\frac{1}{F} \sum_f \left| Y_{f,t} \right|^2 - \frac{1}{F} \alpha \sum_f \hat{N}_{f,t} \right), \tag{31}$$

where F is the total number of frequency bins.

Equation (31) shows that LPS is equivalent to performing spectral subtraction after averaging all the elements in the current frame. Due to the averaging process, the whole spectral subtraction scheme become more robust since both speech and noise estimate are kind of expectations of the actual signal.

Implementation Details

The proposed algorithm consists of two parts, iterative solution of the nonlinear function and log-power subtraction.

Figure 5 shows the block diagram of the proposed algorithm. The detailed parameter settings are $\alpha = 0.9$, $\alpha_{f,t} = 0.4$, $\beta = 0.8$, $\varepsilon_0 = 10^{-10}$, and the iteration is performed only once. Minimum Statistics (MS) is used for noise estimation [13].

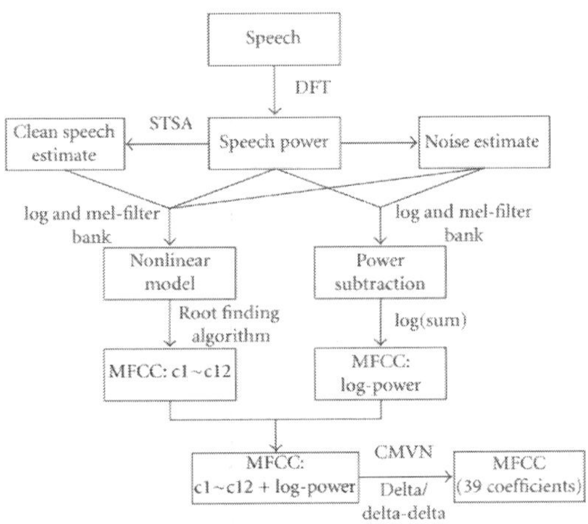

Figure 5: Diagram of the proposed algorithm.

ALGORITHM EVALUATION

Experiment Setup

AURORA2 Database

The AURORA2 database is adopted to evaluate the performance of the proposed method. The AURORA2 data is based on a version of the original TIDigits (as available from LDC) sampled to 8 kHz [14]. Noise is artificially added at several SNRs (20 dB, 15 dB, 10 dB, 5 dB, 0 dB, −5 dB). Set A and Set B are filtered with a G712 [15] characteristic filter, which simulates the response of filters found in the A/D interface of PCM transmission systems. Set C is filtered with MIRS filter to simulate a telephone system. There are two training conditions in AURORA2, clean training set and multi-condition training set. For clean training condition, the training set has no noise added and it consists of 8440 utterances recorded from 55 male and 55 female adults. 4004 utterances from 52 male and 52 female speakers are split equally into 4 subsets with 1001 utterances each, with all speakers being present in each subset. In the multi-condition training set, four types of noises have been added at various SNR levels [14, 16].

System Description

The proposed front-end feature extractor is modified from the MFCC model provided by Voicebox Toolkit [17]. The demo scripts from the AURORA2 database are used for training. In the evaluation experiments, log-energy (log E) together with c1 to c12 is used as the static feature vector, and then the delta and delta-delta features are calculated using the frame-differential.

The same recognizer is used for both the proposed front-end feature extraction algorithm and the baseline system for comparison. Each digit is modeled by a simple left-to-right 18 states (including two non-emitting states) HMM model, with 3 Gaussian mixtures per state. Two pause models are defined. One is "sil", which has 3 HMM states and models the pauses before and after each utterance. The other one is "sp", which is a single state model (tied with the middle state of "sil") and models the pauses among words.

Comparison Targets

The proposed algorithm does not need stereo data input. Therefore, algorithms such as SPLICE [18] are not selected for comparison, since comparison between algorithms with and without clean speech input is unfair. Because the proposed method is developed based on MFCC, it is chosen to be the baseline. The diagram is given in Figure 6.

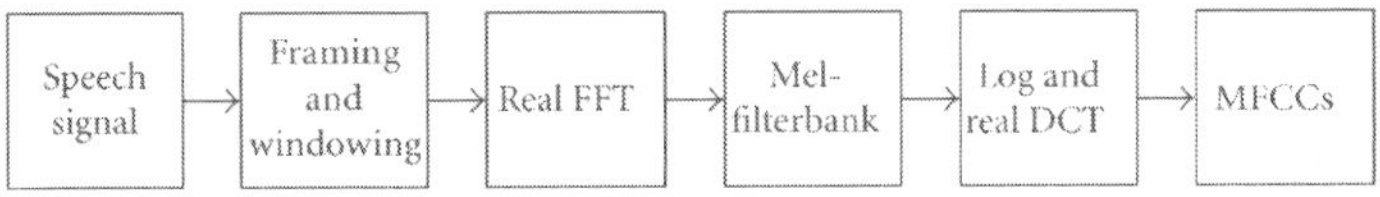

Figure 6: Diagram of MFCC.

MMSE-STSA is the standard MMSE approach for mathematically recovering the clean speech. In this paper, the STSA algorithm is implemented with minimum statistics as the noise estimation part. The log-power subtraction approach is similar to SS, so it is chosen to show that in speech recognition log-power subtraction is much better than SS. MVA is a cepstral domain approach, which is chosen to show the superiority of the proposed algorithm in relevant area. Figure 7 shows the diagram of MVA.

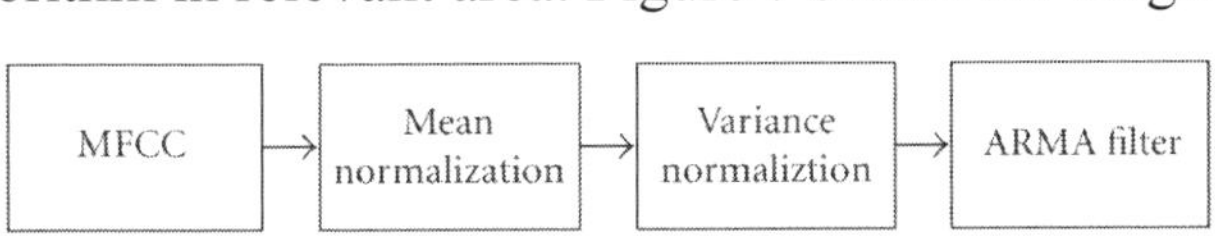

Figure 7: Diagram of MVA.

The ETSI standard advanced front-end feature extraction algorithm (AFE) is also implemented for comparison [9].

Results and Discussion

Experimental Results

Experiments are conducted to show the speech recognition results of the proposed NLPS algorithm with different iterations. Detailed recognition results are given in Table 1. It can be easily found out that the optimal result comes at the second iteration.

Table 1: Detailed recognition rates (%).

Iteration No.	**1**	*2*	**3**	**4**	**5**
Clean	99.09	*99.08*	98.37	98.36	97.23
Avg 0–20	**85.70**	***85.76***	**85.66**	**80.07**	**76.17**
−5 dB	27.80	*27.85*	23.24	23.24	21.31

Comparison is made against MFCC, MMSE-STSA [3], Spectral Subtraction (SS) [8], Cepstral Mean Variance Normalization (CMVN), AFE [9], and MVA [10].

There are two training conditions in the AURORA2 database demo, clean-training condition and multi-training condition. In the multi-training condition noisy speech together with the clean speech are used for training HMMs. Therefore, the recognition results from multi-training condition are very good. For most of the SNR levels, the recognition results are over 90%. It makes all of the above mentioned methods yields similar recognition results, about 92% on average. Actually, it is meaningless to make the recognition results increase from 92.1% to 92.5%. Besides, in real life preparing a noisy database for training HMMs is not realistic. It is because there are infinite types of noise and SNRs, which makes it difficult to generate an effective database for training. Moreover, if the noise encountered is very different from that in the database, bad results will be obtained. Therefore, only the clean training condition results are used for comparison. The experiment results are shown in Tables 2, 3, 4, and 5.

Table 2: Detailed recognition rates (%).

SNR	**Set A**				**Set B**				**Set C**	
	Subway	Bab-ble	Car	Exhi-bition	Station	Restau-rant	Street	Airport	Restau-rant	Street
Clean	98.83	99.09	99.14	99.29	98.83	99.09	99.14	99.29	98.93	99.15
Avg 0–20	**85.96**	**86.72**	**87.77**	**82.81**	**86.80**	**86.84**	**88.33**	**87.94**	**83.15**	**84.82**
−5 dB	29.23	26.18	31.40	29.37	29.63	29.50	31.26	30.64	21.80	26.72

Table 3: Recognition results for different parts of the proposed algorithm.

	Clean	**Avg 0–20**	**−5**
CMVN	99.32	**77.78**	13.90
LPS	99.47	**73.07**	12.92
LPS+CMVN	99.07	**83.30**	20.78
Newton	99.20	**83.83**	25.65
Newton+CMVN	99.25	**84.96**	27.78
NLPS (Newton+LPS+CMVN)	*99.08*	***85.76***	*27.85*

Table 4: Recognition results for comparison targets.

	Clean	**Avg 0–20**	**–5**
MFCC	99.42	**71.80**	13.39
SS	99.32	**72.42**	25.26
CMVN	99.32	**77.78**	13.90
STSA	99.26	**80.12**	20.31
AFE	99.20	**82.23**	24.77
MVA	99.20	**84.15**	26.24

Table 5: Recognition results for comparison targets.

	Avg 0–20	**Relative Imp.**		**Relative Imp.**
MFCC	**71.80**	19.4%	**13.39**	108.0%
SS	**72.42**	18.4%	**25.26**	10.3%
CMVN	**77.78**	10.3%	**13.90**	100.4%
STSA	**80.12**	7.0%	**20.31**	37.1%
AFE	**82.23**	4.3%	**24.77**	12.4%
MVA	**84.15**	1.9%	**26.24**	6.1%

In Table 3, LPS stands for log-power subtraction. LPS + CMVN means only LPS and CMVN are implemented in the speech recognition system. Newton refers to the system with only Newton's iterative method. Newton + CMVN means both methods are implemented. NLPS is the final form of the proposed algorithm which involves the implementation of all the three methods, Newton's method, LPS and CMVN. The experimental results in Table 3 are given to show that the three parts of the proposed algorithm all helps to improve the performance of speech recognition system.

In the following discussion, MFCC denotes the traditional 13 Mel Frequency Cepstral Coefficients together with the corresponding velocity and acceleration parameters. Results are averaged over the noisy test sets with SNRs from 0 to 20 dB, denoted as Avg 0–20. Another point that has to be mentioned is that the clean set results of all the above mentioned algorithms are over 99%. It is also meaningless to attempt to achieve significant improvements at this level. Therefore, discussion will be carried out mainly for Avg 0–20 and SNR −5 dB. Figure 8 shows the experimental results at Avg 0–20 and SNR −5 dB.

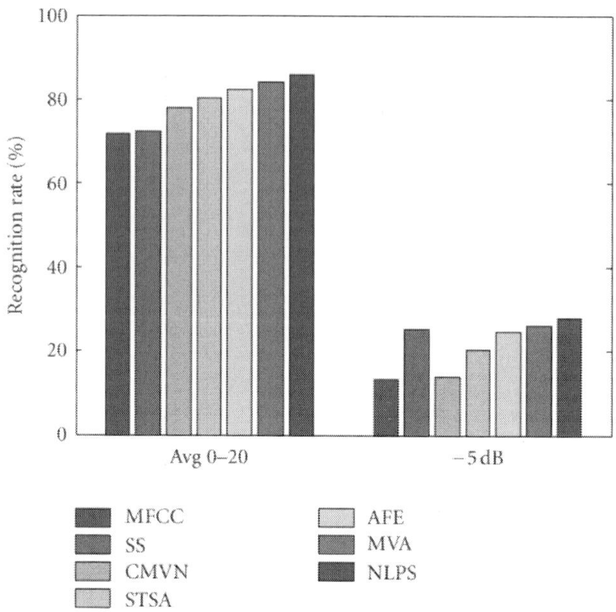

Figure 8: Experimental results.

Results Analysis

Experimental results in Table 3 show that the implementation of LPS and Newton's method greatly improves the recognition results. Besides, the two fundamental parts, LPS and Newton's method, both contribute to the excellent performance of the proposed algorithm. As shown in Table 3, Newton's method alone can reach a recognition rate of 83.83% at Avg 0–20. With the combination of LPS and CMVN, the performance of the speech recognition system is further improved, 84.96% for Newton + CMVN and 85.76% for the proposed NLPS algorithm.

Comparisons in Tables 3 and 4 show that the proposed algorithm significantly improved the performance of speech recognition system. The relative improvement ratios are shown in Table 5. Compared with the baseline MFCC system, the proposed algorithm achieves very impressive improvements, 19.4% in terms of Avg 0–20 and *108*% in SNR −5 dB. For CMVN and STSA, also very significant improvements are reached. In the level of Avg 0–20, the relative improvements are 10.3% over CMVN, and 7% over STSA. When it comes to SNR −5 dB, the improvements become much more significant, *100.4*% over CMVN and 37.1% over STSA.

In speech processing technique, there is a kind of awkward situation when speech enhancement algorithm sometimes cannot improve the speech recognition results even if it manages to improve speech quality in terms of human listening test. SS is just one of the above mentioned methods. Direct implementation of the SS in [8] yields terrible results. Therefore, in our evaluation test, the noise estimation part of SS is replaced by Minimum Statistics [19]. In terms of Avg 0–20, the relative improvement reaches 18.4%. At SNR −5 dB the relative improvement is 10.3%. The performance of SS can successfully support the novelty of the LPS method, which is an indispensible part of the proposed NLPS algorithm. As for MVA, admittedly it is a very successful algorithm. However, the proposed algorithm still yields better results. At Avg 0–20, a 1.9% improvement is reached. For SNR −5 dB, the relative improvement is 6.1%. For the European Telecommunications Standards Institute (ETSI) standard AFE, at Avg 0–20, a relative improvement of 4.3% is reached. For SNR −5 dB, the relative improvement is 12.4%.

CONCLUSION

In this paper, a novel algorithm for robust speech recognition system is presented with its detailed derivation, implementation, and evaluation. It is based on the direct solution of a nonlinear system model together with a novel log-power subtraction method. The novelty of the proposed algorithm lies in four parts. Firstly, the proposed method does not need any additional training process, which makes the computational burden very small. Besides, the proposed method is a blind approach, which means that the proposed method yields good performance at all SNRs and noise types. Another advantage of the proposed algorithm is its ability to adapt to changing environments. The adaptation can be made by simply changing the noise estimation part. Finally, the NLPS algorithm can be easily combined with other algorithm, such as the MVA discussed above. The proposed algorithm is implemented and evaluated with AURORA2 database. Comparison is made against STSA, SS, and MVA. Experimental results demonstrate significant improvement in the recognition accuracy.

SUPPLEMENTARY MATERIALS

Table.1. Experimental Results

SNR/dB		Clean	20	15	10	5	0	-5	Avg 0-20
MFCC (39)	Set A	99.37	97.98	94.84	82.55	56.09	27.59	12.54	**71.81**
	Set B	99.37	98.17	94.97	82.30	56.52	29.39	13.23	**72.27**
	Set C	99.35	95.96	90.73	78.63	55.47	28.20	13.36	**69.80**
	Avg	**99.36**	**97.37**	**93.51**	**81.16**	**56.02**	**28.39**	**13.04**	**71.29**
SS (Boll)	Set A	99.34	95.93	91.57	79.58	50.46	22.61	10.72	**68.03**
	Set B	99.34	96.55	93.08	82.80	58.29	27.98	12.01	**71.74**
	Set C	99.29	95.43	90.80	77.43	51.18	24.10	11.32	**67.79**
	Avg	**99.32**	**95.97**	**91.82**	**79.94**	**53.31**	**24.90**	**11.35**	**69.19**
SS (Martin)	Set A	95.11	90.74	86.63	79.06	65.51	44.02	26.50	**73.19**
	Set B	95.11	91.17	88.13	81.51	67.97	45.75	26.96	**74.90**
	Set C	95.13	89.34	84.08	74.64	59.32	38.44	22.33	**69.16**
	Avg	**95.11**	**90.41**	**86.28**	**78.40**	**64.27**	**42.74**	**25.26**	**72.42**
Newton Only	Set A	99.20	97.90	96.15	91.60	79.35	52.17	24.33	**83.43**
	Set B	99.20	98.14	96.83	93.26	81.95	56.04	28.47	**85.24**
	Set C	99.19	97.37	95.80	90.29	78.82	51.74	24.16	**82.80**
	Avg	**99.20**	**97.80**	**96.257**	**91.71**	**80.04**	**53.32**	**25.65**	**83.83**
Newton + CMVN	Set A	99.26	97.84	95.96	91.33	79.96	56.34	26.77	**84.29**
	Set B	99.26	98.12	96.83	93.33	83.49	59.94	29.31	**86.34**
	Set C	99.235	97.43	95.85	90.96	80.34	56.64	27.26	**84.24**
	Avg	**99.25**	**97.80**	**96.21**	**91.87**	**81.26**	**57.64**	**27.78**	**84.96**
Iterative (Proposed)	Set A	99.09	97.80	96.11	92.13	82.15	60.90	29.05	**85.82**
	Set B	99.09	98.22	96.95	94.07	84.95	63.21	30.26	**87.48**
	Set C	99.04	97.47	95.89	91.50	80.55	54.52	24.26	**83.98**
	Avg	**99.07**	**97.83**	**96.31**	**92.56**	**82.55**	**59.54**	**27.85**	**85.76**

Spectral subtraction is not very suitable for speech recognition. The main problem lies in the noise estimation part. State of the art noise estimation algorithms intends only to estimate the noise in a 'general' way. Therefore, the estimated noise is very 'stationary' compared with the true noise.

$$X = Y - N = Y + (-N)$$

If the noise estimate is 'very different' from the true noise, the spectral subtraction scheme actually is adding new noise, $-N$, into the speech. Besides, from the recognition results in Table 1 it can be easily found out that the proposed algorithm is much better than spectral subtraction. Even the primary form (Newton's method only) yields better results than spectral subtraction at all SNR levels.

Detailed Recognition Results

Experimental results for the comparison targets (including detailed SNR level) are shown below.

Table.2. Experimental Results

SNR/dB		Clean	20	15	10	5	0	-5	Avg 0-20
MFCC (39)	Set A	99.37	97.98	94.84	82.55	56.09	27.59	12.54	**71.81**
	Set B	99.37	98.17	94.97	82.30	56.52	29.39	13.23	**72.27**
	Set C	99.35	95.96	90.73	78.63	55.47	28.20	13.36	**69.80**
	Avg	**99.36**	**97.37**	**93.51**	**81.16**	**56.02**	**28.39**	**13.04**	**71.29**
CMVN	Set A	99.34	97.03	94.48	88.52	72.62	40.98	14.95	**78.72**
	Set B	99.34	97.48	95.21	89.57	73.75	42.56	15.31	**79.71**
	Set C	99.29	96.40	93.29	84.69	67.23	32.99	11.45	**74.92**
	Avg	**99.32**	**96.97**	**94.32**	**87.59**	**71.20**	**38.84**	**13.90**	**77.78**
SS	Set A	95.11	90.74	86.63	79.06	65.51	44.02	26.50	**73.19**
	Set B	95.11	91.17	88.13	81.51	67.97	45.75	26.96	**74.90**
	Set C	95.13	89.34	84.08	74.64	59.32	38.44	22.33	**69.16**
	Avg	**95.11**	**90.41**	**86.28**	**78.40**	**64.27**	**42.74**	**25.26**	**72.42**
STSA	Set A	99.27	96.83	94.18	88.53	76.00	50.07	21.33	**81.12**
	Set B	99.27	97.30	94.69	88.81	75.06	48.54	20.97	**80.88**
	Set C	99.24	96.44	93.25	86.36	71.34	44.35	18.65	**78.35**
	Avg	**99.26**	**96.86**	**94.04**	**87.90**	**74.13**	**47.65**	**20.31**	**80.12**
MVA	Set A	99.25	97.34	95.21	90.49	79.56	56.22	28.36	**83.76**
	Set B	99.25	97.61	95.75	91.67	80.35	57.41	28.78	**84.56**
	Set C	99.12	96.50	93.94	87.42	73.87	46.83	21.58	**79.71**
	Avg	**99.20**	**97.15**	**94.97**	**89.86**	**77.93**	**53.48**	**26.24**	**82.68**

REFERENCES

1. L. Rabiner and B.-H. Juang, *Fundamentals of Speech Recognition*, Prentice-Hall, Englewood Cliffs, Ny, USA, 1993.
2. B. Gold and N. Morgan, *Speech and Audio Signal Processing—Processing and Perception of Speech and Music*, John Wiley & Sons, 2000.
3. Y. Ephraim and D. Malah, "Speech enhancement using a minimum mean-square error short-time spectral amplitude estimator," *IEEE Transactions on Acoustics, Speech, and Signal Processing*, vol. 32, no. 6, pp. 1109–1121, 1984.
4. D. Yu, L. Deng, J. Droppo, J. Wu, Y. Gong, and A. Acero, "Robust speech recognition using a cepstral minimum-mean-square-error-motivated noise suppressor," *IEEE Transactions on Audio, Speech and Language Processing*, vol. 16, no. 5, pp. 1061–1070, 2008.
5. K. M. Indrebo, R. J. Povinelli, and M. T. Johnson, "Minimum mean-squared error estimation of mel-frequency cepstral coefficients using a novel distortion model," *IEEE Transactions on Audio, Speech and Language Processing*, vol. 16, no. 8, pp. 1654–1661, 2008.
6. J. Chen, J. Benesty, Y. Huang, and S. Doclo, "New insights into the noise reduction Wiener filter," *IEEE Transactions on Audio, Speech and Language Processing*, vol. 14, no. 4, pp. 1218–1233, 2006.
7. L. Deng, J. Droppo, and A. Acero, "Estimating cepstrum of speech under the presence of noise using a joint prior of static and dynamic features," *IEEE Transactions on Speech and Audio Processing*, vol. 12, no. 3, pp. 218–233, 2004.
8. S. F. Boll, "Suppression of acoustic noise in speech using spectral subtraction," *IEEE Trans Acoust Speech Signal Process*, vol. 27, no. 2, pp. 113–120, 1979.
9. European Telecommunications Standards Institute (ETSI), ETSI ES 202 050 V1.1.5, 2007.
10. C. Chia-Ping and A. B. Jeff, "MVA processing of speech features," *IEEE Transactions on Audio, Speech and Language Processing*, vol. 15, no. 1, pp. 257–270, 2007.
11. A. Acero, *Acoustical and environmental robustness in automatic speech recognition [Ph.D. thesis]*, Department of Electrical and Computer Engineering, Carnegie Mellon University, 1990.

12. K. Ishizuka, T. Nakatani, M. Fujimoto, and N. Miyazaki, "Noise robust voice activity detection based on periodic to aperiodic component ratio," *Speech Communication*, vol. 52, no. 1, pp. 41–60, 2010.
13. R. Martin, "Noise power spectral density estimation based on optimal smoothing and minimum statistics," *IEEE Transactions on Speech and Audio Processing*, vol. 9, no. 5, pp. 504–512, 2001.
14. H. Hirsch and D. Pearce, "The Aurora experimental framework for the performance evaluations of speech recognition system under noisy conditions," in *Proceedings of the 7th international conference on Information, communications and signal processing (ICICS '09)*, Paris, France, 2000.
15. ITU-T, Recommendation G.712. Transmission Performance Characteristics for Pulse Code Modulation Channels, Geneva, Switzerland, 1996.
16. R. G. Leonard, "A database for speaker independent digit recognition," in *Proceedings of the International Conference on Acoustics, Speech, and Signal Processing (ICASSP '84*, vol. 3, pp. 42–53, 1984.
17. M. Brookes, Voicebox, http://www.ee.ic.ac.uk/hp/staff/dmb/voicebox/voicebox.html.
18. J. Droppo, A. Acero, and L. Deng, "Evaluation of the SPLICE algorithm on the Aurora 2 database," in *Proceedings of the Eurospeech Conference, International Speech Communication Association*, Aalbodk, Denmark, September 2001.
19. R. Martin, "Spectral subtraction based on minimum statistics," in *Proceedings of the European Signal Processing Conference (EUSIPCO '96)*, pp. 1182–1185, 1994.

CHAPTER 4

Deep Neural Learning Adaptive Sequential Monte Carlo for Automatic Image and Speech Recognition

Patcharin Kamsing,[1] Peerapong Torteeka,[2] Wuttichai Boonpook,[3] and Chunxiang Cao[4,5]

[1]Air-Space Control, Optimization and Management Laboratory, Department of Aeronautical Engineering, International Academy of Aviation Industry, King Mongkut's Institute of Technology, Ladkrabang, Bangkok 10520, Thailand

[2]National Astronomical Research Institute of Thailand, ChiangMai 50180, Thailand

[3]Department of Geography, Faculty of Social Sciences, Srinakharinwirot University, Bangkok 10110, Thailand

[4]State Key Laboratory of Remote Sensing Science, Aerospace Information Research Institute, Chinese Academy of Sciences, Beijing 100101, China

[5]University of Chinese Academy of Sciences, Beijing 100094, China

Citation: Patcharin Kamsing, Peerapong Torteeka, Wuttichai Boonpook, Chunxiang Cao, "Deep Neural Learning Adaptive Sequential Monte Carlo for Automatic Image and Speech Recognition", Applied Computational Intelligence and Soft Computing, vol. 2020, Article ID 8866259, 9 pages, 2020. https://doi.org/10.1155/2020/8866259.

ABSTRACT

To enhance the performance of image classification and speech recognition, the optimizer is considered an important factor for achieving high accuracy. The state-of-the-art optimizer can perform to serve in applications that may not require very high accuracy, yet the demand for high-precision image classification and speech recognition is increasing. This study implements an adaptive method for applying the particle filter technique with a gradient descent optimizer to improve model learning performance. Using a pretrained model helps reduce the computational time to deploy an image classification model and uses a simple deep convolutional neural network for speech recognition. The applied method results in a higher speech recognition accuracy score—89.693% for the test dataset—than the conventional method, which reaches 89.325%. The applied method also performs well on the image classification task, reaching an accuracy of 89.860% on the test dataset, better than the conventional method, which has an accuracy of 89.644%. Despite a slight difference in accuracy, the applied optimizer performs well in this dataset overall.

INTRODUCTION

Soft computing is available in several applications due to its usefulness in modeling and optimization. Numerous studies have focused on image and video processing with objectives such as detection and tracking. Various models have been proposed, including neural networks, deep learning, fuzzy logic, and hybrid methods [1]. However, their practical use in applications remains problematic because many applications require higher accuracy than the available models can supply. Hybrid methods that combine two or more soft computing techniques can often enhance the efficiency of image and video retrieval processes [2]. In an image context, a 3D geographical information system (GIS) data plan for the WiMax network was integrated to optimize both the network performance and the investment costs, both of which are relevant to the required number of base stations and sectors [3]. In addition, soft computing plays an important role in GIS research [4–7]. One important aspect of implementing soft computing is the quality of the dataset. Soft computing can also be used to generate meaningful and human-interpretable big datasets by defining an interface between the numerical and categorical spaces, i.e., the data definition and the linguistic space of human reasoning [8]. Furthermore, datasets applied to investigate soft computing methods should use a benchmark dataset intended for validating various methods [1]. One example of applying soft computing for decision making was presented [9]; this is a new method named the neurofuzzy analytical network process. The presented method works based on both fuzzy logic and an artificial neural network. Another implementation of soft computing was proposed for tunneling optimization [10]. This model analyzes the relationship between the target tunneling responses and the impact of input parameters, including both geometrical and geological factors. The proposed implementation is useful in reaching robust and low-cost soft computing solutions in the mining industry [11]. Soft computing can be applied in environmental management to predict vehicular traffic noise using data such as the volume per hour, percentage of heavy vehicles, and average speed of vehicles as inputs to neural networks or random forests [12]. Six methods are used for modeling soil water capacity parameters that are important in environmental management of targeted areas [13]. In the aviation industry, a multilayer perceptron neural network is employed to diagnose aerospace structure defects: the classical method uses signal processing and data interpretation [14]. Soft computing has also been implemented in path categorization of airplanes [15]. Soft computing can also be applied for estimating the position and orientation of spacecraft, which is useful for space technology development [16].

Image classification and speech recognition remain demanding research topics, since they can be applied in various applications [17]. One example of an image classification method is a graph-based multiple rank regression model [18], for which the researchers presented a method that can reduce the losses in matrix data correlations that occur when an image is transformed into a vector suitable for image classification processes. An integrated recurrent neural network and a convolutional neural network (CNN), named the multipath *x-D* recurrent neural network (MxDRNN), has been proposed for image classification [19]. In addition, semisupervised deep neural networks implement a robust loss function to enhance image classification performance [20], and hyperspectral image classification has been widely used in many earth observation tasks, including object detection, object recognition, and surveillance. A new joint spatial-spectral hyperspectral image classification method based on differently scaled two-stream convolutional networks and spatial enhancement achieved improved classification performance [21]. Image classification for very high-resolution imagery (VHRI) is another challenging task because of the rich detail captured in the images. Many studies have focused on object-based convolutional neural networks (OCNNs) and proposed various innovations, such as integrating a multilevel context-guided classification method with an OCNN to achieve higher VHRI classification accuracy [22]. Image classification techniques have also been applied to medical applications such as breast cancer screening through histopathological imaging [23]. In addition, speech recognition research is useful for native language tasks, such as the implementation of deep neural networks for the Algerian dialect [24] and for code-switching among Frisian languages [25]. Other speech recognition research has concentrated on recognizing emotion from speech with regard to age and sex using hierarchical models [26]. A new approach for speech recognition based on the specific coding of time and frequency characteristics of speech using CNNs has been presented [27]. Visual object tracking by using an exponential quantum particle filter and mean shift optimization has been presented as an another challenge for object tracking [28].

The applied method employs the particle filter technique, a state estimation technique, to optimize the gradient descent optimizer. State estimation is often used in navigation and guidance applications and has sometimes been applied to other optimization methods. For example, for real-time traffic estimation, state estimation has been implemented using an extended Kalman filter instead of using Gaussian process regression models with respect to historical data [29]. A particle filter has also been implemented to adjust various parameters to improve image classification [30–32] and for some application such as crack propagation filtering [33]. The gradient descent algorithm is mainly used to optimize an objective [34]. For instance, it was used to implement a demonstration of a morphing wing-tip for an aircraft to reduce low-speed drag [35]. Thermal power plants use state estimation to optimize various parameters [36]. The adaptive technique presented in this paper, which combines a particle filter with the gradient descent optimizer to adjust and improve the performance on image classification and speech recognition tasks, is evaluated using the PlanesNet [37] and TensorFlow speech recognition challenge [38] datasets.

MATERIALS AND METHODS

Materials

PlanesNet Dataset

Future airport designs should provide improved passenger convenience, such as reducing airplane delays or requiring less check-in time. Air traffic management, as the backbone of the aviation industry, is one factor leading airports to become more intelligent [17]. Airplane detection is a fundamental task in tracking, positioning, and predicting the positions of airplanes. PlanesNet is a medium-resolution, labeled, remote sensing image dataset that can serve as training data for training machine learning algorithms [37]. The dataset consists of 20 × 20 RGB images labeled as "plane" or "no-plane" as shown in Figures 1 and 2, respectively. The "plane" images mainly consist of the wings, tail, and nose of the airplane. The images labeled "no-plane" may include land cover features such as water, vegetation, bare earth, or buildings and do not show any part of an airplane. Some example image data are presented in the following figures.

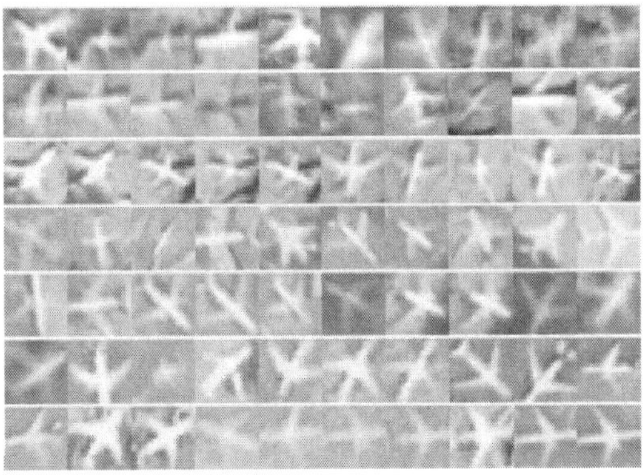

Figure 1: Example of images in the PlanesNet dataset labeled as the "plane" category.

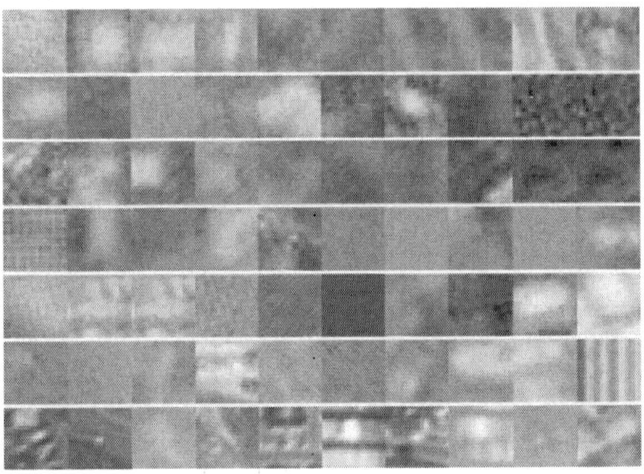

Figure 2: Example of images in the PlanesNet dataset labeled as the "no-plane" category.

Speech Commands Dataset

Another dataset adopted in this study for testing the applied method is a public dataset for single word speech recognition, which was initially compiled for use in the TensorFlow Speech Recognition Challenge [38]. The dataset consists of audio files in which a single speaker says one word. The objective is to predict the audio files in the testing dataset, which are categorized in one of twelve categories: "silence," "unknown," "yes," "no," "up," "down," "left," "right," "on," "off," "stop," and "go." It should be noted that the applied method is based on a CNN, which is normally applied to 2D spatial problems. In contrast, audio is inherently a one-dimensional continuous signal across time. The dataset was preprocessed into images by defining a time window into which the spoken words fit; then, the captured audio signal is converted into an image by grouping the incoming audio samples into short segments, just a few milliseconds long, and calculating the strength of the frequencies across a set of bands. Each set of frequency strengths from a segment is treated as a vector of numbers, and those vectors are arranged in time sequence to form a two-dimensional array. This array of values can then be treated such as a single-channel image called a spectrogram.

Methods

The applied method is implemented based on a combination of a particle filter and minibatch gradient descent optimizer processes as expressed in equation (1) with the goal of obtaining a suitable optimizer for the target dataset:

$$\theta = \theta - \eta \cdot g_\theta J\left(\theta; x^{(i:i+n)}; y^{(i:i+n)}\right), \tag{1}$$

where θ is the weight, η is the learning rate, and gθ is a gradient of the cost function J(θ) with respect to weight changes. Stochastic gradient descent (SGD) performs a parameter update after processing each training example $x^{(i)}$ and label $y^{(i)}$, which means that the batch size is 1. (e cost function in minibatch gradient descent is the average over a small data batch, which usually ranges in size between 50 and 256, but can vary depending on the application.

The applied method uses a generated particle process in combination with variables from the minibatch gradient descent optimizer. Consequently, the applied optimizer performs updates by using the computed variables instead of the conventional variables from the minibatch gradient descent optimizer. The applied method can be expressed as shown in the following equation:

$$\theta = \theta - \left(\eta \cdot g_{\theta} J\left(\theta; x^{(i:i+n)}; y^{(i:i+n)}\right) + K \times \text{learning rate}\right), \tag{2}$$

where K is an adjustment value obtained from the particle filter process. K is multiplied by the deep learning rate before being added to the second equation term of the conventional minibatch gradient descent optimizer in equation (1). Figure 3 illustrates the working process of a particle filter. It works based on historical information from the prior stage. PF works iteratively by generating a particle, propagating it to the next time step t, and then performing an update to obtain an accurate value of the time step. A workflow of the applied method to obtain the K value is depicted in Figure 4.

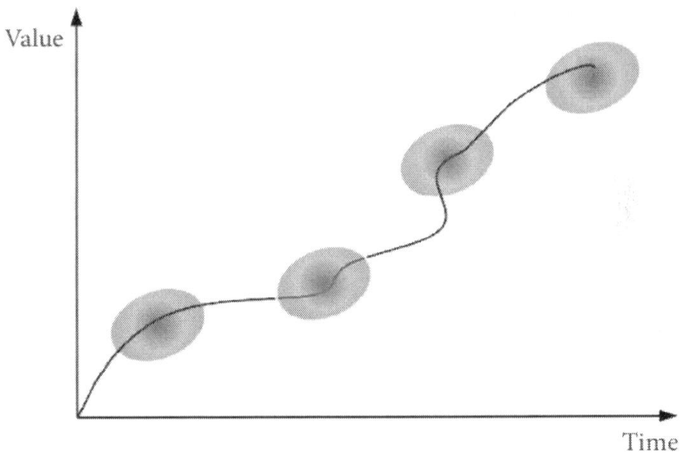

Figure 3: Working process of a particle filter.

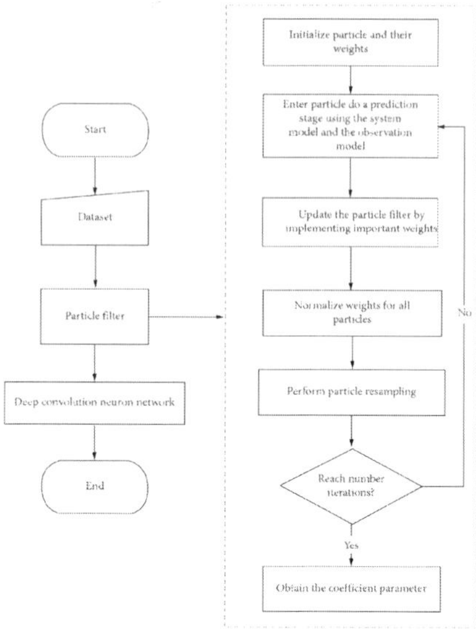

Figure 4: Working processes of the applied method.

The applied method shown in Figure 4 is described as follows [32]:

- Initialization: at t = 0, generate n particles, and set their weights to $\{x_0^i = \mathbf{x}_0, \pi_0^i = 1/n\}_{i=1}^n$
- For t = 1, · · · , end

  a. Input the particle set $\{x_{t-1}^i, \pi_{t-1}^i\}_{i=1}^n$ to obtain the output $\widehat{x}_{t|t-1}^i$ by using the system model equation, which is determined by the particle plus a value from the Gaussian process with zero mean and whose variance is equal to the deep learning rate

  b. Predict the observation value $\widetilde{z}_{t|t-1}^i$ by using $\widehat{x}_{t|t-1}^i$ with the measurement value assigned based on the mean of the prior iteration

  c. Update the particle weight based on the observation vector z_t by $h_t(\cdot)$ or the observation model, which is set to 1. Calculate the importance weight using $\pi_t^i = p(\mathbf{z}_t \mid \widehat{x}_{t|t-1}^i), i = 1, \cdots, n$.

  d. Normalize the weights according to $\widetilde{\pi}_t^i = \pi_t^i / \sum_{j=1}^n \pi_t^j$. Particle rejection or retention depends on the weight (π_t^i) and multinomial resampling, which is determined by the resampling algorithm.

RESULTS AND DISCUSSION

Image Classification Result

This experiment uses the inception_v3 model, which is a pretrained model intended for image classification applications. The PlanesNet dataset deployed in this experiment has a total of 18,085 images divided into two classes (7,995 "plane" images and 10,090 "no-plane" images). The data are divided into a training set with 14,377 images and a testing set with 3,708 images. The training batch size is set to 100, the leaning rate is 0.001, and the deep learning computation requires 10,000 epochs.

The results of the applied method are compared with those of the conventional gradient descent optimizer. The applied method shows three cases (with different numbers of particles and particle filter iterations in parentheses). The results of the applied method and those of the gradient descent optimizer for image classification in Table 1 reveal that iterations using the applied method (180, 300) achieve the best performance as measured by the mean cross entropy in every iteration (0.3193) and by the final test accuracy (89.860%). The applied method (50, 50) achieves the best performance with regard to mean accuracy (87.4291%), which is calculated after every iteration.

Table 1: Results of the applied method and the gradient descent optimizer for image classification.

Method	**Mean accuracy (%)**	**Mean cross entropy**	**Final test accuracy (%)**
The applied method (50, 50)	**87.4291**	0.3196	89.482
The applied method (150, 100)	87.3806	0.3199	89.482
The applied method (180, 300)	87.4269	**0.3193**	**89.860**
The gradient descent method	87.4073	0.3200	89.644

The accuracy and cross entropy after each deep learning iteration are shown in Figure 5. The graphs do not clearly express different model efficiencies because the performance improves only slightly as shown in Table 1. However, both accuracy and cross entropy (Figures 5(a) and 5(b), respectively) present the values of the corresponding trends for the applied method and the conventional method.

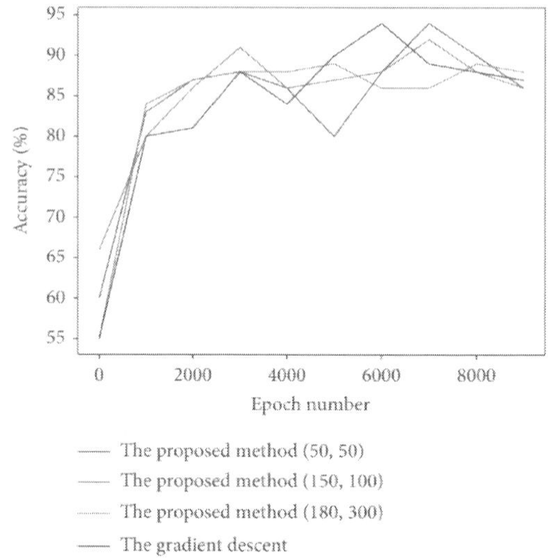

(a)

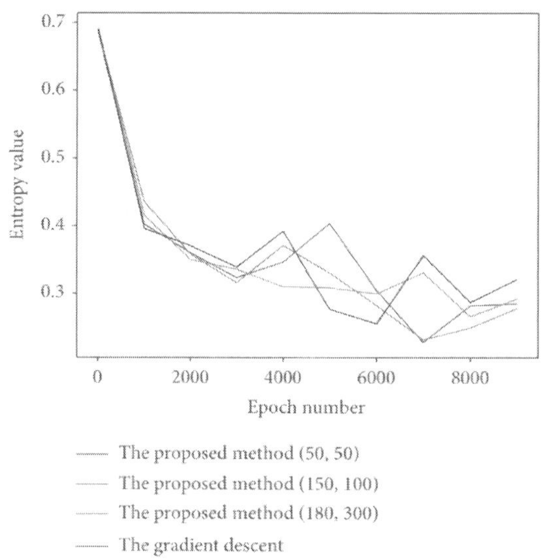

(b)

Figure 5: Image classification performance: (a) accuracy after each learning step; (b) cross entropy after each learning step.

The confusion matrices for all cases are shown in Figure 6, clearly revealing that the applied method with 180 particles and 300 particle filter iterations achieves the best prediction result for the category of "no-plane;" however, it shows poor prediction results for the "plane" category. The confusion matrices for the other three results in Figures 6(a), 6(b), and 6(d) show no large differences in either the "plane" or the "no-plane" categories. These results imply that differences in the number of particles and the number of iterations in the particle filter affect the overall performance of the applied method. Thus, each application should select the most appropriate model based on user requirements and acceptable model accuracy.

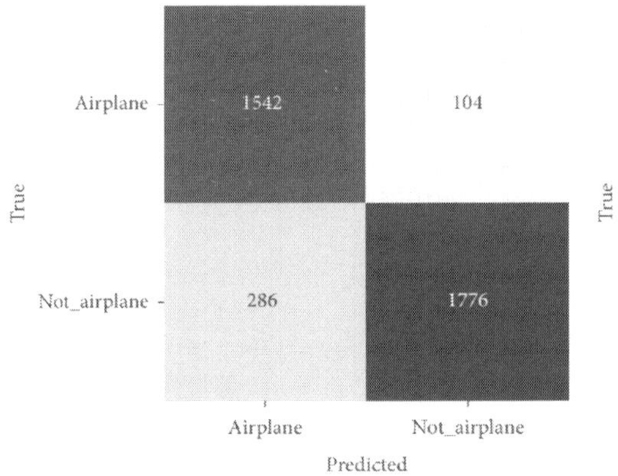

(a)

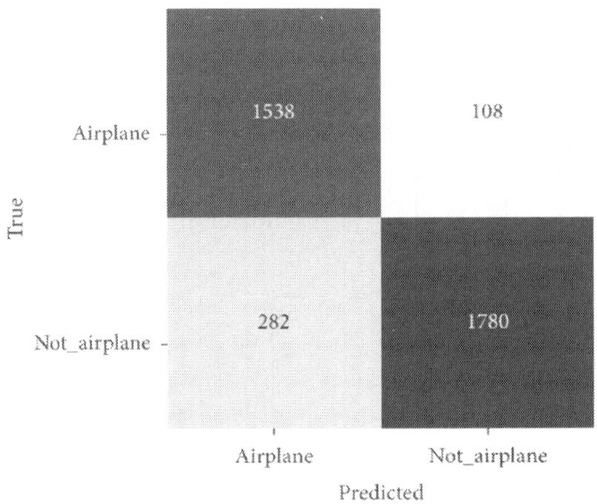

(b)

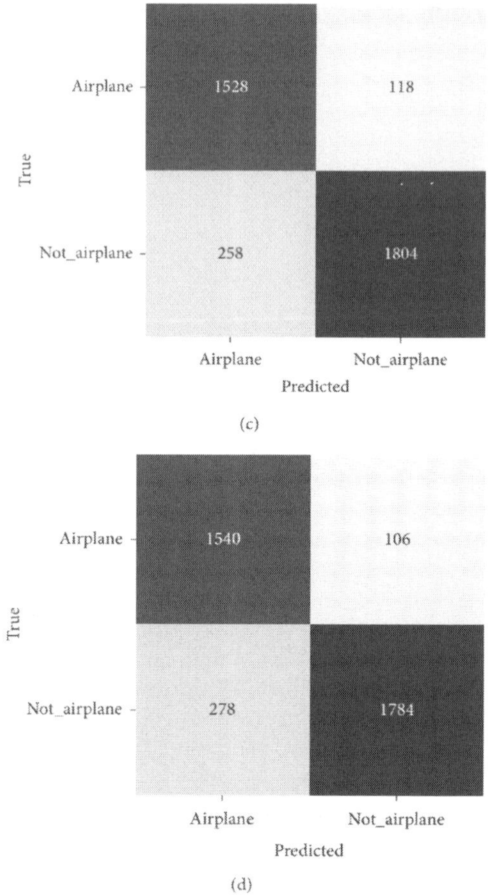

Figure 6: Confusion matrix: (a) the applied method (50, 50); (b) the applied method (150, 100); (c) the applied method (180, 300); (d) the gradient descent method.

Speech Recognition Result

A simple deep CNN is used in this experiment to generate a model for the audio file. The models are trained for 25,000 epochs with a batch size of 100 and a learning rate of 0.001. The audio files include 105,829 individual files: 100,939 in the training dataset and 4,890 in the testing dataset. Similar to the image classification experiment, this experiment compares the results of the applied method under different numbers of particles and particle filter iterations with the results from the conventional minibatch gradient descent optimizer.

The results are presented in Table 2, which show that the applied method (50, 50) achieves exceptional performance compared to the other models and obtains the best mean accuracy (77.8163%), mean cross entropy (0.6772), and final test accuracy (89.693%). The conventional minibatch gradient descent optimizer is the second best. From these results, we can conclude that the applied method configured with an appropriate number of particles and particle filter iterations can achieve a better performance than the conventional method. The accuracy and cross entropy results after each iteration are illustrated in Figure 7, which did not reveal obvious overall differences; therefore, the improvements are listed in Table 2. Confusion matrices are presented in Figure 8. The applied method (50, 50) shows exceptional performance on the "no," "right," and "off" classes. However, the conventional method achieves the best performance on the "yes," "down," and "go" classes. The other two versions of the applied method achieve a good performance on the "unknown" class. Finally, the applied method (150, 100) achieves the best results on the "left" and "on" classes.

Table 2: Results of the applied method and the gradient descent optimizer for speech recognition.

Method	Mean accuracy (%)	Mean cross entropy	Final test accuracy (%)
The applied method (50, 50)	**77.8163**	**0.6772**	**89.693**
The applied method (150, 100)	77.4286	0.6900	89.059
The applied method (180, 300)	77.2724	0.6952	89.141
The gradient descent method	77.4950	0.6853	89.325

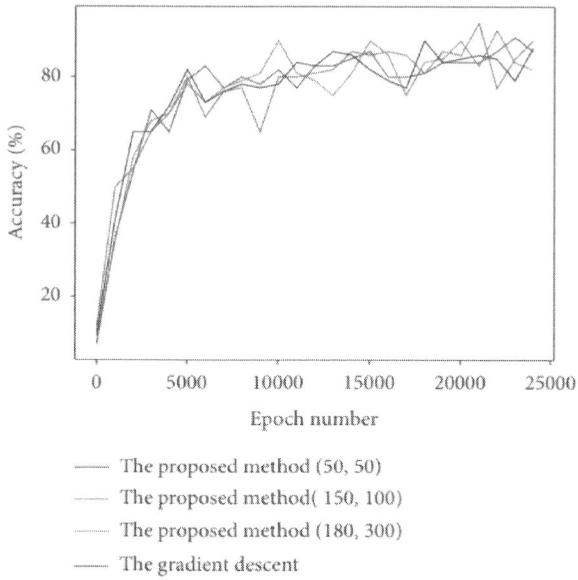

(a)

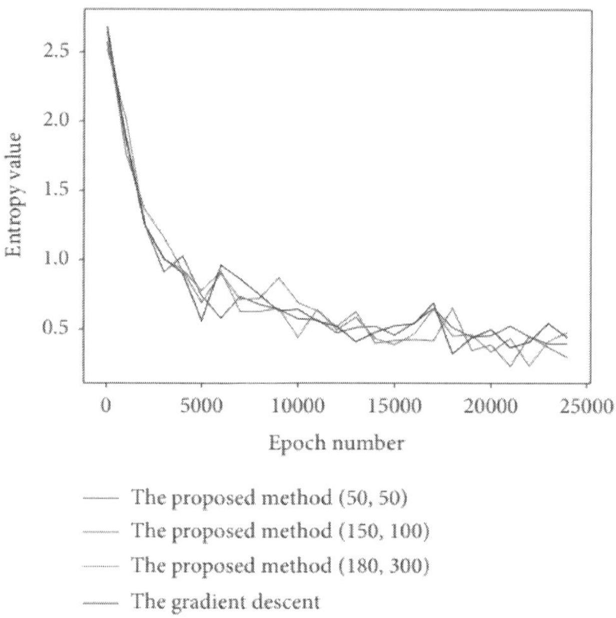

(b)

Figure 7: Speech recognition performance: (a) accuracy after each learning step; (b) cross entropy after each learning step.

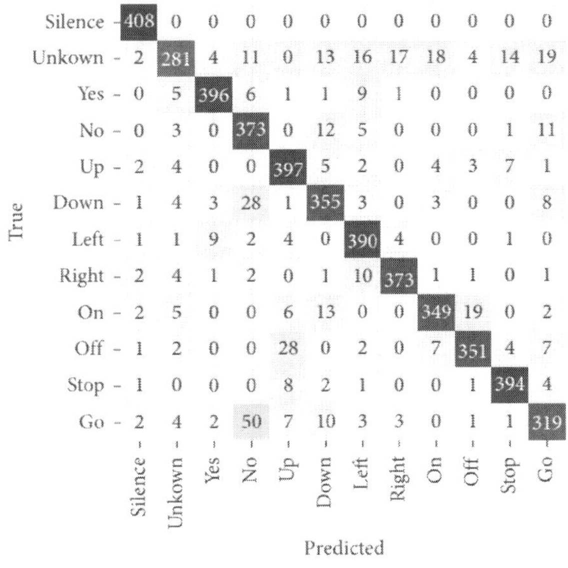
Silence 408 0 0 0 0 0 0 0 0 0 0 0
Unkown 2 281 4 11 0 13 16 17 18 4 14 19
Yes 0 5 396 6 1 1 9 1 0 0 0 0
No 0 3 0 373 0 12 5 0 0 0 1 11
Up 2 4 0 0 397 5 2 0 4 3 7 1
Down 1 4 3 28 1 355 3 0 3 0 0 8
Left 1 1 9 2 4 0 390 4 0 0 1 0
Right 2 4 1 2 0 1 10 373 1 1 0 1
On 2 5 0 0 6 13 0 0 349 19 0 2
Off 1 2 0 0 28 0 2 0 7 351 4 7
Stop 1 0 0 0 8 2 1 0 0 1 394 4
Go 2 4 2 50 7 10 3 3 0 1 1 319
True
Silence Unkown Yes No Up Down Left Right On Off Stop Go
Predicted

(a)

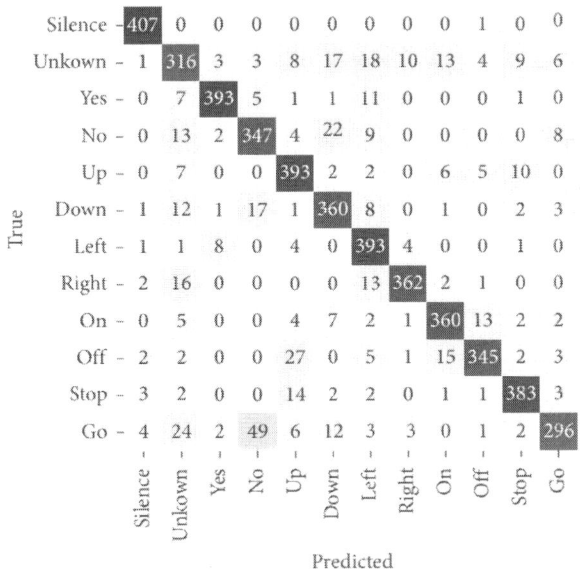
Silence 407 0 0 0 0 0 0 0 0 1 0 0
Unkown 1 316 3 3 8 17 18 10 13 4 9 6
Yes 0 7 393 5 1 1 11 0 0 0 1 0
No 0 13 2 347 4 22 9 0 0 0 0 8
Up 0 7 0 0 393 2 2 0 6 5 10 0
Down 1 12 1 17 1 360 8 0 1 0 2 3
Left 1 1 8 0 4 0 393 4 0 0 1 0
Right 2 16 0 0 0 0 13 362 2 1 0 0
On 0 5 0 0 4 7 2 1 360 13 2 2
Off 2 2 0 0 27 0 5 1 15 345 2 3
Stop 3 2 0 0 14 2 2 0 1 1 383 3
Go 4 24 2 49 6 12 3 3 0 1 2 296
True
Silence Unkown Yes No Up Down Left Right On Off Stop Go
Predicted

(b)

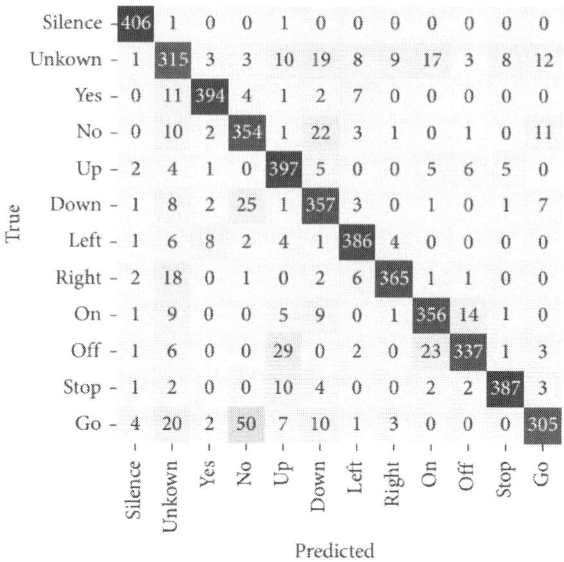

(c)

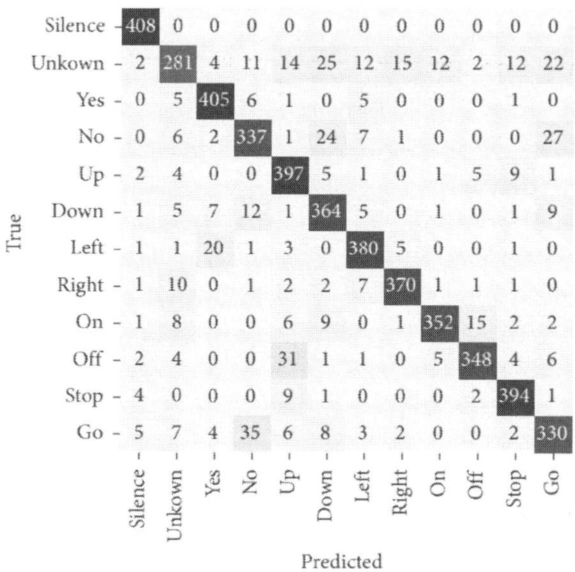

(d)

Figure 8: Confusion matrices: (a) the applied method (50, 50); (b) the applied method (150, 100); (c) the applied method (180, 300); (d) the gradient descent method.

The overall results of the speech recognition experiment show that the applied method performs better than the conventional method in terms of both accuracy and cross entropy. However, the confusion matrix results should be considered in detail before selecting the most suitable model for a given application.

The overall performance of using the applied method with image classification and speech recognition provides better accuracy. However, confusion matrices for both image classification and speech recognition illustrate some failure cases that remain a challenging task for further research. This is a very important consideration for some applications that require high precision of image classification, such as in the health care industry, or high precision of speech recognition, such as in rescue processes. Therefore, the applied method in this experiment, based on state estimation and a well-known optimizer, is helpful to slightly improve performance in both applications. To apply this method in practical applications, more consideration of acceptable cases and failure cases using confusion matrices is required to reach optimal performance.

CONCLUSIONS

The goal of this study was to use the particle filter technique to optimize a variable in a gradient descent optimizer. The applied method was validated by applying it to two different types of public datasets: the PlanesNet dataset (for image classification) and the Speech Commands dataset (for speech recognition). Moreover, three variations of the applied method that use different numbers of particles and different numbers of iterations were tested on those two datasets: the three model variations used 50 particles and 50 particle filter iterations, 150 particles and 100 particle filter iterations, and 180 particles and 300 particle filter iterations, respectively. The overall results show that the applied method achieves exceptional performances on both datasets, obtaining higher accuracy and lower cross entropy than the conventional method. The experiments also showed that the number of particles and the number of iterations used in the particle filter process affect the model's overall performance. Therefore, to build a high-accuracy model, appropriate parameter values should be selected for the particle filter process in the applied method according to each application. A confusion matrix can be used as an assistive tool to select the most suitable model for a given application.

ACKNOWLEDGMENTS

The authors thank the staff of the International Academy of Aviation Industry, King Mongkut's Institute of Technology Ladkrabang, for their contributions to this article. This research was funded by Academic Melting Pot, the KMITL Research Fund, King Mongkut's Institute of Technology Ladkrabang, Bangkok 10520, Thailand.

REFERENCES

1. M. Kaushal, B. S. Khehra, and A. Sharma, "Soft computing based object detection and tracking approaches: state-of-the-art survey," *Applied Soft Computing*, vol. 70, pp. 423–464, 2018.
2. H. Bhaumik, S. Bhattacharyya, M. D. Nath, and S. Chakraborty, "Hybrid soft computing approaches to content based video retrieval: a brief review," *Applied Soft Computing*, vol. 46, pp. 1008–1029, 2016.
3. L. H. Son and P. H. Thong, "Soft computing methods for WiMax network planning on 3D geographical information systems," *Journal of Computer and System Sciences*, vol. 83, no. 1, pp. 159–179, 2017.
4. A. U. Islam, M. J. Khan, K. Khurshid, and F. Shafait, "Hyperspectral image analysis for writer identification using deep learning," in *Proceedings of the International Conference on Digital Image Computing: Techniques and Applications (DICTA)*, pp. 1–7, IEEE, Perth, Australia, December 2019.
5. M. J. Khan, H. S. Khan, A. Yousaf, K. Khurshid, and A. Abbas, "Modern trends in hyperspectral image analysis: a review," *IEEE Access*, vol. 6, pp. 14118–14129, 2018.
6. M. J. Khan, K. Khurshid, and F. Shafait, "A spatio-spectral hybrid convolutional architecture for hyperspectral document authentication," in *Proceedings of the International Conference on Document Analysis and Recognition (ICDAR)*, pp. 1097–1102, IEEE, Sydney, Australia, September 2019.
7. M. J. Khan, A. Yousaf, K. Khurshid, A. Abbas, and F. Shafait, "Automated forgery detection in multispectral document images using fuzzy clustering," in *Proceedings of the 13th IAPR International Workshop on Document Analysis Systems (DAS)*, pp. 393–398, IEEE, Vienna, Austria, April 2018.
8. G. Smits, O. Pivert, R. R. Yager, and P. Nerzic, "A soft computing approach to big data summarization," *Fuzzy Sets and Systems*, vol. 348, pp. 4–20, 2018.
9. D. A. Carrera, R. V. Mayorga, and W. Peng, "A soft computing approach for group decision making: a supply chain management application," *Applied Soft Computing*, vol. 91, Article ID 106201, 2020.
10. S. Isam and Z. Wengang, *Use of Soft Computing Techniques for Tunneling Optimization of Tunnel Boring Machines*, Underground Space, Upper Saddle River, NJ, USA, 2020.

11. C. K. Arthur, V. A. Temeng, and Y. Y. Ziggah, "Soft computing-based technique as a predictive tool to estimate blast-induced ground vibration," *Journal of Sustainable Mining*, vol. 18, no. 4, pp. 287–296, 2019.
12. D. Singh, S. P. Nigam, V. P. Agrawal, and M. Kumar, "Vehicular traffic noise prediction using soft computing approach," *Journal of Environmental Management*, vol. 183, pp. 59–66, 2016.
13. J. Shiri, A. Keshavarzi, O. Kisi, and S. Karimi, "Using soil easily measured parameters for estimating soil water capacity: soft computing approaches," *Computers and Electronics in Agriculture*, vol. 141, pp. 327–339, 2017.
14. G. D'Angelo and S. Rampone, "Feature extraction and soft computing methods for aerospace structure defect classification," *Measurement*, vol. 85, pp. 192–209, 2016.
15. P. Kamsing, P. Torteeka, S. Yooyen et al., "Aircraft trajectory recognition via statistical analysis clustering for Suvarnabhumi international airport," in *Proceedings of the 22nd International Conference on Advanced Communication Technology (ICACT)*, pp. 290–297, IEEE, Phoenix Park, Republic of Korea, February 2020.
16. T. Phisannupawong, P. Kamsing, P. Tortceka, and S. Yooyen, "Vision-based attitude estimation for spacecraft docking operation through deep learning algorithm," in *Procedings of the 22nd International Conference on Advanced Communication Technology (ICACT)*, pp. 280–284, IEEE, Phoenix Park, Republic of Korea, February 2020.
17. P. Kamsing, P. Torteeka, and S. Yooyen, "Deep convolutional neural networks for plane identification on satellite imagery by exploiting transfer learning with a different optimizer," in *Proceedings of the IGARSS 2019 - 2019 IEEE International Geoscience and Remote Sensing Symposium*, pp. 9788–9791, IEEE, Yokohama, Japan, August 2019.
18. H. Yuan, J. Li, L. L. Lai, and Y. Y. Tang, "Graph-based multiple rank regression for image classification," *Neurocomputing*, vol. 315, pp. 394–404, 2018.
19. R. Gao, Y. Huo, S. Bao et al., "Multi-path x-D recurrent neural networks for collaborative image classification," *Neurocomputing*, vol. 397, pp. 48–59, 2020.

20. H. Cevikalp, B. Benligiray, and O. N. Gerek, "Semi-supervised robust deep neural networks for multi-label image classification," *Pattern Recognition*, vol. 100, Article ID 107164, 2020.
21. M. Han, R. Cong, X. Li, H. Fu, and J. Lei, "Joint spatial-spectral hyperspectral image classification based on convolutional neural network," *Pattern Recognition Letters*, vol. 130, pp. 38–45, 2020.
22. C. Zhang, P. Yue, D. Tapete, B. Shangguan, M. Wang, and Z. Wu, "A multi-level context-guided classification method with object-based convolutional neural network for land cover classification using very high resolution remote sensing images," *International Journal of Applied Earth Observation and Geoinformation*, vol. 88, Article ID 102086, 2020.
23. R. Yan, F. Ren, Z. Wang et al., "Breast cancer histopathological image classification using a hybrid deep neural network," *Methods*, vol. 173, pp. 52–60, 2020.
24. M. A. Menacer, O. Mella, D. Fohr, D. Jouvet, D. Langlois, and K. Smaïli, "Development of the Arabic loria automatic speech recognition system (ALASR) and its evaluation for Algerian dialect," *Procedia Computer Science*, vol. 117, pp. 81–88, 2017.
25. E. Yılmaz, H. van den Heuvel, and D. van Leeuwen, "Investigating bilingual deep neural networks for automatic recognition of code-switching Frisian speech," *Procedia Computer Science*, vol. 81, pp. 159–166, 2016.
26. R. Flynn and E. Jones, "Robust distributed speech recognition in noise and packet loss conditions," *Digital Signal Processing*, vol. 20, no. 6, pp. 1559–1571, 2010.
27. M. Kubanek, J. Bobulski, and J. Kulawik, "A method of speech coding for speech recognition using a convolutional neural network," *Symmetry*, vol. 11, no. 9, p. 1185, 2019.
28. P. P. Dash and D. Patra, "An efficient hybrid framework for visual tracking using exponential quantum particle filter and mean shift optimization," *Multimedia Tools and Applications*, vol. 79, no. 29-30, pp. 21513–21537, 2020.
29. J. Jin and X. Ma, "A non-parametric Bayesian framework for traffic-state estimation at signalized intersections," *Information Sciences*, vol. 498, pp. 21–40, 2019.

30. P. Insom, C. Cao, P. Boonsrimuang et al., "A support vector machine-based particle filter for improved land cover classification applied to MODIS data," in *Proceedings of the 2016 IEEE International Geoscience and Remote Sensing Symposium (IGARSS)*, pp. 775–778, IEEE, Beijing, China, July 2016.
31. P. Insom, C. Chunxiang Cao, P. Boonsrimuang et al., "A support vector machine-based particle filter method for improved flooding classification," *IEEE Geoscience and Remote Sensing Letters*, vol. 12, no. 9, pp. 1943–1947, 2015.
32. P. Kamsing, P. Torteeka, and S. Yooyen, "An enhanced learning algorithm with a particle filter-based gradient descent optimizer method," *Neural Computing and Applications*, vol. 32, no. 16, pp. 12789–12800, 2020.
33. S. F. Karimian, R. Moradi, S. Cofre-Martel, K. M. Groth, and M. Modarres, "Neural network and particle filtering: a hybrid framework for crack propagation prediction," *Signal Processing*, vol. 2004, 2020.
34. A. Ratre, "Stochastic gradient descent-whale optimization algorithm-based deep convolutional neural network to crowd emotion understanding," *The Computer Journal*, vol. 63, no. 2, pp. 267–282, 2019.
35. A. Koreanschi, O. Sugar Gabor, J. Acotto et al., "Optimization and design of an aircraft's morphing wing-tip demonstrator for drag reduction at low speed, Part I—aerodynamic optimization using genetic, bee colony and gradient descent algorithms," *Chinese Journal of Aeronautics*, vol. 30, no. 1, pp. 149–163, 2017.
36. A. M. Kler, P. V. Zharkov, and N. O. Epishkin, "Parametric optimization of supercritical power plants using gradient methods," *Energy*, vol. 189, Article ID 116230, 2019.
37. Rhammell, "PlanesNet—planes in satellite imagery," https://www.kaggle.com/rhammell/planesnet/version/2.
38. P. Warden, "Speech Commands: A Public Dataset for Single-word Speech Recognition," https://www.kaggle.com/c/tensorflow-speech-recognition-challenge.

CHAPTER 5

A Fast Learning Method for Multilayer Perceptrons in Automatic Speech Recognition Systems

Chenghao Cai,[1] Yanyan Xu,[2] Dengfeng Ke,[3] and Kaile Su[4]

[1]School of Technology, Beijing Forestry University, No. 35 Qinghua Dong Road, Haidian District, Beijing 100083, China

[2]School of Information Science and Technology, Beijing Forestry University, No. 35 Qinghua Dong Road, Haidian District, Beijing 100083, China

[3]Institute of Automation, Chinese Academy of Sciences, No. 95 Zhongguancun Dong Road, Haidian District, Beijing 100190, China

[4]Institute for Integrated and Intelligent Systems, Griffith University, 170 Kessels Road, Nathan, Brisbane, QLD 4111, Australia

Citation: Chenghao Cai, Yanyan Xu, Dengfeng Ke, Kaile Su, "A Fast Learning Method for Multilayer Perceptrons in Automatic Speech Recognition Systems", Journal of Robotics, vol. 2015, Article ID 797083, 7 pages, 2015. https://doi.org/10.1155/2015/797083.

ABSTRACT

We propose a fast learning method for multilayer perceptrons (MLPs) on large vocabulary continuous speech recognition (LVCSR) tasks. A preadjusting strategy based on separation of training data and dynamic learning-rate with a cosine function is used to increase the accuracy of a stochastic initial MLP. Weight matrices of the preadjusted MLP are restructured by a method based on singular value decomposition (SVD), reducing the dimensionality of the MLP. A back propagation (BP) algorithm that fits the unfolded weight matrices is used to train the restructured MLP, reducing the time complexity of the learning process. Experimental results indicate that on LVCSR tasks, in comparison with the conventional learning method, this fast learning method can achieve a speedup of around 2.0 times with improvement on both the cross entropy loss and the frame accuracy. Moreover, it can achieve a speedup of approximately 3.5 times with only a little loss of the cross entropy loss and the frame accuracy. Since this method consumes less time and space than the conventional method, it is more suitable for robots which have limitations on hardware.

INTRODUCTION

Pattern recognition is one of the most important topics on humanoid robots. To make robots have capabilities of communicating with and learning from the realistic world, recognizing information such as speeches and images is needed. There is much former relevant work. For instance, methods of speech recognition have been used for facilitating interactions between human and humanoid robots for more than ten years [1]. An automated speech recognisor, which has relatively better performance on separating sentences and reducing noises than before, has been then applied to robots [2]. Besides, methods of image recognition have been widely applied to such humanoid robots. A classic example is the use of the robotic vision, such as gesture recognition to realize the direct commanding from humans to robots [3, 4].

However, there are some problems restricting the application of such methods to robots, the chief among which is that the recognising results are not satisfying. Fortunately, deep neural networks (DNNs) can resolve this problem to a great degree. DNNs were first successfully applied to image recognition, bringing evident improvement on the recognition performance [5]. Then they have been used in speech recognition, especially in LVCSR tasks, over the past few years. Former work reveals that automatic speech recognition (ASR) systems based on context dependent Gaussian mixture models (CD-GMMs) and hidden Markov models (HMMs) are improved by replacing GMMs with DNNs [6–10]. Moreover, new usages of DNNs are proposed in recent work [11–18].

An MLP based on a supervised BP learning algorithm is one of the widely used DNNs in ASR systems. However, learning is difficult in the MLP due to the heavy computational burdens of densely connected structures, multilayers, and several epochs of iterations, and thus it requires considerably long time to achieve an essential recognition accuracy. Another drawback of DNNs is that it is hard to decode them as the decoding processes also entail a large amount of time.

Some methods have been proposed to ameliorate these disadvantages. Since graphics processing units (GPUs) have powerful abilities on parallel computations, they have been used to improve the speed of computing matrix multiplications in regard to the dense weight matrices of MLPs [19]. Meanwhile, asynchronous training algorithms have been applied to the training processes, making several computers or processing units work asynchronously so that the training tasks were allocated to parallel simultaneous jobs [20–22]. Moreover, Hessian-free (HF) optimisation focuses on reducing the number of iterations, which makes parameters converge faster than conventional stochastic gradient descent (SGD) [23–25]. Nevertheless, the heavy computational burdens of learning MLPs still exist, especially on realistic tasks that demand markedly sufficient learning to improve the recognition accuracy. To speed up the decoding processes, SVD is used to restructure the models, but it requires extra time for retraining and once again increases the time consumption [26, 27].

In this paper, we propose a fast learning method, reducing the computational burdens of learning MLPs and decoding them. The basic concept of this method is to preadjust roughly the initial MLP and then train the MLP using an unconventional BP algorithm after restructuring weight matrices via SVD. The preadjusting process alters the distributions of singular values before the MLP is accurately trained. Since SVD reduces the dimensionality of weight matrices, the burdens of computing matrix multiplications are lessened.

The rest of this paper is organized as follows. Section 2 describes the fast learning method. Section 3 shows experimental results and discussions and in Section 4 we draw conclusions.

A FAST LEARNING METHOD

A Learning Strategy for the First Epoch

The basic concept of this strategy is to roughly train the MLP before accurate learning. Concretely, it goes through all of the training data only once during the first epoch, using the conventional BP algorithm. During this epoch, the frame accuracy of the MLP is heightened as far as possible.

This strategy first separates averagely the training data into T bunches. When training with the ith bunch data, a dynamically declining learning rate is used, which is

$$\epsilon(i) = \epsilon_0 \alpha^{i-1} \quad (i = 1, 2, 3, \ldots, T), \tag{1}$$

where ϵ_0 denotes the initial learning rate and $0<\alpha<1$. The proportions of these bunches are different, observing a rule based on the cosine function. The proportion of the ith bunch is

$$p(i) = \frac{\pi}{2T} \cdot \cos\left(\frac{\pi}{2T} \cdot i\right) \quad (i = 1, 2, 3, \ldots, T-1). \tag{2}$$

Particularly, to ensure that the rest of data are contained in the last bunch, the proportion of the Tth bunch is

$$p(T) = 1 - \sum_{i=1}^{T-1} p(i). \tag{3}$$

In fact $\sum_{i=1}^{T-1} p(i)$ converges to 1 when T tends to positive infinity, because

$$\lim_{T \to +\infty} \sum_{i=1}^{T-1} \frac{\pi}{2T} \cdot \cos\left(\frac{\pi}{2T} \cdot i\right) = \int_0^{\pi/2} \cos\beta \, d\beta = [\sin\beta]_0^{\pi/2} = 1. \tag{4}$$

It ensures that all bunches observe the rule of the cosine function and all data are used when T tends to positive infinity. Nonetheless, it is impossible to let T tend to positive infinity in reality, so T is set to a big positive integer practically. We particularly name this strategy as preadjusting (PA), as the learning-rates and data arrangement are different from those conventional training methods.

The dynamic declining learning-rate is used due to the fact that the PA process requires going through the training data once and achieving heightened accuracies as far as possible. Relatively high learning-rates learn models effectively, but low precision exists, whereas relatively low learning-rates learn MLPs slowly but achieve high recognition accuracies. In (1), the initial learning-rate is high, facilitating the learning speed at the beginning, and, then, α^{i-1} decays this rate exponentially, ensuring the precisions of the intermediate and last learning.

A BP Algorithm Based on Weight Matrix Restructuring

Weight Matrix Restructuring and Training

An MLP consists of an input layer, several hidden layers, and an output layer. Except the input layer that obtains states directly from input vectors, each of the other layers uses a weight matrix, a set of biases, and an activation function to compute states. The computational burdens are mainly due to the weight matrices. Concretely, both forward and backward computations demand the products of weight matrices and various vectors; thus the time complexity of the MLP is determined by the dimensionality of weight matrices.

SVD is one of the basic and important analysis methods in linear algebra [28], which can be used to reduce the dimensionality of matrices and has the following equation [26, 27]:

$$\begin{aligned}\mathrm{SVD}\left(\mathbf{W}_{(\mathbf{m}\times\mathbf{n})}\right) &= \mathbf{U}_{(\mathbf{m}\times\mathbf{m})}\cdot\boldsymbol{\Sigma}_{(\mathbf{m}\times\mathbf{n})}\cdot\mathbf{V}^{\mathbf{T}}_{(\mathbf{n}\times\mathbf{n})}\\ &\approx \mathbf{U}_{(\mathbf{m}\times\mathbf{l})}\cdot\left(\boldsymbol{\Sigma}_{(\mathbf{l}\times\mathbf{l})}\cdot\mathbf{V}^{\mathbf{T}}_{(\mathbf{n}\times\mathbf{n})}\right)\\ &= \mathbf{W}_{\mathbf{1}(\mathbf{m}\times\mathbf{l})}\cdot\mathbf{W}_{\mathbf{2}(\mathbf{l}\times\mathbf{n})},\end{aligned} \tag{5}$$

where the numbers in "( )" stand for dimensions, $W_{(m\times n)}$ stands for an $m\times n$ weight matrix, $U_{(m\times m)}$, $\Sigma_{(m\times n)}$, and $V^T_{(n\times n)}$ stand for three matrices generated by SVD, $W_{1(m\times l)}$ and $W_{2(l\times n)}$ stand for two new obtained weight matrices, and $l < \max(m, n)$ stands for the number of kept singular values. The time complexity of computing a product of $W_{(m\times n)}$ and a vector k(n) is originally $O(m \times n)$. By replacing $W_{(m\times n)} \cdot k(n)$ with $W_{1(m\times l)} \cdot (W_{2(l\times n)} \cdot k_{(n)})$, the time complexity is reduced to $O((m + n) \times l)$ when $l < m \times n/(m + n)$. Since the effectiveness of SVD, to some extent, depends on the meaningful parameters of weight matrices, the SVD-based method is arranged after preadjusting. In other words, SVD is meaningless to stochastic weight matrices which have not learned anything.

To simplify the discussion, consider a single layer. Let $b_{(m)}$ denote an m-dimensional set that contains m biases, and $\varphi(x)$ denotes an activation function. The forward computation transforms an n-dimensional input vector $i_{(n)}$ to an m- dimensional output vector $o_{(m)}$ by

$$\mathbf{o}_{(\mathbf{m})} = \varphi\left(\mathbf{W}_{\mathbf{1}(\mathbf{m}\times\mathbf{l})} \cdot \left(\mathbf{W}_{\mathbf{2}(\mathbf{l}\times\mathbf{n})} \cdot \mathbf{i}_{(\mathbf{n})}\right) + \mathbf{b}_{(\mathbf{m})}\right). \tag{6}$$

Since the weight matrices are unfolded, the backward computation is required to fit the doubled matrix structure. Let $e_{(m)}$ stand for a received error signal, $\varphi'(x)$ for the derivative of the activation function, $\delta_{(m)}$ for a gradient, $e_{(n)}$ for an error signal that will be transmitted to the beneath layer, $\Delta b_{(m)}$, $\Delta W_{1(m\times l)}$, and $\Delta W_{2(l\times n)}$ for the deltas, and ϵ for a learning-rate. According to the BP theory, the gradient is

$$\boldsymbol{\delta}_{(\mathbf{m})} = \varphi'\left(\mathbf{W}_{\mathbf{1}(\mathbf{m}\times\mathbf{l})} \cdot \left(\mathbf{W}_{\mathbf{2}(\mathbf{l}\times\mathbf{n})} \cdot \mathbf{i}_{(\mathbf{n})}\right) + \mathbf{b}_{(\mathbf{m})}\right) \cdot \mathbf{e}_{(\mathbf{m})}. \tag{7}$$

The update rule of $b_{(m)}$ is

$$\Delta\mathbf{b}_{(\mathbf{m})} = \epsilon \cdot \boldsymbol{\delta}_{(\mathbf{m})}. \tag{8}$$

The update rule of $W_{1(m\times l)}$ is

$$\Delta\mathbf{W}_{\mathbf{1}(\mathbf{m}\times\mathbf{l})} = \epsilon \cdot \boldsymbol{\delta}_{(\mathbf{m})} \cdot \left(\mathbf{W}_{\mathbf{2}(\mathbf{l}\times\mathbf{n})} \cdot \mathbf{i}_{(\mathbf{n})}\right)^{T}. \tag{9}$$

The error signal becomes $W^{T}_{1(m\times l)} \cdot \delta_{(m)}$ through $W_{1(m\times l)}$; thus, the update rule of $W_{2(l\times n)}$ is

$$\Delta\mathbf{W}_{\mathbf{2}(\mathbf{l}\times\mathbf{n})} = \epsilon \cdot \mathbf{W}^{\mathbf{T}}_{\mathbf{1}(\mathbf{m}\times\mathbf{l})} \cdot \boldsymbol{\delta}_{(\mathbf{m})} \cdot \mathbf{i}^{\mathbf{T}}_{(\mathbf{n})}. \tag{10}$$

The error $e_{(n)}$ is

$$\begin{aligned} \mathbf{e}_{(\mathbf{n})} &= \left(\mathbf{W}_{\mathbf{1}(\mathbf{m}\times\mathbf{l})} \cdot \mathbf{W}_{\mathbf{2}(\mathbf{l}\times\mathbf{n})}\right)^{T} \cdot \boldsymbol{\delta}_{(\mathbf{m})} \\ &= \mathbf{W}^{\mathbf{T}}_{\mathbf{2}(\mathbf{l}\times\mathbf{n})} \cdot \left(\mathbf{W}^{\mathbf{T}}_{\mathbf{1}(\mathbf{m}\times\mathbf{l})} \cdot \delta_{(\mathbf{m})}\right). \end{aligned} \tag{11}$$

Input. $\mathbf{W}_{\mathbf{1}(\mathbf{m}\times\mathbf{l})} \in \mathbb{R}^{m\times l}$, $\mathbf{W}_{\mathbf{2}(\mathbf{l}\times\mathbf{n})} \in \mathbb{R}^{l\times n}$, $\mathbf{b}_{(\mathbf{m})} \in \mathbb{R}^{m}$, and $\mathbf{i}_{(\mathbf{n})} \in \mathbb{R}^{n}$, $\varphi(x)$, $\epsilon \in \mathbb{R}$.

Output. $\Delta\mathbf{W}_{\mathbf{1}(\mathbf{m}\times\mathbf{l})} \in \mathbb{R}^{m\times l}$, $\Delta\mathbf{W}_{\mathbf{2}(\mathbf{l}\times\mathbf{n})} \in \mathbb{R}^{l\times n}$, $\Delta\mathbf{b}_{(\mathbf{m})} \in \mathbb{R}^{m}$, and $\mathbf{e}_{(\mathbf{n})} \in \mathbb{R}^{n}$.

(1) $\mathbf{o}_{(\mathbf{m})} \leftarrow \varphi(\mathbf{W}_{1(\mathbf{m}\times\mathbf{l})} \cdot (\mathbf{W}_{2(\mathbf{l}\times\mathbf{n})} \cdot \mathbf{i}_{(\mathbf{n})}) + \mathbf{b}_{(\mathbf{m})})$.

(2) Obtain an error signal $\mathbf{e}_{(\mathbf{m})}$.

(3) $\boldsymbol{\delta}_{(\mathbf{m})} \leftarrow \varphi'(\mathbf{W}_{1(\mathbf{m}\times\mathbf{l})} \cdot (\mathbf{W}_{2(\mathbf{l}\times\mathbf{n})} \cdot \mathbf{i}_{(\mathbf{n})}) + \mathbf{b}_{(\mathbf{m})}) \cdot \mathbf{e}_{(\mathbf{m})}$.

(4) $\Delta\mathbf{W}_{1(\mathbf{m}\times\mathbf{l})} \leftarrow \epsilon \cdot \boldsymbol{\delta}_{(\mathbf{m})} \cdot (\mathbf{W}_{2(\mathbf{l}\times\mathbf{n})} \cdot \mathbf{i}_{(\mathbf{n})})^T$.

(5) $\Delta\mathbf{W}_{2(\mathbf{l}\times\mathbf{n})} \leftarrow \epsilon \cdot \mathbf{W}^{\mathbf{T}}_{1(\mathbf{m}\times\mathbf{l})} \cdot \boldsymbol{\delta}_{(\mathbf{m})} \cdot \mathbf{i}^{\mathbf{T}}_{(\mathbf{n})}$.

(6) $\Delta\mathbf{b}_{(\mathbf{m})} \leftarrow \epsilon \cdot \boldsymbol{\delta}_{(\mathbf{m})}$.

(7) $\mathbf{e}_{(\mathbf{n})} \leftarrow \mathbf{W}^{\mathbf{T}}_{2(\mathbf{l}\times\mathbf{n})} \cdot (\mathbf{W}^{\mathbf{T}}_{1(\mathbf{m}\times\mathbf{l})} \cdot \boldsymbol{\delta}_{(\mathbf{m})})$.

Algorithm 1 illustrates the training process based on weight matrix restructuring. Step (1) is the forward computation. In step (2), the error signal is obtained. In steps (3), (4), (5), and (6), update $W_{1(m\times l)}$, $W_{2(l\times n)}$, and $b_{(m)}$. In step (7), transmit the error to the beneath layer.

After being trained by this algorithm, the final weight matrices can be inversely converted to the original structure via

$$\mathbf{W}_{(\mathbf{m}\times\mathbf{n})} = \mathbf{W}_{1(\mathbf{m}\times\mathbf{l})} \cdot \mathbf{W}_{2(\mathbf{l}\times\mathbf{n})}. \tag{12}$$

Nonetheless, it is not necessary to convert them to the original structure unless being seriously demanded, because converting inversely does not improve the recognition accuracy but increases the computational burdens of recognition.

The Complexity Reduction Theorem

As previously mentioned, the SVD-based method reduces the time complexities of matrix multiplications, which is summarized by the following theorem.

Theorem 2. *Assume that W is an $m\times n$ weight matrix and i is an n-dimensional vector. By applying the SVD-based method on W and keeping l largest singular values, the time complexity of computing W · i is reduced from ($m \times n$) to $O((m + n) \times l)$, when $l < m \times n/(m + n)$.*

Proof. Computing W · i requires $m\times n$ times of real number multiplications, so the time complexity of computing W · i is ($m \times n$). Apply the SVD method on W and obtain W_1 and W_2. After replacing W by $W_1 \cdot W_2$, W $\cdot_i$ is replaced by $(W_1 \cdot W_2) \cdot i$. According to the associative law, we obtain

$$(\mathbf{W}_1 \cdot \mathbf{W}_2) \cdot \mathbf{i} = \mathbf{W}_1 \cdot (\mathbf{W}_2 \cdot \mathbf{i}). \tag{13}$$

Computing $W_2 \cdot i$ requires $l \times n$ times of real number multiplications and gets an l-dimensional vector. Computing the product of W_2, the l-dimensional vector requires $m \times l$ times of real number multiplications, so $W_1 \cdot (W_2 \cdot i)$ requires $(m + n) \times l$ times of real number multiplications. The number of real number multiplications is reduced when

$$m \times l + l \times n < m \times n, \qquad (14)$$

and we obtain

$$l < \frac{m \times n}{(m+n)}. \qquad (15)$$

Therefore, the time complexity is reduced from $(m \times n)$ to $O((m + n) \times l)$, when $l < m \times n/(m + n)$.

The time complexities of learning MLPs are reduced to $((m + n) \times l)$ via (5), (7), (9), (10), and (11), when $l < m \times n/(m + n)$, so the computational burdens are eased in comparison with the conventional training algorithm.

EXPERIMENTS

Experimental Settings

We conduct experiments of LVCSR tasks on a server with 4 Intel Xeon E5-2620 CPUs and 512 GB memory. The training of MLPs is accelerated by an NVIDIA GeForce GTX TITAN Black graphics card. We use hours (h) of speech databases and their transcriptions to train and test acoustic models. The training data contain a 120 h speech database and the testing data contain a 3 h speech database. The texts of the testing data contain 17,221 words. The language model used is a 5-gram ARPA model.

First, GMMs must be trained before replacing GMMs by MLPs. To obtain GMMs, we use Mel-frequency cepstral coefficients (MFCCs) as the features of speeches and then train monophone, triphone, linear discriminant analysis (LDA), and maximum likelihood linear transformation (MLLT) in turn.

Then, MLPs are trained on the basis of GMMs. Featurespace maximum likelihood linear regression (FMLLR) is used as features of speeches for training MLPs. Alignments from GMMs are used as labels of supervised learning. Each MLP has an input layer, five hidden layers, and an output layer. The input layer has 440 units, corresponding to 440-dimensional input vectors. More specifically, each vector contains 40 real numbers that are the features of the corresponding frame of speeches and $40 \times (5 + 5)$ real numbers that are the features of 5 frames before this frame and 5 frames after this frame. Each hidden layer has 1024 units. Sigmoid is chosen as the activation function of the hidden layers. The output layer has 1952 units. To deal with multiclassification problems in ASR systems, softmax is chosen as the activation function of the output layer. All parameters of these layers, including weight matrices and biases, are stochastically initialized. The conventional method and the PA strategy are used to train this initial stochastic MLP, respectively. The number of bunches (T) is set to 20. For the conventional task, the data are averagely separated into bunches, and the learning-rate is set to 0.032. For the PA task, the data are separated by (2) and (3). The initial learning-rate ϵ_0 is set to 0.032 and α in (1) is set to 0.975.

Next, the SVD-based matrix restructuring method is applied to the basic model, keeping 384, 256, and 128 of the largest singular values, respectively. Since the input layer has 440 units, applying the SVD-based method to the first weight matrix will not evidently decrease the time complexity. Therefore, the SVD-based method will not be applied to the first weight matrix, but to all of the other matrices, including the one of the output layer. The structure of the model which keeps 256 singular values is shown in Figure 1 as an example, where the bottleneck means the linear transform. The reason of the numbers of kept largest singular values being set to $384(1024 \times 3/8)$, $256(1024 \times 1/4)$, and $128(1024 \times 1/8)$, respectively, is that the time complexity is reduced when $l < m \times n/(m + n)$, and therefore $l < 512$ if $m = n = 1024$. After that, the BP algorithm illustrated in Section 2.2 is used to train the restructured models. The learning-rates of iterations are decayed from an initial value: when the increment of the frame accuracy on cross validation (The frame accuracy is equal to $(N_{correct}/N_{total}) \times 100$, where $N_{correct}$ denotes the number of correct recognized states on softmax and N_{total} denotes the total number of states.) is not smaller than 0.5, the learning-rate does not change, but when the increment of the frame accuracy on cross validation is smaller than 0.5, the learning-rate is halved. The initial learning-rate is set to 1×10^{-5}.

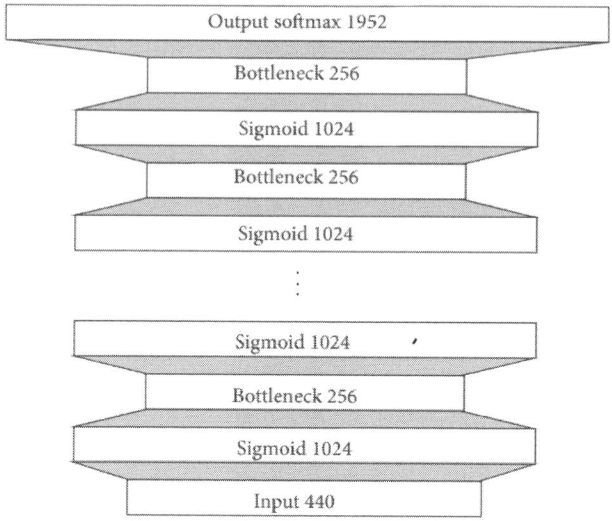

Figure 1: A model restructured by the SVD method.

In these experiments, the cross entropy losses and the frame accuracies on cross validation are used to appraise the performance of MLPs. The word error rate (WER) is used to assess the performance of final CD-MLP-HMMs, which is equal to the number of misrecognized words divided by the total number of words.

Results and Discussions

Figure 2 shows the changes of the cross entropy loss during the first epoch. The curves of the PA task and the conventional task are provided. Both of them first drop sharply, followed by slight decreases after training by 8 bunches. However, the PA task drops more significantly when training by the first 8 bunches, after which it remains stable. By contrast, the cross entropy loss of the conventional task keeps decreasing when training, but finally it is still higher than that of the PA task, which is because the first 8 bunches on the PA task contain more data due to the fact that they are based on the cosine function. Another further contributing factor is that the dynamic learning-rate facilitates the training, which is also the reason why the PA task has a considerable drop when training the 3rd–7th bunches..

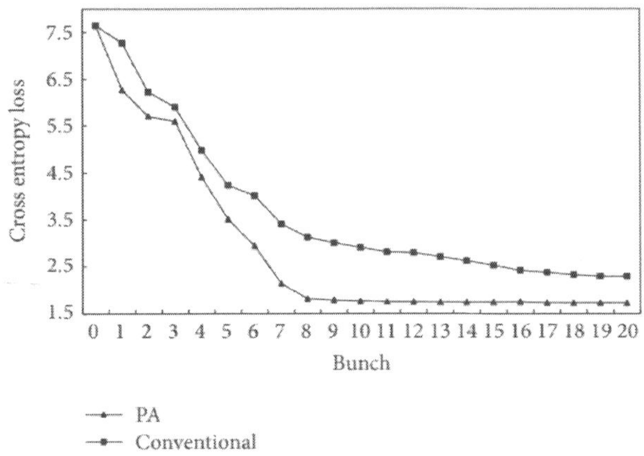

Figure 2: Cross entropy losses during the first epoch.

Figure 3 reveals the changes of frame accuracies on cross validation during the first epoch. Combining with Figure 2, we can see that the frame accuracy increases when the cross entropy loss decreases. However, the changes of frame accuracies are more evident. After training by the first 5 bunches, the frame accuracy of the PA task reaches a very high point, whereas the low point of the cross entropy loss occurs after 8 bunches. A similar phenomenon also occurs on the conventional task. More importantly, the final frame accuracy of the PA task is higher than that of the conventional one. Such a high accuracy facilitates the subsequent training, and it is the reason why we use the PA strategy.

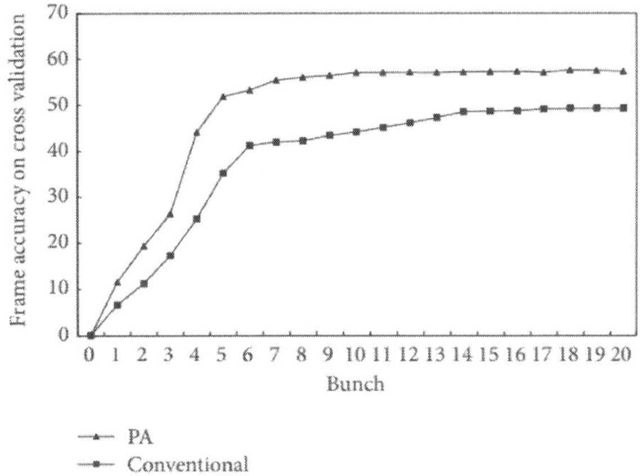

Figure 3: Frame accuracies on cross validation during the first epoch.

A glance at Figure 4 shows some differences on cross entropy losses between the PA-SVD training method and the conventional method. The initial cross entropy loss of the conventional task is significantly higher than those of the PA-SVD tasks due to the fact that the PA strategy has better performance on reducing the cross entropy loss during the first epoch. With regard to the PA-SVD tasks, the initial cross entropy loss is low, and the more bottlenecks mean the lower value. However, the cross entropy losses of the PA-SVD tasks increase during the second epoch, achieving peaks which are dramatically higher than before, which is attributed to the fact that the structures of these models have been altered by the SVD method, and the training algorithm is different from the conventional BP method. After the peaks, marked declines of the cross entropy losses occur to these tasks, followed by sustained decreases. Finally, all of these cross entropy losses become more and more similar to each other. More importantly, the final cross entropy losses of the PA-tasks (PA-SVD-384 and PA-SVD-256) are still slightly lower than that of the conventional task, indicating that the former models have better performance than the latter one.

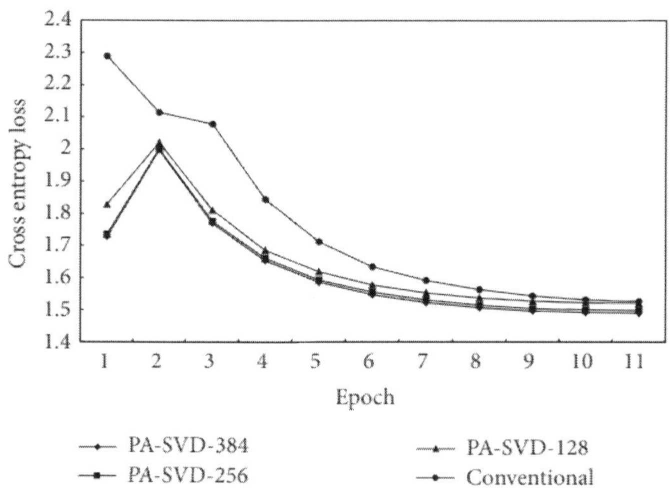

Figure 4: Changes of cross entropy losses.

In fact, on LVCSR tasks, the frame accuracy is more practical, because it directly indicates the proportion of correct recognition results of MLPs. Figure 5 provides the changes of frame accuracies on cross validation. It is easy to note that the initial frame accuracies of PA-SVD tasks are evidently higher than that of the conventional one, which means that the PA strategy improves not only the cross entropy loss (see Figure 4) but also the frame accuracy. Meanwhile, small gaps occur among the three PA-SVD tasks. This phenomenon is attributed to the fact that the SVD method brings loss of information to models, particularly when the number of bottlenecks is small. Then the frame accuracies of the PA-SVD tasks reach minima after the second epoch, and the reason is the same as that of the increasing of the cross entropy loss. After that, the frame accuracies keep increasing till the end of training. With regard to the conventional task, the frame accuracy has a slight decrease during the third epoch, which is because the learning-rate is high during this epoch, and from this point it is halved. Finally, the frame accuracy of the PA-SVD-384 task as well as that of the PA-SVD-256 task is slightly higher than that of the conventional task, whereas the frame accuracy of the PA-SVD-128 task is a little lower. These results again indicate that the PA-SVD-384 model and the PA-SVD-256 model perform better than the conventional model.

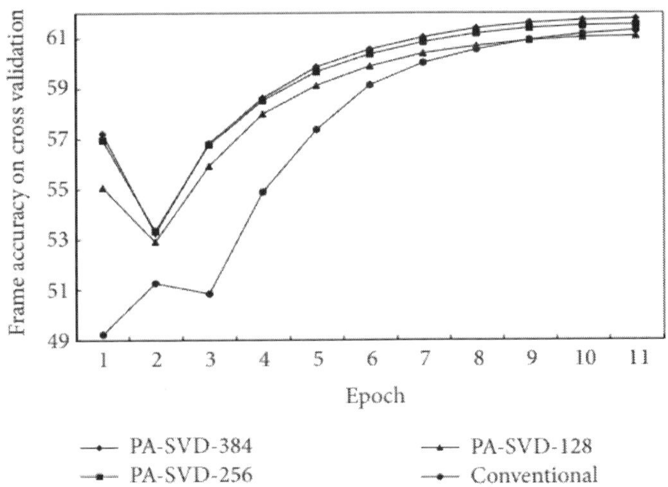

Figure 5: Changes of frame accuracies on cross validation.

Table 1 provides the final results of the overall LVSCR tasks, including the WERs and the numbers of parameters. It is easy to note that the bigger number of parameters means the lower WER, but the gaps among them are very small. In comparison with the previous results, although the PA-SVD-256 task and the PA-SVD-384 task have higher WERs than the conventional task, they have better cross entropy losses and frame accuracies, which is because WERs not only depend on the performance of MLPs but also are affected by the ARPA models above them. For the same MLP, using different ARPA models will bring different results.

Table 1: WERs and model scales.

Task	NUM-PARA (N_{para})	WER
Conventional	≈6.64M	16.32%
PA-SVD-384	≈4.74M	16.48%
PA-SVD-256	≈3.31M	16.55%
PA-SVD-128	≈1.88M	16.71%

With regard to the complexities, the number of computations (including real number multiplications and additions) for both a forward pass and a backward pass is approximately equal to the number of parameters. During training, the computing is on GPUs, and a forward pass and a backward pass are required. Thus, the time complexity for training is

$$O_{tr} = \frac{2 \times N_{para}}{N_{GPU}}, \qquad (16)$$

where N_{GPU} denotes the number of GPU cores which can realistically run parallel (In reality, for some tasks, not all of the GPU cores can work simultaneously, but it is difficult to discuss in this work, as parallel computing is very complicated.). During decoding, only a forward pass is required. The time complexity for decoding is

$$O_{de} = \frac{N_{para}}{N_{GPU}}. \qquad (17)$$

In our experiments, the NVIDIA GeForce GTX TITAN Black graphics card, including 2880 GPU cores, is used. Since N_{GPU} is large, the experiments run relatively fast and are finished in a few days. However, the volume of this graphics card is big (26.67 cm × 11.12 cm × 7.44 cm), so it is hard to embed it into a humanoid robot for decoding. If smaller graphics cards or CPUs are used in the robot, it will take considerable longer time for training and decoding. Thus, it is important to reduce the time complexities.

Equations (16) and (17) reveal that the time cost depends on the number of parameters. Revisiting Table 1, we notice that the PA-SVD tasks have significant less time cost than the conventional task, whereas the WERs are almost the same. Particularlly, the PA-SVD-256 task achieves a 2.0 times speedup and the PA-SVD-128 task achieves a 3.5 times speedup, which provides a way for humanoid robots to learn and recognize speech much more efficiently and effectively. Besides, the memories of robots are much smaller than servers, as robots have restrictions on sizes, weights, and powers. It is easy to note that the final models of the PA-SVD tasks have markedly lower numbers of parameters than the conventional model, which consequently also provides a way for robots to reduce their sizes, weights, and consumptions of energy.

CONCLUSIONS

We propose a fast learning method for MLPs in ASR systems in this paper, which is suitable for humanoid robots whose CPU/GPUs and memories are limited, as its time complexities are low, and the final model sizes are small. First, the PA strategy improves the frame accuracies and the cross entropy losses of the MLP during the first training epoch, based on the cosine function separation of training data and the dynamic learning-rate. The SVD-based method then restructures the weight matrices of the preadjusted MLPs and reduces their dimensionality. After that, the BP algorithm that fits the unfolded weight matrices is used to train the MLP obtained by the SVD restructuring. In the experiments, this method accelerates the training processes to around 2.0 times faster than before with improvements on the cross entropy loss and the frame accuracy, and moreover it accelerates the training processes to around 3.5 times faster than before with just a negligible increase of the cross entropy loss as well as a tiny loss of the frame accuracy.

ACKNOWLEDGMENTS

This work is supported by the Fundamental Research Funds for the Central Universities (YX2014-18), the Beijing Higher Education Young Elite Teacher Project (YETP0768), and the National Natural Science Foundation of China (61472369 and 61103152).

REFERENCES

1. C. Breazeal and L. Aryananda, "Recognition of affective communicative intent in robot-directed speech," *Autonomous Robots*, vol. 12, no. 1, pp. 83–104, 2002.
2. S. Yamamoto, J.-M. Valin, K. Nakadai et al., "Enhanced robot speech recognition based on microphone array source separation and missing feature theory," in *Proceedings of the IEEE International Conference on Robotics and Automation (ICRA '05)*, pp. 1477–1482, April 2005.
3. K. Nickel and R. Stiefelhagen, "Visual recognition of pointing gestures for human-robot interaction," *Image and Vision Computing*, vol. 25, no. 12, pp. 1875–1884, 2007.
4. R. Stiefelhagen, C. Fügen, P. Gieselmann, H. Holzapfel, K. Nickel, and A. Waibel, "Natural human-robot interaction using speech, head pose and gestures," in *Proceedings of the IEEE/RSJ International Conference on Intelligent Robots and Systems (IROS '04)*, pp. 2422–2427, October 2004.
5. G. E. Hinton, S. Osindero, and Y.-W. Teh, "A fast learning algorithm for deep belief nets," *Neural Computation*, vol. 18, no. 7, pp. 1527–1554, 2006. | MathSciNet
6. G. E. Hinton, L. Deng, D. Yu et al., "Deep neural networks for acoustic modeling in speech recognition: the shared views of four research groups," *IEEE Signal Processing Magazine*, vol. 1, no. 6, pp. 82–97, 2012.
7. G. E. Dahl, T. N. Sainath, and G. E. Hinton, "Improving deep neural networks for LVCSR using rectified linear units and dropout," in *Proceedings of the 38th IEEE International Conference on Acoustics, Speech, and Signal Processing (ICASSP '13)*, pp. 8609–8613, May 2013.
8. A.-R. Mohamed, G. E. Dahl, and G. E. Hinton, "Acoustic modeling using deep belief networks," *IEEE Transactions on Audio, Speech and Language Processing*, vol. 20, no. 1, pp. 14–22, 2012.
9. G. E. Dahl, D. Yu, L. Deng, and A. Acero, "Context-dependent pre-trained deep neural networks for large-vocabulary speech recognition," *IEEE Transactions on Audio, Speech and Language Processing*, vol. 20, no. 1, pp. 30–42, 2012.

10. N. Jaitly, P. Nguyen, A. Senior, and V. Vanhoucke, "Application of pretrained deep neural networks to large vocabulary speech recognition," in *Proceedings of the 13th Annual Conference of the International Speech Communication Association (INTERSPEECH '12)*, pp. 2577–2580, September 2012.
11. M. D. Zeiler, M. Ranzato, R. Monga et al., "On rectified linear units for speech processing," in *Proceedings of the 38th IEEE International Conference on Acoustics, Speech, and Signal Processing (ICASSP '13)*, pp. 3517–3521, May 2013.
12. A. Graves, A.-R. Mohamed, and G. Hinton, "Speech recognition with deep recurrent neural networks," in *Proceedings of the 38th IEEE International Conference on Acoustics, Speech, and Signal Processing (ICASSP '13)*, pp. 6645–6649, May 2013.
13. L. Deng, G. E. Hinton, and B. Kingsbury, "New types of deep neural network learning for speech recognition and related applications: an overview," in *Proceedings of the 38th IEEE International Conference on Acoustics, Speech, and Signal Processing (ICASSP '13)*, pp. 8599–8603, IEEE, Vancouver, Canada, May 2013.
14. A. L. Maas, A. Y. Hannun, and A. Y. Ng, "Rectifier nonlinearities improve neural network acoustic models," in *Proceedings of the International Conference on Machine Learning (ICML '13)*, Atlanta, Ga, USA, June 2013.
15. D. Yu, L. Deng, and F. Seide, "The deep tensor neural network with applications to large vocabulary speech recognition," *IEEE Transactions on Audio, Speech and Language Processing*, vol. 21, no. 2, pp. 388–396, 2013.
16. H. Su, G. Li, D. Yu, and F. Seide, "Error back propagation for sequence training of Context-Dependent Deep NetworkS for conversational speech transcription," in *Proceedings of the 38th IEEE International Conference on Acoustics, Speech, and Signal Processing (ICASSP '13)*, pp. 6664–6668, May 2013.
17. D. Yu, G. E. Hinton, N. Morgan, J.-T. Chien, and S. Sagayama, "Introduction to the special section on deep learning for speech and language processing," *IEEE Transactions on Audio, Speech and Language Processing*, vol. 20, no. 1, pp. 4–6, 2012.

18. N. Morgan, "Deep and wide: multiple layers in automatic speech recognition," *IEEE Transactions on Audio, Speech and Language Processing*, vol. 20, no. 1, pp. 7–13, 2012.
19. Z. Luo, H. Liu, and X. Wu, "Artificial neural network computation on graphic process unit," in *Proceedings of IEEE International Joint Conference on Neural Networks (IJCNN '05)*, vol. 1, pp. 622–626, July–August 2005.
20. J. Dean, G. S. Corrado, R. Monga et al., "Large scale distributed deep networks," in *Proceedings of the 26th Annual Conference on Neural Information Processing Systems (NIPS '12)*, pp. 1232–1240, Lake Tahoe, Nev, USA, December 2012.
21. G. Heigold, V. Vanhoucke, A. W. Senior et al., "Multilingual acoustic models using distributed deep neural networks," in *Proceedings of the 38th IEEE International Conference on Acoustics, Speech, and Signal Processing (ICASSP '13)*, pp. 8619–8623, May 2013.
22. S. Zhang, C. Zhang, Z. You, R. Zheng, and B. Xu, "Asynchronous stochastic gradient descent for DNN training," in *Proceedings of the 38th IEEE International Conference on Acoustics, Speech, and Signal Processing (ICASSP '13)*, pp. 6660–6663, May 2013.
23. J. Martens, "Deep learning via Hessian-free optimization," in *Proceedings of the 27th International Conference on Machine Learning (ICML '10)*, pp. 735–742, June 2010.
24. P. L. Dognin and V. Goel, "Combining stochastic average gradient and Hessian-free optimization for sequence training of deep neural networks," in *Proceedings of the IEEE Workshop on Automatic Speech Recognition and Understanding (ASRU '13)*, pp. 321–325, December 2013.
25. J. Martens and I. Sutskever, "Training deep and recurrent networks with Hessian-free optimization," in *Neural Networks: Tricks of the Trade*, vol. 7700 of *Lecture Notes in Computer Science*, pp. 479–535, Springer, Berlin, Germany, 2nd edition, 2012.
26. J. Xue, J. Li, D. Yu, M. Seltzer, and Y. Gong, "Singular value decomposition based low-footprint speaker adaptation and personalization for deep neural network," in *Proceedings of the IEEE International Conference on Acoustics, Speech and Signal Processing (ICASSP '14)*, pp. 6359–6363, Florence, Italy, May 2014.

27. J. Xue, J. Li, and Y. Gong, "Restructuring of deep neural network acoustic models with singular value decomposition," in *Proceedings of the Annual Conference of International Speech Communication Association (INTERSPEECH '13)*, pp. 2365–2369, Lyon, France, 2013.
28. V. C. Klema and A. J. Laub, "The singular value decomposition: its computation and some applications," *IEEE Transactions on Automatic Control*, vol. 25, no. 2, pp. 164–176, 1980.

SECTION 2: SPEECH RECOGNITION FOR DIFFERENT LANGUAGES

CHAPTER 6

Development of Application Specific Continuous Speech Recognition System in Hindi

Gaurav, Devanesamoni Shakina Deiv, Gopal Krishna Sharma, Mahua Bhattacharya

Indian Institute of Information Technology & Management, Gwalior, India

ABSTRACT

Application specific voice interfaces in local languages will go a long way in reaching the benefits of technology to rural India. A continuous speech recognition system in Hindi tailored to aid teaching Geometry in Primary schools is the goal of the work. This paper presents the preliminary work done

Citation: G. Gaurav, D. Deiv, G. Sharma and M. Bhattacharya, "Development of Application Specific Continuous Speech Recognition System in Hindi," Journal of Signal and Information Processing, Vol. 3 No. 3, 2012, pp. 394-401. doi: 10.4236/jsip.2012.33052.

towards that end. We have used the Mel Frequency Cepstral Coefficients as speech feature parameters and Hidden Markov Modeling to model the acoustic features. Hidden Markov Modeling Tool Kit −3.4 was used both for feature extraction and model generation. The Julius recognizer which is language independent was used for decoding. A speaker independent system is implemented and results are presented.

Keywords: Automatic Speech Recognition; Mel Frequency Cepstral Coefficients; Hidden Markov Modeling

INTRODUCTION

To make Information Technology (IT) relevant to rural India, voice access to a variety of computer based services is imperative. Although many speech interfaces are already available, the need is for speech interfaces in local Indian languages. Application specific Hindi speech recognition systems are required to make computer aided teaching, a reality in rural schools. This paper presents the preliminary work done to demonstrate the relevance of a Hindi Continuous Speech Recognition System in primary education.

Automatic speech recognition has progressed tremendously in the last two decades. There are several commercial Automatic Speech Recognition (ASR) systems developed, the most popular among them are Dragon Naturally Speaking, IBM Via voice and Microsoft SAPI. Efforts are on to develop speech recognition systems in different Indian Languages. An isolated word Hindi ASR for small vocabulary is developed and evaluated in [1]. An effort to increase the recognition accuracy of Hindi ASR by online speaker adaptation has been reported in [2]. It is demonstrated that Maximum Likelihood Linear Regression (MLLR) transform based adaptation transforms the acoustic models in such a way that the difference between test and training conditions is reduced, resulting in better performance.

A general approach to identifying feature vectors that effectively distinguish gender of a speaker from Hindi vowel phoneme utterances has been presented in [3,4]. Centre for Development of Advanced computing has developed a domain specific speaker independent continuous speech recognition system for Hindi using Julius recognition engine [5]. They also have built a Hindi ASR for travel domain [6] giving encouraging recognition accuracy.

State likelihood evaluation in Hidden Markov model (HMM) using mixture of Gaussians is one problem that needs to be solved. A novel method using Gaussian Mixture Model (GMM) for statistical pattern classification is suggested to reduce computational load [7]. Development of speech interfaces in Hindi for IT based services is a work in progress [8]. Efforts to compensate for different accents in Hindi are also explored in [9]. Apart from Hindi ASR, speech recognition systems are being developed in other languages like Arabic, Malayalam, Tamil, Bengali, Telugu, etc. [10-14].

IBM Research Laboratory of India has developed a Hindi Speech Recognition system which has been trained on 40 hours of audio data and has a trigram language model that is trained with 3 million words [15]. Efforts are on to develop large speech databases in various Indian Languages for Large Vocabulary Speech Recognition Systems [16]. SRI Language Model (SRILM) extensible toolkit is discussed in [17] which can be used for developing Language model. This toolkit has been used in developing language model for large vocabulary systems in Hindi.

Hidden Markov Model provides an elegant statistical framework for modeling speech patterns and is the most widely used technique [18,19]. Recently the hybrid HMM and Artificial Neural Network (ANN) framework is also used in an effort to overcome the challenges posed by speech variability due to physiological differences, style variability due to co-articulation effects, varying accents, emotional states, context variability etc [20].

Another method to handle the problem of changes in the acoustic environment or speaker specific voice characteristics is by adapting the statistical models of a speech recognizer and speaker tracking. Combining speaker adaptation and speaker tracking may be advantageous, because it allows a system to adapt to more than one user at the same time. Authors in [21] have extended a standard speech recognizer by combining speaker specific speech decoding with speaker identification in an efficient manner. Approximately 20% relative error rate reduction and about 94.6% identification rate are reported.

The system presented here is an application specific Continuous Speech Recognizer in Hindi. It is restricted to the task of computer-aided teaching of Geometry at primary school level. The paper is organized as follows. Section 2 describes the architecture of the speech recognition system with the function of each module. Section 3 explains the training methodology of developing the proposed Hindi CSR. Section 4 details the testing of the system. The results are discussed in Section 5. Section 6 concludes with future direction of the work.

AUTOMATIC SPEECH RECOGNITION SYSTEM

Speech recognition is the process of converting an acoustic signal, captured by a microphone or a telephone into a set of words. The recognized words can be the final result for applications such as commands and control, data entry, and document preparation. They can also serve as the input to further linguistic processing in order to achieve speech understanding. **Figure 1** shows the block diagram of a state of the art automatic speech recognition system.

Speech signal is analog. In the first place analog electrical signals are converted to digital signals. This is done in two steps, sampling and quantization. So a typical representation of a speech signal is a stream of 8-bit numbers at the rate of 10,000 numbers per second. Once the signal conversion is complete, background noise is filtered to keep signal to noise ratio high. The signal is pre-emphasized and then speech parameters are extracted.

Feature Extraction

Mel-Frequency Cepstral Coefficients (MFCCs) are widely used features for automatic speech recognition systems to transform the speech waveform into a sequence of discrete acoustic vectors.

The MFCC technique makes use of two types of filter, namely, linearly spaced filters and logarithmically spaced filters. The Mel frequency scale has linear frequency spacing below 1000 Hz and a logarithmic spacing above 1000 Hz. In the sound processing, the Mel-frequency cepstrum is a representation of the short-term power spectrum of a sound, based on a linear cosine transform of a log power spectrum on a nonlinear Mel-frequency scale.

The procedure by which the Mel-frequency cepstral coefficients are obtained consists of the following steps. **Figure 2** depicts the procedure of extracting MFCC feature vectors from speech.

The signal is passed through a filter which emphasizes higher frequencies. This process will increase the energy of the signal at higher frequency.

The Pre-emphasis of the speech signal is realized with this simple FIR filter

$$H(z) = 1 - az^{-1} \quad (1)$$

where a is from interval [0.9, 1].

The digitized speech is segmented into frames with a length within the range of 10 to 40 ms. The segment of waveform used to determine each parameter vector is usually referred to as a window.

The Hamming window which is used for the purpose is defined by the equation

$$w(n)0.54 - 0.46\cos\left[2\pi n/(N-1)\right] \quad (2)$$

where, $0 \le n \le N-1$

N = number of samples in each frame.

Let Y(n) = Output signal and X(n) = input signal The result of windowing the signal is

$$Y(n) = X(n)W(n) \quad (3)$$

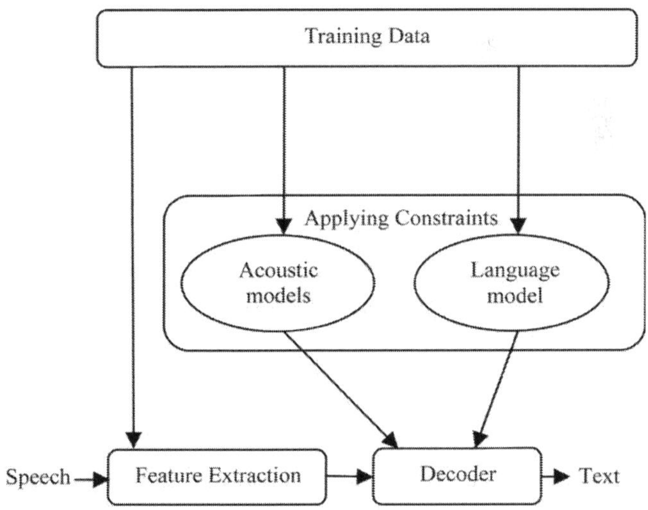

Figure 1. Automatic speech recognition system.

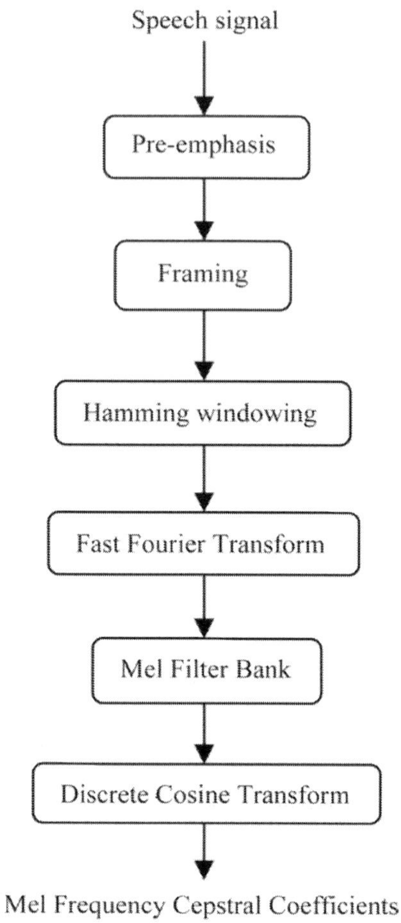

Figure 2. Flow chart of MFCC feature extraction.

Next, the Fast Fourier transform (FFT) is used to convert each frame of N samples from time domain into frequency domain. Thus the components of the magnitude spectrum of the analyzed signal are calculated.

$$Y(\omega) = \mathrm{FFT}\left[h(t) * x(t)\right] = H(\omega)X(\omega) \tag{4}$$

The most important step in this signal processing is Mel-frequency transformation. Compensation for nonlinear perception of frequency is implemented by the bank of triangular band filters with the linear distribution of frequencies along the so called Mel-frequency range. Linear deployment of filters to Mel-frequency axis results in a non-linear distribution for the standard frequency axis in hertz. Definition of the Mel-frequency range is described by the following equation.

$$f_{mel} = 2595 \log_{10}\left(1 + f/100\right) Hz \quad (5)$$

where f is frequency in linear range and f_{mel} the corresponding frequency in nonlinear Mel-frequency range.

The Mel spectrum coefficients and their logarithm are real numbers. Hence they can be converted to the time domain using the discrete cosine transform (DCT). The result is the Mel Frequency Cepstral Coefficients. The cepstral representation of the speech spectrum provides a good representation of the local spectral properties of the signal for the given frame analysis.

$$c_n = \sqrt{2/K} \sum_{j=1}^{N} \left(\log_{mj}\right) \cos\left(\pi n \left(j - 0.5\right)/K\right) \quad (6)$$

n = number of Mel-frequency cepstral coefficients K = number of Mel-frequency band filters (filter bank channels) in the bank of filters.

The Acoustic Model

In a statistical framework for speech recognition, the problem is to find the most likely word sequence, which can be described by the equation

$$\hat{W} = \arg_w \max P\left(W/X\right) \quad (7)$$

Applying the Bayes' equation, we get

$$\hat{W} = \arg_w \max P\left(W/X\right) P\left(W\right) \quad (8)$$

The term P(X/W) in the above equation can be realized by the Acoustic model. An acoustic model is a file that contains a statistical representation of each distinct sound that makes up a spoken word. It contains the sounds for each word found in the Language model.

The speech recognition system implemented here uses Hidden Markov Models (HMM) for representing speech sounds. A HMM is a stochastic model. A HMM consists of a number of states, each of which is associated with a probability density function. The model parameters are the set of probability density functions, and a transition matrix that contains the probability of transitions between states.

HMM-based recognition algorithms are classified into two types, namely, phoneme level model and word-level model. The word-level HMM has excellent performance at isolated word tasks and is capable of representing speech transitions between phonemes. However, each distinct word has to be represented by a separate model which leads to extremely high computation cost (which is proportional to the number of HMM models). The phoneme model on the other hand can help reproduce a word as a sequence of phonemes. Hence new words can be added to the dictionary without necessitating additional models. Hence phoneme model is considered more suitable in applications with large sized vocabularies and where addition of word is a essential possibility.

The phoneme model is used here. The MFCC features extracted from speech and the associated transcriptions are used to estimate the parameters of HMM based acoustic models that represent phonemes. The iterative process of estimating and re-estimating the parameters to achieve a reasonable representation of the speech unit is called ASR system training. The training procedure involves the use of forward-backward algorithm.

The Language Model

The term P(W) in Equation (2) represents the a priori probability of a word sequence based on syntax, semantics and pragmatics of the language to be recognized. It can be realized by the Language Model which contains a list of words and their probability of occurrence in a given sequence, and is independent of the acoustic signal. The probability of a word sequence is given below.

$$p(w_1, w_2, w_3, w_4, w_5, \cdots, w_n) = p(W) \tag{9}$$

By Chain rule the probability of nth word is:

$$p(w_1^n) = p(w_1)\,p(w_2|w_1)\,p(w_2|w_1^2)\cdots p(w_n|w_1^{n-1}) \tag{10}$$

$$p(w_1^n) = \prod_{k=1}^{n} p(w_k|w_1^{k-1}) \tag{11}$$

Language Model or Grammar essentially defines constraints on what the Speech Recognition Engine can expect as input.

The Recognizer

Recognizer is a Software program that takes the sounds spoken by a user and searches the Acoustic Model for the equivalent sounds. When a match is made, the Decoder determines the phoneme corresponding to the sound. It keeps track of the matching phonemes until it reaches a pause in the user's speech. It then searches the Language Model or Grammar file for the equivalent series of phonemes. If a match is made it returns the text of the corresponding word or phrase to the calling program.

THE TRAINING METHODOLOGY

The two major stages involved in the process of Speech Recognition are the training of the ASR and the Testing. The training phase involves the following steps.

The Database

The text corpus consists of chosen application specific sentences, pertaining to teaching Geometry to children. Forty three distinct Hindi sentences about shape geometry using 29 distinct Hindi phonemes were designed as the text corpus. These sentences were spoken in a continuous fashion and recorded using good quality microphones under office noise conditions.

The Wave-surfer software was used for recording. The training corpus contains 1806 utterances spoken by 12 females and 18 males. All the speakers are natives of the Hindi heart-land of India, educated and in the age group of 18 to 30.

Phone Set

Phoneme is the basic unit of sound in any language. Hindi belongs to the Indo Aryan family of languages and is written in the Devanagari script. There are 11 vowels and 35 consonants in standard Hindi. In addition, five Nukta consonants are also adopted from Farsi/Arabic sounds. The phone set that is used here to develop the application specific speech recognition system for Hindi language uses only 29 of the 60 used in large vocabulary systems.

Lexicon

The pronunciation dictionary (lexicon) contains all the distinct words in the corpus and its corresponding pronunciation given as a string of phonemes. Some sample entries are given in **Table 1**. The pronunciation dictionary is case insensitive. This dictionary includes entries for the beginning-of-sentence and the end-of-sentence tokens and respectively as well as the silence.

Transcription

The transcription file contains the sentences or utterances of the spoken text and the corresponding audio files in the following format. Each word in the transcription file is present in the pronunciation lexicon.

Parameterization of Speech Data

The digitized speech signal is subjected to first order preemphasis applied using a coefficient of 0.97. The signal is then segmented into frames and hamming windowed. The HMM Tool Kit (HTK) [22] was used to parameterize the raw speech waveforms into sequences feature vectors.

Table 1. Pronunciation lexicon.

आयत	aa y ax t sp
बैगनी	b ae g n iy sp
बनाओ	b ax n aa ow sp
चतुर्भुज	ch ax t uh r b hh uh jh sp
एक	ey k sp
हरा	hh ax r aa sp
काला	k aa l aasp
लाल	l aa l sp
नारंगी	n aa r ax ng iy sp
नीला	n iy l aa sp
पीला	p iy l aa sp
सफ़ेद	s ax f eh ey dh sp
समान्तर	s ax m aa n t ax r sp
सम्बाहू	s ax m b aa hh uh sp

Mel Frequency Cepstral Coefficients (MFCCs) are derived from FFT-based log spectra. Coding was performed using the tool HCopy configured to automatically convert its input into MFCC vectors. A configuration file specifies all of the conversion parameters [22]. A typical configuration file is seen in **Figure 3**.

The target parameters are to be MFCC using C_0 as the energy component. The standard 39 dimension MFCC, delta and acceleration feature vector is computed for the 16 kHz sampled signals at 10 ms intervals (100 ns). Mel scaled 26 filter banks spanning the 8 kHz frequency range are used for computation of MFCCs.

The output was saved in compressed format, and a crc checksum added. The 39-demensional feature vector consists of 13 Mel Scale Cepstral Coefficients and their first and second derivates. A sample MFCC file is shown below in **Figure 4**.

Acoustic Model Generation

The speech recognition system implemented here employs Hidden Markov Model (HMM) for representing speech sounds. A HMM consists of a number of states, each of which is associated with a probability density function. The parameters of a HMM comprises of the parameters of the set of probability density functions, and a transition matrix that contains the probability of transition between states.

The MFCC feature vectors extracted from speech signals and their associated transcriptions are used to estimate the parameters of HMMs. This process is called ASR system training. HMM Tool Kit, HTK-3.4 was used for training models over 29 context-dependent Hindi phonemes used in the chosen application. The basic acoustic units are context dependent phonemes, that is, tri-phones modeled by left-to-right, 5-state, HMMs.

The output probability distributions of states were represented by Gaussian mixture densities. For every state of every phoneme 256 global Gaussian density functions were used to generate Gaussian mixtures.

Prototype models are built using the flat start approach. With the exception of the transition probabilities, all of the HMM parameters given in the prototype definition are ignored. The purpose of the prototype definition is only to specify the overall characteristics and topology of the HMM. The actual parameters will be computed later.

```
# Coding parameters
SOURCEFORMAT = WAV
TARGETKIND = MFCC_0_D_A
TARGETRATE = 100000.0
SAVECOMPRESSED = T
SAVEWITHCRC = T
WINDOWSIZE = 250000.0
USEHAMMING = T
PREEMCOEF = 0.97
NUMCHANS = 26
CEPLIFTER = 22
NUMCEPS = 12
ENORMALISE = F
```

Figure 3. A typical configuration file.

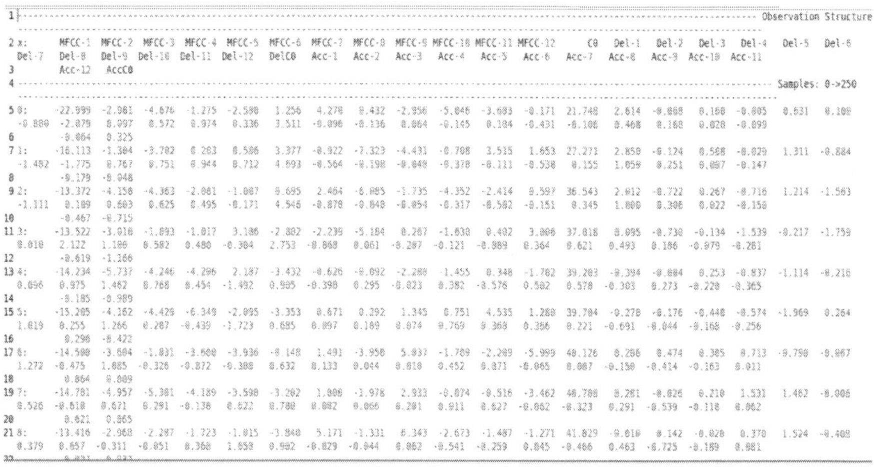

```
---------------------------------------------------------------- Observation Structure
x:  MFCC-1 MFCC-2 MFCC-3 MFCC-4 MFCC-5 MFCC-6 MFCC-7 MFCC-8 MFCC-9 MFCC-10 MFCC-11 MFCC-12 C0 Del-1 Del-2 Del-3 Del-4 Del-5 Del-6
 Del-7 Del-8 Del-9 Del-10 Del-11 Del-12 DelC0 Acc-1 Acc-2 Acc-3 Acc-4 Acc-5 Acc-6 Acc-7 Acc-8 Acc-9 Acc-10 Acc-11
 Acc-12 AccC0
---------------------------------------------------------------- Samples: 0->250
0:  -22.999 -2.981 -4.676 -1.275 -2.580 1.256 4.278 0.432 -2.956 -5.046 -3.683 -0.171 21.748 2.614 -0.008 0.160 -0.805 0.631 0.108
 -0.880 -2.079 0.097 0.572 0.974 0.336 3.511 -0.096 -0.136 0.064 -0.145 0.104 -0.431 -0.106 0.468 0.188 0.028 -0.099
 -0.064 0.325
1:  -16.113 -1.304 -3.702 0.263 0.586 3.377 -0.922 -7.323 -4.431 -0.708 3.515 1.653 27.271 2.850 -0.124 0.588 -0.029 1.311 -0.884
 -1.482 -1.775 0.767 0.751 0.944 0.712 4.693 -0.564 -0.198 -0.048 -0.378 -0.111 -0.538 0.155 1.059 0.251 0.087 -0.147
 -0.179 -0.048
2:  -13.372 -4.158 -4.363 -2.081 -1.087 0.695 2.464 -6.085 -1.735 -4.352 -2.414 0.597 36.543 2.012 -0.722 0.267 -0.716 1.214 -1.563
 -1.111 0.189 0.603 0.625 0.495 -0.171 4.546 -0.878 -0.848 -0.054 -0.317 -0.582 -0.151 0.345 1.000 0.306 0.022 -0.158
 -0.467 -0.715
3:  -13.522 -3.018 -1.093 -1.017 3.186 -2.882 -2.239 -5.184 0.287 -1.030 0.402 3.006 37.018 0.095 -0.730 -0.134 -1.539 -0.217 -1.759
 0.010 2.122 1.180 0.582 0.480 -0.304 2.753 -0.868 0.061 -0.287 -0.121 -0.889 0.364 0.621 0.493 0.186 -0.979 -0.281
 -0.619 -1.166
4:  -14.234 -5.737 -4.246 -4.296 2.187 -3.432 -0.626 -0.092 -2.288 -1.455 0.348 -1.762 39.203 -0.394 -0.884 0.253 -0.837 -1.114 -0.216
 0.096 0.975 1.462 0.768 0.454 -1.492 0.985 -0.398 0.295 -0.023 0.382 -0.576 0.502 0.578 -0.303 0.273 -0.228 -0.365
 -0.185 -0.989
5:  -15.205 -4.162 -4.429 -6.349 -2.095 -3.353 0.671 0.292 1.345 0.751 4.535 1.280 39.704 -0.278 -0.176 -0.448 -0.574 -1.969 0.264
 1.019 0.255 1.266 0.287 -0.439 -1.723 0.685 0.097 0.189 0.074 0.769 0.368 0.356 0.221 -0.691 -0.044 -0.168 -0.256
 0.298 -0.422
6:  -14.500 -3.604 -1.831 -3.600 -3.936 -0.148 1.491 -3.958 5.037 -1.789 -2.289 -5.999 40.126 0.286 0.474 0.385 0.713 -0.798 -0.067
 1.272 -0.475 1.085 -0.326 -0.872 -0.388 0.632 0.133 0.044 0.010 0.452 0.071 -0.065 0.087 -0.150 -0.414 -0.163 0.011
 0.064 0.009
7:  -14.781 -4.957 -5.381 -4.189 -3.598 -3.202 1.006 -1.978 2.933 -0.074 -0.516 -3.462 40.708 0.281 -0.026 0.210 1.531 1.462 -0.006
 0.526 -0.618 0.671 0.291 -0.138 0.622 0.780 0.082 0.066 0.201 0.911 0.627 -0.062 -0.323 0.291 -0.539 -0.118 0.062
 0.621 0.065
8:  -13.416 -2.968 -2.287 -1.723 -1.015 -3.840 5.171 -1.331 0.343 -2.673 -1.487 -1.271 41.829 -0.010 0.142 -0.028 0.370 1.524 -0.408
 0.379 0.657 -0.311 -0.051 0.368 1.658 0.902 -0.829 -0.044 0.062 -0.541 -0.259 0.045 -0.466 0.463 -0.725 -0.189 0.081
```

Figure 4. Screenshot of an MFCC file.

A prototype model is shown in **Figure 5**.

These models were further refined by applying nine iterations of the standard Baum-Welch embedded training procedure. These models are then converted to tri-phone models and two iterations of Baum-Welch training procedure are applied, then the states are tied using decision tree based approach and iterations of Baum-Welch training procedure are applied. **Figure 6** shows the training procedure.

EVALUATION METHODOLOGY

The performance of the ASR is tested while transcribing unknown utterances. A database which is not used for training the system is called unseen data. The test data here is an exclusive set consisting of 344 unseen utterances spoken by 8 speakers (4 males and 4 females) each speaking 43 sentences.

```
~o
<STREAMINFO> 1 39
<VECSIZE>
39<NULLD><MFCC_D_A_0><DIAGC>
~h "proto
<BEGINHMM>
<NUMSTATES> 5
<STATE> 2
<MEAN> 39
-7.055892e+00 -2.760827e+00 -1.855420e+00 .......
<VARIANCE> 39
3.614088e+01 4.895053e+01 6.375173e+01 .......
<GCONST> 1.185559e+02
<STATE> 3
<MEAN> 39
-7.055892e+00 -2.760827e+00 -1.855420e+00 ....
<VARIANCE> 39
3.614088e+01 4.895053e+01 6.375173e+01 .......
<GCONST> 1.185559e+02
<STATE> 4
<MEAN> 39
-7.055892e+00 -2.760827e+00 -1.855420e+00 ......
<VARIANCE> 39
3.614088e+01 4.895053e+01 6.375173e+01 .......
<GCONST> 1.185559e+02
<TRANSP> 5
0.000000e+00 1.000000e+00 0.000000e+00
0.000000e+00 0.000000e+00
0.000000e+00 6.000000e-01 4.000000e-01
0.000000e+00 0.000000e+00
0.000000e+00 0.000000e+00 6.000000e-01
4.000000e-01 0.000000e+00
0.000000e+00 0.000000e+000.000000e+00
7.000000e-01 3.000000e-01
0.000000e+00 0.000000e+00 0.000000e+00
0.000000e+00 0.000000e+00
<ENDHMM>
```

Figure 5. A prototype model.

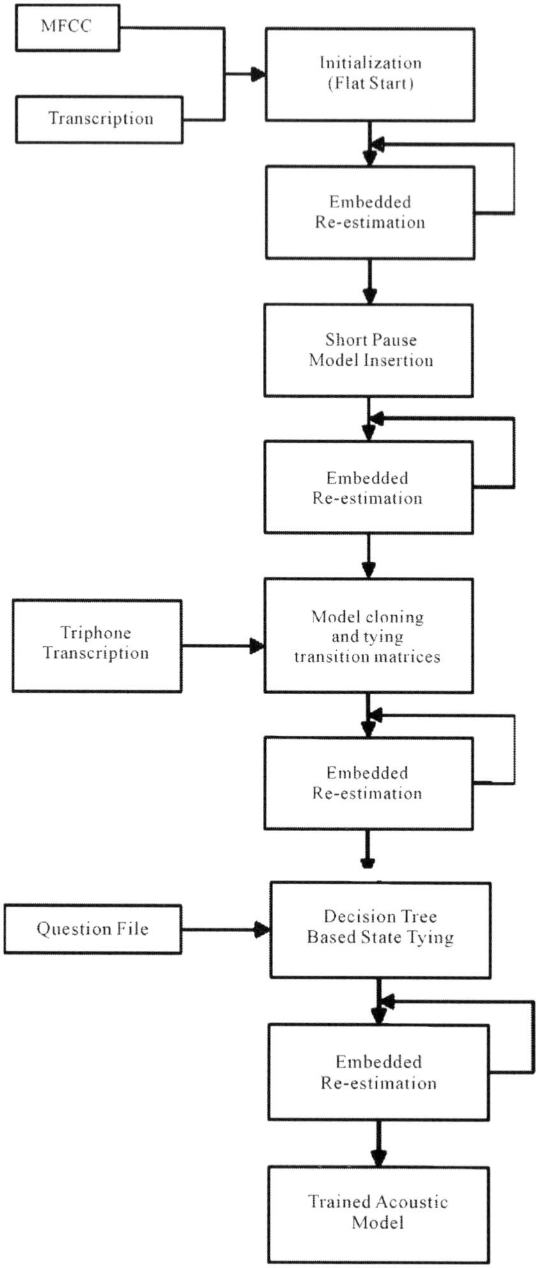

Figure 6. Acoustic model training methodology.

Role of Language Model

In speech recognition the Language Model is used for the task of finding word boundaries, that is, segmentation. The language model or grammar which is an a priori knowledge of the syntax, semantics and pragmatics of the language in question, helps decode the sequence of phonemes into different words in a sentence. An example is given in **Figure 7**.

Here the constraints applied by the Language model helps the Recognizer in decoding the phoneme sequence into words. We have generated our own language model.

The Recognizer

The decoder used for recognition is Julius. Since Julius itself is a language-independent decoding program [23], we can make a recognizer of any language if given an appropriate language model and acoustic model for the target language. The recognition accuracy largely depends on the models. Julius is a real-time, high-speed, accurate recognition engine based on 2-step strategy. It works in two steps. The first step is a high-speed approximate search, which uses a 2-gram frame synchronous beam searching algorithm. In the first step, a treestructured lexicon assigned with the language model probabilities was applied. Pre-computed unigram factoring values are assigned to the intermediate nodes and bi-gram probabilities on the word-end nodes. The second step is a high precision trigram N-best stack decoding. The tree trellis search in the second pass recovers the degradation caused by the rough approximation in the first step. Julius adopts acoustic models in HTK ASCII format, pronunciation dictionary in almost HTK format, and word 3-gram language models in ARPA standard format (forward 2-gram and reverse 3- gram trained from same corpus). The following is a sample output for one of our test utterances.

The Evaluation Parameters

Finally, the recognition accuracy of the Speaker Independent ASR system and the percentage of correct words and percentage of correct sentences were calculated using the following formulae.

$$\%correct = H / N \tag{12}$$

where, H = Number of labels (sentences here) correctly recognized N = Total number of labels

$$\%\text{Recognition Accuracy} = (N - D - S - I)/N \tag{13}$$

D = Number of unrecognized/missed words. (Deletion errors)

[ey k sp s ax m aa n t ax r sp ch ax t uh r b hh uh jh sp b ax n aa ow sp]
एक समान्तर चतुर्भुज बनाओ

Figure 7. The Recognition of series of phonemes into series of words.

S = Number of times a word was misrecognized as another word (Substitution errors)

I = Number of extra words inserted between correctly recognized words (Insertion errors)

N = Total number of words or sentences

RESULTS AND DISCUSSION

The system was trained with 1806 Hindi utterances (sentences) spoken by 18 males and 12 females. The performance of the system was evaluated both for seen and unseen speech data. All the 43 distinct sentences for which the system was trained were uttered by 8 persons (4 males and 4 females). A total of 316 test (unseen) utterances and 1371 seen utterances were used in testing. The % of correct sentences and Recognition Accuracy were calculated using formulae given above and results are shown in **Table 2**.

The Recognition Accuracy for males is better as expected as the ASR is speaker independent and the male speech data is more than that of females. The amount of training data must be increased to achieve better speaker independent model.

CONCLUSION AND FUTURE WORK

We have proposed an approach to implement a continuous speech recognition system in Hindi customized for computer aided teaching of geometry. We have used the MFCC as speech feature parameters and HMM to model the acoustic features. HTK-3.4 was used both for feature extraction and model generation. The Julius recognizer which is language independent was used for decoding.

The present work was limited to 29 phonemes of Hindi. It is mostly demonstrative in nature. The future endeavor will be to make the system full-fledged by increasing vocabulary to include all required words and all the Hindi phonemes. A phonetically balanced and rich database for the said application will be created and used.

More training data will be collected and used to improve the speaker Independent system. Methods to improve the Recognition rate of the speaker Independent Gaurav, Devanesamoni Shakina Deiv, Gopal Krishna Sharma, Mahua Bhattacharya system will be studied and experimented. Feature sets other than MFCC will be tested for reducing speaker and other variability.

Table 2. Recognition accuracies and % of correct words for speakers in training and test sets.

Speakers		% Correct Sentences	% Recognition Accuracy (Words)
	Male (18)	76.84	92.72
Training (Seen)	Female (12)	60.28	84.9
	All (30)	68.56	88.81
Test (Unseen)	All (8 = 4M + 4F)	42.72	79.11

REFERENCES

1. K. Kumar and R. K. Agarwal, "Hindi Speech Recognition System Using HTK," International Journal of Computing and Business Research, Vol. 2, No. 2, 2011, ISSN (Online): 2229-6166.
2. G. Sivaraman and K. Samudravijaya, "Hindi Speech Recognition and Online Speaker Adaptation," Proceedings of ICTSM 2011, Vol. 145, 2011, pp. 233-238.
3. D. ShakinaDeiv, Gaurav and M. Bhattacharya, "Automatic Gender Identification for Hindi Speech Recognition," International Journal of Computer Applications, Vol. 31, No. 5, 2011, pp. 1-8.
4. R. K. Aggarwal and M. Dave, "Implementing a Speech Recognition System Interface for Indian Language," Proceedings of the IJCNLP-2008 Workshop on NLP for Less Privileged Languages, Hyderabad, January 2008, pp. 105-112.
5. R. Mathur, Babita and A. Kansal, "Domain Specific Speaker Independent Continuous Speech Recognition Using Julius," ASCNT 2010.
6. S. Arora, B. Saxena, K. Arora and S. S. Agarwal, "Hindi ASR for Travel Domain," Oriental COCOSDA 2010 Proceedings Centre for Development of Advanced Computing, Noida, 24-25 November 2010.
7. R. K. Aggarwal and M. Dave, "Fitness Evaluation of Gaussian Mixtures in Hindi Speech Recognition System," 2010 First International Conference on Integrated Intelligent Computing, Bangalore, 5-7 August 2010, pp. 177- 183. doi:10.1109/ICIIC.2010.13
8. K. Samudravijaya, "Hindi Speech Recognition," Journal Acoustic Society of India, Vol. 29, No. 1, 2009, pp. 385- 393.
9. K. Malhotra and A. Khosla, "Automatic Identification of Gender & Accent in Spoken Hindi Utterances with Regional Indian Accents," IEEE Spoken Language Technology Workshop, Goa, 15-19 December 2008, pp. 309- 312.
10. R. Gupta, "Speech Recognition for Hindi," M. Tech. Project Report, Department of Computer Science and Engineering, Indian Institute of Technology, Bombay, Mumbai, 2006.
11. B. A. Q. Al-Qatab and R. N. Ainon, "Arabic Speech Recognition Using Hidden Markov Model Toolkit (HTK)," International Symposium in Information Technology, Kuala Lumpur, 15-17 June 2011, pp. 557-562.

12. C. Kurian and K. Balakrishnan, "Speech Recognition of Malayalam Numbers," World Congress on Nature & Biologically Inspired Computing, Coimbatore, 9-11 December 2009, pp. 1475-1479.
13. R. Syama and S. M. Idikkula, "HMM Based Speech Recognition System for Malayalam," The International Conference on Artificial Intelligence, 2008Monte Carlo Resort, Las Vegas, 14-17 July 2008.
14. P. G. Deivapalan and H. A. Murthy, "A Syllable-Based Isolated Word Recognizer for Tamil Handling OOV Words," The National Conference on Communications, Indian Institute of Technology Bombay, 1-3 February 2008, pp. 267-271.
15. C. Neti, N. Rajput and A. Verma, "A Large Vocabulary Continuous Speech Recognition System for Hind," IBM Research and Development Journal, September 2004.
16. G. Anumanchipalli, R. Chitturi, S. Joshi, R. Kumar, S. P. Singh, R. N. V. Sitaram and S. P. Kishore, "Development of Indian Language Speech Databases for Large Vocabulary Speech Recognition Systems," Proceedings of International Conference on Speech and Computer (SPECOM), Patras, October 2005.
17. A. Stolcke, "SRILM—An Extensible Language Modeling Toolkit," Proceedings of the 7th International Conference on Spoken Language Processing, 2002, pp. 901-904. http://www.speech.sri.com/
18. L. R. Rabiner, "A Tutorial on Hidden Markov Models and Selected Applications in Speech Recognition," Proceedings of the IEEE, Vol. 77, No. 2, 1989, pp. 257-286.
19. C. J. Legetter, "Improved Acoustic Modeling for HMMs Using Linear Transformations," Ph.D. Thesis, University of Cambridge, Cambridge, 1995.
20. M. Benzeghiba, R. De Mori, O. Deroo, S. Dupont, T. Erbes, D. Jouvet, L. Fissore, P. Laface, A. Mertins, C. Ris, R. Rose, V. Tyagi and C. Wellekens, "Automatic Speech Recognition and Speech Variability: A Review," Speech Communication, Vol. 49, No. 10-11, 2007, pp. 763-786. doi:10.1016/j.specom.2007.02.006
21. T. Herbig, F. Gerl, W. Minker and R. Haeb-Umbach, "Adaptive Systems for Unsupervised Speaker Tracking and Speech Recognition," Evolving Systems, Vol. 2, No. 3, 2011, pp. 199-214. doi:10.1007/s12530-011-9034-1

22. Steve Young, et al., "The HTK Book," http://htk.eng.cam.ac.uk/docs/docs.shtml [Citation Time(s):2]

23. A. Lee, T. Kawahara and K. Shikano, "Julius—An Open Source Real-Time Large Vocabulary Recognition Engine," Proceedings of 7th European Conference on Speech Communication and Technology, 2001.

CHAPTER 7

Multitask Learning with Local Attention for Tibetan Speech Recognition

Hui Wang , Fei Gao , Yue Zhao , Li Yang , Jianjian Yue , and Huilin Ma

School of Information Engineering, Minzu University of China, Beijing 100081, China

ABSTRACT

In this paper, we propose to incorporate the local attention in WaveNet-CTC to improve the performance of Tibetan speech recognition in multitask learning. With an increase in task number, such as simultaneous Tibetan speech content recognition, dialect identification, and speaker recognition,

Citation: Hui Wang, Fei Gao, Yue Zhao, Li Yang, Jianjian Yue, Huilin Ma, "Multi-task Learning with Local Attention for Tibetan Speech Recognition", Complexity, vol. 2020, Article ID 8894566, 10 pages, 2020. https://doi.org/10.1155/2020/8894566.

the accuracy rate of a single WaveNet-CTC decreases on speech recognition. Inspired by the attention mechanism, we introduce the local attention to automatically tune the weights of feature frames in a window and pay different attention on context information for multitask learning. The experimental results show that our method improves the accuracies of speech recognition for all Tibetan dialects in three-task learning, compared with the baseline model. Furthermore, our method significantly improves the accuracy for low-resource dialect by 5.11% against the specific-dialect model.

INTRODUCTION

Multitask learning has been applied successfully for speech recognition to improve the generalization performance of the model on the original task by sharing the information between related tasks [1–9]. Chen and Mak [6] used the multitask framework to conduct joint training of multiple low-resource languages, exploring the universal phoneme set as a secondary task to improve the effect of the phoneme model of each language. Krishna et al. [7] proposed a hierarchical multitask model, and the performance differences between high-resource language and low-resource language were compared. Li et al. [8] and Toshniwal et al. [9] introduced additional information of language ID to improve the performance of end-to-end multidialect speech recognition systems.

Tibetan is one of minority languages in China. It has three major dialects in China, i.e., Ü-Tsang, Kham, and Amdo. There are also several local subdialects in each dialect. Tibetan dialects pronounce very differently, but the written characters are unified across dialects. In our previous work [10], Tibetan multidialect multitask speech recognition was conducted based on the WaveNet-CTC, which performed simultaneous Tibetan multidialect speech content recognition, dialect identification, and speaker recognition in a single model. WaveNet is a deep generative model with very large receptive fields, and it can model the long-term dependency of speech data. It is very effective to learn the shared representation from speech data of different tasks. Thus, WaveNet-CTC was trained on three Tibetan dialect data sets and learned the shared representations and model parameters for speech recognition, speaker identification, and dialect recognition. Since the Lhasa of Ü-Tsang dialect is a standard Tibetan speech, there are more corpora available for training than Changdu-Kham and Amdo pastoral dialect. Although two-task WaveNet-CTC improved the performance on speech recognition for Lhasa of Ü-Tsang dialect and Changdu-Kham dialect, the three-task model did not improve performance for all dialects. With an increase in task number, the speech recognition performance degraded.

To obtain a better performance, attention mechanism is introduced into WaveNet-CTC for multitask learning in this paper. Attention mechanism can learn to set larger weight to more relevant frames at each time step. Considering the computation complexity, we conduct a local attention using a sliding window on the whole of speech feature frames to create the weighted context vectors for different recognition tasks. Moreover, we explore to place a local attention at the different positions within WaveNet, i.e., in the input layer and high layer, respectively.

The contribution of this work is three-fold. For one, we propose the WaveNet-CTC with local attention to perform multitask learning for Tibetan speech recognition, which can automatically capture the context information among different tasks. This model improves the performance of the Tibetan multidialect speech recognition task. Moreover, we compared the performance of local attention inserted at different positions in the multitask model. The attention component embedded in the high layer of WaveNet obtains better performance than the one in the input layer of WaveNet for speech recognition. Finally, we conduct a sliding window on the speech frames for efficiently computing the local attention.

The rest of this paper is organized as follows: Section 2 introduces the related work. Section 3 presents our method and gives the description of the baseline model, local attention mechanism, and the WaveNet-CTC with local attention. In Section 4, the Tibetan multidialect data set and experiments are explained in detail. Section 5 describes our conclusions.

RELATED WORK

Connectionist temporal classification (CTC) for end-to-end has its advantage of training simplicity and is one of the most popular methods used in speech recognition. Das et al. [11] directly incorporated attention modelling within the CTC framework to address high word error rates (WERs) for a character-based end-to-end model. But, in Tibetan speech recognition scenarios, the Tibetan character is a two-dimensional planar character, which is written in Tibetan letters from left to right, besides there is a vertical superposition in syllables, so a word-based CTC is more suitable for the end-to-end model. In our work, we try to introduce attention mechanism in WaveNet as an encoder for the CTC-based end-to-end model. The attention is used in WaveNet to capture the context information among different tasks for distinguishing dialect content, dialect identity, and speakers. In multitask settings, there are some recent works focusing on incorporating attention mechanism in multitask training. Zhang et al. [12] proposed an attention mechanism for the hybrid acoustic modelling framework based on LSTM, which weighted different speech frames in the input layer and automatically tuned its attention to the spliced context input. The experimental results showed that attention mechanism improved the ability to model speech. Liu et al. [13] incorporated the attention mechanism in multitask learning for computer vision tasks, in which the multitask attention network consisted of a shared network and task-specific soft-attention modules to learn the task-specific features from the global pool, whilst simultaneously allowing for features to be shared across different tasks. Zhang et al. [14] proposed an attention layer on the top of the layers for each task in the end-to-end multitask framework to relieve the overfitting problem in speech emotion recognition. Different from the works of Liu et al. and Zhang et al. [13, 14], which distributed many attention modules in the network, our method merely uses one sliding attention window in the multitask network and has its advantage of training simplicity.

METHODS

Baseline Model

We take the Tibetan multitask learning model in our previous work [10] as the baseline model as shown in Figure 1, which was initially proposed for Chinese and Korean speech recognition from the work of Xu [15] and Kim and Park [16]. The work [10] integrates WaveNet [17] with CTC loss [18] to realize Tibetan multidialect end-to-end speech recognition.

WaveNet contains the stacks of dilated causal convolutional layers as shown in Figure 2. In the baseline model, the WaveNet network consists of 15 layers, which are grouped into 3 dilated residual blocks of 5 layers. In every stack, the dilation rate increases by a factor of 2 in every layer.

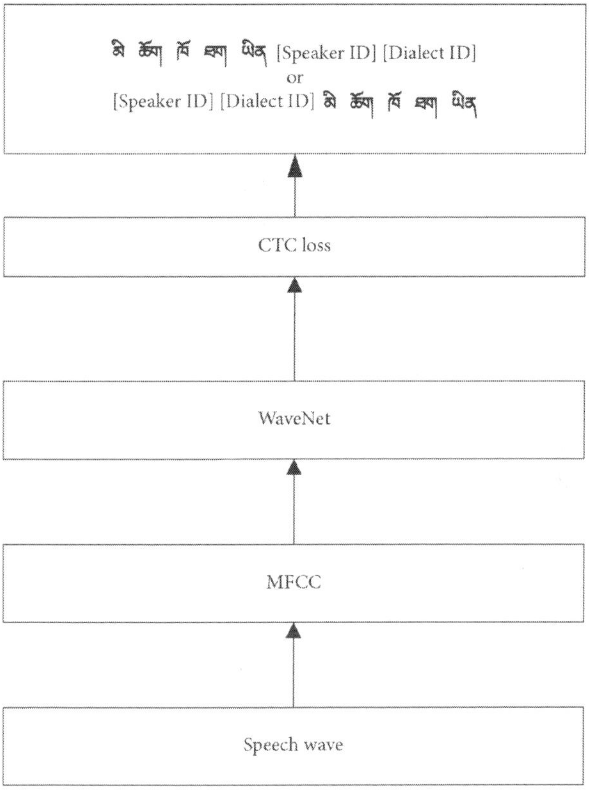

Figure 1: The baseline model.

The filter length of causal dilated convolutions is 2. According to equations (1) and (2), the respective field of WaveNet is 46:

$$\text{Receptive\_field}_{\text{block}} = \sum_{i=1}^{n} \left(\text{Filter}_{\text{length}} - 1\right) \times \text{Dilation}_{\text{rate}_i} + 1. \quad (1)$$

$$\text{Receptive field}_{\text{stacks}} = S \times \text{Receptive field}_{\text{block}} - S + 1. \quad (2)$$

In equations (1) and (2), S refers to the number of stacks, Receptive $\text{field}_{\text{block}}$ refers to the receptive field of a stack of dilated CNN, Receptive $\text{field}_{\text{stacks}}$ refers to the receptive field of some stacks of dilated CNN, and $\text{Dilation}_{\text{ratei}}$ refers to the dilation rate of the i-th layer in a block.

WaveNet also uses residual and parameterized skip connections [19] to speed up convergence and enable training of much deeper models. More details about WaveNet can be found in [17].

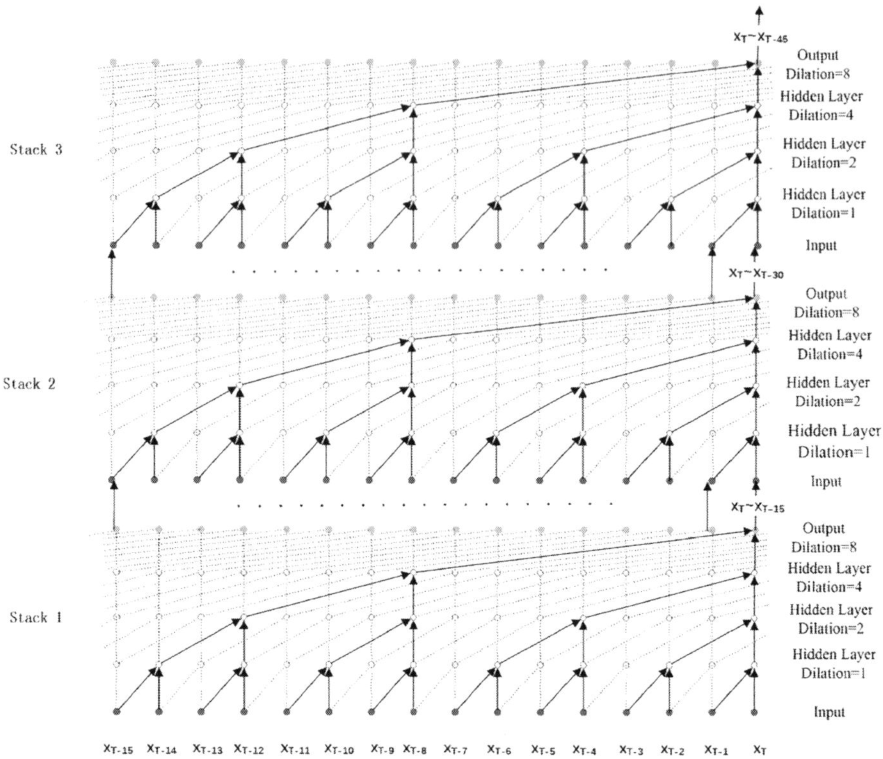

Figure 2: 3 stacks of 5 dilated causal convolutional layers with filter length 2.

Connectionist temporal classification (CTC) is an algorithm that trains a deep neural network [20] for the end-to-end learning task. It can make the sequence label predictions at any point in the input sequence [18]. In the baseline model, since the Tibetan character is a two-dimensional planar character as shown in Figure 3, the CTC modeling unit for Tibetan speech recognition is Tibetan single syllable, otherwise a Tibetan letter sequence from left to right is unreadable.

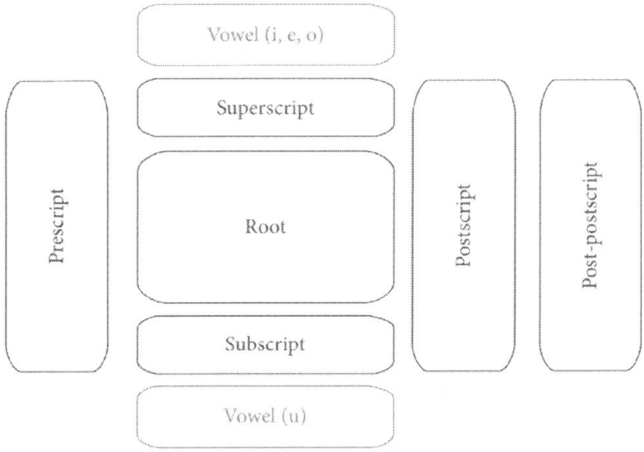

Figure 3: The structure of a Tibetan syllable.

Local Attention Mechanism

Since the effect of each speech feature frame is different for the target label output at current time, considering the computational complexity, we introduce the local attention [21] into WaveNet to create a weighted context vector for each time i. The local attention places a sliding window with the length 2n centered around the current speech feature frame on the input layer and before the softmax layer in WaveNet, respectively, and repeatedly produces a context vector C_i for the current input (or hidden) feature frame $x(h)_i$. The formula for C_i is shown in equation (3), and the schematic diagram is shown in Figure 4:

$$C_i = \sum_{j=i-n, j\neq i}^{i+n} \alpha_{i,j} \cdot x(h)_j, \tag{3}$$

where $\alpha_{i,j}$ is the attention weight, subject to $\alpha \geq 0$ and $\sum_j \alpha_{i,j} = 1$ through softmax normalization. The $\alpha_{i,j}$ calculation method is as follows:

$$\alpha_{i,j} = \frac{\exp(\mathrm{Score}(x(h)_i, x(h)_j))}{\sum_j \exp(\mathrm{Score}(x(h)_i, x(h)_j))}. \tag{4}$$

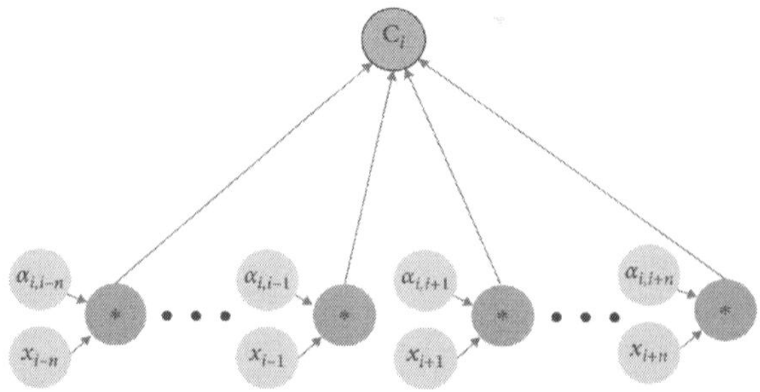

Figure 4: Local attention.

It captures the correlation of speech frame pair ($x(h)_i$, $x(h)_j$, $j \neq i$). The attention operates on n frames before and after the current frame. Score (.) is an energy function, whose value is computed as equation (5) by the MLP which is jointly trained with all the other components in an end-to-end network. Those $x(h)_j$, $j \neq i$ that get larger scores would have more weights in context vector C_i.

$$\text{Score}(x_i, x_j) = v_a^T \tanh(W_a [x(h)_i; x(h)_j]). \tag{5}$$

Finally, $x(h)_i$ is concatenated with C_i as the extended feature frame and fed into the next layer of WaveNet as shown in Figures 5 and 6. The attention module is inserted in the input layer in Figure 5 referred as Attention-WaveNetCTC. The attention module is embedded before the softmax layer in Figure 6 referred as WaveNet-Attention-CTC.

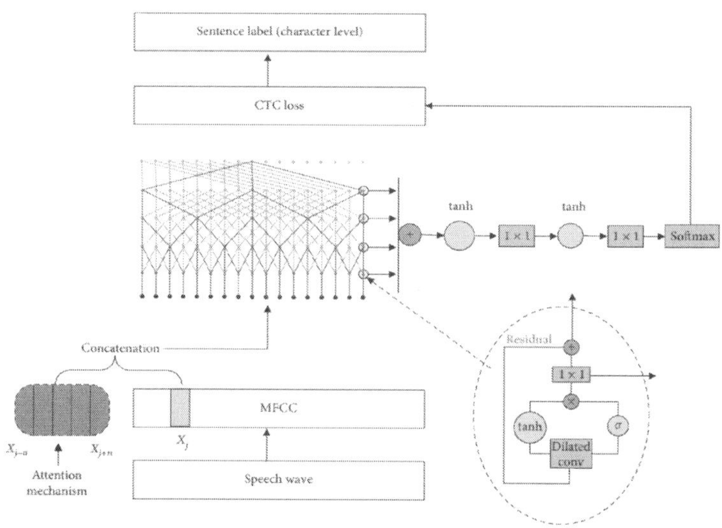

Figure 5: The architecture of attention-WaveNet-CTC.

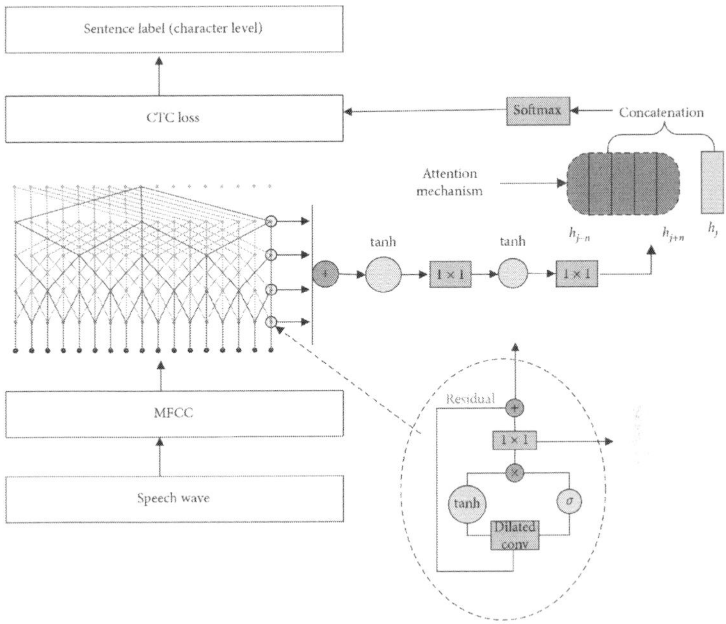

Figure 6: The architecture of WaveNet-attention-CTC.

EXPERIMENTS

Data

Our experimental data are from an open and free Tibetan multidialect speech data set TIBMD@MUC [10], in which the text corpus consists of two parts: one is 1396 spoken language sentences selected from the book "Tibetan Spoken Language" [22] written by La Bazelen and the other part contains 8,000 sentences from online news, electronic novels, and poetry of Tibetan on internet. All text corpora in TIBMD@MUC include a total of 3497 Tibetan syllables.

There are 40 recorders who are from Lhasa City in Tibet, Yushu City in Qinghai Province, Changdu City in Tibet, and Tibetan Qiang Autonomous Prefecture of Ngawa. They used different dialects to speak out the same text for 1396 spoken sentences, and other 8000 sentences are read loudly in Lhasa dialect. Speech data files are converted to 16K Hz sampling frequency, 16 bit quantization accuracy, and wav format.

Our experimental data for multitask speech recognition are shown in Table 1, which consists of 4.4 hours Lhasa-Ü-Tsang, 1.90 hours Changdu-Kham, and 3.28 hours Amdo pastoral dialect, and their corresponding texts contain 1205 syllables for training. We collect 0.49 hours Lhasa-Ü-Tsang, 0.19 hours Changdu-Kham, and 0.37 hours Amdo pastoral dialect, respectively, to test.

Table 1: The experimental data statistics.

Dialect	**Training data (hours)**	**Training utterances**	**Test data (hours)**	**Test utterances**	**Speaker**
Lhasa-Ü-Tsang	4.40	6678	0.49	742	20
Changdu-Kham	1.90	3004	0.19	336	6
Amdo pastoral	3.28	4649	0.37	516	14
Total	9.58	14331	1.05	2110	40

39 MFCC features of each observation frame are extracted from speech data using a 128 ms window with 96 ms overlaps.

The experiments are divided into two parts: two-task experiments and three-task experiments. Three dialect-specific models and a multi-dialect model without attention are trained on WaveNet-CTC.

In WaveNet, the number of hidden units in the gating layers is 128. The learning rate is 2×10^{-4}. The number of hidden units in the residual connection is 128.

Two-task Experiment

For two-task joint recognition, the performances of the dialect ID or speaker ID at the beginning and at the end of output sequence were evaluated, respectively. We set $n=5$ frames before and after the current frame to calculate the attention coefficients for attention-based WaveNet-CTC, which are referred to as Attention (5)-WaveNet-CTC and WaveNet-Attention (5)-CTC, respectively, for the two architectures in Figures 5 and 6. Compared with the calculation of the attention coefficient of all frames, the calculation speed of local attention has been improved quickly, which is convenient for the training of models.

The speech recognition result is summarized in Table 2. The best model is the proposed WaveNet-Attention-CTC with the attention embedded before the softmax layer in WaveNet and dialect ID at the beginning of label sequence. It outperforms the dialect-specific model by 7.39% and 2.4%, respectively, for Lhasa-Ü-Tsang and Changdu-Kham and gets the SER close to the dialect-specific model for Amdo Pastoral, which has the highest ARSER (average relative syllable error rate) for three dialects. The model of dialectID-speech (D-S) in the framework of WaveNet-Attention-CTC is effective to improve multilinguistic speech content recognition. Speech content recognition is more sensitive to the recognition of dialect ID than speaker ID. The recognition of dialect ID helps to identify the speech content. However, the attention inserted before the input layer in WaveNet resulted in the worst recognition, which shows that raw speech feature cannot provide much information to distinguish the multitask.

Table 2: Syllable error rate (%) of two-task models on speech content recognition.

Architecture	**Model**	**Lhasa-Ü-Tsang**		**Changdu-Kham**		**Amdo Pastoral**		
		SER[1]	RSER[2]	SER	RSER	SER	RSER	ASER[3]
Dialect-specific model		28.83	62.56			**17.6**		
WaveNet-CTC		29.55	−0.72	62.83	−0.27	33.52	−15.92	−5.63
WaveNet-CTC with dialect ID or speaker ID (baseline model)	D-S[4]	32.84	−4.01	68.58	−6.02	33.00	−15.40	−8.48
	S-D[5]	26.80	2.03	64.03	−1.47	30.79	−13.09	−4.21
	S-S1[6]	27.21	1.62	64.17	−1.61	29.68	−12.08	−4.02
	S-S2[7]	28.13	0.7	62.43	0.13	28.04	-10.44	−3.20
Attention (5)-Wave Net-CTC	D-S	52.19	−23.36	65.24	−2.68	50.22	-32.62	−19.55
	S-D	55.16	−26.33	67.78	−5.22	55.23	-37.63	−23.06
	S-S1	77.42	−48.59	85.44	−22.88	82.08	-64.48	−45.32
	S-S2	83.32	−54.49	89.15	−26.94	81.47	-63.87	−48.43
WaveNet-Attention (5)-CTC	D-S	**21.44**	**7.39**	**60.16**	**2.40**	20.46	**−2.86**	**2.31**
	S-D	23.79	5.04	62.96	−0.4	24.15	−6.55	−0.64
	S-S1	34.86	−6.03	63.36	−0.8	40.10	−22.50	−9.78
	S-S2	34.83	−6.00	62.70	−0.14	37.63	−20.03	−8.72

[1]SER: syllable error rate, [2]RSER: relative syllable error rate, [3]ARSER: average relative syllable error rate, [4]D-S: the model trained using the transcription with dialect ID at the beginning of target label sequence, like "A ཐུགས་རྗེ་ཆེ," [5]S-D: the model trained using the transcription with dialect ID at the end of target label sequence, [6]S-S1: the model trained using the

transcription with speaker ID at the beginning of target label sequence, and [7]S-S2: the model trained using the transcription with speaker ID at the end of target label sequence.

For dialect ID recognition, in Table 3, we can see that the model with attention mechanism added before the softmax layer performs better than which is added in the input layer, and the dialect ID at the beginning is better than that at the end. From Table 2 and Table 3, it can be seen that the dialect ID recognition influences the speech content recognition.

Table 3: Dialect ID recognition accuracy (%) of two-task models.

Architecture	Model	Lhasa-Ü-Tsang	Changdu-Kham	Amdo Pastoral
DialectID model		97.88	92.24	97.9
WaveNet-CTC with dialect ID	D-S	98.57	95.23	**99.6**
	S-D	99.01	97.61	99.41
Attention (5)-WaveNet-CTC	D-S	**100**	89.28	94.52
	S-D	0	0	0
WaveNet-Attention (5)-CTC	D-S	**100**	**98.8**	99.41
	S-D	**100**	94.04	98.06

We also test the speaker ID recognition accuracy for the two-task models. Results are listed in Table 4. It is worth noting that the Attention-WaveNet-CTC model performs poorly on both tasks of the speaker and speech content recognition. Especially in the speaker identification task, the recognition rate of the speakerID-speech model in all three dialects is very poor. Among the Attention-WaveNet-CTC models, it can be seen that the modelling ability of two models of the dialectID-speech and speakerID-speech model shows big gap, which means the Attention-WaveNet-CTC architecture cannot learn effectively the correlation among multiple frames of acoustic feature for multiple classification tasks. In contrast, the WaveNet-Attention-CTC model has a much better performance on the two tasks. The attention embedded before the softmax layer can find the related and important frames to lead to high recognition accuracy.

Table 4: Speaker ID recognition accuracy (%) of two-task models.

Architecture	**Model**	**Lhasa-Ü-Tsang**	**Changdu-Kham**	**Amdo Pastoral**
SpeakerID model		67.75	93.13	95.31
WaveNet-CTC with speaker ID	S-S1	68.32	92.85	**97.48**
	S-S2	**71.15**	95.23	96.12
Attention (5)-WaveNet-CTC	S-S1	0	0	0
	S-S2	60.64	77.38	85.85
WaveNet-Attention (5)-CTC	S-S1	70.35	92.85	**97.48**
	S-S2	69.40	**100**	96.70

Three-task Experiment

We compared the performances of two architectures, namely, Attention-WaveNet-CTC and WaveNet-Attention-CTC on three-task learning with the dialect-specific model and WaveNet-CTC, where we evaluated $n=5$, $n=7$, and $n=10$, respectively, for the attention mechanism. The results are shown in Table 5.

Table 5: Syllable error rate (%) of three-task models on speech content recognition.

Architecture	**Model**	**Lhasa-Ü-Tsang**		**Changdu-Kham**		**Amdo Pastoral**		
		SER	RSER	SER	RSER	SER	RSER	ASER
Dialect-specific model		**28.83**	62.56			**17.60**		
WaveNet-CTC with dialect ID and speaker ID (baseline model)	S-D-S	30.64	−1.81	64.17	−1.61	34.06	−16.46	-6.62
	D-S-S1	39.64	−10.81	65.10	−2.54	45.15	−27.55	−13.63
	D-S-S2	33.43	−4.60	64.83	−2.27	37.56	−19.96	-8.94
Attention (5)-WaveNet-CTC	S-D-S	48.69	−19.86	68.31	−5.75	63.22	−45.62	−23.74
	D-S-S1	52.57	−23.74	69.38	−6.82	71.42	−53.82	−28.13
	D-S-S2	49.10	−20.27	79.41	−16.85	61.09	−43.49	−26.87
WaveNet-Attention (5)-CTC	S-D-S	30.75	−1.92	69.51	−6.95	34.21	−16.61	−8.49
	D-S-S1	33.17	−4.34	69.51	-6.95	38.49	−20.89	−10.73
	D-S-S2	31.16	−2.33	69.25	−6.69	34.14	−16.54	−8.52

WaveNet-Attention (7)-CTC	S-D-S	30.39	−1.56	70.05	−7.49	32.7	−15.1	−8.05
	D-S-S1	35.28	−6.45	68.12	−5.56	38.03	−20.73	−10.81
	D-S-S2	32.58	−3.75	62.74	−0.18	37.16	−19.56	−7.83
WaveNet-Attention (10)-CTC	S-D-S	30.25	**−1.42**	69.25	−6.69	32.01	**−14.41**	−7.51
	D-S-S1	34.06	−5.23	70.05	−7.49	40.10	−22.50	−11.74
	D-S-S2	31.85	−3.02	**57.45**	**5.11**	33.65	−16.05	**−4.65**

We can see that the three-task models have worse performance compared with the two-task model, and WaveNet-Attention-CTC has lower SERs for Lhasa-Ü-Tsang and Amdo Pastoral against the dialect-specific model, but for Changdu-Kham, a relative low-resource Tibetan dialect, the model of dialectID-speech-speakerID (D-S-S2) based on the framework of WaveNet-Attention (10)-CTC achieved the highest recognition rate in all models, which outperforms the dialect-specific model by 5.11%. We analyzed the reason that maybe is the reduction of generalization error of the multitask model with the number of learning tasks increasing. It improves the recognition rate for small-data dialect, however not for big-data dialects. Since ASER reflects the generalization error of the model, D-S-S2 of WaveNet-Attention (10)-CTC has highest ASER in all models, which shows it has better generalization capacity. Meanwhile, WaveNet-Attention (10)-CTC achieved the better performance than WaveNet-Attention (5)-CTC and WaveNet-Attention (7)-CTC for speech content recognition as shown in Figure 7, where the syllable error rates declined with the number of n increasing for three dialects, and Changdu-Kham's SER has a quickest descent. We can conclude that attention mechanism needs a longer range to distinguish more tasks, and it pays more attention on the low-resource task. It is also observed that WaveNet-Attention (5)-CTC has better performance than Attention (5)-WaveNet-CTC, which demonstrates again that the attention mechanism placed in the high layer can find the related and important information which leads to more accurate speech recognition than when it is put in the input layer.

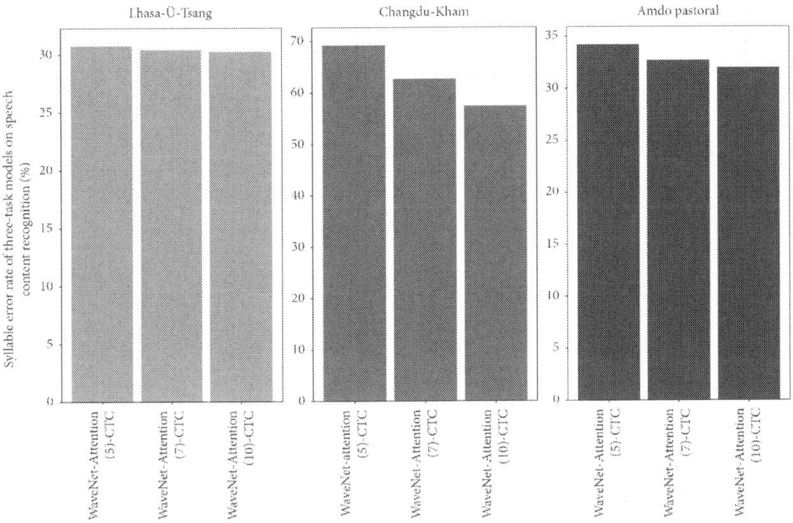

Figure 7: Syllable error rate of WaveNet-Attention-CTC for different lengths of the attention window.

From Tables 6 and 7, we can observe that models with attention have worse performance than the ones without attention for dialect ID recognition and speaker ID recognition, and longer attention achieved the worse recognition for the language with large data. It also shows that in the case of more tasks, the attention mechanism tends towards the low-resource task, such as speech content recognition.

Table 6: Dialect ID recognition accuracy (%) of three-task models.

Architecture	Model	Lhasa-Ü-Tsang	Changdu-Kham	Amdo Pastoral
DialectID model		97.88	92.24	97.9
WaveNet-CTC with dialect ID and speaker ID	D-S-S1	98.01	**98.8**	99.41
	D-S-S2	99.73	96.42	**99.61**
	S-D-S	99.25	95.23	99.03
Attention (5)-WaveNet-CTC	S-D-S	**100**	76.19	91.27
	D-S-S1	**100**	90.47	94.18
	D-S-S2	**100**	82.14	93.02
WaveNet-Attention (5)-CTC	S-D-S	**100**	89.28	93.79
	D-S-S1	**100**	85.71	93.79
	D-S-S2	**100**	95.23	94.18

WaveNet-Attention (7)-CTC	S-D-S	0	85.71	91.66
	D-S-S1	0	89.98	93.88
	D-S-S2	0	89.28	95.34
WaveNet-Attention (10)-CTC	S-D-S	0	85.71	95.54
	D-S-S1	0	94.04	93.99
	D-S-S2	0	0	0

Table 7: Speaker ID recognition accuracy (%) of three-task models.

Architecture	**Model**	**Lhasa-Ü-Tsang**	**Changdu-Kham**	**Amdo pastoral**
SpeakerID model		67.75	93.13	95.31
WaveNet-CTC with dialect ID and speaker ID	S-D-S	**72.91**	**98.8**	96.12
	D-S-S1	70.21	95.23	93.6
	D-S-S2	70.35	96.42	96.89
Attention (5)-WaveNet-CTC	S-D-S	61.08	83.33	89.53
	D-S-S1	62.12	83.33	87.01
	D-S-S2	61.99	84.52	90.11
WaveNet-Attention (5)-CTC	S-D-S	61.99	85.71	92.05
	D-S-S1	62.53	82.14	91.08
	D-S-S2	61.18	89.28	92.44
WaveNet-Attention (7)-CTC	S-D-S	60.91	85.71	91.66
	D-S-S1	62.04	84.31	92.01
	D-S-S2	58.49	86.90	90.69
WaveNet-Attention (10)-CTC	S-D-S	58.49	84.52	92.05
	D-S-S1	59.43	83.33	91.27
	D-S-S2	63.47	92.85	**97.86**

In summary, combining the results of the above experiments, whether two task or three task, the multitask model can make a significant improvement on the performance of the low-resource task by incorporating the attention mechanism, especially when the attention is applied to the high-level abstract features. The attention-based multitask model can achieve the improvements on speech recognition for all dialects compared with the baseline model. With an increase in the task number, the multitask model needs to increase the range for attention to distinguish multiple dialects.

CONCLUSIONS

This paper proposes a multitask learning mechanism with local attention based on WaveNet to improve the performance for low-resource language. We integrate Tibetan multidialect speech recognition, speaker ID recognition, and dialect identification into a unified neural network and compare the attention effects on the different places in architectures. The experimental results show that our method is effective for Tibetan multitask processing scenarios. The WaveNet-CTC model with attention added into the high layer obtains the best performance for unbalance-resource multitask processing. In the future works, we will evaluate the proposed method on larger Tibetan data set or on different languages.

AUTHORS' CONTRIBUTIONS

Hui Wang and Yue Zhao contributed equally to this work.

ACKNOWLEDGMENTS

This work was supported by the National Natural Science Foundation under grant no. 61976236.

REFERENCES

1. Z. Tang, L. Li, and D. Wang, "Multi-task recurrent model for speech and speaker recognition," in *Proceedings of the 2016 Asia-Pacific signal and Information Processing Association Annual Summit and Conference (APSIPA)*, pp. 1–4, Jeju, South Korea, December 2016.
2. O. Siohan and D. Rybach, "Multitask learning and system combination for automatic speech recognition," in *Proceedings of the 2015 IEEE Workshop on Automatic Speech Recognition and Understanding (ASRU)*, pp. 589–595, Scottsdale, AZ, USA, December 2015.
3. Y. Qian, M. Yin, Y. You, and K. Yu, "Multi-task joint-learning of deep neural networks for robust speech recognition," in *Proceedings of the 2015 IEEE Workshop on Automatic Speech Recognition and Understanding (ASRU)*, pp. 310–316, Scottsdale, AZ, USA, December 2015.
4. A. Thanda and S. M. Venkatesan, "Multi-task learning of deep neural networks for audio visual automatic speech recognition," 2020, http://arxiv.org/abs/1701.02477.
5. X. Yang, K. Audhkhasi, A. Rosenberg, S. Thomas, B. Ramabhadran, and M. Hasegawa-Johnson, "Joint modeling of accents and acoustics for multi-accent speech recognition," in *Proceedings of the 2018 IEEE International Conference on Acoustics, Speech and Signal Processing (ICASSP)*, Calgary, Canada, April 2018.
6. D. Chen and B. K.-W. Mak, "Multitask learning of deep neural networks for low-resource speech recognition," *IEEE/ACM Transactions on Audio, Speech and Language Processing*, vol. 23, no. 7, pp. 1172–1183, 2015.
7. K. Krishna, S. Toshniwal, and K. Livescu, "Hierarchical multitask learning for ctc-based speech recognition," 2020, http://arxiv.org/abs/1807.06234.
8. B. Li, T. N. Sainath, Z. Chen et al., "Multi-dialect speech recognition with a single sequence-to-sequence model," 2017, http://arxiv.org/abs/1712.01541.
9. S. Toshniwal, T. N. Sainath, B. Li et al., "Multilingual speech recognition with a single end-to-end model," 2018, http://arxiv.org/abs/1711.01694.

10. Y. Zhao, J. Yue, X. Xu, L. Wu, and X. Li, "End-to-end-based Tibetan multitask speech recognition," *IEEE Access*, vol. 7, pp. 162519–162529, 2019.

11. A. Das, J. Li, R. Zhao, and Y. F. Gong, "Advancing connectionist temporal classification with attention," in *Proceedings of the 2018 IEEE International Conference on Acoustics, Speech and Signal Processing (ICASSP)*, Calgary, Canada, April 2018.

12. Y. Zhang, P. Y. Zhang, and H. Y. Yan, "Long short-term memory with attention and multitask learning for distant speech recognition," *Journal of Tsinghua University (Science and Technology)*, vol. 58, no. 3, p. 249, 2018, in Chinese.

13. S. Liu, E. Johns, and A. J. Davison, "End-to-end multi-task learning with attention," in *Proceedings of the IEEE Computer Vision and Pattern Recognition (CVPR)*, Long Beach, CA, USA, June2019.

14. Z. Zhang, B. Wu, and B. Schuller, "Attention-augmented end-to-end multi-task learning for emotion prediction from speech," in *Proceedings of the IEEE International Conference on Acoustics, Speech and Signal Processing (ICASSP)*, Brighton, UK, May 2019.

15. S. Xu, "Speech-to-text-wavenet: end-to-end sentence level Chinese speech recognition using deepmind's wavenet," 2020, https://github.com/CynthiaSuwi/Wavenet-demo.

16. Kim and Park, "Speech-to-text-WaveNet," 2016, https://github.com/buriburisuri/ GitHub repository.

17. A. van den Oord, A. Graves, H. Zen et al., "WaveNet: a generative model for raw audio," 2016, http://arxiv.org/abs/16 09.03499.

18. A. Graves, *Supervised Sequence Labelling with Recurrent Neural Networks*, Springer, New York, NY, USA, 2012.

19. M. Wei, "A novel face recognition in uncontrolled environment based on block 2D-CS-LBP features and deep residual network," *International Journal of Intelligent Computing and Cybernetics*, vol. 13, no. 2, pp. 207–221, 2020.

20. A. S. Jadhav, P. B. Patil, and S. Biradar, "Computer-aided diabetic retinopathy diagnostic model using optimal thresholding merged with neural network," *International Journal of Intelligent Computing & Cybernetics*, vol. 13, no. 3, pp. 283–310, 2020.

21. M.-T. Luong, H. Pham, and C. D. Manning, "Effective approaches to attention-based neural machine translation," 2020, http://arxiv.org/abs/1508.04025.
22. B. La, "Tibetan spoken language," 2005, in Chinese.

CHAPTER 8

Arabic Speech Recognition System Based on MFCC and HMMs

Hussien A. Elharati[1], Mohamed Alshaari[2], Veton Z. Këpuska[2]

[1]Electrical Engineering Department, High Institute of Science and Technology, Sūqal-Jum'a, Tripoli, Libya

[2]Electrical & Computer Engineering Department, Florida Institute of Technology, Melbourne, FL, USA

ABSTRACT

Speech recognition allows the machine to turn the speech signal into text through identification and understanding process. Extract the features, predict the maximum likelihood, and generate the models of the input speech

Citation: Elharati, H. , Alshaari, M. and Këpuska, V. (2020), Arabic Speech Recognition System Based on MFCC and HMMs. Journal of Computer and Communications, 8, 28-34. doi: 10.4236/jcc.2020.83003.

signal are considered the most important steps to configure the Automatic Speech Recognition System (ASR). In this paper, an automatic Arabic speech recognition system was established using MATLAB and 24 Arabic words Consonant-Vowel Consonant-Vowel Consonant-Vowel (CVCVCV) was recorded from 19 Arabic native speakers, each speaker uttering the same word 3 times (total 1368 words). In order to test the system, 39-features were extracted by partitioning the speech signal into frames ~ 0.25 sec shifted by 0.10 sec. in back-end, the statistical models were generated by separated the features into number of states between 4 to 10, each state has 8-gaussian distributions. The data has 48 k sample rate and 32-bit depth and saved separately in a wave file format. The system was trained in phonetically rich and balanced Arabic speech words list (10 speakers * 3 times * 24 words, total 720 words) and tested using another word list (24 words * 9 speakers * 3 times *, total 648 words). Using different speakers similar words, the system obtained a very good word recognition accuracy results of 92.92% and a Word Error Rate (WER) of 7.08%.

Keywords: Speech Recognition, Feature Extraction, Maximum Likelihood, Gaussian Distribution, Consonant-Vowel

INTRODUCTION

Speech is a way to express ourselves, it's a complex naturally acquired human motor ability [1]. Speech recognition is the capability of a device to receive, identify, and recognize the speech signal [2]. Speech recognition process fundamentally functions as a pipeline that converts the sound into recognized text, as shown in Figure 1. Based on spectral, the input signal is converted into a sequence of training and testing feature vectors saved in unique files. Given all the observations in the training data, Baum-Welch algorithm can learn and generate the HMM models equal to the number of the words to be recognized. In testing process, pattern matching provides likelihoods of a match of all sequences of speech recognition units to the input speech. Decision making generated according to the best path sequence between the models and testing data. Speech recognition system involved in several applications such as: call routing, automatic transcriptions, information searching, data entry, Speech to Text conversion, Text to Speech conversion etc. [3].

Arabic is the native language for over 300 million speakers and considered one of the official languages in many countries around the world. It has a unique set of diacritics that can change the meaning [4]. Arabic

ASR received little attention compared to other languages, and research was oblivious to the diacritics in most cases. Omitting diacritics circumscribes the Arabic ASR system's usability for several applications such as voice-enabled translation, text to speech, and speech-to-speech [5].

Feature Extraction is accomplished by changing the waveform speech form to a form of parametric representation with a relatively low data rate for subsequent processing and analysis. Subsequently, the acceptable classification in the training and testing part is derived from the quality features [6]. Therefore, the most popular speech methods, Mel Cepstral frequency coefficients (MFCC) and Hidden Markov Model have been selected and tested in order to provide a high level of reliability and acceptability of the Arabic ASR.

MEL FREQUENCY CEPSTRAL COEFFICIENTS (MFCC)

MFCC is a feature widely used in automatic speech and speaker recognition has been used to extract spectral features from frame sequences [7] [8].

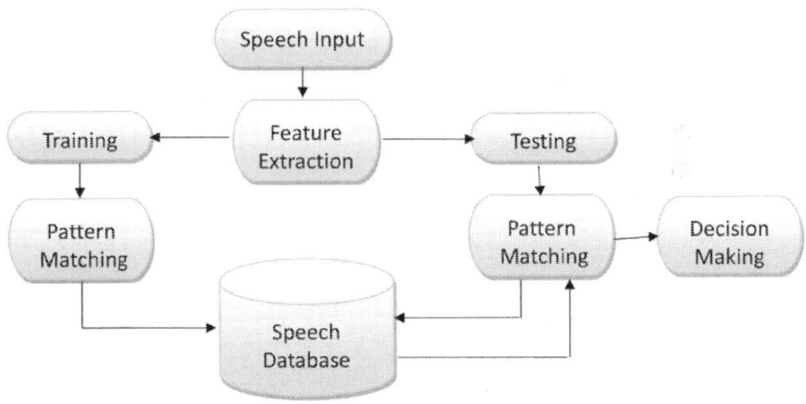

Figure 1. Speech recognition process.

Fast Fourier Transform (FFT) has been used to transfer the signal into frequency domain using the Equation (2.1). After pre-emphases, blocking, and windowing the input signal, FFT applies on the speech frames to obtain 256-point certain parameters, converting the power-spectrum to a Mel-frequency spectrum using Equations (2.2) and (2.3), and finally taking the logarithm of that spectrum and computing its inverse Fourier transform as shown in Figure 2.

$$X(k) = \sum_{N=0}^{N-1} x[n] e^{-j2\pi nk/N}, \quad 0 \le k < N \tag{2.1}$$

$$F_{mel} = 2595 \cdot \log_{10}\left(1 + \frac{f_{Hz}}{700}\right) \tag{2.2}$$

$$F_{Hz} = 700 \cdot \left(10^{\frac{F_{mel}}{2595}} - 1\right). \tag{2.3}$$

HIDDEN MARKOV MODEL (HMM)

HMM is used to classify the features and generate the correct decision. HMM considered the powerful statistical tool used in speech recognition and speaker identification systems, due to the ability to model non-linearly aligning speech and estimating the model parameters [9]. Gaussian Mixtures also used to model the emission probability distribution function inside each state.

In training process, the observation parameters, transition probability matrix, the prior probabilities, and Gaussian distribution were re-estimated in order to get good parameters at each iteration as shown in Figure 3. As a result, all the previous HMM parameters are used to generate the likelihood scores, which are used to find the best path between the frames in order to recognize the unknown word [10] [11].

Evaluation Process

Given the observation sequence (O) and the model parameters (λ), Forward (α) and Backward (β) algorithms were used to find the probability of the observation sequence given the model P(O|λ)P(O|λ) [12]. As shown in Figure 4, forward and backward probabilities are added to evaluate the probability that any sequence of states has produced the sequence of observations.

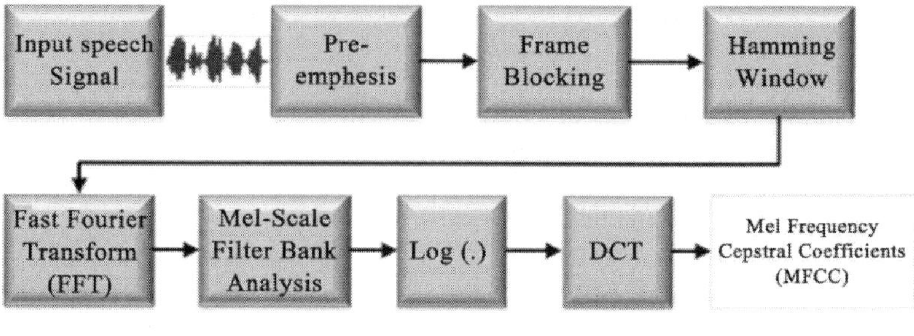

Figure 2. Mel Frequency Cepstral Coefficients (MFCC) block diagram.

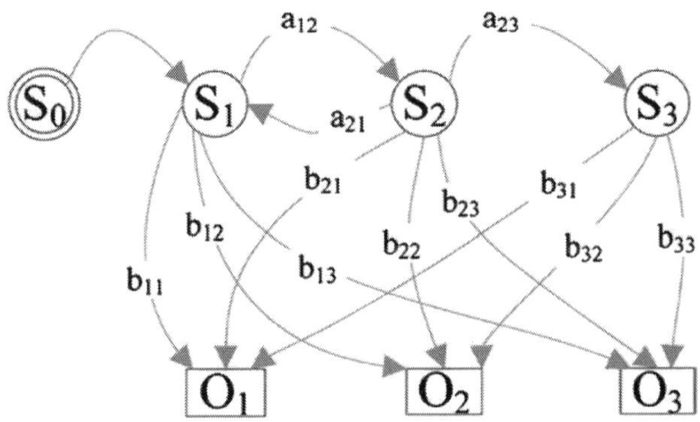

Figure 3. Three states hidden Markov model.

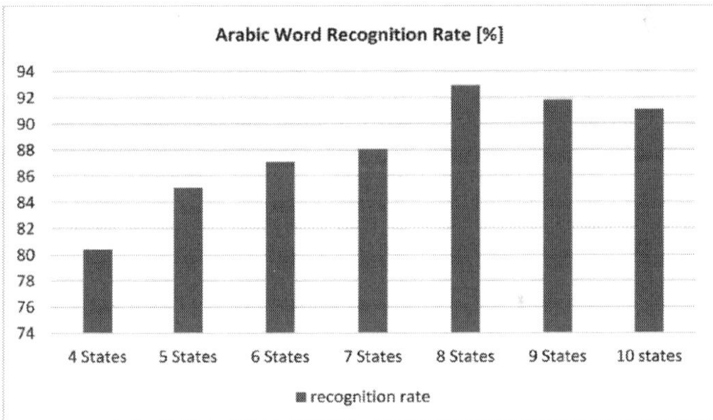

Figure 4. Recognition rate using different state numbers based on MFCC.

Training Process

Given the observation sequence (O) and the model parameters (λ), Baum-Welch algorithm was used to re-adjust and re-estimate the transition probability matrix and Gaussian mixture parameters (mean and covariance) that best describe the process [13] [14]. Baum welch algorithm also used to learn and encode the characteristics of the observation sequence in order to recognize a similar observation sequence.

Decoding Process

Viterbi algorithm has been used to comparing between the training and the testing data and find the optimal scoring path of state sequence by selecting the high probabilities between the model and the testing data [15] [16]. The maximal probability of state sequences is defined using the Equation (3.1), and the optimal scoring path of state sequence selected is calculated using the following MATLAB function.

start_recognition ("testing_list.mat", dim).

$$\delta t(i) = \max\left(P\left(q(1), q(2), \cdots, q(t-1); o(1), o(2), \cdots, o(t) \mid \lambda\right)\right) \tag{3.1}$$

EXPERIMENTAL RESULTS

Using the automatic ASR system, several experiments were carried out using 24 (CVCVCV) Arabic isolated words as shown in Table 1. The feature vectors have been extracted for each sound using MFCC algorithm and saved, and the statistical models were generated using Hidden Markov Model classifier to match the data. The performance evaluation of the Arabic ASR system was obtained by finding the maximum word recognition rate.

In this work, (24 words * 3 times) Arabic CVCVCV words, small vocabulary data set are recorded from 19 adult male speakers (total 1368) divided into training and testing files. Table 2 shows the confusion matrix of the average classification results, which obtained using convenient features in training and testing sessions. Each experiment conducted by dividing the data into 4, 5, 6, 7, 8, 9, and 10 number of states and modeled using 8 multi-dimensional Gaussians Hidden Markov Model.

Table 1. CVCVCV arabic words.

Number	Word	Number	Word	Number	Word	Number	Word
1	فَعَلَ	7	فَعِلَ	13	فَعُلَ	19	فُعِلَ
2	رَفَعَ	8	بَخِلَ	14	بَلُغَ	20	ذُكِرَ
3	ذَكَرَ	9	عَمِلَ	15	صَلُحَ	21	جُمِعَ
4	ذَهَبَ	10	حَفِظَ	16	سَهُلَ	22	خُلِقَ
5	شَرَحَ	11	سَمِعَ	17	كَبُرَ	23	كُتِبَ
6	كَتَبَ	12	فَرِحَ	18	كَرُمَ	24	حُشِرَ

Table 2. Recognition rate using different state numbers based on MFCC.

State No.	Wrong words											
	1	2	3	4	5	6	7	8	9	10	11	12
4	3	4	12	5	0	8	27	8	2	2	0	3
5	6	1	11	4	0	6	1	0	0	2	0	1
6	4	3	4	0	0	5	0	0	4	0	1	5
7	12	0	4	2	1	3	4	3	2	0	2	2
8	3	0	1	1	1	3	0	0	1	0	0	0
9	0	1	2	1	0	1	3	1	0	0	0	1
10	8	0	2	1	0	0	0	0	0	2	0	1
State No.	**Wrong words**											
	13	14	15	16	17	18	19	20	21	22	23	24
4	5	0	7	3	0	10	3	6	0	0	11	22
5	17	0	10	3	2	0	16	8	0	0	3	16
6	4	1	5	10	5	0	21	7	0	1	1	12
7	11	0	5	9	3	0	6	5	0	0	0	12
8	10	0	4	4	0	1	9	2	0	0	1	10
9	9	0	8	4	2	0	4	8	0	0	1	13
10	13	2	4	3	0	0	13	0	0	1	7	7

Table 3. Recognition rate summary based on MFCC.

State No.	Total error count	Total correct count	Recognition rate
4	141	579	80.4166667
5	107	613	85.1388889
6	93	627	87.0833333
7	86	634	88.0555556
8	51	669	92.9166667
9	59	661	91.8055556
10	64	656	91.1111111

During the experiments, the speech signal pre-reemphasis using 0.975 factor, covered by 25 milliseconds hamming window, and 10 milliseconds overlapping. The 256-point Fast Fourier Transform (FFT) was applied to the signal to transform 200 samples of speech from time to frequency domain. The summary of the resulting confidence level intervals for the recognition rate obtained in decoding process are listed in Table 3 and the chart in Figure 1 summarizes the recognition rate obtained for each state number.

CONCLUSION

The primary contribution of this work is to design Arabic ASR system and find the performance of the selected Arabic words is successfully verified and examined. For this purpose, 24 CVCVCV Arabic words were recorded from native speakers, all the experiments are conducted, and the recognition results of the ASR system were investigated and evaluated. The system is designed by MATLAB based on MFCC and discrete-observation multivariate HMM. In this work, the best results are achieved when the acoustic signals are extracted using 10 states and modeled by 8 Gaussian mixtures. The best recognition rate reaches 92.92% (51 total error count from 1368 total words count). According to Figure 3, the recognition rate decreased when using more or less than 10 state numbers.

REFERENCES

1. Rabiner, L.R. and Juang, B.-H. (1993) Fundamentals of Speech Recognition. PTR Prentice Hall, Englewood Cliffs.
2. Këpuska, V. and Klein, T. (2009) A Novel Wake-Up-Word Speech Recognition System, Wake-Up-Word Recognition Task, Technology and Evaluation. Nonlinear Analysis: Theory, Methods & Applications, 71, e2772-e2789. https://doi.org/10.1016/j.na.2009.06.089
3. Këpuska, V.Z. and Elharati, H.A. (2015) Robust Speech Recognition System Using Conventional and Hybrid Features of MFCC, LPCC, PLP, RASTA-PLP and Hidden Markov Model Classifier in Noisy Conditions. Journal of Computer and Communications, 3, 1-9. https://doi.org/10.4236/jcc.2015.36001
4. Satori, H., Harti, M. and Chenfour, N. (2007) Introduction to Arabic Speech Recognition Using CMUSphinx System. https://doi.org/10.1109/ISCIII.2007.367358
5. Hyassat, H. and Zitar, R.A. (2006) Arabic Speech Recognition Using Sphinx Engine. International Journal of Speech Technology, 9, 133-150. https://doi.org/10.1007/s10772-008-9009-1
6. Këpuska, V.Z. and Elharati, H.A. (2015) Performance Evaluation of Conventional and Hybrid Feature Extractions Using Multivariate HMM Classifier. International Journal of Engineering Research and Applications, 5, 96-101.
7. Meng, Y. (2004) Speech Recognition on DSP: Algorithm Optimization and Performance Analysis. The Chinese University of Hong Kong, Hong Kong.
8. Alkanhal, M.I., Al-Badrashiny, M.A., Alghamdi, M.M. and Al Qabbany, A.O. (2012) Automatić Stochastic Arabic Spelling Correction with Emphasis on Space Insertions and Deletions. IEEE Transactions on Audio, Speech, and Language Processing, 20, 2111-2122. https://doi.org/10.1109/TASL.2012.2197612
9. Kumar, M., Aggarwal, R., Leekha, G. and Kumar, Y. (2012) Ensemble Feature Extraction Modules for Improved Hindi Speech Recognition System. International Journal of Computer Science Issues, 9, 175.
10. Abdelali, A., Darwish, K., Durrani, N. and Mubarak, H. (2016) Farasa: A Fast and Furious Segmenter for Arabic. In: HLT-NAACL Demos, Association for Computational Linguistics, San Diego, 11-16. https://doi.org/10.18653/v1/N16-3003

11. Huang, X., Acero, A. and Hon, H.-W. (2001) Spoken Language Processing. Prentice Hall, Englewood Cliffs.
12. Bogert, B.P., Healy, M.J. and Tukey, J.W. (1963) The Quefrency Analysis ofTime Series for Echoes: Cepstrum, Pseudo-Autocovariance, Cross-Cepstrum and Saphe Cracking. Proceedings of the Symposium on Time Series Analysis, Vol. 15, 209-243.
13. Sakoe, H. and Chiba, S. (1978) Dynamic Programming Algorithm Optimization for Spoken Word Recognition. IEEE Transactions on Acoustics, Speech and Signal Processing, 26, 43-49. https://doi.org/10.1109/TASSP.1978.1163055
14. Dhingra, S.D., Nijhawan, G. and Pandit, P. (2013) Isolated Speech Recognition Using MFCC and DTW. International Journal of Advanced Research in Electrical, Electronics and Instrumentation Engineering, 2, 4085-4092.
15. Okamoto, T., Hiroe, A. and Kawai, H. (2017) Reducing Latency for Language Identification Based on Large-Vocabulary Continuous Speech Recognition. Acoustical Science and Technology, 38, 38-41. https://doi.org/10.1250/ast.38.38
16. Ding, N., Melloni, L., Tian, X. and Poeppel, D. (2017) Rule-Based and Word-Level Statistics-Based Processing of Language: Insights from Neuroscience. Language, Cognition and Neuroscience, 32, 570-575. https://doi.org/10.1080/23273798.2016.1215477

CHAPTER 9

Using Morphological Data in Language Modeling for Serbian Large Vocabulary Speech Recognition

Edvin Pakoci,[1,2] Branislav Popović,[1,3] and Darko Pekar[1,2]

[1]Department for Power, Electronic and Telecommunication Engineering, Faculty of Technical Sciences, University of Novi Sad, 21000 Novi Sad, Serbia

[2]AlfaNum Speech Technologies, 21000 Novi Sad, Serbia

[3]Department for Music Production and Sound Design, Academy of Arts, Alfa BK University, 11000 Belgrade, Serbia

ABSTRACT

Serbian is in a group of highly inflective and morphologically rich languages that use a lot of different word suffixes to express different grammatical, syntactic, or semantic features. This kind of behaviour usually produces a lot of recognition errors, especially in large vocabulary systems—even when, due to good acoustical matching, the correct lemma is predicted by

Citation: Edvin Pakoci, Branislav Popović, Darko Pekar, "Using Morphological Data in Language Modeling for Serbian Large Vocabulary Speech Recognition", Computational Intelligence and Neuroscience, vol. 2019, Article ID 5072918, 8 pages, 2019. https://doi.org/10.1155/2019/5072918.

the automatic speech recognition system, often a wrong word ending occurs, which is nevertheless counted as an error. This effect is larger for contexts not present in the language model training corpus. In this manuscript, an approach which takes into account different morphological categories of words for language modeling is examined, and the benefits in terms of word error rates and perplexities are presented. These categories include word type, word case, grammatical number, and gender, and they were all assigned to words in the system vocabulary, where applicable. These additional word features helped to produce significant improvements in relation to the baseline system, both for n-gram-based and neural network-based language models. The proposed system can help overcome a lot of tedious errors in a large vocabulary system, for example, for dictation, both for Serbian and for other languages with similar characteristics.

INTRODUCTION

There are two main components in any contemporary automatic speech recognition (ASR) system. The first is the acoustic model (AM), which describes acoustical characteristics of different speech components (most often context-dependent phonemes) for a single speaker (in speaker-dependent or speaker-adapted systems) or multiple speakers (in speaker-independent systems). The other component, on which this manuscript will be focused, is the language model (LM), which describes the vocabulary and sentence forming rules of the language or speech domain in question. The language model is used to provide the speech recognizer with allowed word sequences in limited-vocabulary and grammar-based environments, as well as to help the acoustic model to decide on the correct word sequence by introducing costs for all different sequences (i.e., language model costs, or scores), where the more likely sequences will have a lesser cost (a better score). In a lot of applications, a well-trained language model can even overcome certain flaws in the acoustic model, by eliminating unnatural, unlikely word sequences from the list of recognition result possibilities. It has been shown that language models have the capability to become very close to human language understanding [1].

For a long time, the best language models in existence were statistical models based on n-grams—frequencies or probabilities of individual word sequences up to and including length n [2]. These LMs proved to be highly effective for an array of applications, even though they had several known problems, e.g., data sparsity (smoothing requirement [3]) and modeling of longer contexts (more than *n* words long). Recently, approaches based on recurrent neural networks (RNNs) have been proposed to overcome *n*-gram issues without raising the implementation difficulty and computational complexity too much. They have shown their superiority in relation to *n*-grams [4], but still they are computationally more demanding, and that usually results in a lot longer training duration.

For the Serbian language, in the past couple of years, several variants of RNN-based LMs (RNNLMs) as language models were examined and compared [5]. All of them produced big improvements over the baseline *n*-gram system, while the best approach seemed to be the TensorFlow-based LSTM-RNNLM (long short-term memory-based RNNLM) approach with pruned lattice rescoring, both in the resulting word error rates (WERs) and training duration. Unfortunately, a number of problems from the *n*-gram system seemed to remain. The biggest ones were errors where the lemma was correct, but the word ending was wrong, which resulted in a very low character error rate (CER) in comparison to the actual WER. The source of this issue was deemed to be high language inflectivity of Serbian—the same basic word form (lemma) can have a lot of different word suffixes describing different grammatical or syntactic roles (Table 1). In Serbian grammar, there are seven word cases (nominative, genitive, dative, accusative, vocative, instrumental, and locative), which apply to all nouns and most adjectives, as well as some pronouns and numerals, two grammatical numbers (singular and plural), and three grammatical genders (masculine, feminine, and neuter). Grammatical numbers and genders apply to most verbs as well. Cases, numbers, and genders do not apply to invariable words (prepositions, adverbs, conjunctions, particles, and exclamations), even though certain prepositions are always followed by certain cases.

Table 1: Morphological categories for words in the Serbian language.

Morphological category	**Possible category values**
Word type	Noun, pronoun, adjective, numeral, verb (variable), preposition, adverb, conjunction, particle, exclamation (invariable)
Word case	Nominative, genitive, dative, accusative, vocative, instrumental, locative
Grammatical number	Singular, plural
Grammatical gender	Masculine, feminine, neuter

In this manuscript, incorporation of the mentioned morphological features into both *n*-gram based and RNN-based language models for Serbian is examined, and the obtained results are presented on the largest Serbian audio database for acoustic modeling, as well as all the currently available textual materials in Serbian for language model training.

The following sections will describe relevant previous work, details of the available resources, training methods, the experimental setup, and the results, followed by conclusions.

RELEVANT PREVIOUS WORK

There were several approaches for incorporation of morphology knowledge into speech recognition systems for other languages, and most of them require some sort of a parser (word decomposer) to determine significant morphological units (morphemes, affixes, etc.) to represent lexical items and word classes, and then that information is used to provide additional constraints to the decoder (in combination or instead of regular words in the conventional approach). A lot of morphologically rich languages face similar issues [6–10].

Another approach is using factored language models (FLMs) [11], which explicitly model relationships between morphological and lexical items in a single language model, and a generalised back-off procedure is used during training to improve the robustness of the resulting FLM during decoding, especially for rarely seen words and *n*-grams. In the approach in this manuscript, additional morphological information about all the words in the textual corpus for LM training is explicitly embedded into the words themselves, and the LM training is performed on this modified vocabulary. Given the fact that Serbian is a fusional language, which are distinguished from agglutinative languages by their tendency to use a single inflectional morpheme to denote multiple grammatical, syntactic, or semantic features (and that has been a problem for some morphology models [8]), and the planned usage of the ASR system in question in large but relatively finite vocabulary environments (specific domains with a lot of expected words and phrases), such an approach is justifiable, but future research should look into the possibilities of creating open vocabulary systems as well [12, 13].

MATERIALS AND METHODS

Audio Database

For all the experiments, the recently expanded speech database for Serbian was used. This database consists of three smaller parts (Table 2). The first part contains audio book recordings, recorded in studio environment by professional speakers. A large part of this database was already mentioned in previous papers [14], but lately it has been expanded by several new audio books. This database part is responsible for 168 hours of data in total, out of which about 140 hours is pure speech (the rest is silence). There are 32 different male and 64 different female recognized speakers (with a slight possibility that a few of them are actually the same speaker), but male speakers had a lot more material by speaker on average. The original data for each speaker were further separated into chunks of 30–35 minutes at most, and all chunks except the first were modified by a carefully chosen combination of speech tempo or pitch changes, basically producing new, mutually distinct subspeakers. The purpose of this procedure was to equalize the amount of material per speaker, as in the original data some speakers have several hours of speech, while others have half an hour or even less. In this way, the trained acoustic models should not be biased towards those speakers with a lot of material. The described procedure resulted in 398 distinct subspeakers. The second part of the database contains radio talk show recordings, separated by speaker. This part totals 179 hours of data, 150 of which are nonsilence, and there are 21 male and 14 female speakers in total, again with a lot more material for males. Speaker equalization (in the same manner as above) was also performed here to produce 420 subspeakers. These recordings contain mostly more spontaneous speech, with a lot more background noise, mispronounced words, etc., but are crucial for better modeling of conversational speech. The final database part is the so-called Serbian "mobile" speech database, also mentioned in previous papers [15], and consists of mobile phone recordings of read commands, questions, numbers, dates, names, locations, spellings, and other inquiry-based utterances, like those to be expected in an interaction with a voice assistant type application on a smartphone. These are also more freely spoken, but the utterances are a lot shorter than those in previous database parts, the vocabulary is very domain-oriented and relatively small, and the material is already evenly distributed among speakers. This part contains 61 hours of material, out of which 41 are pure speech, and there are 169 male and 181 female distinct speakers. All audio data for acoustic model training were sampled at 16 kHz, 16 bits per sample, mono PCM.

Table 2: Audio database overview.

Database part	Amount of data (h)	Amount of speech (h)	Male (sub) speakers	Female (sub) speakers
Audio books	168	140	208	190
Radio talk shows	179	150	350	70
Phone recordings	61	41	169	181
Total	408	331	727	441
For training	379	308	677	410

In addition to this, for testing purposes, 29 hours of material was extracted in total (between 5% and 10% from all database parts), 23 of which is speech, from 81 total test subspeakers. All subspeakers used in the test set were completely used for testing (i.e., excluded completely from training) to avoid biased test results.

Textual Corpus

All the language models that are going to be mentioned were trained on the same textual corpus. The largest part of it are texts previously collected for Serbian language model training [5, 15], divided into segments corresponding to different functional styles—the largest journalistic corpus, followed by literary, administrative, scientific, popular-scientific, and conversational segments. The whole corpus was used in an attempt to cover as much variability as possible, as it has been shown that sentence structures in different functional styles can differ significantly [16]. Additionally, the transcriptions of the training part of the audio data for acoustic modeling were appended to the existing corpus. In total, there are about 1.4 million sentences and 26 million words. Out of these, 20000 sentences were used only for evaluation (the development, or "dev" set), while the rest were used in the language model training procedure (Table 3).

Table 3: Textual database overview.

Corpus part	#Sentences	#Words	#Characters
Journalistic	737k	17M	94M
Literary	303k	3.9M	18M
Scientific	23k	503k	3M
Administrative	15k	378k	2M
Popular-scientific	18k	357k	2M
Conversational	38k	128k	530k
Transcriptions	251k	3.2M	15M
Total	1.4M	26M	135M
"Dev" set	20k	470k	2.6M

Training Method—Acoustic Model

The used acoustic models were subsampled time-delay neural networks (TDNNs), which are trained using cross-entropy training within the so-called "chain" training method [17]. For this purpose, the Kaldi speech recognition toolkit [18] was used. The trained neural network is 9 layers deep, with 625 neurons per layer. The initial layers (1–5) were spliced in a $\{-1, 0, 1\}$ manner (they see 3 consecutive frames), while $\{-3, 0, 3\}$ splicing was used for the most hidden layers (layers 5–9; they also see 3 frames, but separated by 3 frames from each other). Using this configuration, the most hidden layers need to be evaluated only every 3 frames. No artificial data expansion was used for these experiments. The training was performed in 5 epochs (145 iterations based on the amount of data). Alignments for the deep neural network (DNN) training were provided by a previously trained speaker-adaptive HMM-GMM (hidden Markov model—Gaussian mixture model) system [19] with 3500 states and 35000 Gaussians. Acoustic features used for DNN training were 40 high-resolution MFCC features (Mel-frequency cepstral coefficients), alongside their first- and second-order derivatives, as well as 3 pitch-based features—weighted log-pitch, delta-log-pitch, and warped normalized cross-correlation function (NCCF) value (which is originally between −1 and 1, and higher for voiced frames), and their derivatives, producing a 129-dimensional feature vector, which is a configuration already used in other experiments [5, 15, 17]. The context dependency tree used for the "chain" training with its special model topology that allows a subsampling factor of 3 had 2000 leaves (output states). The effective learning rate was in the range from 0.001 (initial) to 0.0001 (final).

Training Method—Language Models

The referent *n*-gram language model is a 3-gram model trained on the described textual data using the SRILM toolkit [20], with Kneser-Ney smoothing and previously optimized pruning cut-off parameter of 10^{-7} [15]. The vocabulary for the LM was chosen in such a way to include all different words from the acoustic training data transcriptions, plus all other words that are mentioned at least 3 times in the whole textual corpus. Additionally, previously unseen words from the test dataset transcriptions were also added into the vocabulary, so there were no actual out-of-vocabulary (OOV) words, but these transcriptions were not used in probability estimation for the LM. Still, it should be acknowledged that adding OOV words to the LM training vocabulary can affect the recognition accuracy of the ASR system. This approach was related to the planned use of this system (relatively finite-vocabulary domains) and the fact that the experimental results needed to demonstrate the expected WERs in such conditions. Moreover, a similar approach was used previously as well [5, 15], but future research and experiments should measure the WER without adding all the OOV words from the test dataset into the vocabulary and even consider an open vocabulary language model capable of learning new words. The procedure used here resulted in 249809 total words (unigrams), while there were also 1.87 million bigrams and 551 thousand trigrams with the given parameters. The test data perplexity was calculated to be around 634.0.

The RNN-based language model was trained using Kaldi-RNNLM [21], an extension to the Kaldi toolkit, which supports RNN-based language modeling within the Kaldi framework and weighted finite state transducer-(WFST-) based decoding. This method involves subword features; more precisely, letter *n*-gram counts for better prediction of rare words, as well as augmented features such as scaled word unigram log-probability and word length, the former of which is used for better out-of-domain results. Kaldi-RNNLM also shares the input and output embeddings for the neural network based on work given in [22], which alongside subword features can produce good results on very large vocabularies without having data sparsity issues (which is otherwise usually combatted by using shortlists during LM training). Finally, each of the most frequent *N* words receives an additional feature, so the top words end up having a one-hot representation in addition to their letter *n*-gram counts vector and the two augmented features (Table 4).

Table 4: Example of a feature vector in RNNLM experiments for word *sam* (Eng. *am*).

Index	Feature type	Feature	Value	Remarks
0	Constant	Constant	0.01	For math reasons
1–5	Special	Special word feat.	0	For bos/eos/unk/brk/silence
6	Unigram	Unigram prob.	0.00788	Scaled unigram log-prob.
7	Length	Word length	0.00186	Scaled word length
8–36	Word	1-hot vect. elem.	0	—
37	Word	1-hot vect. elem.	0.21	Scale based on unigram prob.
38–97644	Word	1-hot vect. elem.	0	—
97645–97657	Final	Lett. *n*-gram prob.	0	—
97658	Final	3-gram *-am$* pr.	0.12	Scaled letter 3-gram prob.
97659–97758	Final	Lett. *n*-gram prob.	0	—
97759	Final	2-gram *-m$* pr.	0.047	Scaled letter 2-gram prob.
97760–97869	Final	Lett. *n*-gram prob.	0	—
97870–98050	Initial	Lett. *n*-gram prob.	0	—
98051	Initial	2-gram ^*s-* pr.	0.03	Scaled letter 2-gram prob.
98052	Initial	3-gram ^*sa-* pr.	0.069	Scaled letter 3-gram prob.
98053–98144	Initial	Lett. *n*-gram prob.	0	—
98145–98300	Match	Lett. *n*-gram prob.	0	—
98301	Match	2-gram *-am-* pr.	0.064	Scaled letter 2-gram prob.
98302–100451	Match	Lett. *n*-gram prob.	0	—
100452	Match	2-gram *-sa-* pr.	0.057	Scaled letter 2-gram prob.
100453–100459	Match	Lett. *n*-gram prob.	0	—
100460	Match	3-gram *-sam-* pr.	0.11	Scaled letter 3-gram prob.
100461–101306	Match	Lett. *n*-gram prob.	0	—

The baseline RNNLM is a 4-layer combined TDNN plus fast LSTMP (LSTM projected [23]) network, with an embedding dimension of 1024 and both recurrent and nonrecurrent projection dimension of 256. The number of most frequent words to receive a special feature is 97636 (calculated to be up to 100000, but to draw a line under a group of words with the same count in the input data). Letter 2-grams and 3-grams are utilized, the minimum frequency of any letter *n*-gram to be considered a feature was 0.0001, and the training was run for 30 epochs (180 iterations based on input data), with the possibility for the best iteration to be before the last one (best iteration is calculated based on the objective function value on the "dev" dataset previously mentioned in the textual corpus section). For RNNLM rescoring, the pruned lattice rescoring method was used [24] with a 4-gram approximation to prevent lattice explosion and a RNNLM interpolation weight of 0.8 (previously determined to be optimal). The baseline perplexity with this RNNLM on the given test set was calculated using Kaldi tools to be about 119.0.

The approach to incorporation of morphological information into the language model for Serbian in this manuscript is to explicitly embed that information into the words themselves, thus modifying the vocabulary of the ASR system. In order to figure out all the different morphological categories for each word in the input textual corpus sentences, a part-of-speech (POS) tagging tool for Serbian [25] was used, alongside the Serbian morphologic dictionary [26]. Previously, morphological clustering of words into classes using a part of the Serbian textual corpus was examined, where the relevant features were defined for each word type (case, number, and gender, as briefly mentioned in the introduction section of this manuscript, alongside subtype, e.g., proper, common, or abstract for nouns and degree of comparison for adjectives) [27]. Not all the additional features are available for all word types, even within a certain type some words do not behave like others, e.g., there are some invariable adjectives. For the following experiments, word type and case, alongside grammatical number and gender, are chosen as additional word features, and for the final one, the corresponding lemma was taken into account as well.

The POS tagging tool and an additional postprocessing tool were used to convert all input textual data for LM training into sentences with tagged words, i.e., words with one or more delimited suffixes for each word denoting its determined type, case, number, and gender, where applicable. Alongside the ten word types in Serbian, two additional types were introduced—abbreviation and isolated letter (e.g., used when spelling something), since they do not really belong in any other category. Some words were marked by the POS tagger as of unknown type (e.g., badly pronounced words which were written as such in transcriptions or words with typographical errors), so they were not assigned any other morphological features. The POS tagger, with the help of the morphologic dictionary, could distinguish six different cases, as dative and locative in Serbian tend to share the same word form. A case is also assigned to certain prepositions, if they are known to always be followed by a word in a particular case in Serbian. The grammatical number and gender did not receive any special treatment; they are used as already described above (Table 5).

Table 5: Some of the most frequent words, with and without morphology-based suffixes.

Without POS data	With POS data	Explanation
je	je_gl	*gl*agol=verb
i	i_vez	*vez*nik=conjunction
u	da_vez	—
da	u_pred_dat	*pred*log=preposition
se	se_zam	*zam*enica=pronoun
na	na_pred_dat	*dat*ive/locative
koji	koji_zam_nom_jd_mr	*nom*inative
bi	bi_gl_jd	*jed*nina=singular
Srbije	Srbije_im_gen_jd_mr	*im*enica=noun, *gen*itive, *m*uški *r*od=masculine

Using the proposed procedure, the number of different words in the LM vocabulary grew to 380747, as some words could, as expected, have different values of certain POS features (sometimes the same word form could be a different combination of case/number/gender in different sentences, even a different word type in some cases). Using the same parameters for smoothing and pruning, the new 3-gram language model has 2.2 million bigrams and 523 thousand trigrams (relatively similar to the referent 3-gram LM). This time though, the perplexity was calculated to be 378.6, which is a lot better, likely because now there is a distinction between formerly same words that could have completely unrelated functions in sentences. On the other hand, the perplexity for the new RNNLM was a bit larger than that for the referent one—147.1, which may be explained by the implicit vocabulary size increase, which had more effect here in relation to the *n*-gram case (possibly due to applied smoothing and pruning techniques there).

RESULTS AND DISCUSSION

3-Gram Results

The baseline 3-gram language model (250k words, without using morphological information) in combination with the resulting acoustic models trained with the "chain" method produced a word error rate of 8.89%. Problems with the inflectivity of Serbian can be observed when comparing that to the character error rate, which in this experiment was measured to be only 2.63%. The largest number of recognition errors happened in the radio talk show test set (12.64% WER), and the error rate for audio books was in the middle of the road (6.25% WER), while the mobile phone test set produced a very small WER of less than 1% (0.96%), just like in past experiments [15], which can be explained by the very small vocabulary (less than 4000 different words) and repeating word patterns and sentence structures for basically all speakers in this dataset, so the language model could learn to predict such sentences very well. When looking through the list of the most substituted words, on the top of it, the typical confusion between similarly sounding *i* and *je* (Eng. *and*, *be*) can be found, as well as a lot of wrong cases, grammatical genders, and numbers (*koja* instead of *koji*, *koje* or *koju*, and vice versa; Eng. *which*), but also words that have two slightly different but functionally completely equivalent forms (e.g., *kad* and *kada*, Eng. *when*), as well as several obvious typographical errors and words that are often shortened in spontaneous speech (e.g., *znači* and *'nači*, where the starting "*z*" sound is often not pronounced at all, likewise *rekao* and *rek'o*; Eng. *so*, *told*). Some of these errors should be automatically corrected by taking morphological features into account. On the other hand, the typographical errors can only be fixed by carefully looking through all the texts by a group of text checkers.

In comparison, when applying the new 3-gram language model which differentiated POS categories of words, the WER was lowered to 6.90%, and the CER to 2.20%, which is a 22% relative improvement in WER and a 16% relative improvement in CER (Table 6). A breakdown by test database part (audio books, radio talk shows, and phone recordings) shows that the most relative improvement occurred in audio books, possibly due to professionally read texts (no unexpected or mispronounced words and sentence structures most of the time). Somewhat less improvement can be observed for radio talk shows, while a very small deterioration happened for the mobile phone database, even though the error rate is still around the 1% WER mark, probably because of more spontaneity in speech for these two test set parts and likely POS tagger mistakes and/or limitations when used on unconventional word forms encountered there (maybe even transcription errors for talk shows or erroneously recorded audio files for the mobile phone database). The total number of substitutions dropped by more than 25%. The number of wrong-POS-category errors dropped as well, and they were more spaced-out through the list of most common errors (they were more rarely seen in relation to other errors). Insertion rate dropped by 19% and deletion rate by 9%—these errors mostly included very short invariable words, and with the new LM, some occurrences of longer and variable words disappeared from the top of those error lists (Table 7).

Table 6: WER and CER results for 3-gram experiments, without and with additional POS data taken into account. Breakdown by test database part is shown as well.

Result	Total (%)	Books (%)	Shows (%)	"Mobile" (%)
WER 3-gram	8.89	6.25	12.64	**0.96**
WER 3-gram+POS	**6.90**	**4.12**	**10.45**	1.06
CER 3-gram	2.63	1.45	4.11	**0.40**
CER 3-gram+POS	**2.20**	**1.05**	**3.59**	0.42

Table 7: Lists of some of the most frequent word errors by type, with #occurrences (3-gram LM).

Substitutions without POS	Substitutions with POS	Insertions without POS	Insertions with POS	Deletions without POS	Deletions with POS
je→i (88)	je→i (79)	i (271)	je (242)	je (769)	je (742)
i→je (61)	i→je (50)	je (260)	i (235)	i (713)	i (669)
iz→i (48)	iz→i (39)	u (112)	u (88)	u (332)	u (302)
reko→rekao (42)	koji→koju (36)	da (87)	da (85)	da (215)	da (204)
koji→koju (40)	reko→rekao (32)	a (69)	a (54)	a (129)	a (130)
koja→koje (39)	sa→s (29)	na (54)	na (37)	on (121)	on (114)
koju→koje (37)	se→su (28)	po (31)	on (25)	na (99)	na (82)
sa→s (33)	je→oni (27)	o (28)	se (24)	to (76)	to (75)
nači→znači (31)	koji→koje (25)	ne (25)	o (22)	ja (75)	ja (63)
se→su (31)	nači→znači (25)	se (25)	pa (19)	od (63)	se (60)
je→koje (30)	koja→koje (24)	on (23)	od (17)	ne (62)	od (56)

tu⟶to (28)	mi⟶i (23)	—	—	se (61)	mi (54)
—	—	s (11)	ne (14)	—	—
kada⟶kad (22)	kada⟶kad (19)	kaže (10)	s (11)	joj (29)	sam (29)
imo⟶imao (19)	imo⟶imao (18)	koje (10)	kaže (10)	sam (28)	koji (25)
bilo⟶bila (19)	bila⟶bilo (18)	koji (10)	ovo (9)	koji (25)	joj (23)

RNNLM Results

The first RNNLM, without morphological features, already gave improvements across the board in comparison to both 3-gram systems. The average WER of 4.90% is a 46% relative improvement to the baseline 3-gram system and a 29% improvement to the 3-gram-POS system. The CER vas measured to be 1.61%. The biggest step forward occurred in the audio books database part again (2.77% WER), but a large step forward was made for radio shows as well (7.56% WER), and even for mobile phone recordings (0.73% WER). Looking at substitutions, insertions, and deletions, the same distribution of errors exists as for the baseline 3-gram system, there are just a lot less of them in absolute numbers.

The RNNLM system with morphological data taken into account produced further improvements in WER and CER—4.34% WER on average and 1.48% CER (Table 8). Best relative improvement was seen for audio books (21%), while radio show error rate lowering was a bit smaller (8%), and phone recordings suffered a 10% relative WER increment (the absolute error rate is still very low), just like in *n*-gram experiments, and probably for the same reasons. Likelihoods during training, both for the actual training data, and the "dev" data, show consistently slightly better values for the baseline RNNLM, probably due to the same set of reasons as for the difference in perplexities (Figure 1), and it has also been shown that a better perplexity does not necessarily mean a better WER and vice versa [28]. A better way to choose a representative "dev" set should be considered as well. The top list of errors by type, especially the substitutions list, now mostly holds errors that can be categorized as of lower significance. As mentioned before, there are a lot of either typographical errors or badly-pronounced-word errors, words with more than one equivalent similar form in regular usage, etc. The effect is even clearer than in the *n*-gram case.

Table 8: WER and CER results for RNNLM experiments, without and with additional POS data taken into account. Breakdown by test database part is shown as well.

Result	Total (%)	Books (%)	Shows (%)	"Mobile" (%)
WER RNNLM	4.90	2.77	7.56	**0.73**
WER RNNLM+POS	**4.34**	**2.18**	**6.93**	0.81
CER RNNLM	1.61	0.70	2.69	**0.28**
CER RNNLM+POS	**1.48**	**0.59**	**2.52**	0.33

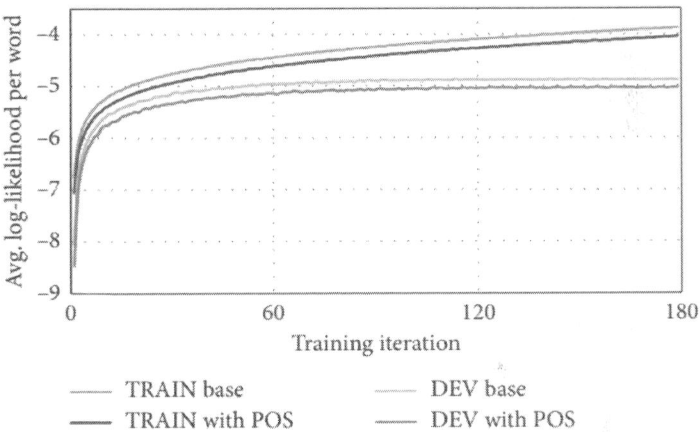

Figure 1: Plot of average log-likelihoods per word during training with respect to training iterations, recorded over 180 iterations in total, for both RNNLM experiments. Likelihoods for the training set (blue lines) and for the "dev" set (red lines) are separated as well.

The last experiment was related to the usage of lemmas, i.e., basic forms of words, as additional information for RNNLM training. Similarly to how the most frequent words had their own feature (a one-hot vector representation as a subvector of their own word features), the most frequent lemmas were also given special features, so the words whose lemmas are in this set had an additional one-hot vector as a feature, representing the lemma. The number of top lemmas was chosen to be equal to the number of top words (97k). This experiment produced the best results on the given test database so far—a WER of 4.23% and CER of 1.45%. Even though the resulting feature and word embedding matrices for the RNNLM are quite larger in this configuration (as there are a lot more individual word features), the decoding speed does not suffer (but memory consumption issues have to be prevented in this case by not using machines with insufficient memory capacity).

Further improvements can be made in several different parts of the ASR system. Firstly, the acoustic models can probably be improved a bit, both with neural network parameter optimization and with audio database augmentation (e.g., by using speech speed perturbance algorithms, or audio with artificially added noise to improve system robustness). There can be improvements in RNNLM training as well—one way is to optimize training parameters a bit more and another is to make more complex networks, but that will lead to slower decoding speeds. Finally, the textual data can be cleaned up and expanded—one way to do the cleaning is by using a simple text processor tool to fix at least the most common mistakes from the top errors lists, which can also be used as a recognition result postprocessor with the current system. Currently, there is an additional textual database in preparation for future trainings. For usage in specific domains, one type of RNNLM training texts can be used with a larger weight, so the final system would prefer sentence structures mostly found in the desired type of text.

CONCLUSIONS

The experiments and the obtained results described in this manuscript show that using additional morphological knowledge for language model training can solve a large part of problems for highly inflective languages, as the Serbian language is. The proposed method incorporated the additional data into the words themselves, and one experiment used additional RNNLM word features on top of that. Big improvements were obtained both in *n*-gram systems and in RNNLM-based systems in relation to baseline systems which did not use any morphological data. The used Kaldi-RNNLM toolkit has also proven to be superior to any other previously used language model training toolkit for Serbian. There is still room for improvement, and there are future plans to create even better both acoustic and language models and even to further optimize the usage of morphological category information in the modeling of the Serbian language. Finally, an open-vocabulary language model capable of learning new words needs to be considered as well.

DATA AVAILABILITY

The audio and textual databases used to support the findings presented in this manuscript are partly available online and partly collected and owned by the Faculty of Technical Sciences in Novi Sad and the AlfaNum Company. All the mentioned data can be made available by the corresponding author upon request.

ACKNOWLEDGMENTS

This paper was supported in part by the Ministry of Education, Science and Technological Development of the Republic of Serbia, within the project "Development of Dialogue Systems for Serbian and Other South Slavic Languages" (TR32035), EUREKA project DANSPLAT, "A Platform for the Applications of Speech Technologies on Smartphones for the Languages of the Danube Region" (E Platf), and the Provincial Secretariat for Higher Education and Scientific Research, within the project "Central Audio-Library of the University of Novi Sad" (114-451-2570/2016-02).

REFERENCES

1. J. T. Goodman, "A bit of progress in language modeling: extended version," Microsoft Research, Redmond, WA, USA, 2001, Tech. Rep. MSR-TR-2001-72.
2. R. Rosenfeld, "Two decades of statistical language modeling: where do we go from here?" *Proceedings of the IEEE*, vol. 88, no. 8, pp. 1270–1278, 2000.
3. R. Kneser and H. Ney, "Improved backing-off for M-gram language modeling," in *Proceedings of 20th International Conference on Acoustics, Speech and Signal Processing (ICASSP)*, pp. 181–184, Detroit, MI, USA, May 1995.
4. T. Mikolov, S. Kombrink, L. Burget, J. H. Černocký, and S. Khudanpur, "Extensions of recurrent neural network language model," in *Proceedings of 36th International Conference on Acoustics, Speech and Signal Processing (ICASSP)*, pp. 5528–5531, Prague, Czech Republic, May 2011.
5. B. Popović, E. Pakoci, and D. Pekar, "A comparison of language model training techniques in a continuous speech recognition system for Serbian," in *Proceedings of 20th International Conference on Speech and Computer (SPECOM)*, pp. 522–531, Leipzig, Germany, September 2018, vol. 11096 of Lecture Notes in Artificial Intelligence.
6. H. Sak, M. Saraçlar, and T. Güngör, "Morphology-based and sub-word language modeling for Turkish speech recognition," in *Proceedings of 35th International Conference on Acoustics, Speech and Signal Processing (ICASSP)*, pp. 5402–5405, Dallas, TX, USA, March 2010.
7. T. Müller, H. Schütze, and H. Schmid, "A comparative investigation of morphological language modeling for the languages of the European Union," in *Proceedings of 12th Annual Conference of the North American Chapter of the Association for Computational Linguistics: Human Language Technologies (HLT-NAACL)*, pp. 386–395, Montréal, Canada, June 2012.
8. R. Sarikaya, M. Afify, Y. Deng, H. Erdogan, and Y. Gao, "Joint morphological-lexical language modeling for processing morphologically rich languages with application to dialectal Arabic," *IEEE Transactions on Audio, Speech, and Language Processing*, vol. 16, no. 7, pp. 1330–1339, 2008.

9. M. Kurimo, A. Puurula, E. Arisoy et al., "Unlimited vocabulary speech recognition for agglutinative languages," in *Proceedings of 8th Annual Conference of the North American Chapter of the Association for Computational Linguistics: Human Language Technologies (HLT-NAACL)*, pp. 104–111, New York, NY, USA, June 2006.
10. O.-W. Kwon and J. Park, "Korean large vocabulary continuous speech recognition with morpheme-based recognition units," *Speech Communication*, vol. 39, no. 3-4, pp. 287–300, 2003.
11. K. Kirchhoff and M. Yang, "Improved language modeling for statistical machine translation," in *Proceedings of ACL 2005 Workshop on Building and Using Parallel Text: Data-Driven Machine Translation and Beyond*, pp. 125–128, Ann Arbor, MI, USA, June 2005.
12. A. Matthews, G. Neubig, and C. Dyer, "Using morphological knowledge in open-vocabulary neural language models," in *Proceedings of 16th Annual Conference of the North American Chapter of the Association for Computational Linguistics: Human Language Technologies (HLT-NAACL)*, vol. 1, pp. 1435–1445, New Orleans, LA, USA, June 2018.
13. L. Qin, "Learning out-of-vocabulary words in automatic speech recognition," Carnegie Mellon University, Pittsburgh, PA, USA, 2013, Ph.D. thesis.
14. S. Suzić, S. Ostrogonac, E. Pakoci, and M. Bojanić, "Building a speech repository for a Serbian LVCSR system," *Telfor Journal*, vol. 6, no. 2, pp. 109–114, 2014.
15. E. Pakoci, B. Popović, and D. Pekar, "Language model optimization for a deep neural network based speech recognition system for Serbian," in *Proceedings of 19th International Conference on Speech and Computer (SPECOM)*, pp. 483–492, Hatfield, UK, September 2017, vol. 10458 of Lecture Notes in Artificial Intelligence.
16. S. Ostrogonac, D. Mišković, M. Sečujski, D. Pekar, and V. Delić, "A language model for highly inflective non-agglutinative languages," in *Proceedings of 10th International Symposium on Intelligent Systems and Informatics (SISY)*, pp. 177–181, Subotica, Serbia, September 2012.
17. E. Pakoci, B. Popović, and D. Pekar, "Improvements in Serbian speech recognition using sequence-trained deep neural networks," *SPIIRAS Proceedings*, vol. 3, no. 58, pp. 53–76, 2018.

18. D. Povey, A. Ghoshal, G. Boulianne et al., "The Kaldi speech recognition toolkit," in *Proceedings of IEEE Workshop on Automatic Speech Recognition and Understanding (ASRU)*, pp. 1–4, Waikoloa, HI, USA, December 2011.
19. D. Povey, H.-K. J. Kuo, and H. Soltau, "Fast speaker adaptive training for speech recognition," in *Proceedings of 9th Annual Conference of the International Speech Communication Association (INTERSPEECH)*, pp. 1245–1248, Brisbane, Australia, September 2008.
20. A. Stolcke, J. Zheng, W. Wang, and V. Abrash, "SRILM at sixteen: update and outlook," in *Proceedings of IEEE Workshop on Automatic Speech Recognition and Understanding (ASRU)*, pp. 5–9, Waikoloa, HI, USA, December 2011.
21. H. Xu, K. Li, Y. Wang et al., "Neural network language modeling with letter-based features and importance sampling," in *Proceedings of 43rd International Conference on Acoustics, Speech and Signal Processing (ICASSP)*, pp. 6109–6113, Calgary, Canada, April 2018.
22. O. Press and L. Wolf, "Using the output embedding to improve language models," in *Proceedings of 15th Conference of the European Chapter of the Association for Computational Linguistics (EACL)*, vol. 2, pp. 157–163, Valencia, Spain, April 2017.
23. H. Sak, A. Senior, and F. Beaufays, "Long short-term memory recurrent neural network architectures for large scale acoustic modeling," in *Proceedings of 15th Annual Conference of the International Speech Communication Association (INTERSPEECH)*, pp. 338–342, Singapore, September 2014.
24. H. Xu, T. Chen, D. Gao et al., "A pruned RNNLM lattice-rescoring algorithm for automatic speech recognition," in *Proceedings of 43rd International Conference on Acoustics, Speech and Signal Processing (ICASSP)*, pp. 5929–5933, Calgary, Canada, April 2018.
25. S. Ostrogonac, "Automatic detection and correction of semantic errors in texts in Serbian," in *Proceedings of 5th International Congress "Applied Linguistics Today," New Tendencies in Theory and Practice*, Novi Sad, Serbia, November 2015.
26. M. Sečujski, "Accentuation dictionary for Serbian intended for text-to-speech technology," in *Proceedings of 4th Conference on Digital Speech and Image Processing (DOGS)*, pp. 17–20, Bečej, Serbia, May 2002.

27. S. Ostrogonac, E. Pakoci, M. Sečujski, and D. Mišković, "Morphology-based vs unsupervised word clustering for training language models for Serbian," *Acta Polytechnica Hungarica: Journal of Applied Sciences*, 2019, In press.
28. D. Klakow and J. Peters, "Testing the correlation of word error rate and perplexity," *Speech Communication*, vol. 38, no. 1-2, pp. 19–28, 2002.

CHAPTER 10

Phoneme Sequence Modeling in the Context of Speech Signal Recognition in Language "Baoule"

Hyacinthe Konan[1], Etienne Soro[1], Olivier Asseu[1,2], Bi Tra Goore[2], Raymond Gbegbe[2]

[1]Ecole Supérieure Africaine des Technologies d'Information et de Communication (ESATIC), Abidjan, C?te d'Ivoire.

[2]Institut National Polytechnique Félix Houphou?t Boigny (INP-HB), Yamoussoukro, C?te d'Ivoire.

ABSTRACT

This paper presents the recognition of "Baoule" spoken sentences, a language of C?te d'Ivoire. Several formalisms allow the modelling of an automatic speech recognition system. The one we used to realize our system is based

---

Citation: Konan, H. , Soro, E. , Asseu, O. , Goore, B. and Gbegbe, R. (2016), Phoneme Sequence Modeling in the Context of Speech Signal Recognition in Language "Baoule". Engineering, 8, 597-617. doi: 10.4236/eng.2016.89055.

on Hidden Markov Models (HMM) discreet. Our goal in this article is to present a system for the recognition of the Baoule word. We present three classical problems and develop different algorithms able to resolve them. We then execute these algorithms with concrete examples.

Keywords: HMM, MATLAB, Language Model, Acoustic Model, Recognition Automatic Speech

INTRODUCTION

The speech recognition by machine has long been a research topic that fascinates the public and remains a challenge for specialists, and it has continued since then to be at the heart of much research. The progress of new information and communications technology has helped accelerate this research. In our first article, we presented a method to separate phonemes contained in a speech signal.

In this article we propose to identify a flow of words often uttered in a more or less background noise. This task is made difficult not only by the deformations induced by the use of a microphone but also by a series of factors inherent in human language, homonyms; local accents; the habits of language; the speed differences between the speakers; the imperfections of a microphone, etc. For our human ear, these factors do not usually represent difficulties. Our brain juggles these deformations of speech by taking into account, almost unconsciously, nonverbal and contextual elements that allow us to eliminate ambiguities. It is only by taking into account these elements that are external to the voice itself that voice recognition software will be able to achieve a high level of reliability. Today, speech recognition softwares that work best are all based on a probabilistic approach. The aim of speech recognition is to reconstruct a sequence of words M from a recorded acoustic signal A. In the statistical approach, we will consider all the consequences of M words that could match the signal A. In this set of possible word sequences, we will then choose the one (M) which is the most likely to maximize the P(M/A) probability that M is the correct interpretation of A, we note:

$$\bar{M} = \underset{M}{\text{Argmax}}\, P(M \mid A) = P(A \mid M)\, P(M)$$

This equation is the key to the probabilistic approach to speech recognition. Indeed, the first term P(A/M) is the probability of observing the acoustic signal A if the M sequence of words is pronounced: it is a purely acoustic problem; the second term P(M) is the probability that this is the result of M words that is actually stated: it is a linguistic problem. The above equation thus teaches us that we can split the speech recognition problem into two independent parts: we will model the acoustic aspects separately and language problems. In the literature, we usually speak of orthogonality between the ACOUSTIC MODELS and LANGUAGE. The succession of possible words that is obtained must be refined and validated by the word patterns and language. The acoustic model can take into account the acoustic and phonetic constraints in a sound or group of sounds. On our part, we have chosen the WORD as decision unit. By integrating also a Markov modeling, which has higher levels of language, it becomes possible to achieve a pronounced phrases discretely recognition system (i.e. in single word).

THE SPEECH SIGNALS

Characteristics of the Speech Signal

PAR is a difficult problem, mainly due to the specific material to interpret: the voice signal. The speech acoustic signal has characteristics that make complex interpretation.

Redundancy: the acoustic signal carries much more information than necessary, which explains its resistance to noise. Of analytical techniques were implemented to extract relevant information without too degrading it.

Variability: the acoustic signal is highly variable from one speaker to the other (gender, age, etc.) but also for a given speaker (emotional state, fatigue, etc.), which makes very difficult the recognition problem speaker's independent speech.

Continuity: the acoustic signal is continuous and contextual effects of sound on elementary visions are considerable.

Processing of the Speech Signal

By speech processing we mean the processing of the information contained in the speech signal. The objective is the transmission or recording of this signal, or its synthesis or recognition. The speech processing is now a fundamental component of the engineering sciences. Located at the intersection of digital signal processing and language processing (that is to say, symbolic data processing), this scientific discipline has known since the 60s a rapid expansion, linked to the development of means and telecommunications techniques. The special importance of speech processing in this broader context is explained by the privileged position of the word as an information vector in our human society.

SYSTEM OVERVIEW

The Acoustic Model

The ACOUSTIC MODEL (Figure 1) reflects the acoustic realization of each modeled element (phoneme, silence, noise, etc.). It is based on the concept of phonemes. Phonemes can be considered as the basic sound units in verbal language. The first stage of speech recognition is to recognize a set of phonemes in words flow. Statistical realization of acoustic parameters of each phone is represented by a Markov model Cache (HMM: Hidden Markov Model). Each phoneme is typically represented by 2 or 3 states and density multigaussienne (GMM: Gaussian Mixture Model) is associated with each state. See Figure 2 below.

The speech signal (picked up using a microphone) is first digitized: it is sampled by a Fourier transformation which calculates the energy levels of the signal in bands of 25 milliseconds, which strips overlap in 10 milliseconds time.

The result is compared with prototypes stored in computer memory in both a standard dictionary and a speaker's own dictionary. This dictionary is constructed by initially sessions dictation standard texts that the speaker must make before effectively use the software. This own dictionary is regularly enriched by self learning during the software uses. It is interesting to note that thus constituted voiceprint is relatively stable for a given speaker and little influenced by external factors such as stress, colds, etc. (Figure 3).

The Language Model

It is generally divided into two part linked to language: a syntactic part and a semantic game. When ACOUSTIC MODEL has identified at best phonemes "heard", we still look the most likely message M corresponding thereto, that is to say, the probability P(M) defined above. It is the role of syntactic and semantic models. See Figure 4 below.

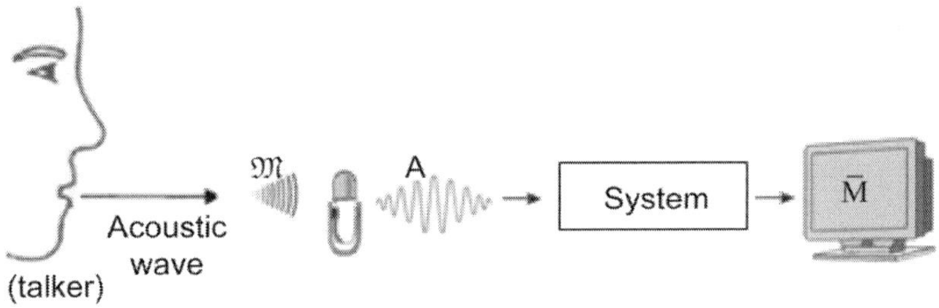

Figure 1. System of speech recognition.

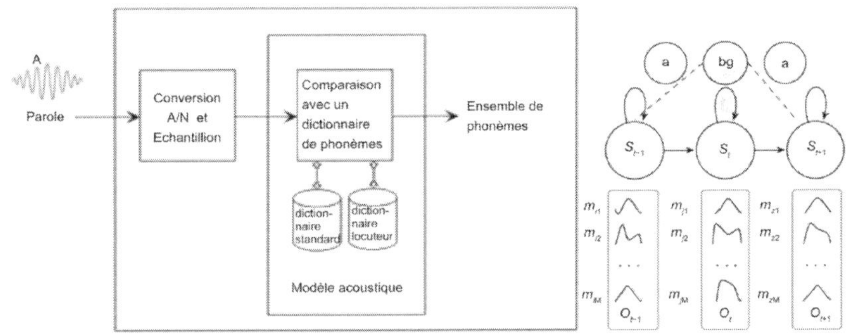

Figure 2. The part of the system using the acoustic model.

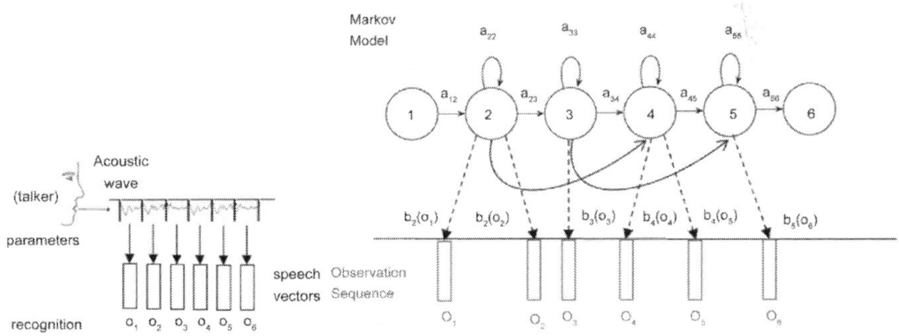

Figure 3. Acoustic model (A phoneme is modeled as a sequence of acoustic vector).

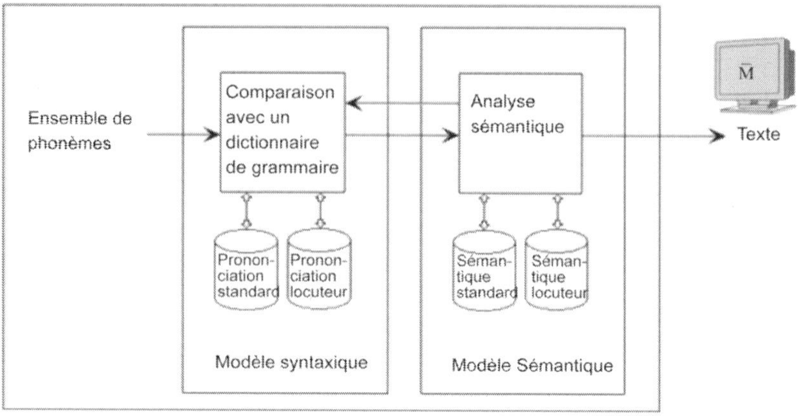

Figure 4. The part of the system using the semantic model.

From the set of phonemes from the ACOUSTIC MODEL The SYNTACTIC MODEL will assemble phonemes into words. This work is also based on a dictionary and grammar standards (The language "Baoule" has one) as well as a dictionary and a grammar own speaker; these reflect the "habits" of the speaker and is continuously enriched. Then SEMANTIC MODEL seeks to optimize the identification of the message by analyzing the context of the words and while basing on both its own common language semantics and on cleanning the speaker semantics (a style). This modeling is usually built from the analysis of sequences of words from a large textual corpus. This clean semantics will be enriched as you use the software. Most softwares also allow enriching the analysis of texts that reflect the stylistic habits of the speaker. These two modules work together and it is easy to conceive that there is a feedback between them.

Initially, the dictionary associated with these two modules were based on fixed syntax language models, that is to say, modeled on a grammar defined by a rigid set of rules (this is not the case in most African languages including the "Baoule" language).

Then, the voice recognition software has evolved into the use of local probabilistic models: recognition no longer performs at a word but at a series of words, called n-gram where n is the length words in a sequence .The statistics of these models are obtained from standard texts and may be enriched gradually. See Figure 5 below.

Here too, Hidden Markov Models are those currently used to describe the probabilistic aspects. the most advanced software tend to combine the advantages of statistical models and fixed syntax models in what is called the "probabilistic grammars", the idea being to derive from fixed grammars of probabilities that can be combined with those of a probabilistic model. In recent approaches, it becomes difficult to distinguish the syntactic model of the semantic model and we rather speak of a single language model.

HIDDEN MARKOV MODEL DISCRETE TIME

Overview and Features

Fundamentals

Hidden Markov Models (HMM) were introduced by Baum and his collaborators in the 60s and the 70s [1] . This model is closely related to Probabilistic Automata (PAs) [2] . A probabilistic automaton is defined by a structure composed of states and transitions, and a set of probability distribution on transitions. Each transition is associated with a symbol of a finite alphabet. This symbol is generated every time the transition is taken. An HMM is also defined by a structure consisting of states and transitions and by a set of probability distribution over the transitions. The essential difference is that the IPs symbol generation is performed on the states, and not on transitions. In addition, is associated with each symbol, not a state, but a probability distribution of the symbols of the alphabet.

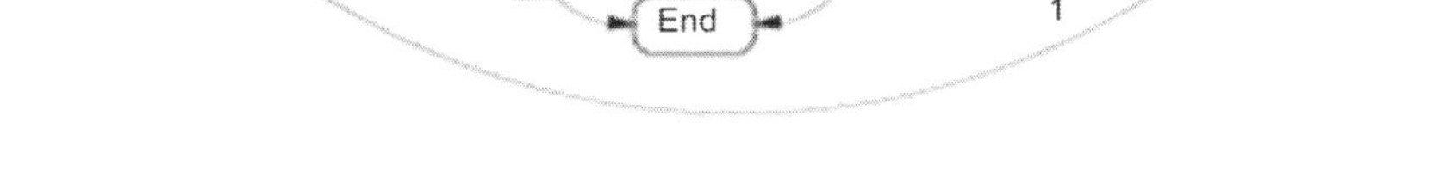

Figure 5. Semantic model.

HMMs are used to model the observation sequences. These observations may be discrete (e.g., characters from a finite alphabet) or continuous (the frequency of a signal, a temperature, etc.). The first area in which the HMMs have been applied is the speech processing in early 1970 [3] [4] . In this area, the HMM will rapidly become the reference model, and most of the techniques for using and implementing HMM have been developed in the context of these applications. These techniques were then applied and adapted successfully to the problem of recognition of handwritten texts [5] [6] and analysis of biological sequences [7] [8] . Theorems, rating and proposals that follow are largely from [9] .

Characteristics of HMM

A sequence $\{X_k\}$ of random variables with values in a finite set E is a Markov chain if the following property holds (Markov property):

$P[X_k = i_k \mid X_0 = i_0, \cdots, X_{k-1} = i_{k-1}] = P[X_k = i_k \mid X_{k-1} = i_{k-1}]$ for any time k and any suite $i_0, \cdots, i_k \in E$

Note that notion generalizes the notion of deterministic dynamical system (finite state machine recurrent sequence, or ordinary differential equation): the probability distribution of the present state X_k depends only on the immediate past state X_{k-1}.

A Markov chain $\{X_k\}$ is entirely characterized by the data

- the original legislation $\upsilon = (v_i);\ v_i := P[X_0 = i]$ for all iεE
- and the transition matrix $\pi = (\pi_{i,j});\ v_i := P[X_0 = i]$ for all I, jεE

supposedly independent of time k (homogeneous Markov chain).

Knowing the transition probabilities that exist between two succesive times is enough to globally characterize a Markov chain.

Proposal

ϑ is a probability on E, and π a Markov matrix E

The probability distribution of the Markov chain $\{X_k\}$ of ϑ original legislation and π transition matrix is given by

$P[X_0 = i_0, \cdots, X_k = i_k] = \upsilon_{i_0} \pi_{i_0,i_1} \cdots \pi_{i_{k-1},i_k}$ for any time k, and any suite $i_0, \cdots, i_k \in E$

In this model the suite is not observed directly after $\{X_k\}$, but observations are available $\{Y_k\}$ with values in a finite space O (if symbolic) or R^d (digital case), collected through a channel without memory, that is to say, conditionally to $\{X_k\}$ states.

i. the observations $\{Y_k\}$ are mutually independent, and

ii. each observation $\{Y_k\}$ depends only on the $\{X_k\}$ at the same time

This property is expressed as follows:

$$P[Y_0 \in dy_0, \cdots, Y_n \in dy_n \mid X_0 = i_0, \cdots, X_n = i_n] = \prod_{k=0}^{n} P[Y_k \in dy_k \mid X_k = i_k]$$

for any result, $i_0, \cdots, i_k \in E$, and every sequence $y_0, \cdots, y_n \in \mathbb{R}^d$

Example

Assume that the observations $\{Y_k\}$ are connected with states $\{X_k\}$ follows $Y_k = h(X_k) + V_k$ where the sequence $\{V_k\}$ is a Gaussian white noise dimension, with zero mean and covariance matrix R reversible, independent of the Markov chain $\{X_k\}$ function h defined on E with values in R^d is characterized by the data of a finite family h=h(i) vectors of R^d, and was

$$P[Y_k \in dy \mid X_k = i] = \frac{1}{\sqrt{\det(2\pi R)}} \exp\left\{-\frac{1}{2}(y - h_h) * R^{-1}(y - h_i)\right\} dy$$

conditionally to $\{X_0 = i_0, \cdots, X_n = i_n\}$, random vectors $Y_0, \cdots, Y_n$ are mutually independent, and each Y_k is a Gaussian random vector of dimension d, medium h_{ik} and R covariance matrix so that no memory channel property is verified.

A hidden Markov model $\{(X_k, Y_k)\}$ is fully characterized by the particular

The original legislation $\upsilon = (v_i);\ v_i := P[X_0 = i]$ for all $i \in E$

The transition matrix $\pi = (\pi_{i,j});\ \pi_{i,j} := P[X_k = j \mid X_{k-1} = i]$ for all $i, j \in E$ and emission densities $g = (g_i);\ g_i(y)dy := P[Y_k \in dy \mid X_k = i]$ for all $i \in E$ for any and all $j \in \mathbb{R}^d$.

So just a local data (transition probabilities between two successive times, and densities of issue at a time) comprehensively characterizes a hidden Markov model, example: for K = 3, it comes:

$$v = \begin{bmatrix} 0.9 \\ 0.1 \\ 0 \end{bmatrix}, \pi = \begin{bmatrix} 0.90 & 0.05 & 0.05 \\ 0.10 & 0.80 & 0.10 \\ 0.05 & 0.15 & 0.80 \end{bmatrix}, h = \begin{bmatrix} -5 \\ 1 \\ 10 \end{bmatrix}, \sigma^2 = \begin{bmatrix} 1 \\ 5 \\ 10 \end{bmatrix}$$

Proposal: The probability distribution of the hidden Markov model $\{(X_k, Y_k)\}$ initial ϑ law of π transition matrix, and g emission densities, is given by $P[X_0 = i_0; \cdots; X_k = i_k; Y_0 \in dy_0; \cdots; Y_k \in dy_k] = v_{i_0} \pi_{i_0, i_1} \cdots \pi_{i_{k-1}, i_k} g_{i_0}(y_0) \cdots g_{i_k}(y_k) dy_0 \cdots dy_k$ for all time k following $i_0, \cdots, i_k \in E$, and every sequence $y_0, \cdots, y_k \in \mathbb{R}^d$ is denoted by $M = (\upsilon; \pi; g)$, the parameters characteristic of the model, and we focus on three issues:

Problem No. 1: Evaluate the model: it comes to efficiently compute the probability distribution of the following observations $(Y_0;\cdots;Y_n)$ (or likelihood function) according to the parameters of the model M. The answer to this problem is provided by the forward Baum equation.

Problem No. 2: Identify the model: given a series of observations $(Y_0;\cdots;Y_n)$, this is to calculate the maximum likelihood estimator for the unknown parameters of the model M. The answer to this problem is provided by the re-estimation formulas of Baum-Welch, defining an iterative algorithm to maximize the likelihood function.

Problem No. 3: Estimate the condition of the system: given a sequence of observations $(Y_0;\cdots;Y_n)$, it is to estimated recursively the state X_n (filtering Song), or a good estimate X_n intermediate state for k = 0,…, n (smoothing Song), or an overall estimate of the sequence of states $(X_0;\cdots;X_n)$, for a given model M. the response to first two problems is provided by the forward and backward equations Baum, which calculate the conditional probability distribution of X_k state given observations $(Y_0;\cdots;Y_n)$.

The answer to the last problem is provided by a dynamic programming algorithm, the Viterbi algorithm, which maximizes the conditional probability distribution of the sequence of states $(X_0;\cdots;X_n)$ given observations $(Y_0;\cdots;Y_n)$.

Equations Forward/Backward Baum

We first present a first method (basic but inefficient) to calculate the probability distribution of observations $(Y_0;\cdots;Y_n)$.

Proposal: The probability distribution of observations $(Y_0;\cdots;Y_n)$ is given (in the digital case) by $P[Y_0 \in dy_0;\cdots;Y_n \in dy_n] = v_{i_0}\pi_{i_0,i_1}\cdots\pi_{i_{k-1},i_k}g_{i_0}(y_0)\cdots g_{i_k}(y_k)dy_0\cdots dy_k$ for any sequence $y_0,\cdots,y_k \in \mathbb{R}^d$.

Note that elementary method provides a first expression for the conditional probability distribution of the sequence of states $(X_0;\cdots;X_n)$ given observations $(Y_0;\cdots;Y_n)$ (in digital case):

$$P[X_0 = i_0,\cdots,X_n = i_n \mid Y_0,\cdots,Y_n] = \frac{v_{i_0}\pi_{i_0,i_1}\cdots\pi_{i_{n-1}i_n}g_{i_0}(Y_0)\cdots g_{i_n}(Y_n)}{\sum_{j_0,\cdots,j_n\in E} v_{j_0}\pi_{j_0,j_1}\cdots\pi_{j_{n-1}j_n}g_{j_0}(Y_0)\cdots g_{j_n}(Y_n)}$$

and the likelihood of the model (obtained using the following observations $(Y_0;\cdots;Y_n)$ in place of dummy variables):

$$L_n = \sum_{i_0,\cdots,i_n \in E} v_{i_0} \pi_{i_0,i_1} \cdots \pi_{i_{n-1} i_n} g_{i_0}(Y_0) \cdots g_{i_n}(Y_n)$$

we deduce the following identities:

$$P[X_0 = i_0, \cdots, X_n = i_n \mid Y_0, \cdots, Y_n] L_n = v_{i_0} \pi_{i_0,i_1} \cdots \pi_{i_{n-1} i_n} g_{i_0}(Y_0) \cdots g_{i_n}(Y_n).$$

Note the number of operations required to calculate the probability distribution of observations $(Y_0; \cdots; Y_n)$ from this basic method is significant for each possible path $(i_0; \cdots; i_n)$ of the Markov chain, you must compute the product of 2(n+1) words, and there is $|E|^{n+1}$ different possible paths the total number of elementary operations (additions and multiplications) thus made is of the order of $2(n+1)|E|^{n+1}$ the number is growing exponentially with the number n of observations. we define the forward $p_k = (p_k^k)$ (seen as a row vector) by $p_k^i = P[X_k = i \mid Y_0, \cdots, Y_k] L_k$ for all $i \in E$.

Note the forward variable used to calculate the conditional probability distribution of the present state X_k given observations $(Y_0; \cdots; Y_n)$: $P[X_k = i \mid Y_0, \cdots, Y_k] = \frac{1}{L_k} p_k^i$ for all $i \in E$. (In this sense, p_k is a distribution of non-normalized probability), and the normalization constant $L_k = \sum_{i \in E} p_k^i$ is interpreted as the likelihood of the model given observations $(Y_0; \cdots; Y_n)$.

Theorem: The sequence { p_k } satisfies the following recurrence equation: $p_k^j = \left[\sum_{i \in E} p_{k-1}^i \pi_{i,j}\right] g_j(Y_k)$ for all $j \in E$ with the initial condition $p_{k-1}^i = v_i g_j(Y_0)$ for any $i \in E$.

Note this statement result component-by-component can also be made for the variable forward view as a row vector $p_k = p_{k-1} \pi G(Y_k)$ and $p_0 = \upsilon G(Y_0)$.

Note the recursive calculation of the variable forward p_n involves only the product matrix/vector, and to calculate more efficiently the probability distribution of observations $(Y_0; \cdots; Y_n)$ simply $|E|(2|E|+1)$ elementary operations (additions and multiplications) to move from time k to time (k+1) the total number of elementary operations to be performed is thus of the order of: $n|E|(2|E|+1)+(2|E|-1)$ this number grows only linearly with the number n of observations.

Digital implementation: Instead of first solving the equation for the forward non-standardized version of the conditional distribution, defined at any time k as $p_k^i = P[X_k = i \mid Y_0, \cdots, Y_k] L_k$ for all $i \in E$ and then deduct the normalization constant (likelihood) and the normalized version of the conditional distribution (filter)

$$L_k = \sum_{i \in E} p_k^i \quad \text{and} \quad \overline{p}_k^i = \frac{p_k^i}{\sum_{j \in E} p_k^j} = P[X_k = i \mid Y_0, \cdots, Y_k]$$

It is more efficient, on a digital point of view, spread directly log-likelihood and filter.

Proposal: Following $\{\overline{p}_k\}$ Verie the following recurrent equation:

$\overline{p}_k^j = \frac{1}{c_k}\left[\sum_{i \in E} \overline{p}_k^j \pi_{i,j}\right] g_j(Y_k)$ for all $j \in E$ with the initial condition $\overline{p}_0^i = \frac{1}{c_0} v_i g_j(Y_0)$ for any $i \in E$.

where the normalization constants are defined by $c_k = \sum_{i,j \in E} \overline{p}_{k-1}^i \pi_{i,j} g_j(Y_k)$ and $c_0 = \sum_{i \in E} v_i g_j(Y_0)$.

Note this result statement component-by-component may also be formulated for the normalized forward variable seen as a row vector $\overline{p}_k = \frac{1}{c_k} \overline{p}_{k-1} \pi G^{Y_k}$ and $\overline{p}_0 = \frac{1}{c_0} \upsilon G^{Y_0}$

where the normalization constants are defined by $c_k = \overline{p}_{k-1} \pi g^{Y_k}$ and $c_0 = \upsilon g^{Y_0}$.

Note: Following $\{\log L_k\}$ truth the following recurrent equation: $\log L_k = \log L_{k-1} + \log c_k$ with the initial condition $\log L_0 = \log c_0$ and iterating log $\log L_k = \sum_{k=0}^{n} \log c_k$. For all intermediate time k, less than the final instant n, is defined $q_k^i = P[X_k = i \mid Y_0, \cdots, Y_n] L_n$ for all $i \in E$.

Note: That variable allows to calculate the conditional probability distribution of the present state X_k knowing all comments $(Y_0; \cdots; Y_n)$, $P[X_k = i \mid Y_0, \cdots, Y_n] = \frac{1}{L_n} q_k^i$

for all $i \in E$ with the normalization constant $L_n = \sum_{i \in E} q_k^i$.

Note: Fix the state at time k allows a break between the past up to time (k-1) and the future from time (k+1). This justifies the introduction of the variable backward $v_k = \left(v_k^i\right)$ (seen as a column vector) and defined as:

$v_k^i = \sum_{i_{k+i},\cdots,i_n \in E} \pi_{i,i_{k+1}} \cdots \pi_{i_{n-1},i_n} g_{i_{k+1}}\left(Y_{k+1}\right) \cdots g_{i_n}\left(Y_n\right)$ for any $i \in E$

and in particular $v_{n-1}^i = \sum_{j \in E} \pi_{i,j} g_j\left(Y_n\right)$ for all $i \in E$ with this definition, is obtained $q_k^i = p_k^i v_k^i$ for all $i \in E$.

Note: Conditionally (X_k = i) the X_ suite $X_{k+1}; X_{k+2}; \cdots$ to come hidden states is a Markov chain, from initial law $\pi_{i,\blacksquare}$ (line i the π matrix), that is to say that $P\left[X_{k+1} = j \mid X_k = i\right] = \pi_{i,j}$ for all $j \in E$ and π transition matrix it follows that the backward variable can be interpreted as the likelihood of the model derived from the X_k = i state at time k given observations $\left(Y_{k+1}, \cdots, Y_n\right)$.

Theorem:

After $\{v_k\}$ Verie recurrent retrograde following equation:

$v_{k-1}^i = \sum_{j \in E} \pi_{i,j} g_j\left(Y_k\right) v_k^j$ for all $i \in E$ with the initial condition: $v_n^i = 1$ for all $i \in E$.

Note: This result statement component-by-component can also be formulated for the backward view variable as a column vector $v_{k-1} = \pi G\left(Y_k\right) v_k$ and $v_n \equiv 1$.

Proposal: the forward and backward equations are dual to one another:

$\sum_{i \in E} p_0^i v_0^i = \sum_{i \in E} p_k^i v_k^i = \sum_{i \in E} p_n^i = L_n$ not dependent of the time in question

Proposal: For the distribution of conditional probability of transition $\left(X_{k-1}, \cdots, X_n\right)$ at an intermediate time given observations $\left(Y_0, \cdots, Y_n\right)$ until the final moment is given by:

$$P\left[X_{k-1} = i, X_k = j \mid Y_0, \cdots, Y_n\right] = \frac{1}{L_n} p_{k-1}^i \pi_{i,j} g_j\left(Y_k\right) v_k^j \quad \text{for all i, } j \in E$$

By summing for all $j \in E$ and using the equation backward, or by summing for all i ∈ E and using the forward equation, we find the following results in

terms of product component-by-component variables forward and backward.
Corollary: the conditional probability distribution of the present state X_k knowing all comments $(Y_0,\cdots,Y_n)$ is given by $P[X_k = i \mid Y_0,\cdots,Y_n] = \frac{1}{L_n} q_k^i$ with the definition $q_k^i = p_k^i v_k^i$ for all $i \in E$.
Note: Verie one that constant Standards

$$\sum_{i,j\in E} p_{k-1}^i \pi_{i,j} b_j^{Y_k} v_k^j = \sum_{j\in E}\left[\sum_{i\in E} p_{k-1}^i \pi_{i,j}\right] b_j^{Y_k} v_k^j = \sum_{j\in E} p_k^j v_k^j = L_n$$

and $\sum_{i\in E} q_k^i = \sum_{i\in E} p_k^i v_k^i = L_n$

do not depend on the time in question, and are interpreted as the likelihood of the model given observations $(Y_0,\cdots,Y_n)$. instead of first solve the backward and forward equation equation separately, and to successively deduct the non-normalized version of the conditional distribution, defined at any instant k as $q_k^i = p_k^i v_k^i = P[X_k = i \mid Y_0,\cdots,Y_n] L_n$ for all $i \in E$

then the normalized version of the conditional distribution (smoother)

$$\overline{q}_k^i = \frac{q_k^i}{\sum_{j\in E} q_k^j} = \frac{p_k^i v_k^i}{\sum_{j\in E} p_k^j v_k^j} = \frac{\overline{p}_k^i v_k^i}{\sum_{j\in E} \overline{p}_k^j v_k^j} = P[X_k = i \mid Y_0,\cdots,Y_n].$$

.

It is more efficient on a digital point of view, spread directly log-likelihood and filter, then spread the variable defined at any time k as $\overline{v}_k^i = \frac{v_k^i}{\sum_{j\in E} \overline{p}_k^j v_k^j}$ for any $i \in E$.

Note: That with normalization of the backward variable, the conditional probability distribution of X_k state given observations $(Y_0,\cdots,Y_n)$ is expressed as

$P[X_k = i \mid Y_0,\cdots,Y_n] = \overline{p}_k^i \overline{v}_k^i = \overline{q}_k^i$ for all $i \in E$.

Proposal: Following $\{\overline{v}_k\}$ Verie recurrent retrograde following equation:

$\overline{v}_{k-1}^{i} = \frac{1}{c_k} \sum_{j \in E} \pi_{i,j} g_j(Y_k) \overline{v}_k^{j}$ for all $i \in E$, with the initial condition: $\overline{v}_k^{i} = 1$ for all $i \in E$ where the normalization constants are those already defined for the normalization of the variable forward.

Note: This result statement component-by-component can also be formulated for backward standardized variable viewed as a column vector $\overline{v}_{k-1} = \frac{1}{c_k} \pi G(Y_k) \overline{v}_k$ and $\overline{v}_n \equiv 1$ where the normalization constants are those already defined for the normalization of the variable forward.

Note: It is noted that $\frac{1}{L_n} p_{k-1}^{i} v_k^{j} = \frac{L_{k-1}}{L_n} \overline{p}_{k-1}^{i} = \frac{1}{c_k} \overline{p}_{k-1}^{i} \overline{v}_k^{j}$ for all i, $j \in E$

And postponing this identity in the expressions obtained above, we Verie that the conditional probability distribution of the transition $(X_{k-1}, \cdots, X_k)$ given observations $(Y_0, \cdots, Y_n)$ is expressed as

$$P[X_{k-1} = i, X_k = j \mid Y_0, \cdots, Y_n] = \frac{1}{c_k} \overline{p}_{k-1}^{i} \pi_{i,j} g_j(Y_k) \overline{v}_k^{j} = \overline{q}_k^{i} \quad \text{for} \quad i, j \in E.$$

for i, $j \in E$.

Viterbi Algorithm

Forward and backward variables used to calculate the conditional probability distribution of the state this X_n, or X_n state at an intermediate moment, given observations $(Y_0, \cdots, Y_n)$ defined by $P[X_n = i \mid Y_0, \cdots, Y_n] = \frac{1}{L_n} p_n^{i}$ for all $i \in E$, and $P[X_k = i \mid Y_0, \cdots, Y_n] = \frac{1}{L_n} q_k^{i}$ for any $i \in E$ respectively, where the normalization constant $L_n = \sum_{i \in E} p_n^{i} = \sum_{i \in E} p_k^{i} v_k^{i} = \sum_{i \in E} q_k^{i}$ does not depend on the time in question, and interprets as the likelihood of the model given observations $(Y_0, \cdots, Y_n)$. it is not necessary to calculate the conditional average, but can be used however the estimator of maximum a posteriori, which minimizes the likelihood of the estimation error given observations $(Y_0, \cdots, Y_n)$ and defined for the present state $X_N^{LMAP} = \arg\max_{i \in E} P[X_n = i \mid Y_0, \cdots, Y_n] = \arg\max_{i \in E} p_n^{i}$

and for the state to an intermediate time by $X_k^{LMAP} = \arg\max_{i \in E} P[X_k = i \mid Y_0, \cdots, Y_n] = \arg\max_{i \in E} q_k^i$ it may happen that the sequence $\left(X_0^{LMAP}, \cdots, X_n^{LMAP}\right)$ generated is inconsistent with the model, in the following sense: it can happen that is obtained $X_{k-1}^{LMAP} = i$ and $X_k^{LMAP} = j$ for two successive times, while $\pi_{i,j} = 0$ for the same pair (i,j), which meant that the transition from state i to state j is just impossible for the model for this reason, rather it uses another estimator, called trajectoriel maximum a posteriori estimator, defined by $\left(X_0^{LMAP}, \cdots, X_n^{LMAP}\right) = \arg\max_{i_0, \cdots, i_n \in E} P[X_0 = i_0, \cdots, X_n = i_n \mid Y_0, \cdots, Y_n]$.

And minimizes the probability of the estimation error of the sequence of hidden states given observations $(Y_0, \cdots, Y_n)$ it is of course not possible to perform this maximization exhaustive manner, listing all $|E|^{n+1}$ possible trajectories: the efficient calculation of this estimator is provided by a dynamic programming algorithm called Viterbi algorithm.

Re-Estimation Formulas Baum-Welch

So far, the focus was on the estimation of a hidden condition or because of successive hidden states, from a series of observations and for a given model. The goal here is to identifier the model, that is to say, to estimate the parameters of the model characteristics, from a series of observations, and the approach taken is that of estimation maximum likelihood.

In the digital case, we look at the case of the Gaussian emission densities characterized by the data of finite $h = (h_i)$ $\mathbb{R}^d$ vectors and of finite Family $R = (R_i)$ matrices invertible covariance, that is to say:

$$g_i(y) = g(h_i, R_i, y) = \frac{1}{\sqrt{\det(2\pi R_i)}} \exp\left\{-\frac{1}{2}(y - h_i) * R_i^{-1}(y - h_i)\right\}$$

The likelihood function of the model $\boldsymbol{M} = (v; \pi; h; R)$ admits expression

$$L_n = \sum_{i_0, \cdots, i_n \in E} v_{i_0} \pi_{i_0, i_1} \cdots \pi_{i_{n-1} i_n} g_{i_0}(Y_0) \cdots g_{i_n}(Y_n)$$

obtained with the basic method, and we will study an iterative algorithm to maximize L_n likelihood function with respect to the parameters $(v; \pi; h; R)$ model of either $\boldsymbol{M}' = (v'; \pi'; h'; R')$ another model, for which the likelihood function takes the value

$$L'_n = \sum_{i_0,\cdots,i_n \in E} v'_{i_0} \pi'_{i_0,i_1} \cdots \pi'_{i_{n-1}i_n} g'_{i_0}(Y_0) \cdots g'_{i_n}(Y_n)$$

the (log) likelihood ratio between the **M** and the **M'** is reduced by

$$Q_n = E'\left[\log \frac{v_{X_0} \pi_{X_0,X_1} \cdots \pi_{X_{n-1}X_n} g_{X_0}(Y_0) \cdots g_{X_n}(Y_n)}{v'_{X_0} \pi'_{X_0,X_1} \cdots \pi'_{X_{n-1}X_n} g'_{X_0}(Y_0) \cdots g'_{X_n}(Y_n)} \mid Y_0, \cdots, Y_n\right]$$

which vanishes when the model **M** coincides with the model **M'**.

Maximize Q_n compared with parameters $(v; \pi; h; R)$ of the model **M** thus ensures that the likelihood of the model which achieved maximum Q_n will be greater than the likelihood L'_n current model **M'** re-formulas Baum-Welch -Estimated allow explicitly find the parameters of the new model based on parameters $(v; \pi; h; R)$ of the current model **M'** by repeating this procedure, we construct a sequence of increasing likelihood models, and ideally this sequence converges to a model that reaches the maximum likelihood function.

Theorem

In the digital case with densities of Gaussian issue, the iterative algorithm for esti- mating the maximum likelihood of the model parameters from the observations$(Y_0, \cdots, Y_n)$, is given by explicit formulas re-estimate

$$v_i = \overline{p}_0'^i \overline{v}_0'^i \quad \text{and} \quad \pi_{i,j} = \pi'_{i,j} \frac{\sum_{k=1}^{n} \frac{1}{c'_k} \overline{p}_{k-1}'^i g'_j(Y_k) \overline{v}_k'^j}{\sum_{k=1}^{n} \overline{p}_{k-1}'^i \overline{v}_{k-1}'^i} \quad \text{and}$$

$$h_i = \frac{\sum_{k=0}^{n} Y_k \overline{p}_k'^i \overline{v}_k'^i}{\sum_{k=0}^{n} \overline{p}_k'^i \overline{v}_k'^i} \quad \text{and} \quad R_i = \frac{\sum_{k=0}^{n} (Y_k - h_i)(Y_k - h_i) * \overline{p}_k'^i \overline{v}_k'^i}{\sum_{k=0}^{n} \overline{p}_k'^i \overline{v}_k'^i}$$

for all i, $j \in E$ where the two sequences $\{\overline{p}'_k\}$ and $\{\overline{v}'_k\}$ are the standard equations of forward and backward solutions respectively for values $(v'; \pi'; h'; R')$ parameters.

Note: Concretely, if $M_{s-1} = (v_{s-1}; \pi_{s-1}; h_{s-1}; R_{s-1})$ denotes the current model in step (s-1) of the algorithm, then for values $(v'; \pi'; h'; R') = (v_{s-1}; \pi_{s-1}; h_{s-1}; R_{s-1})$ the para- meters are calculated standardized solutions $\{\overline{p}'_k\}$ and $\{\overline{v}'_k\}$ of equations forward and backward respectively the parameters $(v_s; \pi_s; h_s; R_s) = (v; \pi; h; R)$ is calculated using the formulas to re-estimate what defines the new model $M_s = (v_s; \pi_s; h_s; R_s)$ to s next step of the algorithm.

IMPLEMENTATION

Our model is based on acoustic signal parameters. These parameters are obtained by calculating cepstral coefficients according to a Mel scale (MFCC Mel Frequency Cepstral Coefficients). Statistical realization of acoustic parameters of each phoneme is represented by a Hidden Markov model. Each phoneme is typically represented by 2 or 3 states, and multigaussienne density (GMM: Gaussian Mixture Model) is associated with each state. GMM densities with a large number of components designed to address multiple sources of variability that are affecting the speech signals (sex and age of the speaker, accent, noise).

For example: With the following data: Number of States (K = 2); π = [0.95 0.05; 0.05 0.95]; h = [−1 1]; σ^2 = [3 3]; υ = [0.5 0.5]; we have the Figure 6 below.

A robust speech recognition system combines accuracy of identification with the ability to filter noise and adapt to other acoustical conditions such as speech and emphasis of the speaker. The design of a robust speech recognition algorithm is a complex task which requires detailed knowledge of signal processing and statistical modeling.

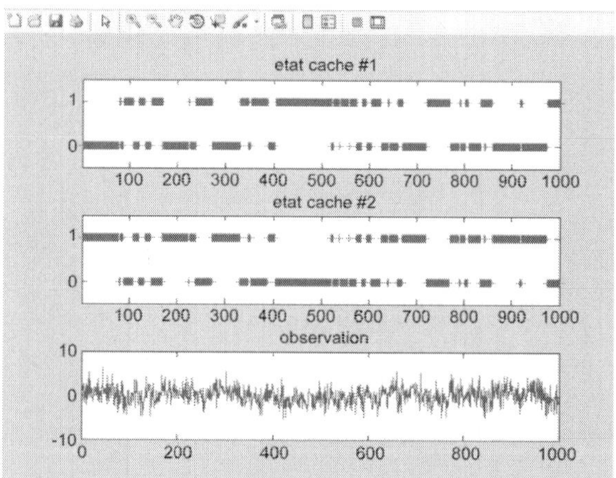

Figure 6. Graphic representation of the Hidden Markov Model.

Most speech recognition systems are classified as isolated or continuous. The isolated word recognition requires a short pause between each spoken word, while the speech recognition does not continue. Speech recognition systems can be classified as a dependent or speaker-independent. Speaker dependent system recognizes only the word of the voice of a particular speaker, while an independent speaker system can recognize any voice. The implementation presented here uses features integrated into MATLAB and related products to develop the recognition algorithm. There are two main steps in the recognition of isolated words:

- a learning phase and
- a test phase.

The learning phase teaches the system by building its dictionary, an acoustic model for each word that the system has to recognize. In our example, the dictionary includes the numbers "zero" to "nine" in "Baoule" language. The test phase uses acoustic models of these numbers to recognize isolated words using a classification algorithm. We start with the the speech signal acquisition, and then we end with its analysis.

Speech Signal Acquisition

During the learning phase, it is necessary to record the repeated statements of each digit in the dictionary. For example, we repeat the word "nnou" (which means five in "Baoule" language) many times with a pause between each statement. That word will be saved in the file 'cinq.wav'. Using the following MATLAB code with a sound card standard PC, we capture ten seconds of speech from a microphone to 8000 samples per second. We obtained y that is a matrix of 8000 rows and one column. This approach works well for training data.

```
Fs = 8000; Duration = 10; y = wavrecord(Duration*Fs, Fs);
```

Acquired Speech Signal Analysis

We first develop a word-detection algorithm that separates each word of ambient noise. We then obtain an acoustic model that provides a strong representation of each word in the stage of learning. Finally, we select an appropriate classification algorithm for testing.

The Development of a Word-Detection Algorithm

The word-detection algorithm continuously reads 160 samples frames from the data of "speech". To detect single digits, we use a combination of the signal energy and have zero crossing for each speech frame.

The signal energy works well to detect sound signals, while the zero-crossing numbers work well for detecting non-voice signals. The calculation of these measures is simple using mathematical operators and MATLAB basic logic. To avoid identifying the ambient noise of speech, we assume that each individual word will last at least 25 milliseconds. In Figure 7 below, we plot the speech signal "five" and the power of short duration and zero crossing measurement.

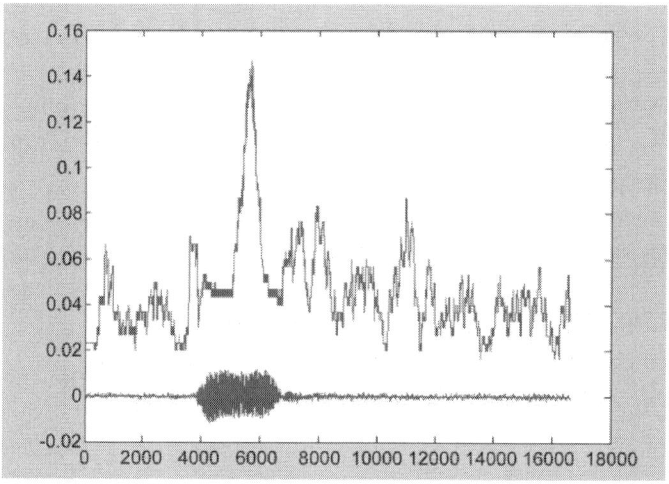

Figure 7. Speech signal "five" and the power of short duration and zero crossing measurement.

```
cinq=wavread('cinq.wav'); N = 300; Px = stpower(cinq, N);
Zx = stzerocross(cinq, N); plot([Px*1e-5 Zx cinq])
```

Development of the Acoustic Model

A good acoustic model should be derived from the word of features that allow the system to distinguish different words in the dictionary. We know that different sounds are produced by varying the shape of the human vocal tract, and these different sounds can each have different frequencies. To investigate the frequency characteristics, we examine the density estimates Spectral Power (CSP) various spoken digits. Since the human vocal tract can be modeled as a filter on all poles, we use the parametric spectral estimation technique Yule-Walker of the window Signal Processing Toolbox to calculate the DSP. After importing a statement of a single digit in the variable "word" we use the MATLAB code below to view the DSP estimate: here there is the speech signal that we have acquired (Figure 8).

```
order = 12; nfft = 512; Fs = 8000; pyulear(cinq, order, nfft, Fs)
```

Because the Yule-Walker algorithm adapts a linear prediction filter model autoregression to the signal, you must supply an order of this filter. We select an arbitrary value of 12, which is typical for voice applications.

Figure 9 shows the PSD estimate of three different expressions of the words "one" and "two". We can see the tops of the PSD remain consistent for a particular number, but differ from one figure to another. This means that we can draw the acoustic models in our system from the spectral characteristics.

A set of spectral characteristics commonly used in voice applications because of its robustness is Mel Frequency Cepstral Coefficients (MFCC). MFCC give a measure of the energy in overlapping boxes frequency of a deformed spectrum by (Mel) Frequency scale 1.

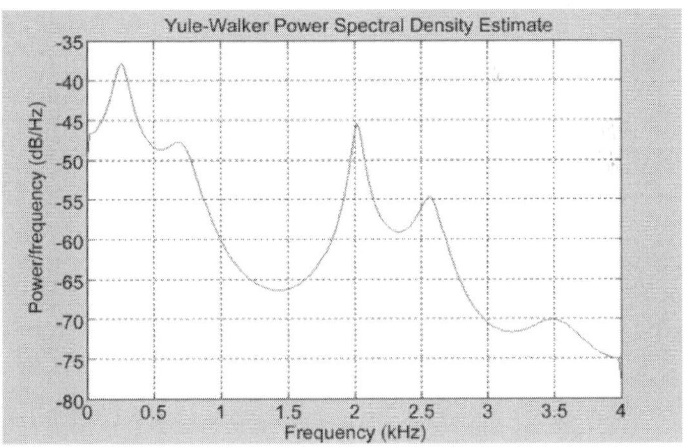

Figure 8. Estimate of the PSD (Yule Walker) the word "five".

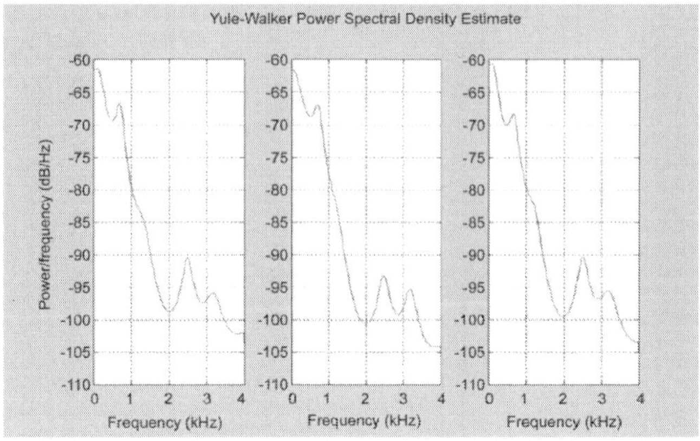

(a)

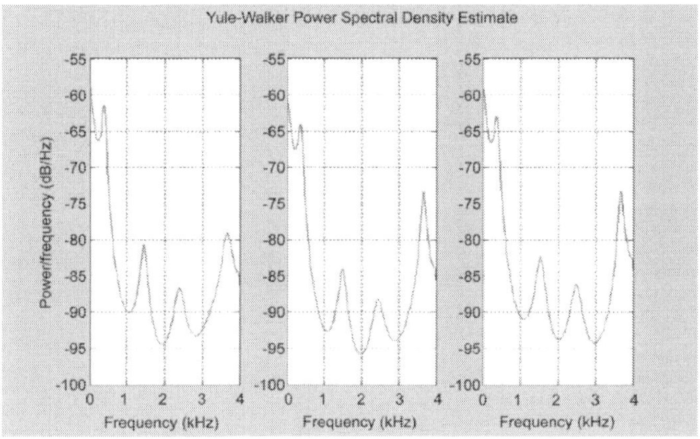

(b)

Figure 9. (a) Estimating the PSD (Yule Walker) in three different expressions of the word "one."; (b) estimating the PSD (Yule Walker) in three different expressions of the word "two".

In the short term, the floor can be considered as stationary, MFCC characteristics of the vectors are calculated for each speech frame detected. Using many statements of a number and by combining all of the feature vectors, we can estimate a multidimensional probability density function (PDF) vectors to a specific figure. Repeating this process for each digit, the acoustic model is obtained for each digit. During the test phase, we extract the MFCC vectors figure test and use a probabilistic measure to determine the number of the source with the maximum likelihood.

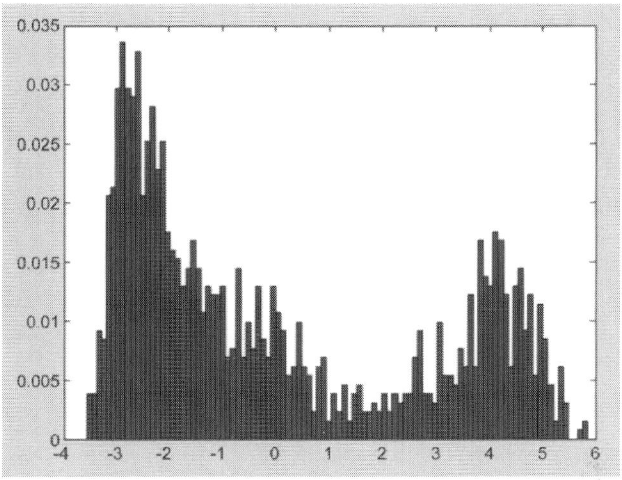

(a)

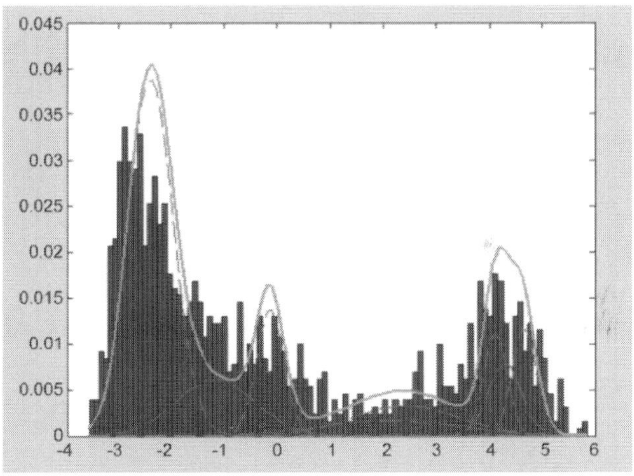

(b)

Figure 10. (a) The distribution of the first dimension of MFCC feature vectors for the digit "one."; (b) Overlay estimated Gaussian components (red) and all Gaussian mixture model (green) for distribution in (4a).

Figure 10 shows the distribution of the first dimension of MFCC feature vectors extracted from the training data for the digit "one." We could use dfittool in StatisticsToolbox adapt to a PDF, but the distribution seems quite arbitrary, and standard distributions do not provide a good fit.

-One solution is to adjust a mixture of Gaussian model (GMM), a sum of weighted Gaussian (Figure 10(b)). The total density of Gaussian mixture is set by the weight of the mixture, the mean vectors and covariance matrices from all densities of the components. For the recognition of isolated digits, each digit is represented by the parameters of the GMM.

To estimate the parameters of a GMM for a set of MFCC feature vectors extracted from the figure when learning, we use an expectation maximization (EM) iterative algorithm for maximum likelihood (ML) estimation. Given some MFCC training data in MFCC train data variable (equal to five here), we use the GMM distribution Statistics Toolbox function for estimating GMM parameters. This function is all that is needed to perform the EM iterative calculations.

```
%Number of Gaussian component densities
M = 8; model = gmdistribution.fit(cinq, M);
```

Selecting a Classification Algorithm

After estimating a GMM for each digit, we have a dictionary for use in the testing phase. Given some test speech, we extracted again MFCC feature vectors of each frame of the detected word. The goal is to find the model numbers of the maximum a posteriori probability for all the long delivery tests, which reduces to maximize the value of log-likelihood.

Given a GMM model (equal to model here) model numbers and some feature vectors tests test data (equal to five here), the log-likelihood value is easily calculated using the post office in Statistics Toolbox: [P, log_like] = later (model, five); we repeat this calculation using the model of each digit. The test speech is classified as revenues at the MGM produce the maximum log-likelihood.

CONCLUSIONS

In this article we presented an overview of HMM: their applications and conventional algorithms used in the literature, the generation probability calculation algorithms in a sequence by an HMM, the path search algorithm optimum, and the drive algorithms.

The speech signal is a complex form drowned in the noise. Its learning is part of complex intelligent activity [10] . By learning a starting model, we will build gradually an effective model for each of the phonemes of the "Baoule" language.

Note finally that HMMs have established themselves as the reference model for solving certain types of problems in many application areas, whether in speech recognition, modeling of biological sequences or for the extraction of information from textual data. However other formalisms such as neural networks can be used to improve the modeling. Our future work will focus on the modeling of the linguistic aspect of the "Baoule" language.

ANNEXES

```
function [valeur,ante,dens] = Viterbi(X,A,p,m,sigma2,K,T)
begin
% densite d'emission
dens = ones(T,K);
dens =
exp(-0.5*(X'*ones(1,K)-ones(T,1)*m).^2./(ones(T,1)*sigma2))./
sqrt(ones(T,1)*sigma2);
% fonction valeur
valeur = ones(T,K);
valeur(1,:) = p.*dens(1,:);
for t=2:T
[c,I] = max((ones(K,1)*valeur(t-1,:)).*A,[],2);
valeur(t,:) = c'.*dens(t,:);
valeur(t,:) = valeur(t,:)/max(valeur(t,:));
ante(t,:) = I;
end
end
function [alpha,beta,dens,ll] = ForwardBackward(X,A,p,m,sigma2,K,T)
% densite d'emission
dens = ones(T,K);
dens =
exp(-0.5*(X'*ones(1,K)-ones(T,1)*m).^2./(ones(T,1)*sigma2))./
sqrt(ones(T,1)*sigma2);
% variable forward
alpha = ones(T,K);
alpha(1,:) = p.*dens(1,:);
c(1) = sum(alpha(1,:));
```

```
alpha(1,:) = alpha(1,:)/c(1);
for t=2:T
alpha(t,:) = alpha(t-1,:)*A;
alpha(t,:) = alpha(t,:).*dens(t,:);
c(t) = sum(alpha(t,:));
alpha(t,:) = alpha(t,:)/c(t);
end
ll = cumsum(log(c));
% variable backward
beta = ones(K,T);
for t=T-1:-1:1
beta(:,t) = beta(:,t+1).*(dens(t+1,:))';
beta(:,t) = A*beta(:,t);
beta(:,t) = beta(:,t)/(alpha(t,:)*beta(:,t));
end
function [X,Y] = gen(A,p,m,sigma2,T)
begin
sigma = sqrt(sigma2);
Y(1) = multinomiale(p);
for t=2:T
q = A(Y(t-1),:);
Y(t) = multinomiale(q);
end
w = randn(1,T);
for t=1:T
moyenne = m(Y(t));
ecart_type = sigma(Y(t));
X(t) = moyenne+ecart_type*w(t);
end
end
function Px = stpower(x,N)
```

```
begin
M = length(x);
Px = zeros(M,1);
Px(1:N) = x(1:N)'*x(1:N)/N;
for m=(N+1):M
Px(m) = Px(m-1) + (x(m)^2 - x(m-N)^2)/N;
end
end
function Zx = stzerocross(x,N)
begin
M = length(x);
Zx = zeros(M,1);
Zx(1:N+1) = sum(abs(sign(x(2:N+1)) - sign(x(1:N))))/(2*N);
for (m=(N+2):M)
Zx(m) = Zx(m-1) + (abs(sign(x(m)) - sign(x(m-1))) ...
- abs(sign(x(m-N)) - sign(x(m-N-1))))/(2*N);
end
end
```

REFERENCES

1. Baum, L.E., Petrie, T., Soules, G. and Weiss, N. (1970) A Maximization Technique Occurring in Statistical Analysis of Probabilistic Functions in Markov Chains. The Annals of Mathematical Statistics, 41, 164-171. http://dx.doi.org/10.1214/aoms/1177697196
2. Casacuberta, F. (1990) Some Relations among Stochastic Finite State Networks Used in Automatic Speech Recognition. IEEE Ttransactions on patern Analysis and Machine Intelligence, 12, 691-695. http://dx.doi.org/10.1109/34.56212
3. Lekoundji, J.-B.V. (2014) Modèles De Markov Cachés. Université Du Québec À Montréal.
4. Rabiner, L.R. (1989) A Tutorial on Hidden Markov Models and Selected Application in Speech Recognition. Proceedings of the IEEE, 77, 257-286. http://dx.doi.org/10.1109/5.18626
5. Kundu, A., He, Y. and Bahl, P. (1988) Recognition of Handwritten Word: First and Second Order Hiden Markov Model Based Approach. IEEE Computer Society Conference on Computer Vision Pattern Recognition, CVPR'88, Ann Arbor, 5-9 June 1988, 457-462. http://dx.doi.org/10.1109/CVPR.1988.196275
6. Schenkel, M., Guyon, I. and Henderson, D. (1994) On-Line Cursive Script Recognition Using Time Delay Neural Networks and Hidden Markov Models. Proceedings of 1994 IEEE International Conference on Acoustics, Speech, and Signal Processing, ICASSP'94, Adelaide, 19-22 April 1994, II-637-II-640. http://dx.doi.org/10.1109/icassp.1994.389575
7. Haussler, D., Krogh, A., Mian, S. and Sjolander, K. (1992) Protein Modeling Using Hidden Markov Models: Analysis of Globins. Technical Report UCSC-CRL-92-23.
8. Durbin, R., Eddy, S., Krogh, A. and Mitchison, G. (1998) Biological Sequence Analysis Probabilistic Models of Proteins and Nucleic Acids. Cambridge University Press, Cambridge. http://dx.doi.org/10.1017/CBO9780511790492
9. In François Le Gland (2014-2015) Télécom Bretagne Module F4B101A Traitement Statistique de l'Information. http://www.irisa.fr/aspi/legland/telecom-bretagne/
10. Corge, C. (1975) Elément d'informatique. Informatique et demarche de l'esprit. Librairie Larousse, Paris.

SECTION 3: APPLICATIONS WITH SPEECH RECOGNITION

CHAPTER 11

An Overview of Basics Speech Recognition and Autonomous Approach for Smart Home IOT Low Power Devices

Jean-Yves Fourniols, Nadim Nasreddine, Christophe Escriba, Pascal Acco, Julien Roux, Georges Soto Romero

Laboratory for Analysis and Architecture of Systems, LAAS, University of Toulouse, Toulouse, France

ABSTRACT

Automatic speech recognition, often incorrectly called voice recognition, is a computer based software technique that analyzes audio signals captured by a microphone and translates them into machine interpreted text. Speech processing is based on techniques that need local CPU or cloud computing

Citation: Fourniols, J., Nasreddine, N., Escriba, C., Acco, P., Roux, J. and Romero, G. (2018), An Overview of Basics Speech Recognition and Autonomous Approach for Smart Home IOT Low Power Devices. Journal of Signal and Information Processing, 9, 239-257. doi: 10.4236/jsip.2018.94015.

with an Internet link. An activation word starts the uplink; "OK google", "Alexa", ... and voice analysis is not usually suitable for autonomous limited CPU system (16 bits microcontroller) with low energy. To achieve this realization, this paper presents specific techniques and details an efficiency voice command method compatible with an embedded IOT low-power device.

Keywords: Voice Recognition, Speech Processing, Voice Command, Embedded Device

INTRODUCTION

Human Machine interface based on speech recognition systems is a reality made possible through an Internet link and multi-threaded, multi-pipelined processor architecture or open source applications. This paper aims to analyze the development of a low cost and low power speech recognition system. The main challenge in this project is to realize the speech recognition system on embedded hardware, using limited resources (computing power, embedded energy) and based on a very small microcontroller (16 bits). This is a difficult task taking into account that a speech recognition system requires high processing power for the audio signal treatment [1] [2] .

The developed system is able to successfully distinguish and recognize short basic voice commands composed from a few words. Also, the language is used for recognition it doesn't matter, the accuracy and reliability of the system remain almost the same in every case. The system is designed to be speaker independent, so it is capable in recognizing voice commands spoken by different persons.

The goal of the system is to help people with disabilities in making their lives easier, by letting them control different things only with voice commands. As well, it can be implemented to simplify the usage of different appliances which have too many hardware buttons for a high number of inputs [3] [4] . This paper is divided in five main parts. These describe the state of art, then the analytical description of the system, followed by the algorithm description, and the recognition technique to conclude with results of the recognition.

OVERVIEW STATE OF THE ART

Speech recognition appeared in 1950 when the first digit recognition system was developed, a fully wired device and very unreliable. By 1960, the introduction of numerical methods and computer usage had entirely change research dimension.

However, the results were very poor because everyone had largely underestimated the realization difficulty of the whole system, particularly for the continuous speech type of recognition system [5] [6] .

Around 1970, the need to use linguistic constraints in automatic speech decoding had been regarded as an engineering problem [7] . But in the end of the 70s the first generation of speech recognition system based on isolated words started to be commercialized.

The following generations have started to take advantage of the increasing and increasing power calculation of the computers [8] , showing very promising results [9] . "Dragon speaking" is one of the best computer software in speech recognition commercialized today. Nowadays, "OK Google", "Alexa", "Siri" and "S-voice" services offered by Apple and Samsung prove to have very good speech recognition accuracy on their mobile devices [10] .

Most publications show the usage of this recognition is computer-based systems [6] [9] [10] . Many embedded software exist but they need a high computing power like 32/64 bits microcontrollers or a Raspberry Pi [11] . Few of them propose this integration on a limited embedded system but, actually, the voice recognition is deported [12] or the system has a high consumption [13] . Our following algorithm is designed to be implemented in a power-limited system by limiting the calculation time and the energetic consumption.

In general, speech recognition systems are devised in 3 important stages as follows:

- Audio capture: a transducer (e.g.: microphone) that captures the audio signal, when a user is talking, and transforms it in electrical signal
- Sound analysis and parameterization: it will analyze, decode and parameterize the audio signal captured by the sensor. This step is a mathematical treatment of signal and it is done in time, frequency and intensity domains. Here the audio signatures of the words will be extracted from the actual audio signal.
- The identification: the decision in choosing the right spoken voice commands is done in this step. Basically, here the program will

compare the audio signatures of the speech commands spoken by the user with the ones already learned (stored) in the system.

Figure 1 resumes these three stages on a schematic.

Voice Characteristics

Human voice properties should be taken in account in developing a speech embedded recognition system:

- The bandwidth of the speech signal is around 4 kHz.
- The speech signal is periodic and has a fundamental frequency between 80 Hz and 350 Hz.
- Peaks exist in the spectral distribution of energy of the voice signal. The frequencies around these values are called formant frequencies.

$F_{peaks}=(2n-1)\times 500Hz$ with $n=1,2,3,$ (1)

- Depending on the shape of the vocal tract the frequency of the formants, especially the first and second, will change, therefore they will characterize the way vowel are articulated.
- The envelope of the voice power spectrum also decreases with the increase of frequency with about 6 dB per octave.

Parametrization

First step is to configure the speaker's voice signal looking for a "signature" to be founded for recognition. In order to do this, several methods exist.

First type consists of spectral analysis. It is based on the frequency decomposition of the signal without a prior knowledge of its fine structure. The best and most used method is the one using Fast Fourier Transform (FFT), more precise the Discrete Fourier Transform calculation (DFT):

$$X(k)=\sum_{n=0}^{N-1} x(n) e^{-\frac{i2\pi nk}{N}} \quad (2)$$

Applying the DFT to a complex sound, and repeating this procedure, a graphic will be drawn showing time amplitude and frequency evolution, as we can see at Figure 2. This will define the sound audio signature. Specific characteristics are extracted and used from this calculation, or even the whole result, in the form of vectors or matrix later in the processing and identification stages.

The second method consists on identification by understanding the mechanisms of sound production. The most commonly used approachis based on linear predictive coding (LPC). The basic idea is that the mouth channel is constituted by a cylindrical tube with varying sections. The adjustment of the parameters of this model allows determining at almost any moment the transfer function. Afterwards, this provides an approximation of the spectrum envelope of the audio signal at the instant analysis. Then, it easily identifies the formant frequencies, with the help of the resonant frequencies of the vocal tract. They correspond to the maximum energy in the spectrum. By repeating this method continuously, the audio signature of the sound will start to show. A LPC representation is shown in Figure 3.

Once the audio signature is obtained, the speech recognition procedure can move to the next step.

Isolated Word Recognition

Speech recognition systems can be configured to work on isolated words or even on continuous speech [14] [15] . The most used is the one on isolated words because it has the highest rate of accuracy and also it doesn't require a powerful hardware as the complex method of continuous speech does, making it suitable for a low budget system. The absence of indicators in speech signal for the boundaries of phonemes and words is a major difficulty in speech recognition. Thus pronouncing words with an artificially isolation, a small silence exceeding a few tenths of a second, in speech commands represents a significant simplification of the problem.

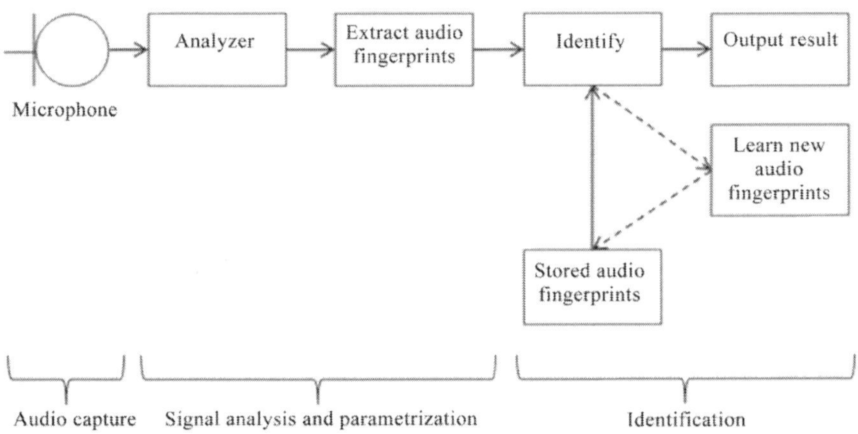

Figure 1. Stages in a speech recognition system.

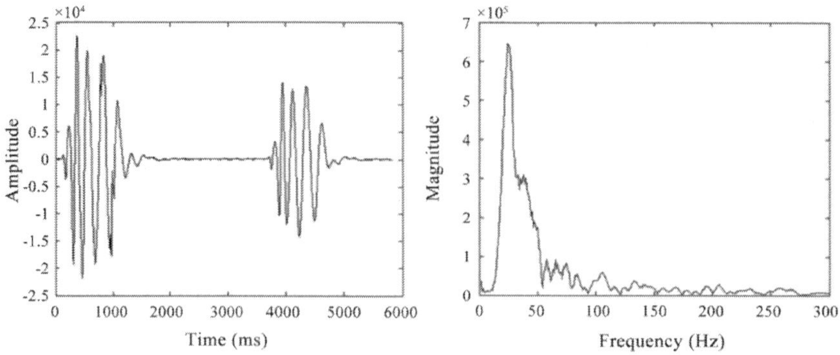

Figure 2. DFT calculation of an audio signal.

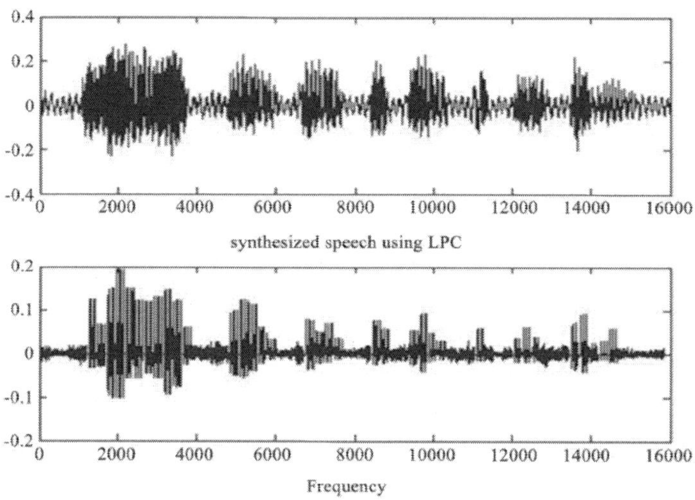

Figure 3. LPC calculation of an audio signal.

Two types of this system currently exist:

- The speaker dependent system—it can be used only by one user and it needs to be trained. A person should dictate a set of words, which maximizes the recognition rate and extend the vocabulary used. The disadvantage is that it can be used by one person only.
- The speaker independent system—it uses a database containing averages of audio signatures allowing the recognition of speech commands spoken by different persons. The main drawback is that the system is not equipped with learning capabilities and the number of words limited.

To increase the recognition rate of the system, by making it work even if the person speaks on different tonalities (different octaves) or if more than one person is used, a normalization process must be implemented. This will be done before the system will start to decode voice commands into phonemes, syllables or words depending on the technique of the system.

Recognition Techniques

Recognition technique is based on two approaches, the global and the analytical method [16] [17] .

In the global approach (entire word), the basic unit is often the word seen as a global entity that is not decomposed. The idea of this method is to give the system an acoustic image of each word that will have to identify it later. This operation is done during the training phase, were each word is pronounced one or more times. This method has the advantage of avoiding the effects of articulation. It is however limited to small vocabulary by a limited number of speakers.

The analytical approach (structure of the word), which takes advantage of the linguistic structure of words, attempts to detect and identify the basic components (phonemes and syllables). These are the basic units to recognize. This method is simpler because only the features of the base units, instead of the whole words, have to be registered in the memory.

In fact, both approaches basically are the same; the difference is the entity to be recognized, "the word" for the first and the "phoneme" or syllable for the second.

Working Principle

The structure of the isolated word speech recognition system can be distinguished in two phases:

The training phase—a user dictates the entire vocabulary used in the voice commands in order to create the reference audio signatures of the commands. But for the analytical the user will only dictate some specific words which contain important successions of phonemes. For an independent speaker system, this does not exist.

The recognition phase—the user says the actual voice command which contain the words from the stored vocabulary. Then, the word recognition system is typical problem of pattern recognition. The calculation done in the recognition phase, when comparing speech commands, is not that simple because words can have different forms depending on the user and speech rate. A speaker cannot pronounce several times the same speech sequence with exactly the same rate and same duration.

Also, time alignment is a problem because the user cannot repeat the same speech commands with the same pause between the words. It is very important that a special time warping algorithm is implemented in order to manage this problem.

Comparison methods by dynamic programming have been widely used for recognition of isolated words. The most commonly calculations used for this method are: the Euclidean squared distance, hidden Markov models and neuro-mimetic models. Classifying the calculation techniques after the required processing power, the Euclidean squared distance needs the least of them all. This makes it suitable for every speech recognition system which has a limited hardware budget. The Euclidean squared distance it is the simplest way to determine the similarity between words in speech commands. If the parameterization is done correctly, then the results obtained with this formula can have very high rate accuracy in the identification of the right spoken voice command. To be more precise, with this formula it can be calculated the actual difference between two vectors containing different audio DFT results for example [18] .

OUR METHODOLOGY

With the main characteristics of speech recognition systems presented in the previous paragraphs, the challenge is to put all of those features into a low cost hardware and energy consuming. The system is configured to work on recognizing isolated words based on the global technique, the words being the unit for recognition. The words in the voice commands must have a small pause between them. As well, they are also aligned and delimited by the system. Audio signatures are extracted with the DFT spectral method.

With the help of the normalization process implemented, the system can be considered speaker independent, even though, before usage, the system has to be trained with the actual voice commands that will be used afterwards. Also, by using normalization process, the successful recognition rate is increased.

Users are able to use and store on our system a defined number of voice commands. A voice command has a defined length of 2 seconds, enough for a person to say a few keywords for a command. For the speech recognition system, it's important to be able to distinct commands even though they are said on different tonalities and by different users, thus a normalization process is implemented in the system. This is done on every signature that is stored and that is currently being processed for command identification. Sometimes the speech commands have the same words in their composition. To avoid confusion between commands the system does the identification routine for the whole sentences and individually for each corresponding word in the sentences. Then it compares on how many words have been identified from the spoken command with the ones in a stored voice command. So, the voice command with the most identified words it's taken in account. The Euclidean squared distance formula is used to calculate the similarities between the audio signature of a spoken command and the audio signatures of the stored voice commands. Depending on which result is the smallest or which one is under a predefined level, the right voice command is recognized.

$$d(c,s) = d(s,c) = \sum_{i=1}^{n} (c_i - s_i)^2 \qquad (3)$$

d—distance (similarity between commands)

c—current spoken voice command

s—stored voice command

n—number of sound signatures (time slots) in a voice command

The 8-kHz frequency sampling rate it's chosen because it will offer a frequency range between 0 and 4 kHz and it will match the human voice, which has a frequency range from 300 Hz to 3.3 kHz. A sampling frequency beyond that value will be useless. Figure 4 presents a vocal command represent relative to the time and Figure 5 presents four different DFT applied on this signal.

As it can be seen from the DFT simulation (Figure 5) in the majority of the cases, every time 2 or 3 important frequency peaks with big density stand out. Also, this thing can vary by a little bit, depending on the language that is spoken. In English 3 peaks stand out.

Because the DSP engine in the microcontroller is optimized to do a 256-point length type DFT [19] [20] , this spectral solution is chosen to extract the voice commands signatures. For an incoming audio signal, with a sample rate of 8 kHz, the 256 point length DFT is done every 32 ms, thus for a time window of 2 seconds are obtained about 64 DFT results, from which the voice commands signatures can be extracted.

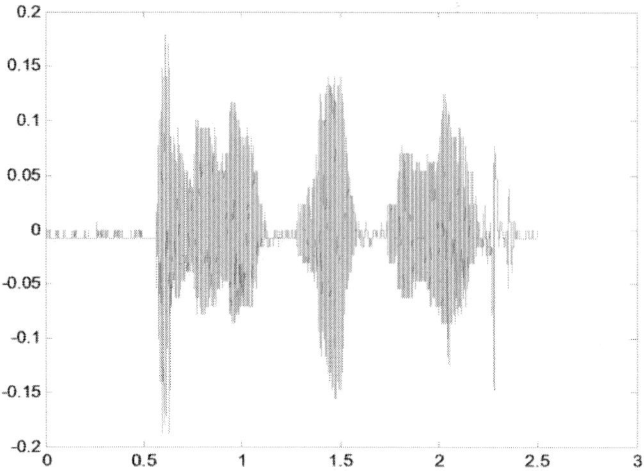

Figure 4. Voice command "Open the window" composed of 3 words.

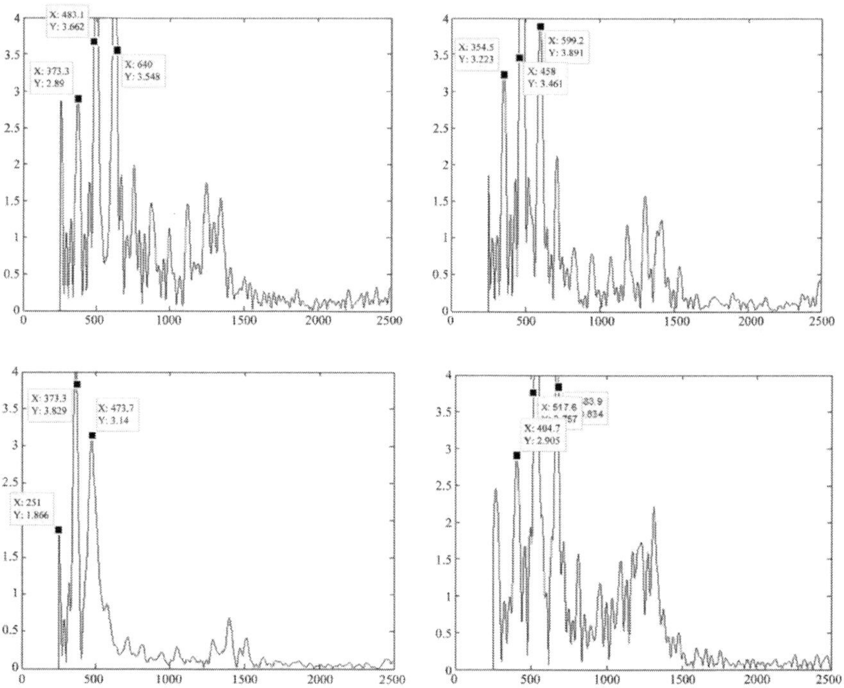

Figure 5. Different 32 ms DFT time windows of a voice command.

$$\mathrm{DFT}_{\mathrm{length}} \div \mathrm{Frequency}_{\mathrm{sample}} = \mathrm{DFT}_{\mathrm{period}}$$

$$256\mathrm{points} \div 8000\mathrm{Hz} = 32\mathrm{ms}$$

$$2048\mathrm{ms} \div 32\mathrm{ms} = 64\mathrm{DFT\ results} \tag{4}$$

The sound signatures with its three important high peaks define the audio signature. These are gathered from each successive 32 ms DFT calculation for a time of 2 seconds resulting in the final voice command audio signature.

To compare, the execution time of a DFT in a not-DSP microcontroller is very long. This time depends of the length of the processed data. For 8 Mhz clocked microprocessor, the execution time of an implementation of a DFT can be calculated by a polynomial expression.

$$t_{\mathrm{execution(ms)}} = 0.065N^2 + 0.2937N + 2.8 \tag{5}$$

For a data of 256 points, the execution lasts 4338 ms which consumes 28.3 μA.h. A DSP, for the 256 points DFT, consumes 0.18 μA.h. For our application, only the DSP can be chosen because of the slowness of the regular microcontroller. Moreover, the electric consumption is reduced by 150, another advantage of using the DSP.

For our algorithm on a DSP, a recognition of a three-second-long text costs 17.28 μA.h. This consumption is compatible with embedded systems. For example, using a button cell CR-2032 (210 mA.h), we can recognize 972 sentences of 3 seconds that gives an equivalent autonomy of more than a month in continuous mode.

ALGORITHM DESCRIPTION

The analog to digital converter is set to process the data captured by the microphone at a sampling rate of 8 kHz and to transfer it into a temporary buffer. Every time this buffer is filled, it triggers a function which starts to do the 256-point length DFT calculation.

At this DFT length and audio sample rate, one unit (frequency bin) of the resulted DFT calculation has a range of frequency of 31.25 Hz. This bin represents the frequency resolution and it contains the actual magnitude of the audio signal in that specific frequency range.

$$\mathrm{Frequency}_{\mathrm{sample}} \div \mathrm{DFT}_{\mathrm{length}} = \mathrm{Frequency}_{\mathrm{resolution}}$$

$$8000\mathrm{Hz} \div 256\mathrm{points} = 31.25\frac{\mathrm{Hz}}{bin} \tag{6}$$

The whole result of the calculation is stored in a vector with a length of 128 values. This contains all the frequency bins and has a frequency range of 0 - 4 kHz. Because this range is too wide for the human voice, it is cropped into a 91-length vector, which corresponds to the range of 280 Hz to 3 kHz. Also, this crop is done in order to eliminate the noise from the low frequency spectrum, caused sometimes by the microphone. The obtained vector represents the magnitude of the raw audio signal in that frequency range for a time of 32 ms.

All DFT calculations and most vector manipulations are done with the DSP engine, integrated in the microcontroller. This vastly reduces the processing time and frees the CPU workload.

In the following step, 3 frequency bins, which have the highest magnitude and represent the highest peaks of the audio signal, are extracted from the resulted vector of the DFT calculation. It is important that, between the selected frequency bins, a distance of at least 3 bins (93.75 Hz) exists, so the system will not pick up values from the same frequency peak.

After the 32 ms sound signature is created, the system is verifying in a loop, for every DFT calculation, if the magnitude of the highest frequency bin is different from 0. In this way, the system knows if something has been spoken by the user and that it is ready to proceed to the following processing steps.

If the system has detected any sign of voice, it starts to record, in a "First-in-First-Out" algorithm, the 3 important high peaks of the 32 ms DFT calculation, for a time length of 2 seconds. For 2 a second length and a 32 ms DFT, the FIFO process will store in total 192 values, which means 64 values for each 3 important frequency peaks. In the same, the LEDs on development board will turn on for 2 seconds to show the user that the audio data is being recorded and also to help him fit his voice command in that time window.

After the recording stops, the values from the FIFO algorithm are distributed in order into 3 separate vectors, each one having a length of 64 values. In one vector are stored the values containing the first highest peak frequency bins, in the second vector are stored the other values containing the second highest peak frequency bins, and in the final vector are stored the third highest frequency bins. These 3 vectors represent the audio signature of the spoken voice command.

Because everyone differs in how they speak, by pronouncing the words at different frequencies and magnitudes, and in order to make the system a speaker independent one, the 3 vectors are normalized. The normalization process is done separately for every vector. It is done by calculating the average of all values from a vector and then by dividing each value with the calculated average.

In the next step the vectors are passed to a time warping process. This process fixes the words length to 12 values (time slots), in each vector, and separates the words at a defined distance. The system is configured to detect and identify a word in a vector, if more than 5 consecutive values of 0 exist after 2 consecutive values different from 0. In this way, the vectors containing the audio signature of the voice command have their words synchronized and can be compared with others.

As the audio signature of the 2-second-long voice command is now processed, the system moves to the next step of comparing the current audio signature with the ones already stored on the flash memory.

If the system has not been trained, no audio signatures are stored on the flash memory; it will just compare the current audio signature with blank audio signatures, resulting in an unidentified voice command. If it has commands stored, it will compare the current signature with stored ones.

The comparison between the audio signatures is done by different techniques using the Euclidean squared distance. Depending on the results, the current voice command is identified, or not, with one of the stored voice commands.

The speech recognition system is configured to have a master voice command in order to prevent the system from mistakenly recognizing different voice commands. This command activates the system for a recognition session, a time window of 10 seconds, in which the user can say his actual voice commands. After the 10 second timer expires, the system deactivates and the user is obliged to repeat the master command in order to resume. The master voice command has the same properties, as the rest of the commands, and it also needs to be stored in the training phase, just like the others.

Finally, after all the processing and calculations are done, the user can now choose to store his desired voice command in order to train the system, if no audio signatures are stored on the flash memory, or to retrain the system, if the user is not satisfied with the already stored voice commands.

RECOGNITION TECHNIQUE

The technique used in recognizing the voice commands is based on the Euclidean squared distance. This formula can be applied in many ways between the audio signatures of the voice commands, but after many experiments, the following two calculation methods have been chosen and they are presented in the Figure 6:

Global distance—this is done by calculating the distance between the whole vectors of the audio signatures. After the 3 vectors are processed, containing first, second and third highest peaks of the 64 time slots of a voice command, they are ready for the distance calculation. First calculation is done between the first vector, containing the first highest peak, of the current processed voice command and the corresponding first vector of a stored voice command. This continues by calculating in the same way for the second and third vectors. In the end three values are obtained representing the distances between the first, second and third vectors of two voice commands. These values are then averaged in ordered to obtain the final distance/difference between vectors.

This calculation is done individually between the current voice command and each voice command stored. If one of the final results is under the value 150 and it's the smallest from the rest of the final values, then the voice command stored, corresponding to the obtained result, is considered the recognized command.

Word distance—this is done by calculating the distance between the words from vectors of the audio signatures. This method was chosen, in addition to the previous one, in order to avoid confusions made by the system in the scenario when the voice commands contain the same words. Also, as the previous method, this calculation is done after the vectors containing the audio signatures are processed. This method begins by calculating the distance between the first word from the first vector, of the current processed voice command, and the corresponding first word from the first vector, of a stored voice command. Then, it continues by calculating in the same way for the next words in the first vector of the voice command, obtaining in total five word distances.

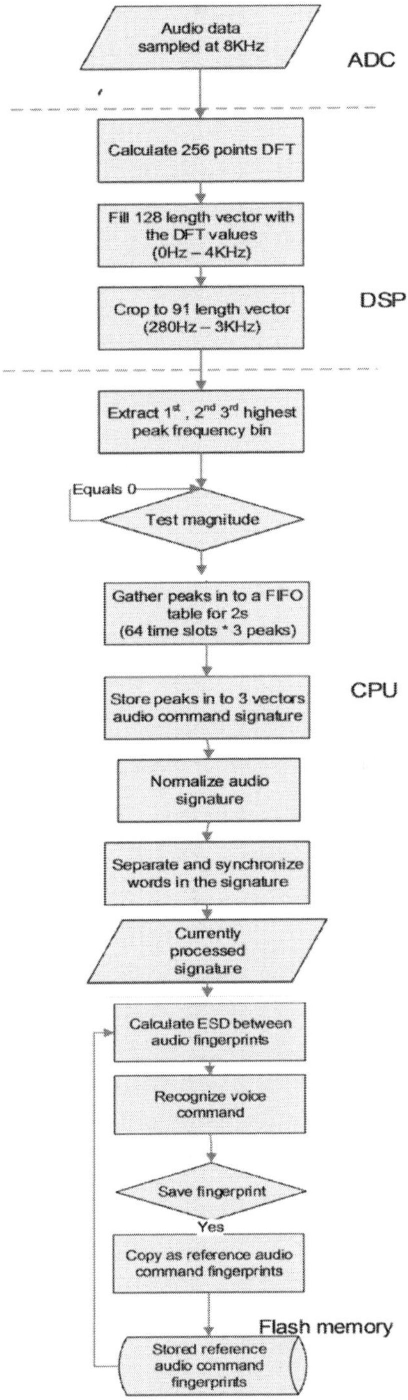

Figure 6. Algorithm description of the speech recognition system.

The calculation is done for the next two vectors, resulting in another ten values and in total fifteen values. These are then averaged, taking in account the words they correspond to, obtaining 5 final distances.

As the previous method, this calculation is done individually between the current voice command and each voice command stored. Depending on which voice command has the biggest number of smallest final distances between words that is considered the recognized voice command.

After calculating both methods in parallel, the voice commands chosen and recognized by the calculation methods are compared in order to make the right decision, resulting in three cases as follows:

- Case 1: If both voice commands identified by the two methods match, then the resulted voice command is recognized.
- Case 2: If the voice commands identified by two methods do not match, then the system will partially recognize the voice command resulted from the global Euclidean squared distance method and it will ask the user to repeat the voice command.
- Case 3: If the value resulted from the global Euclidean squared distance method it's above 150, it will not identify anything and the result from the second calculation method will not be taken in account anymore, forcing the system to not recognize any voice command at all.

Table 1 resumes the results of these three cases.

RESULTS

The developed speech recognition system was tested in order to calculate its accuracy and reliability. Tests were done with English language, a worldwide language [21] [22] . We present here English language, in a quiet and in a noisy environment, with one person and with two persons. The system was trained with the following three voice commands spoken ten times:

Table 1. Voice commands recognition technique.

	Method I (global) result - priority	**Method II (word) result**	**Final result**
Case 1	voice command "a" recognized	voice command "a" recognized	voice command "a" recognized => recognition
Case 2	voice command "b" recognized	voice command "c" recognized	voice command "b" partially recognized => confusion
Case 3	No voice command recognized (>150)	Not taken in account anymore	No recognition

- 1st voice command: "Turn on the light"
- 2nd voice command: "Close the window"
- 3rd voice command: "Open the door"

Speech Test in a Quiet Environment

Output results from the two recognition methods for the first voice command "Turn on the light" are presented in Figure 7 and in Figure 8.

It can be observed Figure 7 that the spoken voice command has the smallest value every time and it's easy to take decision in recognizing the right voice command. A small exception being in the 5th case, when the distance is above the minimum required value of 150 and the system will not recognize anymore the voice command.

For the same spoken voice command, but now with the second method, it can be observed that the spoken voice command has the biggest amount of recognized words every time. So, taking in account that the first method has priority, and by combining the results, it turns out that accuracy of the system for the first spoken voice command is 90%.

Figure 9 and Figure 10 presents the results with the second voice command "Close the window".

It can be noticed that not each the time the spoken voice command has the smallest value in this chart, so in order to improve the accuracy it has to be taken in account the second method. Also, in 2nd and 6th case the values are above 150, so they are not taken in account anymore. Worse, in the 5th case another voice command has the smallest value, decreasing even more the recognition rate.

The second method for the same spoken voice command helps in clarifying which test number has the biggest number of recognized words and confirms the results from the first method. The final successful recognition rate is 70% for this voice command.

Output results from the two recognition methods for the third voice command "Open the door" are shown in Figure 11 and Figure 12.

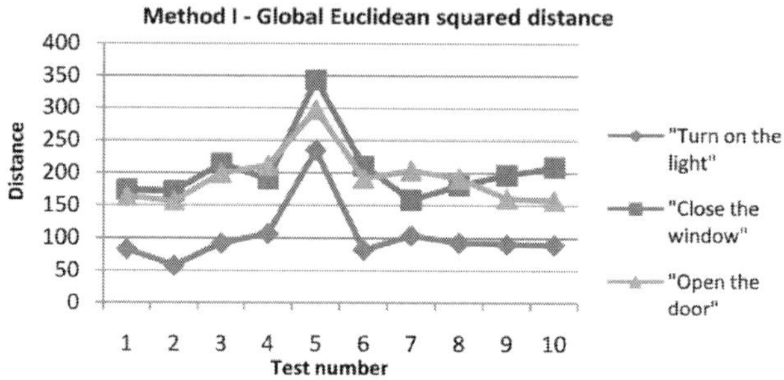

Figure 7. "First training command" first result.

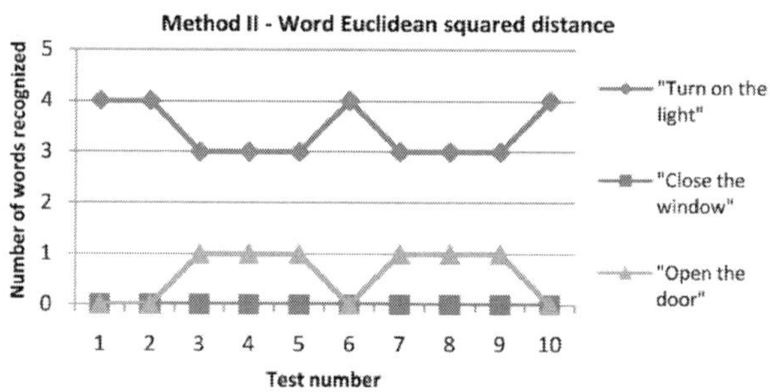

Figure 8. "First training command" second results.

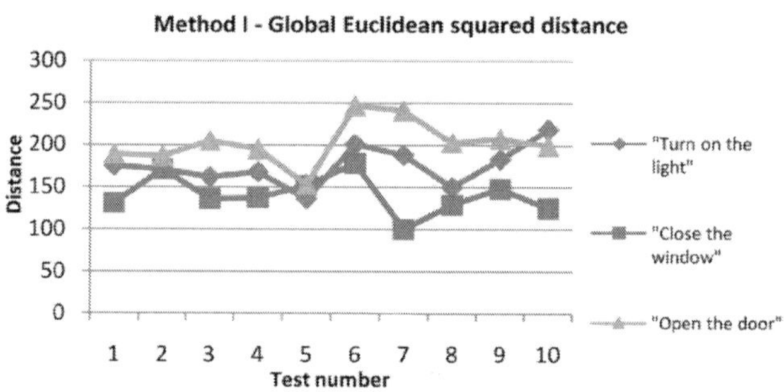

Figure 9. "Second training command" first results.

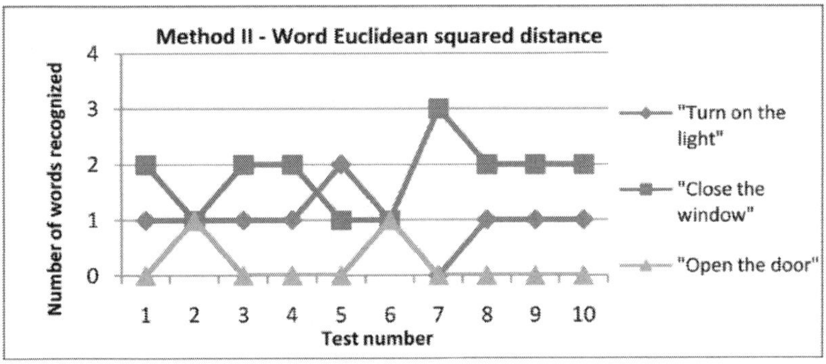

Figure 10. "Second training command" second results.

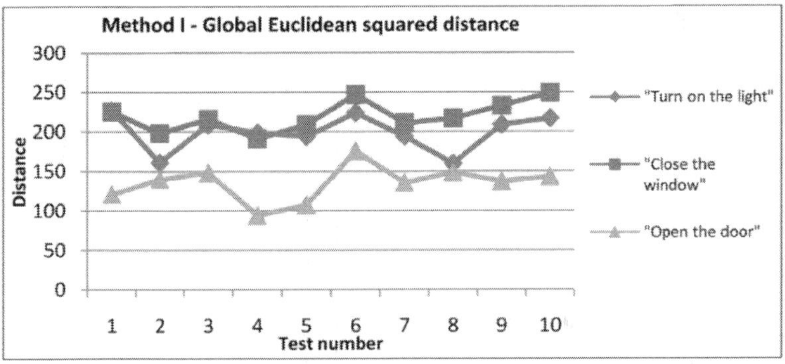

Figure 11. Third training command first results.

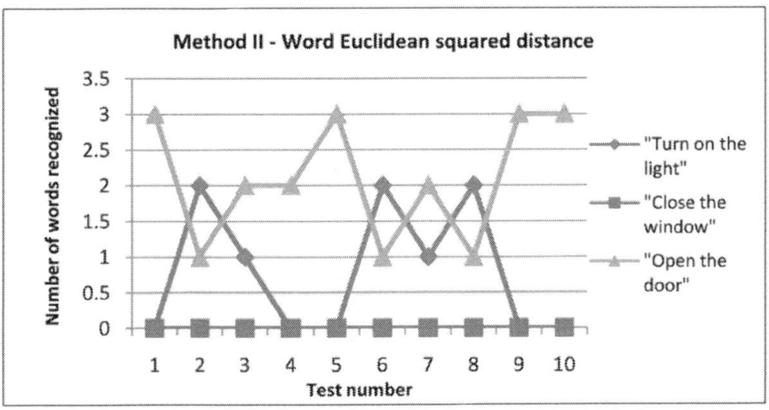

Figure 12. Third training command second results.

In this chart, it can be seen that the spoken voice command has all the time the smallest value. Even though, the distance is pretty big in the 6th test, being above 150, it's easy for the system to take a decision in recognizing the right command. Now it only needs confirmation from the second method.

The second method confuses three times the spoken voice command with another command but it confirms for the rest of the tests. This is the reason why the first method has priority in the final decision. The recognition rate for this command is 70%.

The final results depend very much on how the user pronounces the actual voice command in comparison with the stored voice command. This is the reasons why is better to have two recognition methods and to compare their results in order to take the final decision in recognizing the voice commands

After reviewing and combining all the results in Table 2, obtained from the tests done, it can be concluded that the speech recognition system has achieved successful recognition rate of 90.0%.

Speech Test in a Noisy Environment

To test how the system will perform in a noisy environment, the system was trained in a quiet environment with the same English voice commands from the previous test. Then, the voice commands were spoken ten times each by the same person, but in a noisy environment this time.

The environment noise consisted from white noise and a couple of music files. They were played through a pair of loudspeakers which are capable of outputting 4 watts of power. Table 3 presents the results in this noisy environment.

After the test was completed and all the results were analysed, the system showed a 85% accuracy in recognition, a little bit under accuracy showed in the test with a quiet environment.

Speech Test with Different Persons

To test how it will perform as speaker independent system, the system was trained again in a quiet environment with the same English voice commands from the first test. Then, in the recognition phase, the voice commands were repeated ten times each in a quiet environment, but by a different person this time. Table 4 shows the recognition rate for this test.

Table 2. Test gathered results.

Voice commands	Good recognition	Bad recognition	Confusion	No recognition
"Turn on the light"	90%	5%	5%	0%
"Close the window"	90%	5%	0%	5%
"Open the door"	90%	5%	5%	0%
Total successful recognition: 90.0%				

Table 3. Test gathered results in a noisy environment.

Voice commands	Good recognition	Bad recognition	Confusion	No recognition
"Turn on the light"	85%	5%	10%	0%
"Close the window"	85%	5%	10%	0%
"Open the door"	85%	5%	10%	0%
Total successful recognition: 85%				

Table 4. Test gathered results with different persons.

Voice commands	Good recognition	Bad recognition	Confusion	No recognition
"Turn on the light"	85%	10%	5%	0%
"Close the window"	85%	5%	10%	0%
"Open the door"	85%	5%	10%	0%
Total successful recognition: 85%				

Analyzing the obtained results, the speech recognition system showed still maintaining a good reliability, even though different persons were used for the training phase and recognition phase.

CONCLUSION

The developed speech recognition system has performed with an almost identical accuracy with few words for several users. This system has equivalent results in a quiet and in a noisy environment. It can support different persons too. So this system can be easily deployed in a house. Further, the system can be adapted to another language by changing its processing parameters, like the number of time slots reserved for every word.

REFERENCES

1. Kamarudin, M.R., et al. (2013) Low Cost Smart Home Automation via Microsoft Speech Recognition. International Journal of Engineering & Computer Science IJECS, IJECS-IJENS, 13.
2. Vacher, M., Istrate, D., Portet, F. Joubert, T. (2011) The Sweet-Home Project: Audio Technologyin Smart Homes to Improve Well-Being and Reliance. 2011 Annual International Conference of the IEEE Engineering in Medicine and Biology Society.
3. Georgoulas, C., Raza, A., Güttler, J., Linner, T. and Bock, T. (2014) Proceedings of the International Symposium on Automation and Robotics in Construction, Vilnius, Vol. 31, 1-9.
4. Rabiner, L. and Jaung, B. (1993) Fundamentals of Speech Recognition. Prentice-Hall, Englewood Cliffs.
5. Becchetti, C. and Ricotti, K.P. (2008) Speech Recognition: Theory and C++ Implementation (With CD). John Wiley & Sons.
6. Thiang, D.W. (2009) Limited Speech Recognition for Controlling Movement of Mobile Robot Implemented on ATmega162 Microcontroller. International Conference on Computer and Automation Engineering.
7. Amodei, D., Ananthanarayanan, S. and Anubhai, R. Deep Speech 2: End-to-End Speech Recognition in English and Mandarin. Proceedings of Machine Learning Research, 48.
8. Verma, A., Kumar, A. and Kaur, I. (2018) Automatic Speech Recognition Using Mel-Frequency Cepstrum Coefficient (MFCC) and Vector Quantization (VQ) Techniques for Continuous Speech. International Journal of Advanced and Applied Sciences, 5, 73-78.
9. Kumar, S. (2014) Ubiquitous Smart Home System Using Android Application. International Journal of Computer Networks & Communications, 6, 33-43.
10. Sonia, B. and Sridhar, D.S. (2018) Implementation of Voice Recognition Technology in Hospitals Using Dragon NaturallySpeaking Software. Biometrics and Bioinformatics, 10.
11. Vojtas, P., Stepan, J., Sec, D., Cimler, R. and Krejcar, O. (2018) Voice Recognition Software on Embedded Devices. In: Nguyen, N.T., Hoang, D.H., Hong, T.-P., Pham, H. and Trawiński, B., Eds., Intelligent Information and Database Systems, Vol. 10751, Springer International Publishing, Cham, 642-650.

12. Lai, C.-H. and Hwang, Y.-S. (2018) The Voice Controlled Internet of Things System. 1-3.
13. Basyal, L., Kaushal, S. and Singh, G. (2018) Voice Recognition Robot with Real Time Surveillance and Automation. International Journal of Creative Research Thoughts (IJCRT), 6, 11-16.
14. Newman, M.J. et al. (2015) Embedded System for Construction of Small Footprint Speech Recognition with User-Definable Constraints. Patent US9117449B2, 2015-08-25.
15. Perez-Cortes, J.C. and Guardiola, J.L. (2009) Pattern Recognition with Embedded Systems Technology: A Survey. 20th International Workshop on Database and Ex- pert Systems Application.
16. Jiang, H., et al. (2014) Convolutional Neural Networks for Speech Recognition. IEEE/ACM Transactions on Audio, Speech, and Language Processing, 22, 1533-1545.
17. Deng, L. and Li, X. (2013) Machine Learning Paradigms for Speech Recognition: An Overview. IEEE Transactions on Audio, Speech, and Language Processing, 21, 1060-1089. https://doi.org/10.1109/TASL.2013.2244083
18. IEEE (2012) IEEE Systems, Man, and Cybernetics Society. IEEE Transactions on Systems, Man, and Cybernetics, Part C (Applications and Reviews), 42, C2.
19. Sinha, P. (2009) CPU Architectures for Speech Processing. In: Speech Processing in Embedded Systems, Springer International Publishing, Boston, MA, 55-74
20. Nedevschi, S., Patra, R.K. and Brewer, E.A. (2005) Hardware Speech Recognition for User Interfaces in Low Cost, Low Power Devices. Proceedings of 42nd Design Automation Conference, Anaheim, CA, USA, 13-17 June 2005.
21. Schafer, E.C., et al. (2017) Speech Recognition in Noise in Adults and Children Who Speak English or Chinese as Their First Language. Journal of the American Academy of Audiology. https://doi.org/10.3766/jaaa.17066
22. Li, K., Mao, S., Li, X., Wu, Z. and Meng, H. (2018) Automatic Lexical Stress and Pitch Accent Detection for L2 English Speech Using Multi-Distribution Deep Neural Networks. Speech Communication, 96, 28-36. https://doi.org/10.1016/j.specom.2017.11.003

CHAPTER 12

BigEar: Ubiquitous Wireless Low-Budget Speech Capturing Interface

Stefano Gorla, Sara Comai, Andrea Masciadri, Fabio Salice

Department of Electronics, Information and Bioengineering of the Politecnico di Milano, Como, Italy

ABSTRACT

This article presents BigEar, a wireless low-cost speech capturing interface that aims to realize unobtrusive and transparent context-aware vocal interaction for home automation. The speech recognition process implemented in BigEar system considers noise sources including possible

Citation: Gorla, S. , Comai, S. , Masciadri, A. and Salice, F. (2017), BigEar: Ubiquitous Wireless Low-Budget Speech Capturing Interface. Journal of Computer and Communications, 5, 60-83. doi: 10.4236/jcc.2017.54005.

holes in the reconstructed audio stream and tries to overcome them by means of inexactness toleration mechanisms to improve intelligibility of the reconstructed signal. Key contribution of this work is the use of extremely low cost devices to realize a modular flexible and real-time wireless sensor network. On-field implementation and experiments show that the proposed solution can perform real-time speech reconstruction, while listening tests confirm the intelligibility of the reconstructed signal.

Keywords: Wireless Sensor Networks, Speech Capture, Degraded Speech Recognition, Ubiquitous Systems, Low Cost Architectures

INTRODUCTION

The ageing of world's population will raise the demand and challenges of elderly care in coming years. Based on a study of the US census, the number of people aged over 65 will increase by 101 percent between 2000 and 2030, at a rate of 2.3 percent each year; during that same period, the number of family members who can provide support for them will increase by only 25 percent, at a rate of 0.8 percent each year. Several approaches have been devised to deal with the needs of older people proactively.

Assistive domotics represents a relatively recent effort in this direction addressing the needs of people with disability, older persons, and people with little or no technical affinity, and offers new levels of safety, security and comfort, and thereby the chance to prolong their safe staying at home.

The BRIDGe[1] (Behaviour dRift compensation for autonomous InDependent livinG) project [1] , carried out at Politecnico di Milano-Polo di Como, aims to build strong connections between a person living independently at home and his/her social environment (family, caregivers, social services) by implementing a system that provides focused interventions according to the user's needs.

BRIDGe addresses the needs of people with mild cognitive or physical impairments and, more generally, fragile people whose weakness threatens their autonomy, health or other important aspects of their life. Fragile people need mutual reassurance: they typically want to be independent and autonomous, but they also know that often somebody else must be present to help them.

BRIDGe's core is a wireless sensor-actuator network that supports house control and user behavior detection through a rich and flexible communication system between the person and his/her social environment, aiming at reassuring both the family and the user. BRIDGe is based on a modular architecture that can be easily configured to satisfy the single user needs, including: house control e.g., lighting and shutter control; home appliance monitoring for user activity recognition and energy consumption measurements purposes; presence detection, i.e. identifying the presence of people in specific areas of the house; indoor localization along with status (moving, sitting, falling, and so on); eventand status-based information transmission to inform caregivers promptly about specific events, such as when a fall is detected.

Target of this work is to model, realize and implement a distributed audio acquisition system called BigEar (uBiquitous wIreless low-budGet spEech cApturing inteRface) to support vocal interaction between the user and the assistive environment, for example, to vocally control some parts of a dwelling like lights, doors, etc. BigEar has been built according to the following Wireless Sensor Network [2] requirements:

The adopted technology (hardware and software) has to consider the economical possibilities of people.

The absence of power and/or signal cables is a strong requirement in order to lower costs for house adaptation. Moreover, wireless systems can ensure a higher degree of flexibility and configurability than wired systems.

The key for pervasiveness is distributed computing [3] , an interaction model in which the devices concur in building a result whose information content is more than the sum of single contributions. Moreover, sensors are completely independent and an eventual failure will not completely compromise the result of the sensor network collaboration.

The system should be implemented using a modular approach in order to be scalable and quickly configurable to match the environment characteristics and the user's needs.

Speech recognition should be immediate, so speed of processing is a crucial requirement in order to give the user an immediate feedback; assistive domotic interaction has to be as fast as possible.

The proposed system consists of different modules that take into account the acquisition environment with its acoustic characteristics and the behavior of the sensor-network model. Such modules have been simulated to investigate the archiecture capabilities of the system. Then, a Reconstruction Algorithm reconstructing the audio signal starting from the audio packets received by the microphones has been developed. This work is organized as follows: after a brief analysis of existent solutions in literature (Section 2), in Section 3 the architecture of BigEar system is described, focusing on the characterization of the context of use, on the features of the prototyping board, and on the communication protocol among the components of the system. Section 4 describes the speech acquisition model that has been simulated to define the working parameters before the realization of the system and the real-world implementation. Section 5 explains operating principles of the BigEar Reconstruction Algorithm, focusing on crucial aspects such as energy compensation, time-delay analysis and streams superposition. The audio data captured by means of the real-world prototype have been compared with the ones generated by the simulated model, and results of this comparison are discussed in Section 6. Speed of processing and the quality of the reconstructed speech signal are evaluated in Section 7. Finally, in Section 8 final remarks conclude the paper and look out over the future works.

RELATED WORK

Different solutions have been proposed in the literature exploiting audio in smart homes, briefly described in the following subsections.

Sweet-Home Project

The Sweet-Home project [4] aims at designing a smart home system based on audio technology focusing on three main goals: to provide assistance via natural man-machine interaction (voice and tactile command), to ease social e-inclusion, and to provide security reassurance by detecting situations of distress. The targeted smart environments are multi-room homes with one or more microphones per room set near the ceiling.

To show the results of the project, a smart home was set up. It is a thirty square meters suite flat including a bathroom, a kitchen, a bedroom and a study; in order to acquire audio signals, seven microphones were set in the ceiling. All the microphones were connected to a dedicated PC embedding an 8-channel input audio card. The authors based the architecture on a multichannel audio card; in general dedicated hardware increases costs and reduces flexibility. Moreover, a wired approach is hard to implement since it requires to fix wires onto walls or into existing electrical pipes. BigEar project is based on low-cost hardware and wireless connections in order to preserve flexibiliy, ease of installation and reduce costs.

Wireless Sensor Networks for Voice Capture in Ubiquitous Home Environments

The authors in Palafox and García-Macias [5] present a voice capture application using a wireless sensor network (WSN). The WSN nodes (each node is a MicaZ mote with a high sensitivity microphone) are grouped in clusters with a special node (cluster-head) coordinating the cluster activities in order to avoid to capture and transmit the same voice command by two or more nodes; the authors consider the command duplication unacceptable. Each cluster-head collects audio data from their cluster nodes and relays it to a base station. Each node continuously senses audio signals at 2 kHz sampling frequency; if the sensed signal intensity exceeds a predetermined threshold, the node sends a notification to the cluster-head. The cluster-head selects a node to capture the command; the selected node enters into 8 kHz sampling frequency, captures three seconds of audio (with 8 bit resolution) and transfers the audio data to the cluster-head node which, in turn, relays it to the base station where a computer processes speech recognition tasks. The authors implement two capturing techniques: capture and send without coordination (consisting of human voice detection, three seconds of audio recording and transmission of the data packet to the cluster-head) and coordinate (consisting of human voice detection, node selection by the clusterhead, three seconds of audio recording and transmission of the data packet to the cluster-head). The main limit of this solution, beside having a quite high cost, is the sampling of three seconds instead of having a continuous voice detection and reconstruction. Our solution improves such limitation.

Exploiting WSN for Audio Surveillance Applications: The VoWSN Approach

The work in Alesii et al. [6] focuses on the analysis of fundamental issues about the transmission of the voice using a wireless sensor network (WSN). The paper is based on the MicaZ wireless sensor nodes. The prototype of the system has been developed through the use of the CrossBow MicaZ-TinyOS_ v1.5. and a PC has been used for listening and the analysis of recorded data. The work focuses on audio surveillance systems (i.e. continuous or event-driven audio monitoring tailored to voice signals that have to be archived and/or postprocessed) and on multi-point sampling to make proper signals (or noises) cancellations. BigEar nodes are based on Wixel prototyping boards, that allow to reduce significantly costs with respect of the solution implemented from the authors, that is based on MicaZ motes [7] [8] .

Differentiating Emergency Voice Traffic in Indoor Wireless Activity Monitoring Network

Demir et al. [9] propose an indoor wireless activity monitoring network (WAMN) to transmit data in real time to a monitoring application. The architecture is based on a personal device where data from an accelerometer are transmitted to the sink for the detection of current physical activities (e.g. lying and sitting); an acoustic sensor was located close to the bed of the older person, to transmit short voice commands (e.g. need help, open the door etc.) for emergency attendance. The paper aims at experimenting a network which treats the voice data as emergency traffic and tries to achieve a certain Quality of Service. The system is only simulated considering the voice and activity data into two different Quality of Service classes: class 1 for voice and class 2 for activity data. The voice data segment (55 bytes) is periodically sent in every 3.57 ms and each voice command is represented by 800 data segment while 55 byte activity data segment is periodically sent in every 2.7 s; they assume each captured voice command is digitized with a sampling rate of fs=8KHzfs=8KHz and bit depth of 8-bit. The authors consider only a single voice source for detecting the user command; compared to this approach we use a set of microphones, which are contemporaneously active. In this way, BigEar solution implements a wireless unobtrusive network that takes advantage of the simultaneous multi-sensor acquisition to reconstruct the speech signal regardless of the position of the source with respect to the sensors.

The Research and Design on Time Division Duplex (TDD) Voice WSN

Rong-lin et al. [10] present an architecture (including hardware architecture of voice node, routing node and gateway node) for Voice Wireless Sensor Networks (VoWSN). The main goal of this paper is the quality of the transmitted voice; such an objective justifies both costs and the energy consumption of the presented hardware solution. The voice node includes a voice circuit (with signal amplifier, filtering, acquisition, quantization, encoding and decoding, A/D and D/A conversion), a digital signal processing circuit (with real-time voice digital signal processing including ADPCM encoding to reduce data rate), and a ZigBee module; the routing node includes only the ZigBee wireless communication module, while the gateway nodes includes the ZigBee communication module, the CDMA module, and an ARM processing circuit. The authors implement the time division duplex (TDD) method to achieve duplex voice communications; in particular, they use the same frequency but different time slots for data sending and receiving.

Blind Alignment of Asynchronously Recorded Signals for Distributed Microphone Array

In this work, Ono et al. [11] present an architecture of independent recording devices that is used as a distributed microphone array. The main goal is to introduce a novel method for the alignment of recorded signals to estimate the localization of microphones and sources. The authors implemented only a simulative experiment with 9 microphones and 8 sources randomly positioned. As source signals, real-recorded hand claps were used and each source was not overlapped each other. The sampling frequency used by the authors was 44,100 Hz and the signal length was 5.0 s. High sampling frequency force the use of devices with high computing capabilities that reflects on costs of the overall architecture. Moreover, it requires high bandwidth in order to transmit data between nodes. BigEar solution focuses on vocal signals and minimizes bandwidth requirements. As it will be discussed in following sections, our approach ensures a proper alignment of audio streams generated by different sensors.

BigEar Approach

The approach proposed in this work tries to improve the current state of the art by providing a faster and flexible access to the transmission channel that allows a more widespread acquisition, based on a low cost solution. Among non functional requirements we have considered that house adaptation should be avoided to ensure high degree of modularity and configurability. Moreover, closed systems and dedicated hardware have been considered as second-best choices not only for their licensing costs, but mainly to keep high levels of flexibility.

BIGEAR ARCHITECTURE

Figure 1 illustrates the architecture of the BigEar system. It is composed of a network of audio sensors that distributively capture audio in a room. The speech is sent to a main receiver (BigEar Receiver), acting as an interface that converts speech packets received via radio channel into serial data to be sent to the Base Station. The Base Station contains the application logic to handle speech packets. Since the audio sensors perform a space-time sampling of the audio inside a room, the application logic tries to reconstruct a good-quality speech stream starting from packets that arrive to the base station with different timestamps and with different physical characteristics. Indeed, each sensor samples the audio signal that reaches the microphone after undergoing variations due to the physical model of the environment: different delays and amplitudes that depend on the position of the person with respect to the sensors, and reflections diffusions due to the geometry of the room and materials of the walls and furniture.

Granularity of space-time sampling is influenced by:

- Number of audio sensors w.r.t the dimensions of the room: the bigger is the number of sensors spread in the room, the finer is the granularity of space sampling.
- Audio sensor internal characteristics and constraints: each sensor needs time in order to sample data (depending on ADC type), store them into buffers and send them to the main receiver.
- Network communication protocol characteristics and constraints: the number of packets sent to the main receiver is affected by the number of collisions that may happen on the channel and also by the protocols themselves (handshaking, request-response timings, timeslot allocations).

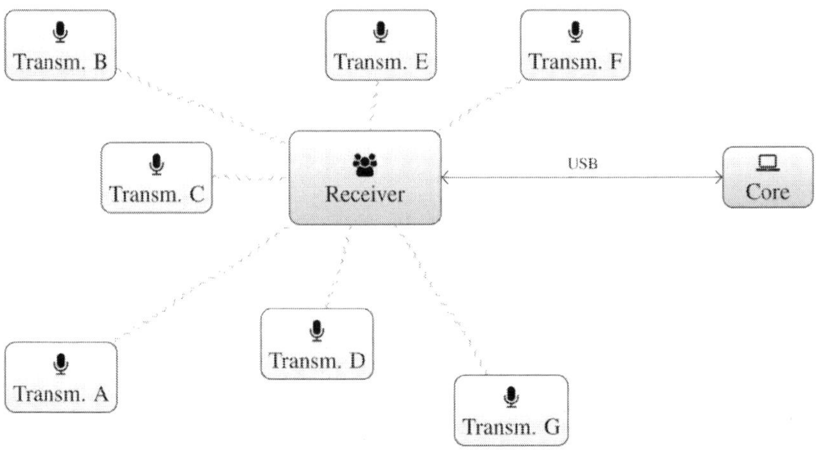

Figure 1. Overview of the BigEar architecture.

BigEar Audio Sensors

The leaf nodes of the architecture are represented by the audio sensors, that are built using Wixel Programmable USB Wireless Modules, general-purpose boards featuring a 2.4 GHz radio and USB port. The Wixel is designed around the CC2511F32 System-on-Chip (SoC) from Texas Instruments, which has an integrated radio transceiver, 32 KB of flash memory, 4 KB of RAM, and a fullspeed USB interface.

Wixel's ADC is connected to a simple signal acquisition and conditioning stage that captures audio signals. ADC resolution represents an important design choice: the higher is the resolution, the lower is the quantization error. On the one hand, low resolutions allow high sampling frequency and so a higher temporal resolution with the drawback of a lower number of quantization levels; on the other hand, high resolutions reduce quantization error granularity. This is an important key factor in signal post-processing.

BigEar Receiver

The only task of the BigEar Receiver is to act as a Radio-to-USB interface (and vice versa) between BigEar Audio Sensors and the Base Station. It mainly receives radio packets from the sensors, transforms them into hexadecimal nibbles and sends them to the Base Station via the USB port. When the Base Station needs to send commands to the sensors (or to reply to protocol messages), BigEar Receiver receives hexadecimal nibbles through the USB port, converts them into bytes and sends them using the built-in radio module. Like BigEar Audio Sensors, also the BigEar Receiver is based on a Wixel Programmable Module.

CC2511F32 SoC has been programmed in order to handle up to 256 different radio channels [12] . All the sensors share the same channel used by the BigEar Receiver; if the network architecture requires channels separation (e.g., to reduce the number of collisions), a second BigEar Receiver connected to another USB port of the Base Station is needed.

Base Station

The Base Station is the device that collects data from the sensors and arranges packets in order to produce a clear and intelligible speech signal. In order to receive packets from audio sensors, it needs to be connected via USB port to the BigEar Receiver, which acts as a bidirectional Radio-to-USB dongle between the Base Station and the wireless audio sensors.

The Base Station receives radio packets containing each one a set of bufferized audio samples tagged with a timestamp and the sensor ID; for each sensor, audio samples are arranged according to their timestamp. In this way, for each sensor a coherent but incomplete stream is obtained: indeed, audio samples are in the right time position with respect to the sensor timestamp, but there is no guarantee that the transmission time is less than, or at most equal to, the sampling time.

Once the samples have been sorted by their timestamps, the application performs a time delaying-or-advance of the audio streams coming from the sensors in order to remove the delays caused by the different distances between the mouth of the user and the sensors. Therefore, in-phase audio contributions are obtained; they can be summed each other in order to produce a seamless stream.

During the alignment process the different energy contribution of the sensors are considered: the closer is the sensor to the user, the bigger will be the signal amplitude and vice versa.

Figure 2 summarizes the Speech Reconstruction Logic carried out by the Base Station: in the left plot in Figure 2(a), audio packets can be seen as received from the Base Station. Then, the Base Station exploits timestamp information carried by each audio packet to arrange audio samples onto the sensor's timeline (right plot in Figure 2(a)). Figure 2(b) illustrates the operating principles of cross-correlation analysis that allows the Base Station to obtain the in-phase contributions that will be superposed to generate a unique, coherent and intelligible speech signal.

Network Protocols

Network protocols have a big impact on the efficiency of the whole system: collisions, granularity of the network of sensors and presence of protocol messages can affect the number of audio packets transmitted and received successfully. In general, when the granularity of the network increases, also the likelihood of collisions grows. At the same time, the number of service messages to implement synchronization mechanisms have to be increased in order to reduce the number of collisions. This can be done at the expense of the channel availability and software complexity.

The simplest protocol that can be adopted in this scenario is ALOHA [13] . Our application has been tested using the pure ALOHA protocol (without acknowledge) in order to exploit and examine system capabilities with the simplest communication protocol.

SPEECH ACQUISITION MODEL AND IMPLEMENTATION

Figure 3 shows a functional view of the BigEar application within its acquisition environment. It is composed of four interconnected modules: the Audio Model block performs the acoustic simulation of the acquisition environment, the Sensor Network Model (which is in turn composed of two inner blocks) simulates the behavior of the transmitters-receiver network; finally, the Speech Reconstruction block performs the reconstruction of the speech signal.

While the first three blocks concerning the behavior of the sensor-receiver network have been simulated, the Speech Reconstruction block has been implemented and its prototype will be described and discussed in Section 5.

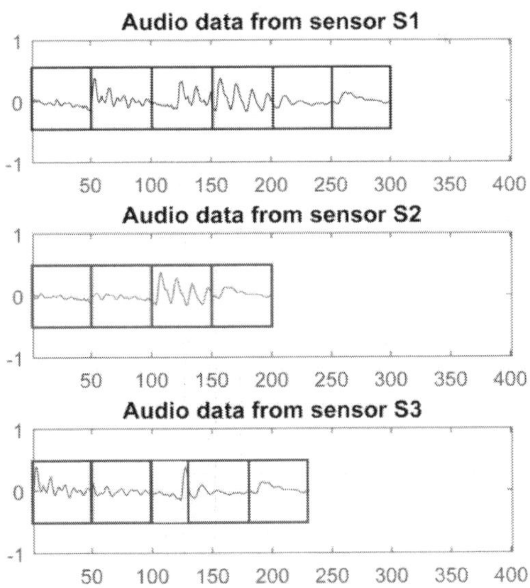

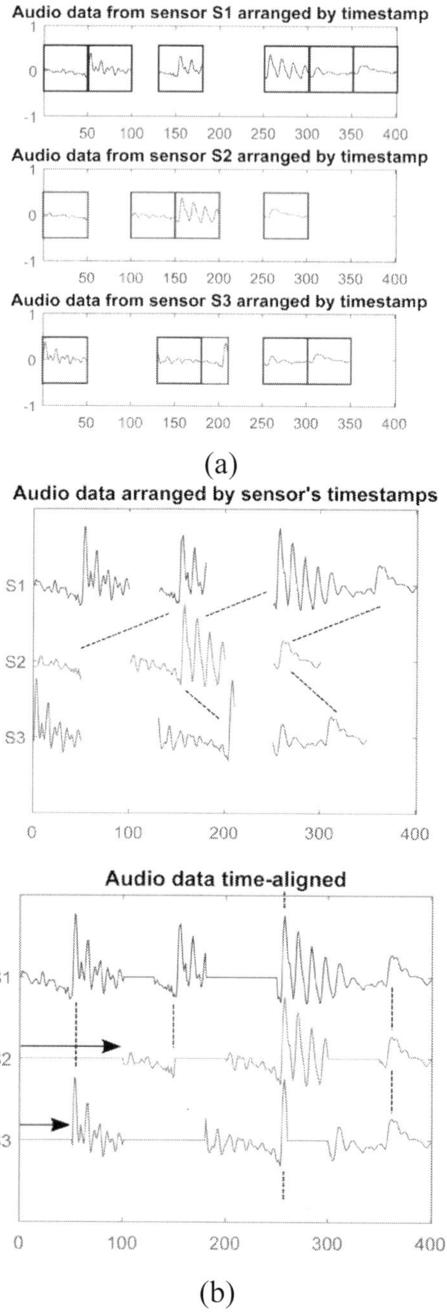

Figure 2. Base station reconstruction logic. (a) Audio packets arranged w.r.t. their timestamp; (b) Audio packets are aligned exploiting cross-correlation between signals.

Audio Model

The Audio Model block models the acoustic environment and sets: the room dimensions (and optionally other parameters such as reflection and diffraction coefficients of walls), the location of the sensors and of the audio source. Once an input audio file is provided, the block produces an audio stream for each sensor. Each stream differs for its amplitude, delay and diffusion, depending on the acoustics characteristics of the room and on the position of the sensor with respect to the source.

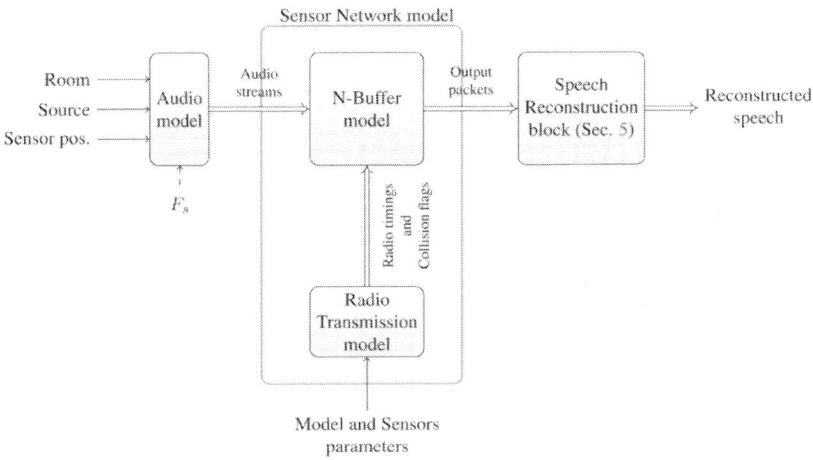

Figure 3. Architecture model.

In order to create an audio model of the typical use case, we made some assumptions about the typical environment where the system may work. The room is modeled as a parallelepiped represented by a three-dimensional space bounded by six surfaces (four walls, ceiling and floor). Each room surface has its own absorption and scattering (diffusion) coefficients. Sound scattering due to furniture and other objects in the room can be approximated by higher levels of overall room diffuseness. Audio modeling is performed by means of MCRoomSim multichannel acoustics MATLAB simulator [14] .

Sensor Network Model

This module recreates a realistic simulation of the behavior of the network where each sensor samples audio signals, buffers them into packets of a specific size and sends them according to a network communication logic. The module is internally split in two parts: the Radio Transmission model, that implements the communication protocol including possible interactions between a receiver and the transmitters or between transmitters, and the N-buffer model, that carries out the internal buffer mechanism of each transmitter.

The Sensor Network module receives in input the audio streams generated by the audio simulator described in Section 4.1, and provides as output the packets of audio sampled and transmitted by each sensor.

Radio Transmission model This block implements the pure ALOHA protocol described in Section 3.4, where each transmitter sends data whenever there is a packet to send and then waits for a random delay before sending another packet. Since audio data are time-dependent, for our purposes it is worthless to re-transmit audio packets, so the transmitter will not wait for any acknowledgment from the receiver. The random delay between transmissions is obtained by the internal random number generator of each transmitter and it is chosen between 0 and a maximum value $T_{maxDelay}$.

The model also checks for collisions. Given the time instant $t_{(i,j)}$ in which the jth transmitter starts to transmit the ith packet, and called t_{busy} the duration of the transmission, all the transmissions started in the interval $[t_{(i,j)}-t_{busy}, t_{(i,j)}+t_{busy}$, where t_{busy} are marked as colliding.

N-Buffer model This block implements the buffering system internal to each transmitter. In a real world, data are continuously sampled and buffered by each transmitter in order to be ready to send them when needed; during the simulation, instead, the time instants in which transmission occurs are known, but we need to model the buffering structures to know which data are ready for being transmitted. This block produces in output the audio samples packed as if they were coming from real transmitters. The structure of each packet is described in Figure 4: each packet contains the ID of the transmitter, the timestamp of the first sample of the packet and a number of samples that correspond to the frame size of each buffer. Only the timestamp of the first sample is sent, since the timestamps of other samples can be inferred by adding $\tau i=i/F_s$, where ii is the (0-based) index of ith sample in the packet and F_s is the sampling frequency. Multiple buffering allows the sensor to work simultaneously on read and write sides: a periodical interrupt routine acquires the signal and stores samples into the write frame, while the main loop can read from the read frame for the transmission.

Real-World Implementation

The three modules described so far compose the virtual model that has been used in order to define the working parameters before the realization of the prototypes. In the real world, the system is composed of a set of audio sensors that perform a space-time sampling of a room. Before sampling, the audio signal converted by each microphone capsule has to be amplified and biased in order to match to ADC characteristics. Each audio sensor samples the signal and packs data into frames in order to send them to the receiver. The multi-buffer internal structure of each transmitter allows an efficient application logic where the sampling stage is managed by means of a timer-handled interrupt routine, and the network logic is handled by the main loop of the applications. Network structure can be layered onto several radio channels in order to reduce the number of collisions. A separate BigEar Receiver is needed for each radio channel.

Tr. ID	Timing data of first sample		FRAME_SIZE samples
ID	Timestamp	T4CNT	1st sample ... N-th sample
1 byte	4 bytes	1 byte	FRAME_SIZE · size(sample) bytes

Figure 4. BigEar data field structure.

Once the packets arrive to the BigEar receiver, they are converted into hexadecimal nibbles and serially sent to the Base Station by means of the USB port. The Base Station, in its experimental form, is composed of a pipelined application that listens to each BigEar Receiver connected to the USB ports of the machine, receives audio packets and stores them into an ordered sequence of files that are processed by means of a MATLAB script that reconstructs the audio data using the reconstruction principles described in Section 5.

SPEECH RECONSTRUCTION

This section illustrates how audio packets are processed in order to produce the best speech signal in terms of intelligibility.

Starting point of the Speech Reconstruction is constituted by the audio packets received by the Base Station from each audio sensor. Due to sound propagation laws, the closer is the sensor to the source, the higher will be the power of captured audio signal; so, in order to preserve energy of the reconstructed signal, audio packets are unbiased and normalized. Then, audio samples are arranged using timestamp information contained in each packet (as already illustrated in Figure 4).

Delays introduced by the different distances between the source and the audio sensors (the closer is the sensor to the source, the lower will be the time of arrival of pressure wave to the microphone) are compensated in the streams alignment stage using cross-correlation analysis.

When the signals have been properly aligned they can be superposed with several summing or replacing methods in order to preserve the signal energy and not to introduce energy variations due to the different number of contributions that are summed at the same time.

The flowchart in Figure 5 illustrates the operation performed by the Speech Reconstruction module; they are described in the next subsections.

Energy Compensation

Audio packets have to be processed in terms of energy compensation to prevent distortions. In particular, the following steps are performed:

- Bias removal, in order to eliminate possible incorrect polarization of the input stage.
- Normalization of input signals, to remove the amplitude attenuation due to the different distances between the speech source and the sensors.

Bias Removal

Incorrect polarization of the input signal can affect the result of the reconstruction block, that is based on the summation of contributions that vary randomly in time. Audio signals coming from different sensors are affected by different polarization. The summation of different DC components corresponds to the superposition to the audio signal of a square wave whose frequency and amplitude are randomly changing, introducing in this way harmonic distortion to the speech signal, as illustrated in Figure 6.

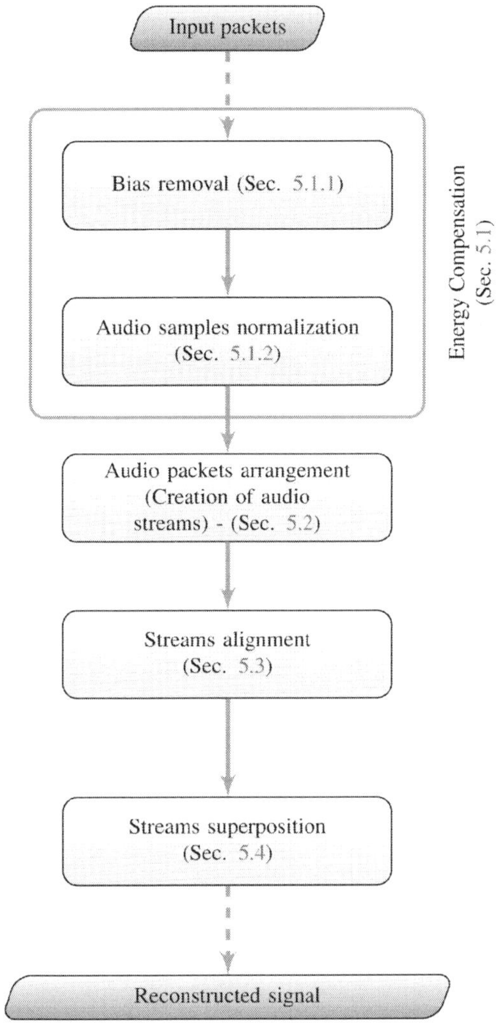

Figure 5. Flowchart of the signal reconstruction block.

$$a_{(i,\bar{j})} = a_{(i,\bar{j})} - \mathbb{E}\left[a_{(i,\bar{j})} \right] = a_{(i,\bar{j})} - \sum_{k=1}^{N} \frac{a_{(i,\bar{j})}}{N}, \tag{1}$$

where N is the number of sensors.

Normalization

Normalization removes energy dependence on the distance between the speech source and the sensor. In this way, neglecting differences in frequency response of microphones and small variations in spectral content due to room acoustics, contributions of different sensors can be summed without compensations coefficients:

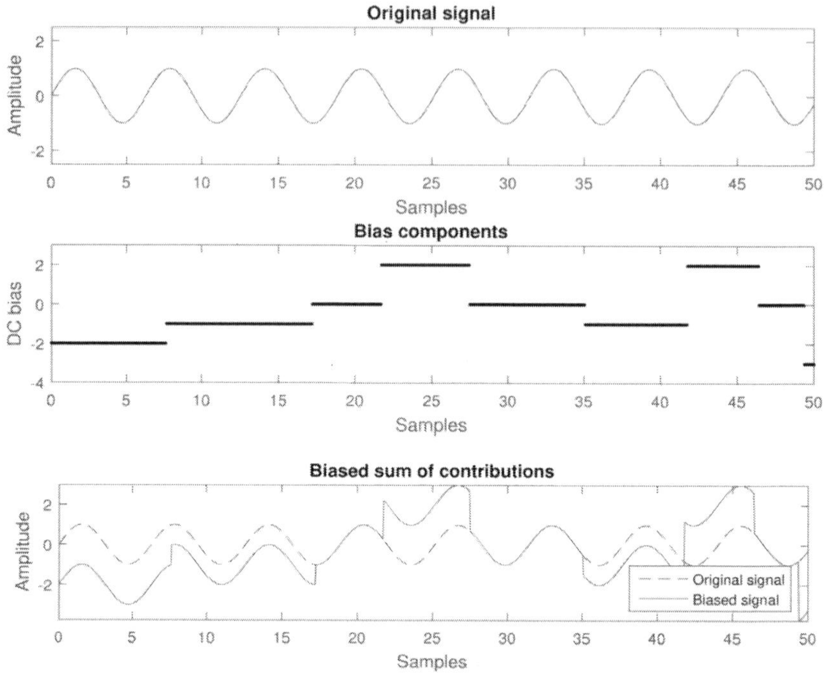

Figure 6. The image shows the effect of the acquisition of the same signal by means of different sensors, each one characterized by a different DC bias.

$$a_{(i,j)} = \frac{a_{(i,j)}}{\max\limits_{1 \le k \le N} a_{(k,j)}} \quad \forall j \in (1, N). \tag{2}$$

Audio Packets Arrangement

The second step of Speech Reconstruction is the arrangement of audio packets. Audio samples are extracted from each packet and get ready for processing using two matrices: A and P , where each element a(i,j)∈A represents the ith sample transmitted by the jth sensor and the corresponding element $p_{(i,j)}$∈P represents the position of the audio sample in the stream expressed in discretetime units:

$$p_{(i,j)} = \left\lfloor F_s \cdot \left(t_{(i,j)} - t_{\min(j)}\right)\right\rfloor \quad \text{where} \quad t_{\min(j)} = \min_{j=\overline{j}}\left(t_{(i,j)}\right). \tag{3}$$

Using position information, audio samples are correctly spaced on the sensor's timeline. For each sensor $j: 1 < j \leq N$, a vector y_j of samples is created:

$$y_j\left(p_{(i,j)}\right) = a_{(i,j)} \,. \quad (4)$$

The elements in y_j where no audio samples are present are 0-filled.

Streams Alignment

The streams generated from audio data coming from sensors are aligned to reduce the delay due to the distance of the speech source with respect to the position of the sensors. The alignment is obtained by using the cross-correlation function [15] . In order to apply it efficiently, the audio streams are processed according to their informative contribution: they are sorted by their normalized power in descending order to allow the cross-correlation algorithm to work in the best condition.

Cross-correlation is a measure of similarity of two series as a function of the lag of the one relative to the other. For two generic discrete functions f[m] and g[m] , cross-correlation measure is defined as:

$$R_{fg}[n] = (f \star g)[n] \triangleq \sum_{m=-\infty}^{+\infty} f^*[m]g[m+n], \quad (5)$$

where f* denotes the complex conjugate of f . The equation essentially slides the gg function along the x-axis, and calculates the integral of their product at each position. When the functions match, the value of (f⋆g) is maximized. Thus, applying cross-correlation to the streams y_i and y_j generated by two different sensors i and j means to find the delay n (expressed in number of samples) that should be applied to y_j to obtain the best in-phase superposition with y_i .

Envelopes Cross-Correlation

A drawback of Cross-correlation function is the inability in discriminating between the true signal and noise or holes.

Cross-correlation function operates on signals that, for their origin, are noisy and holey. If holes and noise are negligible, cross-correlation gives expected results; if sequence of zeros (holes) are much bigger than the signal itself, or if the signal is subject to particular types of noises such as impulse trains, the Cross-correlation function would produce wrong results. To overcome this problem, instead of applying Cross-correlation function directly on noisy or holey signals, it has been applied to the positive envelopes of the signals themselves. A positive envelope is a particular representation of a signal that evidences the shape of the signal. Figure 7 illustrates the result of the alignment step of the envelopes. On the image, for the sake of readability, envelopes of the streams coming from different sensor have been shifted along y-axis. It can be noted that peaks and valley of the signals are globally aligned. This alignment technique offers higher robustness with highly noisy or highly depleted streams, although the effort for a better alignment could be frustrated from the lower intelligibility of the speech signal.

Streams Superposition

Once audio streams obtained by sensor acquisition have been made uniform by means of unbiasing and normalizations, and they have been delayed to make them coherent, they need to be superposed in order to reconstruct the recorded speech signal. Two methods have been implemented: Weighted Sum of Contribution and Holes Replacement.

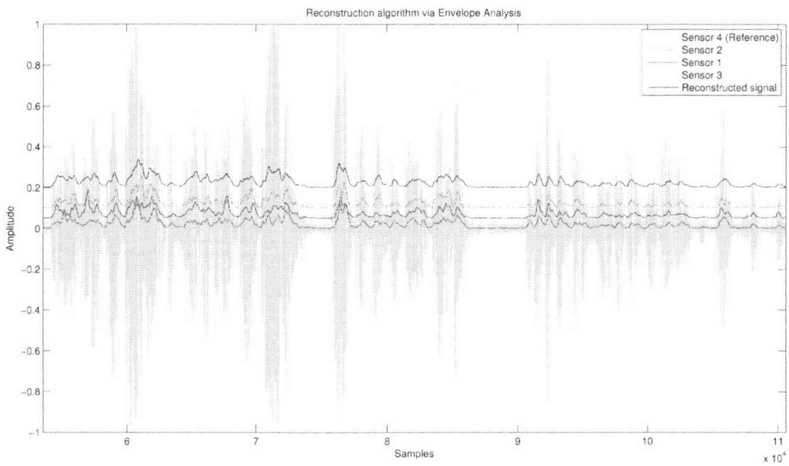

Figure 7. Cross-correlation analysis and alignment on signal's envelopes.

Weighted Sum of Contributions

Contribution coming from different sensors are summed and scaled to prevent amplitude artifacts. Given $y_{(i,j)}$ the ith sample of the audio stream coming from jth sensor and w(i) the number of sensors that contribute to the ith sample, the ith sample of the resulting stream y_{sum} is given by:

$$y_{\text{sum}}(i) = \frac{\sum_{j=1}^{N}(y_{i,j})}{w(i)}. \qquad (6)$$

Weighted Sum is needed for energy preservation and for avoiding harmonic distortions due to the summation of contributions. Figure 8 illustrates an example of distortion caused by the sum of multiple contributions without weighting.

Holes Replacement

Weighted Sum of Contribution presents some drawbacks: it does not take into account the big differences in the spectrum of signals and in the environment contributions between sensors located in different places. Each BigEar Audio Sensor is subject to an environment contribution that depends on:

- The distance between the sensors and the speech source;
- The position of the sensors in the environment.

Contributions can be very different in terms of signal spectrum and of reverberation. In general, the closer the sensors, the lower will be the overall effect of the environment-inducted artifacts since spectrum of the signals will be similarly colored and reverberation tails will be alike.

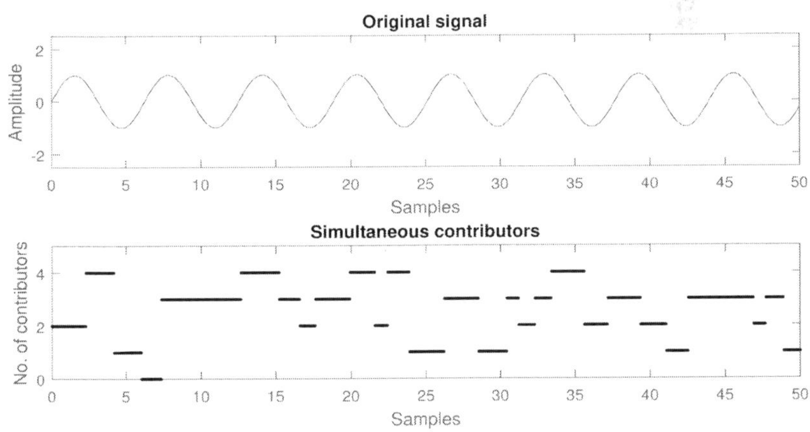

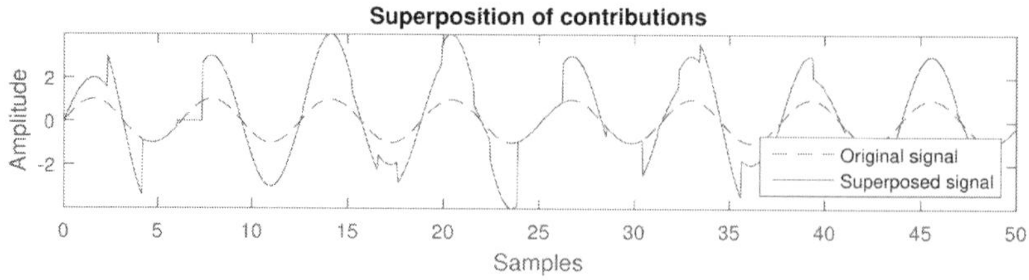

Figure 8. Harmonic distortion due to unweighted sum of contributions.

For this reason, an alternative superposition policy has been tested: instead of performing a weighted sum of each contribution, only the holes in the most powerful audio stream are filled with contributions coming from other sensors. This method reduces the number of summation artifacts, provided that the reference signal (the one on which the holes will be replaced with samples coming from other sensors) has the higher number of valid samples, otherwise there is the risk that replacing artifacts will become prominent with respect to summing artifacts. A comparison metric between Weighted Sum and Holes Replacement will be discussed in Section 7.2.

BIGEAR SIMULATION AND MODEL VALIDATION

Once the system has been implemented and the prototype realized, some metrics have been defined to compare the data captured by means of the BigEar prototype and the data obtained by means of the BigEar simulated model described in Section 4.

This Section focuses on the quality of reconstructed signal analyzing amount of overlapping data between the stream generated by each sensor, while Section 7 illustrates system capabilities in terms of speed of processing and outlines qualitative aspects of the reconstructed speech.

Metrics Definition

The metrics defined in this sections provide quantitative measures concerning the reconstructed speech signal. As already mentioned in Section 5, the success of speech recognition is influenced by the number and the size of holes in the reconstructed signal. Moreover, the BigEar Reconstruction algorithm convergence is influenced by the amount of information that can be overlapped for the Cross-correlation alignment. The following metrics are therefore defined:

$$Fill\_ratio = \frac{\text{No} \cdot \text{of samples}}{N} \quad \text{where } N = \text{Length of the stream}\left(\text{in samples}\right).$$

Referring to the reconstructed signal, it represents the amount of samples with respect to the total length of the stream. The more the value is close to 1, the more the reconstructed signal is complete.

$NoH = \text{Normalized number of } 0 - ed \text{ sequences}$

$SoH = \text{Average size of } 0 - ed \text{ sequences.}$

Since reconstructed signal is given by the superposition of audio packets sampled by different sensors at random time instants, it can be affected by sequences of empty samples. In conjunction with NoH , SoH characterizes the distribution of empty samples (holes) into the reconstructed signal. In case of constant Fill_ratio, SoH and SoH allow to compare whether empty samples are gathered into few big blocks or are diffused into many small blocks.

Sf=Averagenumberofcontributorpersample.

Sf gives a measure of the contribution of each single transmitter to the construction of the final speech signal. $Sf \in (0, N_{TX}]$ where N_{TX} is the number of transmitters. The higher Sf , the higher the overlapping of the streams obtained by the different transmitters.

Simulation Setup

Simulations have been performed using the BigEar Simulator described in Section 4 in a MATLAB 2015b environment [16] using McRoomSim v. 2.14 [14] and varying some parameters in order to study system behavior under different configurations. The parameters that have been changed are: the number of sensors, their positions in the room, the radio channel configuration (how many transmitters communicating on the same radio channel), and the maximum delay between adjacent transmission of the same transmitter.

From these simulations, Statistic data and Metrics have been calculated according to Section 6.1. These data will be compared with real data obtained from On-field setup (Subsection 6.3) and discussed in Section 6.4.

On-Field Setup

Near-field Tests During Near-field tests, the consistence between the simulated model and the real world has been probed. In this setup, BigEar Audio Capture boards were placed side by side on a plane surface, and the speaker has been asked to talk at a distance of about 0.6 m far from the microphones. Then data have been captured using different configurations:

- Number of transmitters and channel configuration. Character sequences indicate the number of channel and how many transmitters are transmitting on the same channel (e.g. AAB means two transmitters on radio channel A and one transmitter on radio channel B):
  - One transmitter: A.
  - Two transmitters: AA-AB.
  - Three transmitters: AAA-AAB.
  - Four transmitters: AAAA-AAAB-AABB.
- Maximum delay between adjacent transmissions from the same transmitter ($T_{maxDelay}$ parameter): 1-3-7-15-31-63 ms.

Far-field Tests During Far-field tests, the focus has shifted on the Reconstruction Algorithm. This is a test stage close to real situation since BigEar Audio Capture boards have been fixed to poles 1.60 m high from ground level and have been placed in a medium-size room. The talker has been asked to speak from an asymmetric position to examine the signal power differences between the different streams.

Figure 9 shows the obtained plots; black asterisks mark real values obtained from the prototypes, while lines indicate the simulated ones. By varying the $T_{maxDelay}$ parameter and the number of transmitters, the obtained curves are asymptotic. Differences are notable when $T_{maxDelay} \in \{1,3,7\}$, i.e., when the average distance between adjacent transmissions of the same transmitter are comparable with the duration of a frame of samples

$$(samples\_per\_frame \cdot sampling\_period = 20 \times \frac{1}{6040\,\text{Hz}} = 3.31\,\text{ms}).$$

This difference is due to the modular structure of the BigEar Simulator: the N-buffer Internal model (Section 4.2) does not communicate to its predecessor the Radio Transmission model (Section 4.2)-any information about the buffer status. In the real world, if the buffer is empty, no transmission happens; instead, the Radio Model makes no considerations on the buffer status, with the result that virtual transmitters that have no data to transmit also contribute to the saturation of the audio channel and then to the valid packet loss.

Looking at Fill_ratio, it can be observed that in most cases the real Fill_ratio is slightly higher than the simulated Fill_ratio. The motivation is due to the fact that the model adopts $T_{busy} = 1$ ms as duration of the transmission, while for the prototype the measured duration of a transmission is 0.937 ms.

In general, the increase of the number of transmitters leads to an increment of the overlap between sampled data, while the increase of the used radio channel leads to the reduction of the collisions between packets traveling on the same channel. By comparing Figure 9(a) with Figure 9(b) it can be observed that doubling the number of transmitters and working on 2 channels instead of 1, a big increment in Fill_ratio and in Sf (support factor) are obtained, thus improving the quality of signal (in term of size of holes) and the support factor, i.e. the quantity of overlapped samples between the streams.

EXPERIMENTAL RESULTS AND EVALUATION

In this section experimental results will be evaluated to test the reactivity of the system and the accuracy of the speech recognition process.

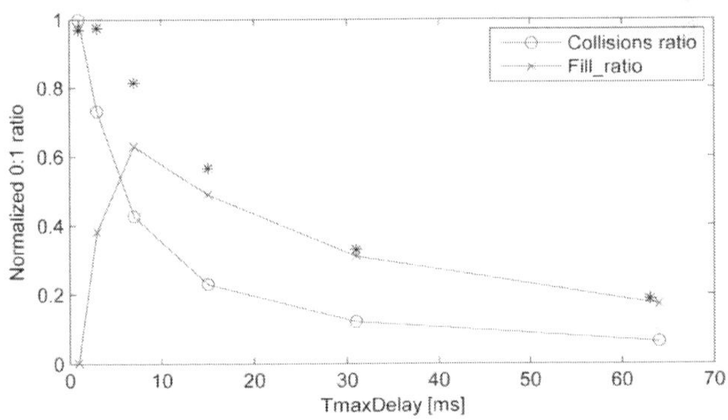

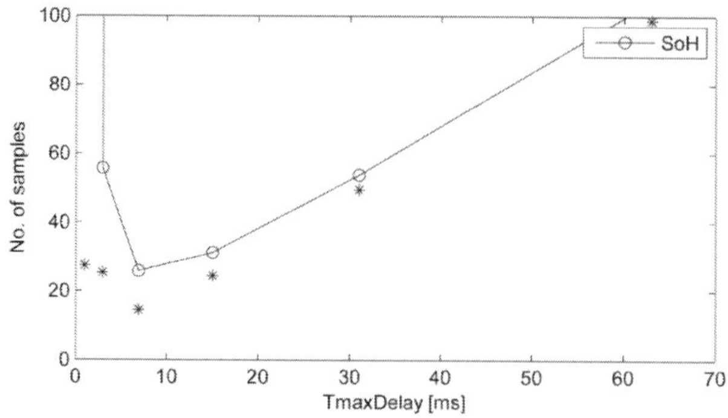

(a)

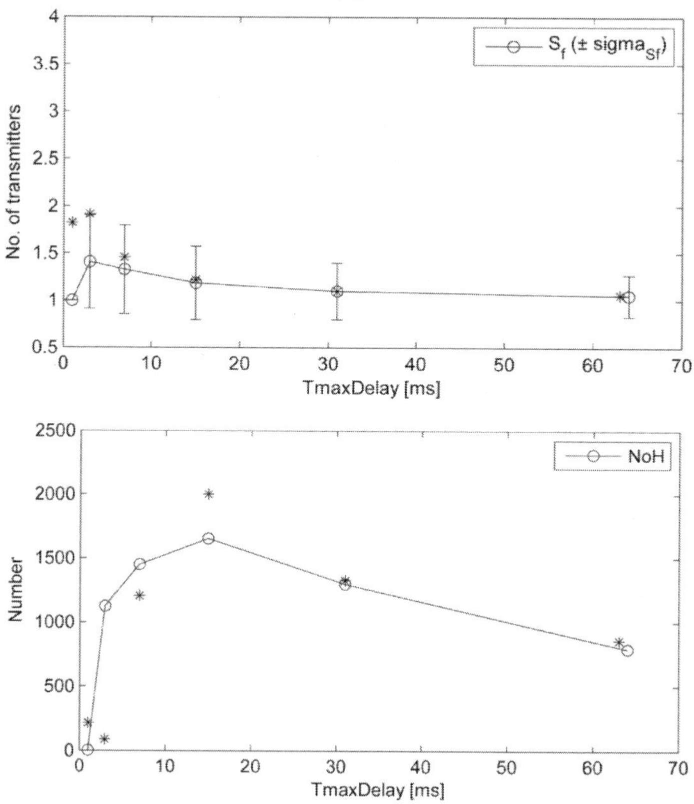

(b)

Figure 9. Metrics of the reconstructed signal plotted as a function of $T_{maxDelay}$ parameter. (a) Test case: 2 transmitters on the same channel (AA); (b) Test case: 4 transmitters on the two channels (AABB).

Speed of Processing Evaluation

System reactivity can be considered as the system's ability to interact with the user in real-time, i.e. to perform an action as soon as possible. Due to the modular architecture of the system, the reactivity can be analyzed from different points of view.

Clock Tests During the implementation of the hardware part of the BigEar prototype, the timer stability have been verified since one of the crucial points of the application is that every BigEar Audio Capture board samples the analog signal at the right sampling frequency Fs . Moreover, it is important to observe that the N-Buffer mechanism works perfectly in order to avoid corrupted data that could generate unattended behaviors in the reconstruction step. All the tests confirmed the clock stability.

Speed of Speech Reconstruction Algorithm The speed of the Speech Reconstruction Algorithm can be expressed as the ratio of the length of the considered audio segment ΔT_{rec} over the duration of the elaboration process ΔT_{elab}. This metric, called Realtime Performance Ratio (RPR), is defined as:

$$\text{RPR} = \frac{\Delta T_{\text{rec}}}{\Delta T_{\text{elab}}} = \frac{(\text{length of reconstructed signal}) \cdot \frac{1}{F_s}}{\Delta T_{\text{elab}}}. \tag{7}$$

This measure depends on the number of transmitters, since with a higher number of transmitters, there is also a higher data flow. So the metric can be used as a global trade-off parameter: $\text{RPR}>1$ states that the whole system is able to buffer, send and process data faster than sampling. For each test case discussed in Section 10, RPR has been measured. For all the tests $\text{RPR} \gg 1$, i.e. the processing speed of the BigEar Reconstruction Algorithm is faster than the sampling speed.

Reconstruction Quality Metric

During Far field tests, the speech signal was reconstructed using both Weighted Sum method (Section 5.4.1) and Holes Replacement method. Listening tests have denoted big differences in reconstructed speech signal depending on the superposition policy adopted. As explained in Section 5.4.2, the higher the distances between BigEar Audio Capture boards, the higher the differences in the audio signals due to different environment reflections and diffusions. These differences cause discontinuity artifacts in the reconstructed signal at the positions where different contributions are superposed in the attempt to fill the holes in the reconstructed signal (described in Section 5).

In order to examine how superposition methods could affect the presence of artifacts, Potential Artifact Ratio metric counts the number of positions where artifacts could be generated and normalizes it with respect to the length of the signal, obtaining thus a comparable metric.

$$A_{WS} = \sum_{k=1}^{N_{TX}} \frac{\text{edges}_k}{N},$$

where $\text{edges}_k = 2 \cdot \text{NoH}_k$ and NoH_k = no·of holes in the stream produced by k^{th} sensor.

$$A_{hr} = \sum_{k=1}^{N_{TX}} \frac{\left(\text{edges}_k - \text{edges}_k^{h<k}\right)}{N},$$

where $\text{edges}_k^{h<k}$=edgesinthe k^{th} stream covered by samples of previous streams.

Since number of potential artifacts is dependent on the chosen superposition policy, two different calculation methods are needed: A_ws is the metric used for Weighted Sum reconstruction and A_{hr} is the one used for Holes Replacement method.

Figure 10 shows that for each $T_{maxDelay}$ set, Weighted Sum method (whose Artifact Ratio is denoted with A_{ws}) is more prone to artifacts creation than Holes Replacement method. Moreover, as expected, Potential Artifacts Ratio grows with the number of transmitters that compose the system, in particular when multiple transmitters operate on multiple channel: since there is high overlapping between audio packets, Weighted Sum has more data to superpose.

The approach of the Holes Replacement policy (Section 5.4.2) is different: it adopt as reference the more powerful signal, then it uses other streams for holes replacement. In this way, the Potential Artifacts Ratio metric gives better results, keeping low the number of points in which an artifact could be generated.

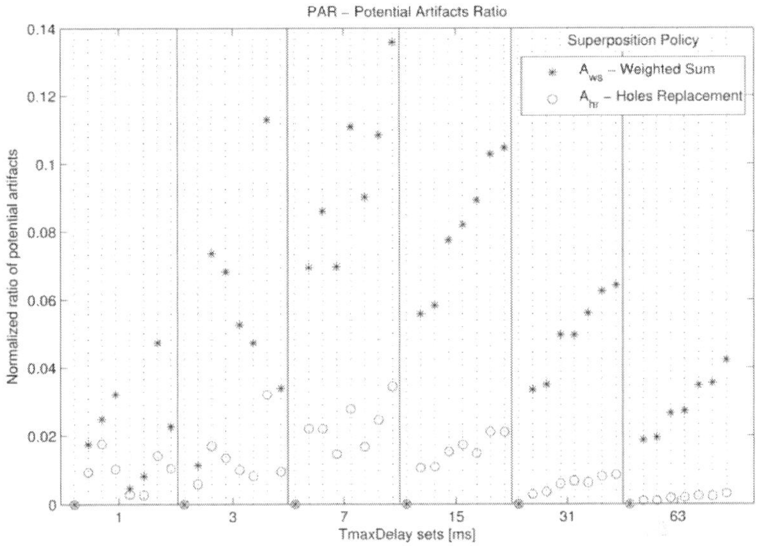

Figure 10. Potential Artifacts Ratio plotted for different test cases, divided by $T_{maxDelay}$ sets.

CONCLUSIONS AND FUTURE WORKS

In this paper, we have presented an application based on a distributed wireless sensor network that performs a space-time audio sampling of an environment. It is based on the low cost technology, i.e. on Wixel Prototyping boards, whose cost is around 20 $ each one; cost for speech acquisition circuit is under 10 $ per board[2].

A virtual model of the architecture has been first implemented, including an Audio Model that performs the acoustic simulation of the acquisition environment and a Sensor Network Model simulating the behavior of the transmittersreceiver network: this BigEar Simulator can be used to perform an apriori analysis to identify the best parameters (such as number of sensors, position of sensors, number of channels, software-configurable parameters) for a specific use case, minimizing production and installation costs. A real-world system has also been implemented to examine its real behavior and capabilities. A speech reconstruction algorithm has been proposed to reconstruct the audio signal coming from different microphones; finally, since in case of speech recognition, the reconstructed stream may contain holes; an inexactness toleration mechanism has been included in the speech recognition process to improve recognition accuracy. The whole architecture is scalable and it can be easily reconfigured by adding or removing sensors from the sensor network. Results show that the BigEar Reconstructor algorithm can perform real-time speech reconstruction, and listening tests confirm the intelligibility of the reconstructed signal. As future work, we plan to improve the BigEar Reconstruction Algorithm to properly feed GSR by filtering only vocal commands. Some experiments have shown that the differential information of power and delay of the signals acquired by the sensors can be used to make a coarse-grain localization of the source. Further studies will lead to a significant increase in localization accuracy to associate each keyword to a spatial information. In order to neutralize effects of superposition artifacts, filtering or far-field speech processing methods can be integrated into the BigEar Reconstructor algorithm; moreover, periodical training stages can be adopted for identifying physical and spectral characteristics of the ambient noise. Finally, the Network Interaction Model could be extended to other network protocols than pure ALOHA family in order to explore how Reconstructed Signal Metrics are influenced by different Network Interactions. In particular, different Network Protocols might help in reducing superposition artifacts; furthermore, Network Protocol could include synchronization mechanisms to prevent sensor clock drift.

REFERENCES

1. Mangano, S., Saidinejad, H., Veronese, F., Comai, S., Matteucci, M. and Salice, F. (2015) Bridge: Mutual Reassurance for Autonomous and Independent Living. IEEE Intelligent Systems, 30, 31-38. https://doi.org/10.1109/MIS.2015.58
2. Akyildiz, I.F., Su, W., Sankarasubramaniam, Y. and Cayirci, E. (2002) Wireless Sensor Networks: A Survey. Computer Networks, 38, 393-422.
3. Coulouris, G., Dollimore, J., Kindberg, T. and Blair, G. (2011) Distributed Systems: Concepts and Design. 5th Edition, Pearson Education, London.
4. Lecouteux, B., Vacher, M. and Portet, F. (2011) Distant Speech Recognition in a Smart Home: Comparison of Several Multisource ASRs in Realistic Conditions. Interspeech 2011, International Speech Communication Association, Florence, August 2011, 2273-2276. https://hal.archives-ouvertes.fr/hal-00642306
5. Palafox, L.E. and Garcia-Macias, J.A. (2009) Wireless Sensor Networks for Voice Capture in Ubiquitous Home Environments. 4th International Symposium on Wireless Pervasive Computing, Melbourne, 11-13 February 2009, 1-5. https://doi.org/10.1109/iswpc.2009.4800614
6. Alesii, R., Gargano, G., Graziosi, F., Pomante, L. and Rinaldi, C. (2009) WSN-Based Audio Surveillance Systems. In: Mastorakis, N., Mladenov, V. and Kontargyri, V.T., Eds., Proceedings of the European Computing Conference, Springer US, 675-681. https://doi.org/10.1007/978-0-387-84814-3_67
7. Ciuca, D., Pomante, L. and Rinaldi, C. (2012) A Speech Indicator for the VoWSN Approach. 5th International Symposium on Communications Control and Signal Processing, Rome, 2-4 May 2012, 1-4. https://doi.org/10.1109/isccsp.2012.6217759
8. Pomante, L. and Santic, M. (2016) Methodologies, Tools and Technologies for Location-Aware AAL. IEEE 2nd International Forum on Research and Technologies for Society and Industry Leveraging a Better Tomorrow (RTSI), Bologna, 7-9 Sep tember 2016, 1-4. https://doi.org/10.1109/RTSI.2016.7740566
9. Demir, A.K., Turkes, O. and Baydere, S. (2014) Differentiating Emergency Voice Traffic in Indoor Wireless Activity Monitoring Network. IEEE 10th International Conference on Wireless and Mobile

Computing, Networking and Communications (WiMob), Larnaca, 8-10 October 2014, 598-603. https://doi.org/10.1109/wimob.2014.6962231

10. Hu, R.-L., Yin, J.-R., Gu, X.-J., Gu, X.-P. and Chen, L.-Q. (2010) The Research and Design on TDD Voice WSN. 2010 International Conference on Multimedia Technology (ICMT), Ningbo, 29-31 October 2010, 1-4. https://doi.org/10.1109/icmult.2010.5629848
11. Ono, N., Kohno, H., Ito, N. and Sagayama, S. (2009) Blind Alignment of Asynchronously Recorded Signals for Distributed Microphone Array. IEEE Workshop on Applications of Signal Processing to Audio and Acoustics, New Paltz, 18-21 October 2009, 161-164. https://doi.org/10.1109/aspaa.2009.5346505
12. Pololu Corp. (2015) Wixel SDK Documentation. http://pololu.github.io/wixel-sdk/
13. Abramson, N. (1970) The Aloha System: Another Alternative for Computer Communications. Proceedings of the Fall Joint Computer Conference, Houston, 17-19 November 1970, 281-285. https://doi.org/10.1145/1478462.1478502
14. Wabnitz, A., Epain, N., Jin, C. and van Schaik, A. (2010) Room Acoustics Simulation for Multichannel Microphone Arrays. Proceedings of the International Symposium on Room Acoustics, Melbourne, 29-31 August 2010, 1-6.
15. Rhudy, M., Bucci, B., Vipperman, J., Allanach, J. and Abraham, B. (2009) Microphone Array Analysis Methods Using Cross-Correlations. ASME 2009 International Mechanical Engineering Congress and Exposition, Lake Buena Vista, Florida, 13-19 November 2009, 281-288. https://doi.org/10.1115/imece2009-10798
16. MATLAB, Version 8.6.0 (2015) Natick, Massachusetts: The MathWorks Inc., 2015.

CHAPTER 13

Using Speech Recognition in Learning Primary School Mathematics via Explain, Instruct and Facilitate Techniques

Ab Rahman Ahmad, Sami M. Halawani, Samir K. Boucetta

Faculty of Computing and Information Technology-Rabigh, King Abdulaziz University, Rabigh, KSA

ABSTRACT

The application of Information and Communication Technologies has transformed traditional Teaching and Learning in the past decade to computerized-based era. This evolution has resulted from the emergence of the digital system and has greatly impacted on the global education

Citation: Ahmad, A., Halawani, S. and Boucetta, S. (2014), Using Speech Recognition in Learning Primary School Mathematics via Explain, Instruct and Facilitate Techniques. Journal of Software Engineering and Applications, 7, 233-255. doi: 10.4236/jsea.2014.74025.

and socio-cultural development. Multimedia has been absorbed into the education sector for producing a new learning concept and a combination of educational and entertainment approach. This research is concerned with the application of Window Speech Recognition and Microsoft Visual Basic 2008 Integrated/Interactive Development Environment in Multimedia-Assisted Courseware prototype development for Primary School Mathematics contents, namely, single digits and the addition. The Teaching and Learning techniques—Explain, Instruct and Facilitate are proposed and these could be viewed as instructors' centered strategy, instructors'—learners' dual communication and learners' active participation. The prototype is called M-EIF and deployed only users' voices; hence the activation of Window Speech Recognition is required prior to a test run.

Keywords: Explain, Instruct and Facilitate Techniques, Multimedia-Assisted Courseware, Primary School Mathematics, Visual Natural Language, Window Speech Recognition

INTRODUCTION

Teaching and Learning (T & L) is an activity or process in connection with the dissemination of knowledge or specific skills. It covers planning, management, delivery, supervision and evaluation in order to effectively disseminate knowledge. The model [1] divides T & L process into Teaching Objectives, Available Knowledge, Teaching Method and Performance Evaluation as shown in Figure 1.

The model in Figure 1 indicates that T & L includes a range of decisions and practices which might require personal contacts between instructors-learners; however, instructors' personality is not the central element in T & L. The use of technological devices, team teaching and non-graded instruction will definitely modify the nature of contacts between instructors-learners. Depending on the requirement of the T&L situations, particularly on the knowledge available, the future classroom will provide for rather different personal contact to the present conventional classroom. The model implies a greater emphasis on instructors' competence rather than personal charisma; however, it is useful to have these combinations.

The facilitation technique [2] is using questions. Previous research has shown that questioning is a key strategy that facilitators use to promote discussion in Problem-Based Learning (PBL). In this study, different types of questions is examined that experienced facilitators asked to promote discussion of teaching problems in professional development for science teachers. PBL sessions facilitated by three pairs of experienced facilitators are recorded. Data analysis showed that facilitators asked a set of questions to initiate and solicit ideas, to reframe ideas, to clarify ideas, to push for elaboration, to check for interpretation, and to connect to teachers' classroom practice. This study has implications for the development of PBL facilitators.

T & L strategies can be classified as three key elements: instructors' centered, concentration and learners' centralization learning. These strategies are sometimes intertwined to each other in T&L process. The 5E model [3] —Engage, Explore, Explain, Elaborate and Evaluate—is modified by inserting a conscious pause in a learning cycle. It is called as an express phase to assess and ensure that learners progress adequately through early phases of the cycle. Ultimately, this revised cycle enables learners to meet the standards addressed in a particular lesson by providing differentiated opportunities.

Various technologies have been used to convey knowledge and the use of checklist [4] is common in Teaching and Learning (T & L) conventional qualitative studies. It is pointed out that the problem must be translated into mathematical terms and mathematical language before it is completed as the concepts contained in the structure of the problem. Some difficulties in T & L may arise, however, problems and difficulties [5] [6] might be overcome by using Information and Communication Technology (ICT). ICT environment [7] is urged to become personalized for T&L and it should be a full multimedia with an almost perfect online for community. T & L might be delivered in various forms and modes, such as entertainment and games. This makes T & L process [8] more interesting, interactive and fun.

The study [9] discussed on teachers' educational beliefs, namely, constructivist and traditional as antecedent of computer use while controlling for the impact of technology-related variables in computer experience and general computer attitudes with demographical variables of sex and age. A multilevel modelling has been used in identifying differences in determinants of computer use in the classroom. For measuring primary teachers' use of computers to support T & L process, a modified version of the Class Use of Computers scale [10] was used. The study supports the hypothesis that teacher beliefs are significant determinants in explaining reasons for adopting computers in the classroom. The impacts of computer experience, general computer attitudes and gender have shown positive constructivist beliefs on the classroom use of computers as opposed to traditional beliefs.

Multimedia is viewed as a dynamic approach when absorbed into education sectors for producing a new T&L concept with a combination of educational and entertainment approach. The rapid development in mobile computing, digital memory, internet resources, audio, video transmission, virtual imaging and wireless communication have created new possibilities for the use of technology in T & L. Multimedia technology [11] which combines computer technologies, compact disc players; video and audio systems yield a better enhanced interaction among end users. Interactive multimedia in the context of education has played a vital role in developing a T & L process towards a more dynamic and quality. Moreover, this technology creates a big and deep impact in the field of communication and education by representing numbers with pictures and animations. This is supported by computer abilities in presenting information and also T&L applications [12] . To date, ICT is often associated with education where the technology provides various facilities in T & L process and increase learners' interest in the subject being taught.

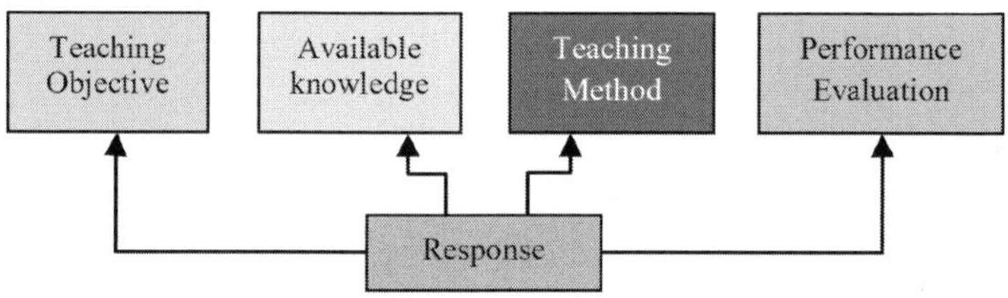

Figure 1. Robert Glaser Model.

The goal in [13] is to acquire how multimedia video case studies can support the professionalization of primary school Mathematics educators. The use of multimedia is investigated to support educators in learning to mathematize, didactize and to learn how to use multimedia with students-teachers. The research study has an exploratory character; presents a framework for the use of multimedia as a tentative answer, grounded in the researchers' experiments and design activities. Finding from the study is of one course result in a six-step framework for working with multimedia cases.

Building an accurate sign language recognition system [14] is of a great importance in order to efficiently facilitating communication between normal and deaf communities. The study is the development of speech recognition for Arabic Sign Language using Window Speech Recognition (WSR). The grammar is developed and embedded in Microsoft Visual Basic

2008 (MSVB2008). The Arabic alphabets and single numbers with their respective signs and avatar images are stored in different directories and invoked upon receiving a word uttered by a user. The system is a visual natural language model that might be used for communication by both groups in Arabic speaking countries.

Automatic speech recognition has now becomes a great benefit both to normal people and those with various disabilities. The study in [15] described T & L in an application of Talk Maths which used the output from a commonly-used conventional automatic speech recognition system. It enables users to dictate mathematical expressions in a relatively straightforward way. These are then converted into electronic formats and embedded in a document to be displayed in an editor or web browser. The process is used for preparing Mathematic teaching materials for online tests. By this, the learning should be relatively straightforward for users whose do not have extensive knowledge on computer or mathematics. The way in which the spoken mathematical expressions are analyzed, converted and encoded is a novel approach.

The current research [14] [15] shows the Speech Recognition application in some disciplines and with right T & L pedagogy and techniques, this surely will enhance the education for everyone. Though mathematics is seen as an abstract of study such as quantity, structure, space and change, it is feasible to be transformed into a WSR-assisted courseware for T & L. The presence of an Integrated/Interactive Development Environment (IDE) provides comprehensive facilities to computer programmers for software or courseware development. This research is concerned with the development of Primary Mathematics courseware prototype using Explain, Instruct and Facilitate Techniques (M-EIF) via WSR and MSVB2008 as IDE platform. The single digits and basic facts addition for these digits are used as the test bed materials for prototype development. The prototype could only be run by users' voice uttering the selected words.

MATERIALS AND METHODS

Windows Speech Recognition

In general, a speech recognition process [14] consists of processing the speech which is in acoustic, extracting feature and recognizing the speech. The process is based on a model as shown in Figure 2.

In this research, Windows 7 Speech Recognition [16] is applied since users' voice can be recognized automatically by the system. Users are required to perform the following training in order to acquire the maximum possible recognized speech. In the system, a voice can be used to control a computer by simply saying commands that a computer responds to and also dictating texts to it. A microphone should be connected to a computer prior to the execution the steps in setting up WSR.

The success of speech recognition depends on the quality of the microphone and the headset and desktop microphones are commonly used. Headset microphones are considered better since they are less prone to picking up extraneous sounds. A 30 minutes WSR training tutorial will assist users to exploit the commands used. Figure 3 shows WSR pop-up widgets display for Starting Speech Recognition.

There is a unique voice profile used by WSR engine to recognize users' voice and spoken commands. Once

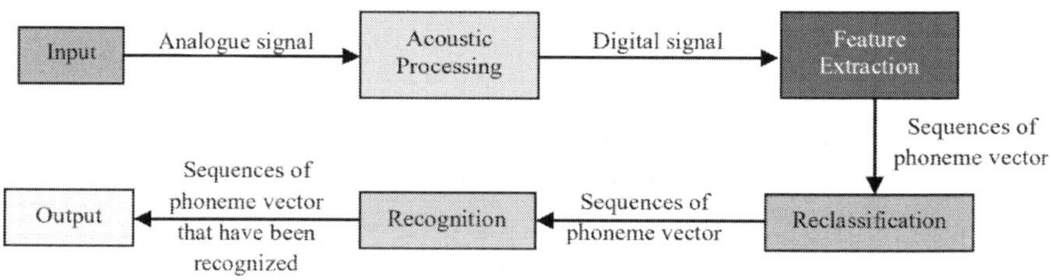

Figure 2. A speech recognition process.

Figure 3. A WSR pop-up widget.

WSR is utilized, users' voices profile gets more detailed and consequently improving computer's ability to understand the voices.

The WSR implementation

The implementation [17] written for C# provides an overview and examples in Windows Forms application by the following operations:

1) Initialize the speech recognizer.

Speech Recognizer SR = new Speech Recognizer().

2) Create a WSR grammar.

The grammar is created by using the constructors and methods on the Grammar Builder and Choices classes. For a simple grammar, an element is added in a Choices object using the Add method. Then the Grammar Builder instance is created and using the Append method to insert the elements in that instance. Finally, the Grammar Builder instance is the initialized. A user must speak exactly one of the elements added by the Choices instance in order to attain the match between user speech and the grammar.

3) Load the grammar into the speech recognizer.

The grammar created in the previous operation must be loaded and passed into the speech recognizer by calling the Load Grammar (Grammar) method.

4) Register for speech recognition event notification.

The speech recognizer raises a number of the Speech Recognized events during its operation, when it accepts a user utterance with a grammar. A notification of this event is registered by appending an Event Handler instance via SR_Speech Recognized the name written by a developer.

5) Create a handler for the speech recognition event.

A handler created for the Speech Recognized event displays the text of the recognized word or phrase using the Result property on the Speech Recognized Event Args parameter, e.

Primary School Mathematics

Mathematics is the study of measurements, properties, and relationships of quantities and sets, using numbers and symbols. It is a group of related sciences, including algebra, geometry, and calculus. It concerns with the study of quantity, shape, and space and their interrelationships by using specialized notations. These notations called mathematical operations and the process is to look for solutions to problems or studies of some scientific field. In this research, Primary Mathematics contents taught in Elementary Schools, Saudi Arabia [18] are considered. Figure 4 shows some materials taken from Class 1 book.

The basic topics in elementary mathematics are arithmetic and geometry. Elementary mathematics is used in everyday life activities such as dining, cooking, buying and selling things. It is also an essential first step on the path to understanding science. The contents presented are only covered basic digits 0 to 9 and addition operation for two single digits known as basic facts. By definition, the basic facts are any numbers or mathematical facts or ideas that can be instantly recalled without having to resort to a strategy to derive it. Table 1 shows the details for addition operation basic facts for two single digits from 0 to 9.

Figure 4. Part of Mathematics for Grade 1 contents.

Table 1. The basic facts addition operation for digit 0 to 9.

Addition operation for digit 0 to 9									
0 + 0 = 0	1 + 0 = 1	2 + 0 = 2	3 + 0 = 3	4 + 0 = 4	5 + 0 = 5	6 + 0 = 6	7 + 0 = 7	8 + 0 = 8	9 + 0 = 9
0 + 1 = 1	1 + 1 = 2	2 + 1 = 3	3 + 1 = 4	4 + 1 = 5	5 + 1 = 6	6 + 1 = 7	7 + 1 = 8	8 + 1 = 9	9 + 1 = 10
0 + 2 = 2	1 + 2 = 3	2 + 2 = 4	3 + 2 = 5	4 + 2 = 6	5 + 2 = 7	6 + 2 = 8	7 + 2 = 9	8 + 2 = 10	9 + 2 = 11
0 + 3 = 3	1 + 3 = 4	2 + 3 = 5	3 + 3 = 6	4 + 3 = 7	5 + 3 = 8	6 + 3 = 9	7 + 3 = 10	8 + 3 = 11	9 + 3 = 12
0 + 4 = 4	1 + 4 = 5	2 + 4 = 6	3 + 4 = 7	4 + 4 = 8	5 + 4 = 9	6 + 4 = 10	7 + 4 = 11	8 + 4 = 12	9 + 4 = 13
0 + 5 = 5	1 + 5 = 6	2 + 5 = 7	3 + 5 = 8	4 + 5 = 9	5 + 5 = 10	6 + 5 = 11	7 + 5 = 12	8 + 5 = 13	9 + 5 = 14
0 + 6 = 6	1 + 6 = 7	2 + 6 = 8	3 + 6 = 9	4 + 6 = 10	5 + 6 = 11	6 + 6 = 12	7 + 6 = 13	8 + 6 = 14	9 + 6 = 15

0 + 7 = 7	1 + 7 = 8	2 + 7 = 9	3 + 7 = 10	4 + 7 = 11	5 + 7 = 12	6 + 7 = 13	7 + 7 = 14	8 + 7 = 15	9 + 7 = 16
0 + 8 = 8	1 + 8 = 9	2 + 8 = 10	3 + 8 = 11	4 + 8 = 12	5 + 8 = 13	6 + 8 = 14	7 + 8 = 15	8 + 8 = 16	9 + 8 = 17
0 + 9 = 9	1 + 9 = 10	2 + 9 = 11	3 + 9 = 12	4 + 9 = 13	5 + 9 = 14	6 + 9 = 15	7 + 9 = 16	8 + 9 = 17	9 + 9 = 18

The Explain, Instruct and Facilitate (EIF) Techniques

Learning methods are frequently referred to as ways through which instructors deliver instructions and learners access these instructions. Several learning methods are described as traditional learning, e-Learning, blended learning, mobile learning, and personalized learning. These methods [19] accompanied with the advancements in technology and the paradigm shift from traditional learning to personalized learning methods. The proposed EIF technique, Explain (E), Instruct (I) and Facilitate (F) involves the development of theory and interactive courseware. Figure 5 shows that each stage has a different approach that involves a different role in T & L.

The Explain (E) stage is the process of explaining concepts for topics delivered. Many examples and other explanations are used to clarify in learning the concepts. Consequently, this stage can be viewed as presenting a text book for topics are being studied. For a courseware development, it is like an electronic book and the questions can be varied using a random function, especially involving numbers. It is useful for self-learning for those who haven't learned the concept presented. Instructors' presence might be required to clarify or clear any doubts.

The Instruct (I) stage is a dual communication where the session is benefited by answering the given questions. Instructors provide the questions according to levels, from easy to difficult. It is a test of knowledge and should be nurtured so that they will not hesitate to answer any questions. The courseware developed is seen as semi-interactive exercise book of students' involvement in response to questions displayed on a computer screen. The numbers are delivered randomly and answers provided by students will be verified by computer. For any difficulties the level Explain (E) can be referred again.

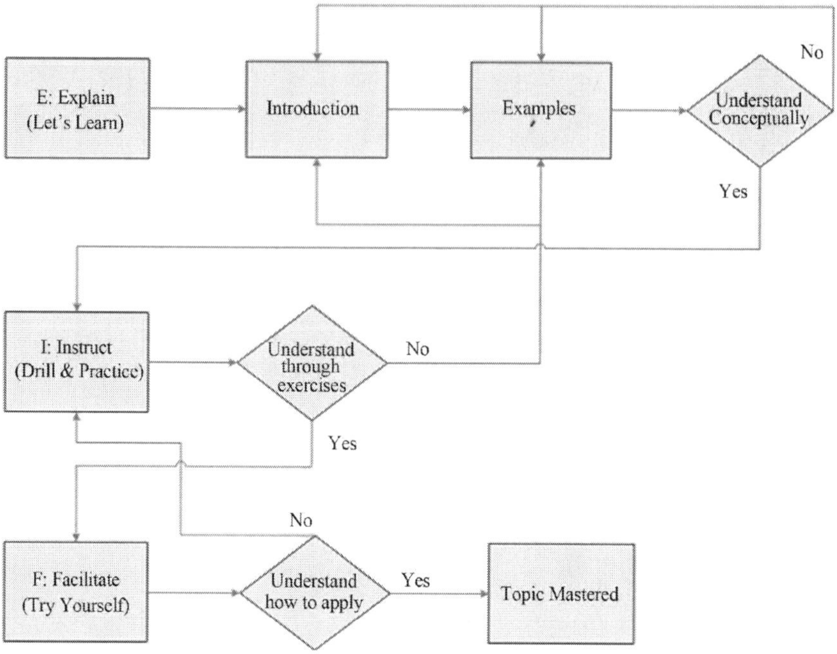

Figure 5. The EIF flow diagram.

Learners' full participation is needed at the Facilitate (F) level. They are required to utter both questions and answers whilst instructors' tasks are to guide or act as facilitators. It is a full of interactive T & L session and a courseware developed at this stage requires knowledge for concepts of topics taught. In addition, the use of logic should be considered as computers assumed instructors jobs. At any higher level of difficulties, some tips for guiding learners should be provided. For the materials chosen in Figure 4 and Table 1, learners are required to pose questions and replied with answers which are verified by computers. Table 2: shows a general T & L process to be used in the developed software using EIF Techniques.

A courseware development requires methods and techniques appropriate to T & L that can help to improve learners' understanding. The hardware and software specifications have to be determined as this has to be consistent with the requirements used for the development. Any cases relating to T & L should be studied to see the strategies are compatible with a computer-aided learning. In this research, the tools used are WSR and MSVB2008 running on a standard personal computer.

The Algorithm

By using WSR and MSVB2008, the idea is to build a language grammar that allocates word phonemes for a user's voice to be recognized. The system is designed as such answers will only be accepted preceded by questions uttered. Table 3 contains the suggested words list and these are used in the source codes in section 3.2 and the respective interface in Section 3.3. The flow diagrams in Figure 6 and Figure 7 used the words mentioned in Table 3 and transferred into the source codes presented in Section 3.2.

RESULTS AND DISCUSSIONS

Creating M-EIF Speech Recognition Grammar

The idea is to build the language grammar that allocates word phonemes in Table 3 for a user's voice to be recognized. Figure 8 shows the M-EIF architecture.

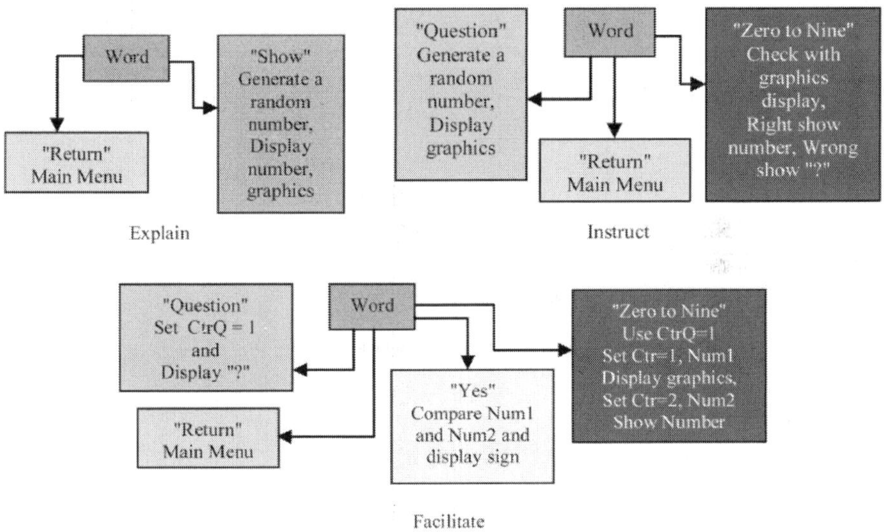

Figure 6. The flow diagram for numbers.

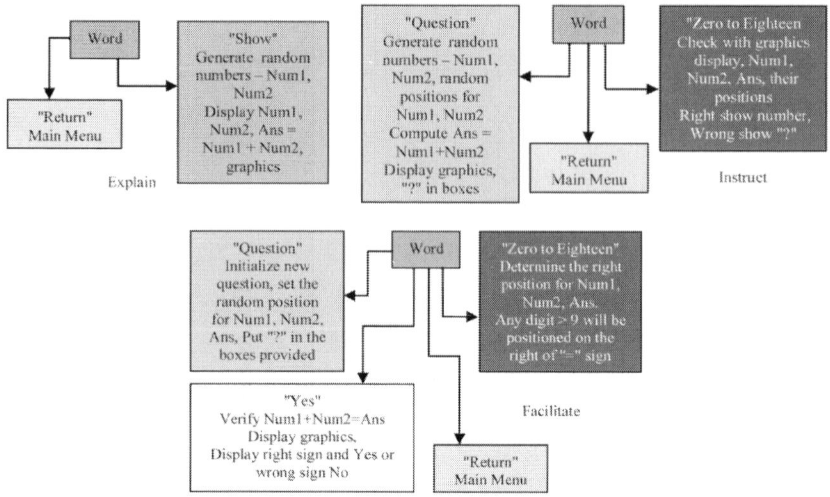

Figure 7. The flow diagram for addition.

Table 2. T & L process.

T & L		
Strategy	Approach	Technique
Ÿ Material Centered Ÿ Teacher Centered Ÿ Student Centered	Ÿ From Simple to Complex Ÿ From General to Specific Ÿ Multiple Stage Understanding	Ÿ Explain (E) Ÿ Instruct (I) Ÿ Facilitate (F)

Table 3. The words list used in the source codes for each interface.

Interface		**Words list**
Main Menu		See, Say, Do, Learn, Check, Attempt, Numbers, Books, Flow, Exit
Numbers	Explain	Show, Return
	Instruct	Question, Zero, One, Two, Three, Four, Five, Six, Seven, Eight, Nine, Return
	Facili-tate	Question, Zero, One, Two, Three, Four, Five, Six, Seven, Eight, Nine, Yes, Return

Addition	Explain	Show, Return
	Instruct	Question, Zero, One, Two, Three, Four, Five, Six, Seven, Eight, Nine, Ten, Eleven, Twelve, Thirteen, Fourteen, Fifteen, Sixteen, Seventeen, Eighteen, Return
	Facilitate	Question, Zero, One, Two, Three, Four, Five, Six, Seven, Eight, Nine, Ten, Eleven, Twelve, Thirteen, Fourteen, Fifteen, Sixteen, Seventeen, Eighteen, Yes, Return
EIF Flowchart		Return
Numbers up to 100		Return
Material used		Return

In this research, a speech recognition application in [17] [20] is adapted to perform the following operations and based on MS-VB2008 structure. The following details are for the M-EIF:

1) The definition for M_EIF as a new Speech Recognition is defined as Dim WithEvents M_EIF As New Recognition. SpeechRecognizer.

2) The definitions for the grammar, alphabets, and loading them are presented as Dim WordFacts As New Recognition.SrgsGrammar. SrgsDocument.

Dim WordRule As New Recognition.SrgsGrammar.SrgsRule ("M_EIF").

DimWordList As New Recognition.SrgsGrammar.SrgsOneOf ("See", "Say", "Do", "Learn", "Check", "Attempt", "Numbers", "Books", "Flow", "Exit").

WordRule.Add(WordList).

WordFacts.Rules.Add (WordRule).

WordFacts.Root = WordRule.

M_EIF.LoadGrammar (New Recognition.Grammar (WordFacts)).

3) The events, whether the defined M_EIF is recognized according to the grammar prescribed in Step 2, or otherwise and these require a subprogram defined as Private Sub M_EIF _ SpeechRecognized (ByVal sender As Object, ByVal e As System. Speech. Recognition. Recognition EventArgs) Handles M_EIF. SpeechRecognized.

which returns the value in e as e.Result.Text 4) The values in Step 2 are connected to the chosen location to display an interface, digit or picture for words designated in Step 3. For example, on uttering the word "See", the system executes frmNumberShow.show. The message "What was that?" in the widget is displayed when no matching is attained.

The Source Codes

The following source codes are based on the algorithm derived in Section 2.4. Figure 9 and Figure 10 show the source codes for M-EIF Main Menu and its Speech Recognizer (SR) procedure.

The source codes for other interfaces and their respective SR procedures are as follows. The words list used for each form is as given in Table 3.

Number-Explain: "See", Figure 11 and Figure 12.

Number-Instruct: "Say", Figure 13 and Figure 14.

Number-Facilitate: "Do", Figure 15 and Figure 16.

Addition-Explain: "Learn", Figure 17 and Figure 18.

Addition-Instruct: "Check", Figure 19 and Figure 20.

Addition-Facilitate: "Attempt", Figure 21 and Figure 22.

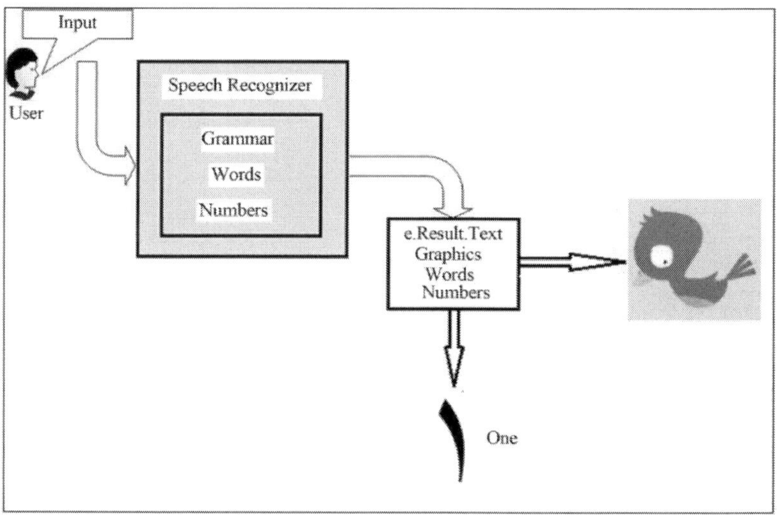

Figure 8. The M-EIF architecture.

```
Imports System.Speech

Public Class frmIntro

    Dim WithEvents M_EIF As New Recognition.SpeechRecognizer

    Private Sub frmIntro_Load(ByVal sender As System.Object, ByVal e As System.EventArgs) Handles My!

        Dim WordFacts As New Recognition.SrgsGrammar.SrgsDocument
        Dim WordsRule As New Recognition.SrgsGrammar.SrgsRule("M_EIF")
        Dim WordsList As New Recognition.SrgsGrammar.SrgsOneOf("See", "Say", "Do", "Learn", "Check",
                                                             "Flow", "Exit")
        WordsRule.Add(WordsList)
        WordFacts.Rules.Add(WordsRule)
        WordFacts.Root = WordsRule
        M_EIF.LoadGrammar(New Recognition.Grammar(WordFacts))
        lblWord.Visible = True
        lblWord.Text = "See Say Do Learn Check Attempt Numbers Books Flow Exit"
    End Sub
```

Figure 9. M-EIF main menu.

```
M_EIF

    Private Sub M_EIF_SpeechRecognized(ByVal sender As Obje

        Select Case e.Result.Text
            Case "See"
                frmNumberShow.Show()
            Case "Say"
                frmNumberTry.Show()
            Case "Do"
                frmNumberSay.Show()
            Case "Learn"
                frmAdd1to9.Show()
            Case "Check"
                frmInstr1to9.Show()
            Case "Attempt"
                frmDo1to9.Show()
            Case "Numbers"
                frmNumbers.Show()
            Case "Books"
                frmBooks.Show()
            Case "Flow"
                frmEIFChart.Show()
            Case "Exit"
                End
        End Select
        Me.Hide()

    End Sub
```

Figure 10. M-EIF SR procedure.

```
Imports System.Speech

Public Class frmNumberShow

    Dim WithEvents ShowNumber As New Recognition.SpeechRecognizer
    Dim Num1 As Integer

    Private Sub frmNumberShow_Load(ByVal sender As System.Object, ByVal e As System

        Dim NumberGrammar As New Recognition.SrgsGrammar.SrgsDocument
        Dim NumbersRule As New Recognition.SrgsGrammar.SrgsRule("ShowNumber")
        Dim NumbersList As New Recognition.SrgsGrammar.SrgsOneOf("Show", "Return")
        NumbersRule.Add(NumbersList)
        NumberGrammar.Rules.Add(NumbersRule)
        NumberGrammar.Root = NumbersRule
        ShowNumber.LoadGrammar(New Recognition.Grammar(NumberGrammar))
        Randomize()
        clearbirds()
        lblWord.Text = "Show Return"
     End Sub
```

Figure 11. Number-explain main.

```
ShowNumber                                              SpeechRecognized

    Private Sub ShowNumber_SpeechRecognized(ByVal sender As Object, ByVal e As System.Sp

        Label2.Visible = True
        Label2.Text = e.Result.Text
        clearbirds()

        Select Case e.Result.Text
            Case "Return"
                frmIntro.Show()
                Me.Hide()
                clearbirds()
            Case "Show"
                Num1 = Rnd() * 10
                Showbirds(Num1)
                If Num1 = 0 Then
                    Label2.Text = "Zero"
                    pbxArabic.BackgroundImage = System.Drawing.Image.FromFile("D:\SayNum
                ElseIf Num1 = 1 Then
                    Label2.Text = "One"
                    pbxArabic.BackgroundImage = System.Drawing.Image.FromFile("D:\SayNum
                ElseIf Num1 = 2 Then
                    Label2.Text = "Two"
                    pbxArabic.BackgroundImage = System.Drawing.Image.FromFile("D:\SayNum
```

Figure 12. Number-explain SR.

```
Imports System.Speech

Public Class frmNumberTry

    Dim WithEvents TryNumber As New Recognition.SpeechRecognizer
    Dim Num1 As Integer

    Private Sub frmNumberTry_Load(ByVal sender As System.Object, ByVal e As System.EventAr

        Dim NumberGrammar As New Recognition.SrgsGrammar.SrgsDocument
        Dim NumbersRule As New Recognition.SrgsGrammar.SrgsRule("TryNumber")
        Dim NumbersList As New Recognition.SrgsGrammar.SrgsOneOf("Question", "Zero", "One",
                                                                  "Seven", "Eight", "Nine",
        NumbersRule.Add(NumbersList)
        NumberGrammar.Rules.Add(NumbersRule)
        NumberGrammar.Root = NumbersRule
        TryNumber.LoadGrammar(New Recognition.Grammar(NumberGrammar))
        Randomize()
        lblWord.Text = "Question Zero One Two Three Four Five Six Seven Eight Nine Return"
        clearbirds()
    End Sub
```

Figure 13. Number-instruct main.

```
TryNumber                                                    SpeechRecognized

    Private Sub TryNumber_SpeechRecognized(ByVal sender As Object, ByVal e As System.

        Label2.Text = e.Result.Text

        Select Case e.Result.Text
            Case "Return"
                frmIntro.Show()
                Me.Hide()
                clearbirds()
            Case "Question"
                clearbirds()
                Num1 = Rnd() * 10
                If Num1 > 0 Then
                    Showbirds(Num1)
                End If
                pbxArabic.BackgroundImage = System.Drawing.Image.FromFile("D:\SayNumb
            Case "Zero"
                If Num1 = 0 Then
                    pbxArabic.BackgroundImage = System.Drawing.Image.FromFile("D:\Say
                Else
                    pbxArabic.BackgroundImage = System.Drawing.Image.FromFile("D:\Say
                End If
            Case "One"
```

Figure 14. Number-instruct SR.

```
Imports System.Speech

Public Class frmNumberSay

    Dim WithEvents SayNumber As New Recognition.SpeechRecognizer
    Dim Num1, Num2, Ctr, CtrQ As Integer

    Private Sub frmNumberSay_Load(ByVal sender As System.Object, ByVal e As System.EventArgs) I

        Dim NumberGrammar As New Recognition.SrgsGrammar.SrgsDocument
        Dim NumbersRule As New Recognition.SrgsGrammar.SrgsRule("SayNumber")
        Dim NumbersList As New Recognition.SrgsGrammar.SrgsOneOf("Question", "Zero", "One", "T
                                                                  "Seven", "Eight", "Nine", "Ye
        NumbersRule.Add(NumbersList)
        NumberGrammar.Rules.Add(NumbersRule)
        NumberGrammar.Root = NumbersRule
        SayNumber.LoadGrammar(New Recognition.Grammar(NumberGrammar))
        Randomize()
        clearbirds()
        lblWord.Visible = True
        lblWord.Text = "Question Zero One Two Three Four Five Six Seven Eight Nine Yes Return"
        Ctr = 1
        CtrQ = 0
```

Figure 15. Number-facilitate main.

```
(frmNumberSay Events)                                           Load

    Private Sub SayNumber_SpeechRecognized(ByVal sender As Object, ByVal e

        Label2.Text = e.Result.Text

        Select Case e.Result.Text
            Case "Question"
                CtrQ = 1
                clearbirds()
                Label2.Visible = True
                pbxArabic.Visible = True
                pbxArabic.BackgroundImage = System.Drawing.Image.FromFile
            Case "Yes"
                If Num1 = Num2 Then
                    pbxCheck.BackgroundImage = System.Drawing.Image.FromF
                Else
                    Label2.Text = "No"
                    pbxCheck.BackgroundImage = System.Drawing.Image.FromF
                End If
                pbxCheck.Visible = True
                CtrQ = 0
            Case "Zero"
                If (CtrQ = 1) And (Ctr = 1) Then
                    Num1 = 0
```

Figure 16. Number-facilitate SR.

```
Imports System.Speech

Public Class frmAdd1to9

    Dim WithEvents ShowAdd As New Recognition.SpeechRecognizer
    Dim Num1, Num2, Ans As Integer

    Private Sub frmAdd1to9_Load(ByVal sender As System.Object, ByVal e As System.E

        Dim NumberGrammar As New Recognition.SrgsGrammar.SrgsDocument
        Dim NumbersRule As New Recognition.SrgsGrammar.SrgsRule("ShowAdd")
        Dim NumbersList As New Recognition.SrgsGrammar.SrgsOneOf("Show", "Return")

        NumbersRule.Add(NumbersList)
        NumberGrammar.Rules.Add(NumbersRule)
        NumberGrammar.Root = NumbersRule
        ShowAdd.LoadGrammar(New Recognition.Grammar(NumberGrammar))
        Randomize()
        lblWord.Text = "Show Return"
        clearallbirds()
        clearNumbers()
    End Sub
```

Figure 17. Addition-explain main.

```
ShowAdd                                                    SpeechRecognized

   Private Sub ShowAdd_SpeechRecognized(ByVal sender As Object, ByVal e As System.

       clearallbirds()

       Select Case e.Result.Text
           Case "Return"
               frmIntro.Show()
               Me.Hide()
               clearallbirds()
           Case "Show"
               Num1 = Rnd() * 10
               If Num1 > 0 Then
                   Displaybird1(Num1)
               End If
               If Num1 = 0 Then
                   lblNum1.Text = "Zero"
                   pbxNum1.Visible = True
                   pbxNum1.BackgroundImage = System.Drawing.Image.FromFile("D:\Say
               ElseIf Num1 = 1 Then
                   lblNum1.Text = "One"
                   pbxNum1.BackgroundImage = System.Drawing.Image.FromFile("D:\Say
               ElseIf Num1 = 2 Then
                   lblNum1.Text = "Two"
```

Figure 18. Addition-explain SR.

```
Imports System.Speech

Public Class frmInstrito9

    Dim WithEvents TryAdd As New Recognition.SpeechRecognizer
    Dim Num1, Num2, Ans1, Ans2, Ans3, Ans, QType As Integer

    Private Sub frmInstrito9_Load(ByVal sender As System.Object, ByVal e As System.EventArgs) Handles MyBase.Load

        Dim NumberGrammar As New Recognition.SrgsGrammar.SrgsDocument
        Dim NumbersRule As New Recognition.SrgsGrammar.SrgsRule("TryAdd")
        Dim NumbersList As New Recognition.SrgsGrammar.SrgsOneOf("Question", "Zero", "One", "Two", "Three", "Four", "Five", "Six", _
                                                        "Seven", "Eight", "Nine", "Ten", "Eleven", "Twelve", "Thirteen", _
                                                        "Fourteen", "Fifteen", "Sixteen", "Seventeen", "Eighteen", "Return")
        NumbersRule.Add(NumbersList)
        NumberGrammar.Rules.Add(NumbersRule)
        NumberGrammar.Root = NumbersRule
        TryAdd.LoadGrammar(New Recognition.Grammar(NumberGrammar))
        Randomize()
        lblWord.Text = "Question Zero One Two Three Four Five Six Seven Eight Nine Ten Eleven Twelve Thirteen Fourteen Fifteen Sixtee
        clearallbirds()
        clearNumbers()
    End Sub
```

Figure 19. Addition-instruct main.

```
'TryAdd

    Private Sub TryAdd_SpeechRecognized(ByVal sender As Object, ByVal

        Select Case e.Result.Text
            Case "Question"
                clearallbirds()
                Ans1 = 0
                Ans2 = 0
                Ans3 = 0
                Num1 = Rnd() * 10
                Num2 = Rnd() * 10
                Ans = Num1 + Num2
                QType = Rnd() * 3 + 1
                If QType = 1 Then
                    If Num1 > 0 Then
                        Displaybird1(Num1)
                    End If
                    If Num2 > 0 Then
                        Displaybird2(Num2)
                    End If
                ElseIf QType = 2 Then
                    If Num2 > 0 Then
                        Displaybird2(Num2)
                    End If
```

Figure 20. Addition-instruct SR.

```
Imports System.Speech

Public Class frmDoito9

    Dim WithEvents DoAdd As New Recognition.SpeechRecognizer
    Dim Num1, Num2, Ans1, Ans2, Ans3, Ans As Integer
    Dim QPlace, QPlace1, QPlace2, QPlace3 As Integer

    Private Sub frmDoito9_Load(ByVal sender As System.Object, ByVal e As System.EventArgs) Handles MyBase.Load

        Dim NumberGrammar As New Recognition.SrgsGrammar.SrgsDocument
        Dim NumbersRule As New Recognition.SrgsGrammar.SrgsRule("DoAdd")
        Dim NumbersList As New Recognition.SrgsGrammar.SrgsOneOf("Question", "Zero", "One", "Two", "Three", "Four", "Five", "Six", _
                                                                 "Seven", "Eight", "Nine", "Ten", "Eleven", "Twelve", "Thirteen", _
                                                                 "Fourteen", "Fifteen", "Sixteen", "Seventeen", "Eighteen", "Yes", _
                                                                 "Return")

        NumbersRule.Add(NumbersList)
        NumberGrammar.Rules.Add(NumbersRule)
        NumberGrammar.Root = NumbersRule
        DoAdd.LoadGrammar(New Recognition.Grammar(NumberGrammar))
        Randomize()
        clearallbirds()
        PutQuestions()
        lblWord.Visible = True
```

Figure 21. Addition-facilitate main.

```
DoAdd                                                          SpeechRecognized

    Private Sub DoAdd_SpeechRecognized(ByVal sender As Object, ByVal e As System.Spe

        Select Case e.Result.Text
            Case "Question"
                clearallbirds()
                QReset()
                PutQuestions()
                pbxCheck.Visible = False
            Case "Yes"
                If ((Ans1 = 1) And (Ans2 = 1) And (Ans3 = 1)) Then
                    Displaybird1(Num1)
                    Displaybird2(Num2)
                    Displaybird3(Ans)
                    If (Num1 + Num2) = Ans Then
                        pbxCheck.BackgroundImage = System.Drawing.Image.FromFile("D:
                    Else
                        pbxCheck.BackgroundImage = System.Drawing.Image.FromFile("D:
                    End If
                    pbxCheck.Visible = True
                End If
            Case "Zero"
                If (QPlace1 = 1) And (Ans1 = 0) Then
                    pbxNum1.BackgroundImage = System.Drawing.Image.FromFile("D:\SayN
```

Figure 22. Addition-facilitate SR.

The M-EIF Testing

The aim of this research is to develop T & L prototype in basic Mathematics, M_EIF based on techniques called EIF, Explain (E), Instruct (I) and Facilitate (F) using WSR and MSVB2008. The contents used are part of Elementary School Mathematics Curriculum, Saudi Arabia. Figure 23 shows the First Form upon executing M-EIF. The prototype only accepts users' voice, hence WSR are required to be installed prior to the testing. The other forms with the details are as follows.

1) Number: Explain—"See"

Figure 24 is shown upon uttering the word "See". By uttering the word "Show", the Number-Explain form randomly displays a digit from 0 to 9, the corresponding graphics birds and word depending on the digit that appeared. Figure 25 and Figure 26 show some sample output "Return" forces the lessons back to M-EIF Main Menu, Figure 23.

Figure 23. M-EIF first form.

Figure 24. Number-explain main.

Figure 25. Number-explain “Zero”.

Figure 26. Number-explain “Nine”.

2) Number-Instruct—“Say”

Upon uttering the word “Say”, the Number-Instruct form as in Figure 27 appears. The word “Question” must be uttered next for a computer to show randomly a digit ranging from 0 to 9. Figure 28 shows a sample output. And for a right answered, the display is as Figure 29, otherwise the “?” is unchanged.

3) Number: Facilitate—“Do”

The screen displays the interface as in Figure 30, upon uttering the word “Do”. Users have to utter “Question” and a number (0 - 9), then the graphics bird is displayed. For the answer, they have to count the number of birds and say the number again, then “Yes” to validate. Figures 31-34 shows the details for the right answer where Q and A stand for Question and Answer respectively. Figures 35-37 is the display the wrong answer.

Figure 27. Number-instruct main.

Figure 28. Number-instruct "Question".

Figure 29. Number-instruct "Seven".

Figure 30. Number-facilitate main.

Figure 31. Number-facilitate—“Question”.

Figure 32. Number-facilitate (Q)—“Seven”.

Figure 33. Number-facilitate (A)—"Seven".

Figure 34. Number-facilitate—"Yes".

Figure 35. Number-facilitate (Q)—"Six".

Figure 36. Number-facilitate (A)—“Five”.

Figure 37. Number-facilitate (A)—“Yes”.

4) Addition: Explain—“Learn”

The word “Learn” will show the main form, Figures 38-41 shows the random outputs by uttering the word “Show”.

5) Addition: Instruct—“Check”

By uttering the word “Check”, the display as in Figure 42 will be shown. The word “Question” will randomly show the position of bird graphics between the three different locations, i.e., Figures 43-48 are a right combination for answers to a random question in Figure 43.

6) Addition: Facilitate—"Attempt"

Figure 49 shows the Main form for Addition-Facilitate upon uttering the word "Attempt". From Figure 49, users are required to utter the first number and the computer will choose the location. For any number bigger than 9, the number will be inserted on the right hand side of the equation. Then, the rest has to be completed in turn with the final word is "Yes" to validate the answer. Figures 50-53 shows the details for correct answer whilst Figure 54 and Figure 55 are for the wrong and correct answer respectively.

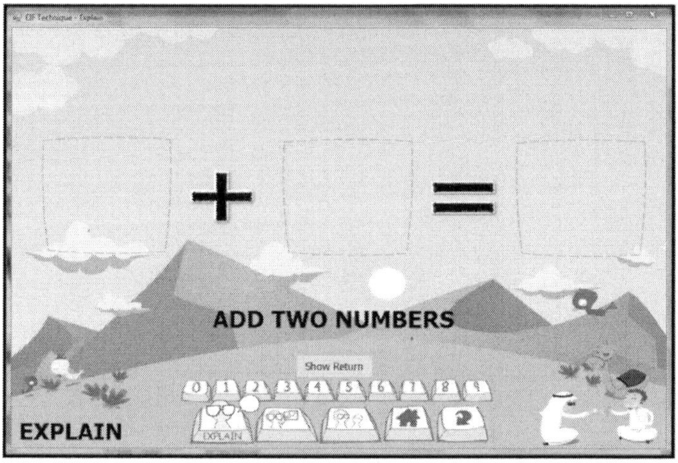

Figure 38. Addition-explain main.

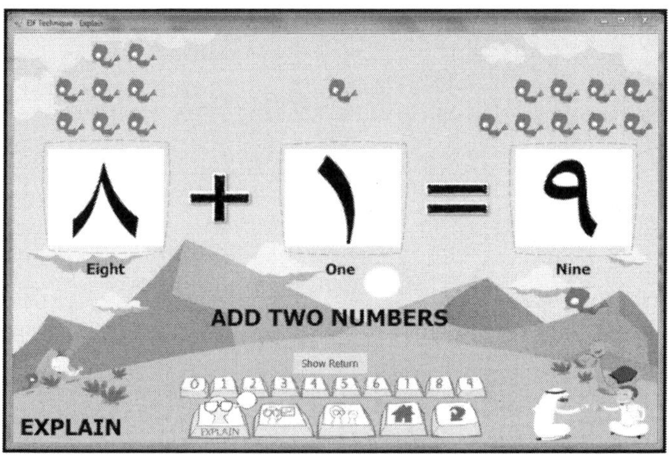

Figure 39. Addition-explain "Show".

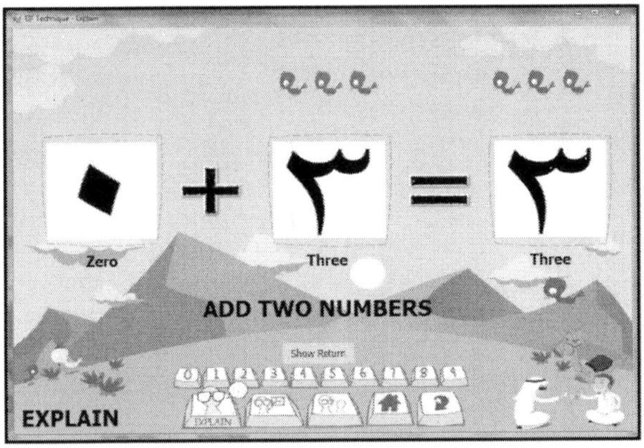

Figure 40. Addition-explain “Show”.

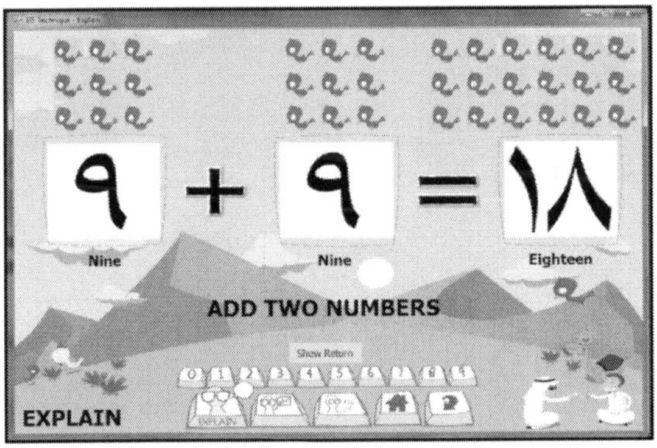

Figure 41. Addition-explain “Show”.

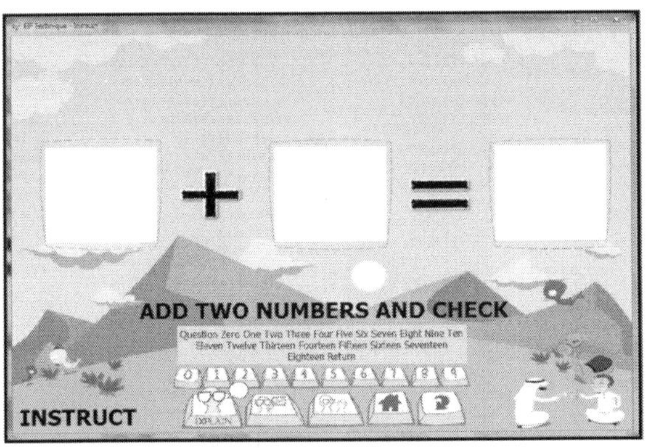

Figure 42. Addition-instruct main.

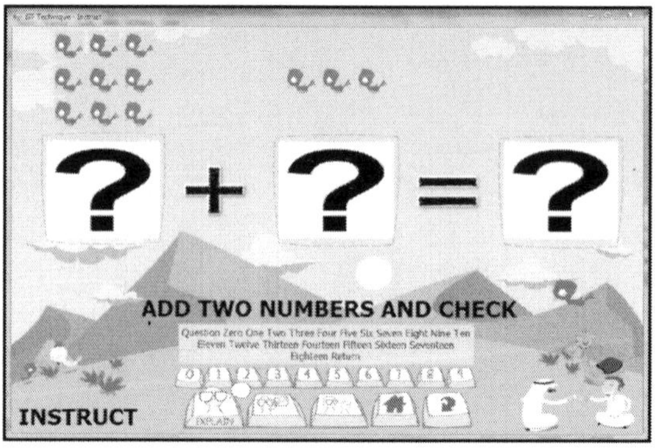

Figure 43. Addition-instruct "Question"

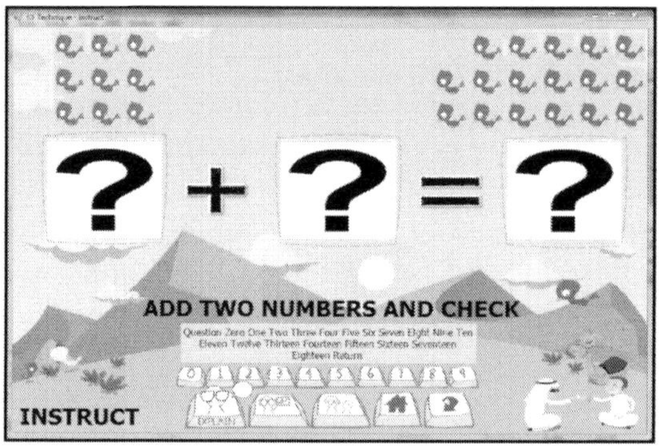

Figure 44. Addition-instruct "Question".

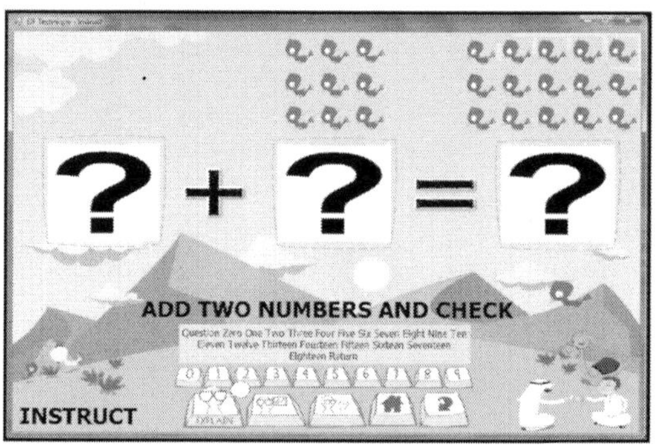

Figure 45. Addition-instruct "Question".

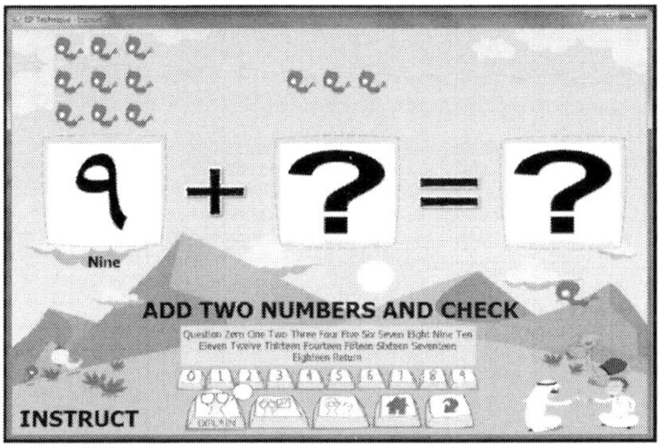

Figure 46. Addition-instruct "Nine".

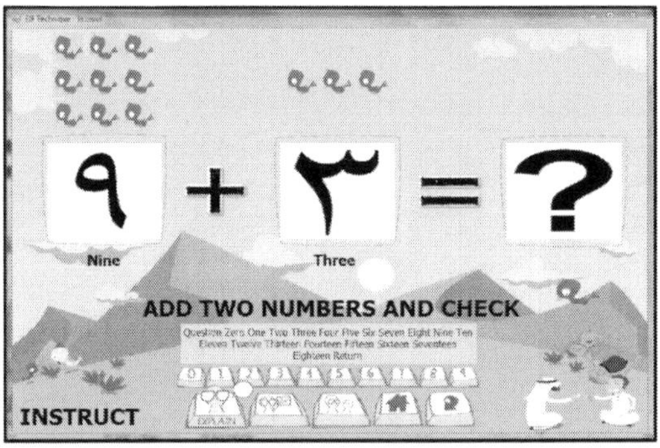

Figure 47. Addition-instruct "Three".

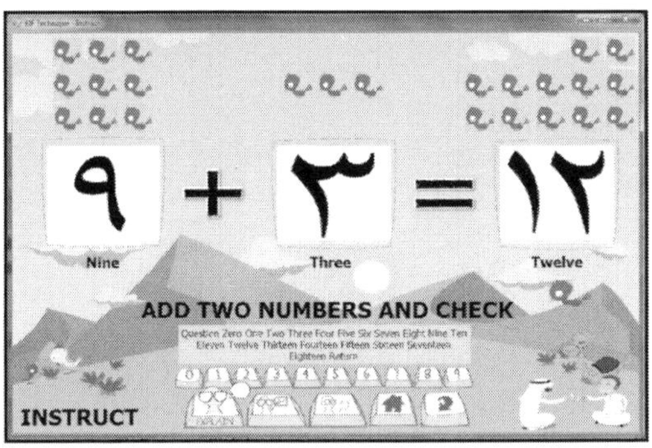

Figure 48. Addition-instruct "Twelve".

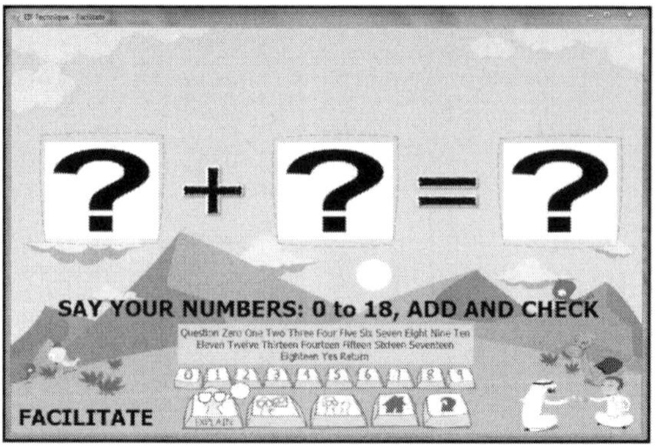

Figure 49. Addition-facilitate main.

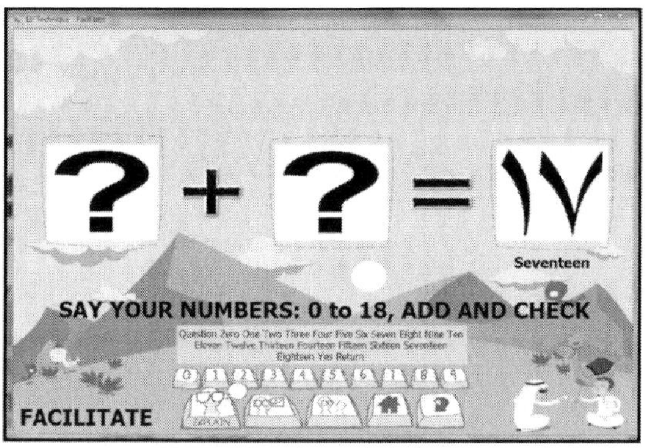

Figure 50. Addition-facilitate "Seventeen".

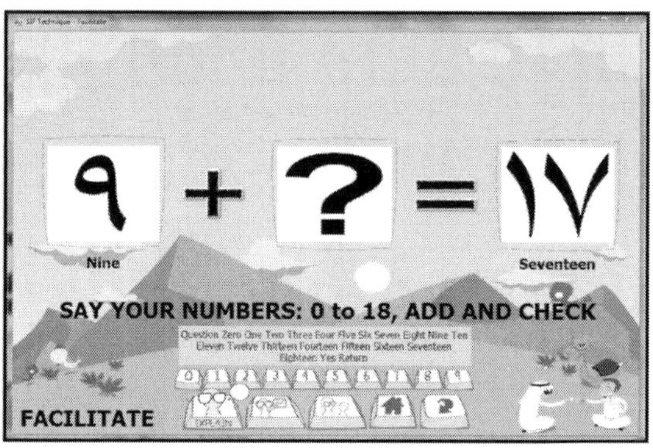

Figure 51. Addition-facilitate "Nine".

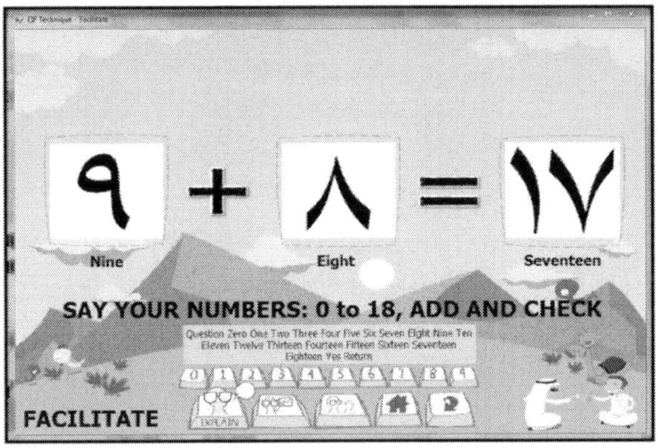

Figure 52. Addition-facilitate "Eight".

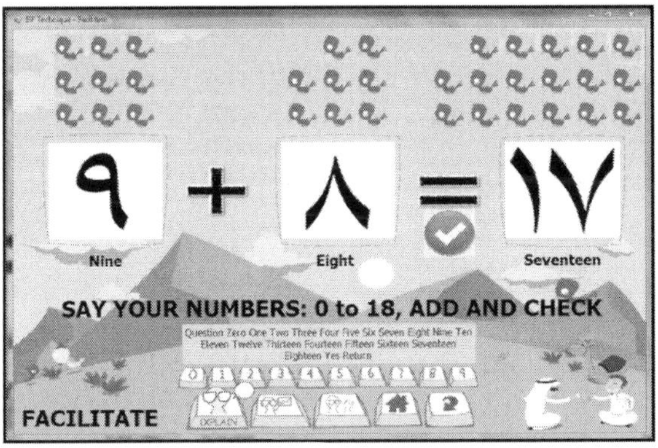

Figure 53. Addition-facilitate "Yes".

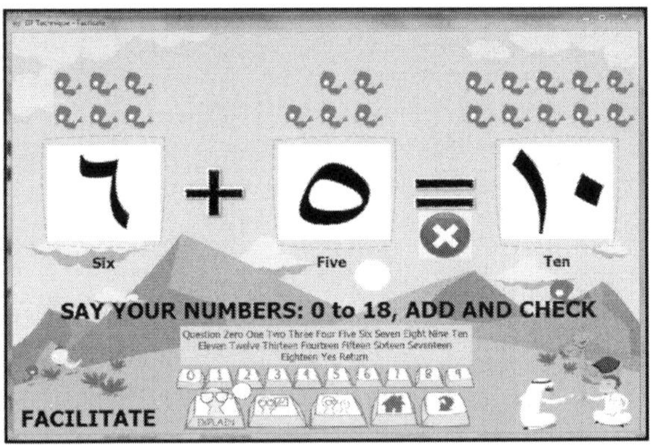

Figure 54. Addition-facilitate "Yes".

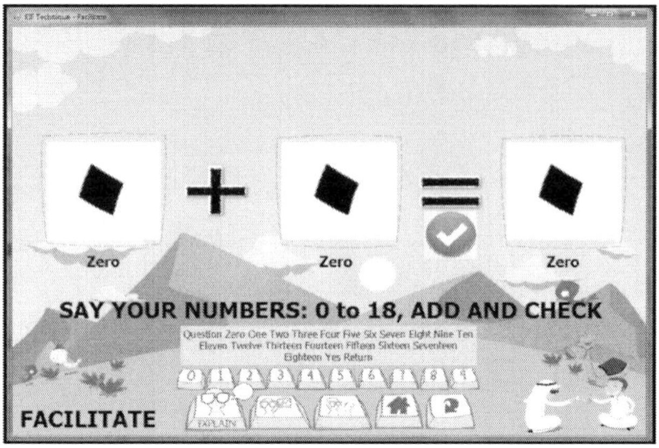

Figure 55. Addition-facilitate "Yes".

CONCLUSIONS AND RECOMMENDATIONS

The rapid change in mathematics education in as many decades implies a wind of change in society. Starting from behavioral theory the 1950-1970, Cognitive Science (1970-1980) and from 1980 to the present theory, the constructivism has been on the trust. Besides, the e-learning system becomes an alternative educational tool that promises to play a prominent role in years ahead. An interactive approach in T&L Mathematics using Explain, Instruct and Facilitate (EIF) technique is expected to open a new wave in mathematical education. The prototype used the multimedia technology to support the viability and significant of the approach. The EIF technique could be deployed in a developed multimedia courseware and implemented at schools for T & L. Learners as beginners on Mathematics or otherwise will benefit from the courseware whilst instructors act an aide to facilitate them.

One of the criteria that are essential in developing multimedia courseware is attractive interfaces and graphic designs. These features should be compatible with the local environment and user friendly. The consistency between learning objectives and content of instruction are required for conveying the right pedagogy with the chosen materials. In this research, M-EIF is successfully developed with the contents consist of single digits (0 to 9) and the basic facts for addition operation with the graphics specially designed for the local environment. The concept of interactive techniques has been much emphasized via EIF. M-EIF could be used to assist learners in mathematics and also English. Regardless of their competencies, M-EIF provides random examples and questions in enriching T & L. M-EIF has been developed for some topics in Primary Mathematics with simple graphics representation and voices using WSR. To develop better courseware, the expertise in Mathematics or chosen subjects, educational psychology, programming, graphics and animations are much required and work as a group. By this, then the rest of the contents either simple or abstract such as mathematical proofs could be done subsequently for the entire curriculum and followed by some tests in schools to acquire the feedbacks. The EIF techniques could also be applied in the higher levels of education, at secondary schools and university to judge its effectiveness. In addition, this technique could also be implemented and tested in other courses. With the availability of financial resources and manpower, further improvement on M-EIF is certainly viable. The use of web technology might be considered in facilitating T & L to anyone, in everywhere and anytime. M-EIF might be regarded as the opening for the development of more sophisticated Multimedia–WSR assisted courseware in the future.

ACKNOWLEDGEMENTS

Ab Rahman Ahmad, Sami M. Halawani, Samir K. Boucetta (DSR), King Abdulaziz University, Jeddah, under grant No. 27-004/430. The authors, therefore, acknowledge with thanks DSR technical and financial support.

REFERENCES

1. Glaser, R. (1976) Components of a Psychology of Instruction: Toward a Science of Design. Review of Educational Research, 46, 1-24. http://www.jstor.org/stable/1169916 http://dx.doi.org/10.3102/00346543046001001
2. Zhang, M., Lundeberg, M., McConnell, T.J., Koehler, M.J. and Eberhardt, J. (2010) Using Questioning to Facilitate Discussion of Science Teaching Problems in Teacher Professional Development, Interdisciplinary Journal of Problem-Based Learning, 4, 57-82. http://dx.doi.org/10.7771/1541-5015.1097
3. Duran, E., Duran, L., Haney, J. and Scheuermann, A. (2011) A Learning Cycle for All Students: Modifying the 5E Instructional Model to Address the Needs of all Learners. The Science Teacher, 78, 56-60. www.scilinks.org
4. Frels, R.K., Sharma, B., Onwuegbuzie, A.J., Leech, N.L. and Stark, M.D. (2011) The Use of a Checklist and Qualitative Notebooks for an Interactive Process of Teaching and Learning Qualitative Research. The Journal of Effective Teaching, 11, 62-79. http://uncw.edu/cte/et/articles/Vol11_1/index.htm
5. Al Ghamdi, Y.A.S. (1987) The Effectiveness of Using Microcomputers in Learning Algebraic Precedence Conventions. Doctoral Dissertation, Florida State University, Florida.
6. Alessi, S.M. and Trollip, S.R. (2000) Multimedia for learning: Methods and Development. 3rd Edition, Allyn and Bacon, Boston.
7. Coelho, A.C.C. (2010) Interactive Textbooks and Student's Learning, e-TEALS: An E-Journal of Teacher Education and Applied Language Studies, 1, 13-43.
8. Funkhouser, C. (1993) The Influence of Problem Solving Software on Student Attitudes about Mathematics. Journal of Research on Computing in Education, 25, 339-346.
9. Hermans, R., Tondeur, J., van Braak, J. and Valcke, M. (2008) The Impact of Primary School Teachers' Educational Beliefs on the Classroom Use of Computers. Computers & Education, 51, 1499-1509. http://dx.doi.org/10.1016/j.compedu.2008.02.001
10. van Braak, J., Tondeur, J. and Valcke, M. (2004) Explaining Different Types of Computer Use among Primary School Teachers. European Journal of Psychology of Education, 19, 407-422. http://dx.doi.

org/10.1007/BF03173218

11. Harun, J. and Tasir, Z. (2000) Pengenalan Kepada Multimedia. Venton Publishing, Kuala Lumpur.
12. Rashid, A.R.A. (2000) Wawasan Dan Agenda Pendidikan. Utusan Publications and Distributors Sdn. Bhd., Kuala Lumpur.
13. Dolk, M., den Hertog, J. and Gravemeijer, K. (2002) Using Multimedia Cases for Educating the Primary School Mathematics Teacher Educator: A Design Study. International Journal of Educational Research, 37, 161-178, http://dx.doi.org/10.1016/S0883-0355(02)00058-7
14. Halawani, S.M., Daman, D., Kari, S. and Ahmad, A.R. (2013) An Avatar Based Translation System from Arabic Speech to Arabic Sign Language for Deaf People. International Journal of Computer Science & Network Security, 13, 43-52. http://paper.ijcsns.org/07_book/201312/20131207.pdf
15. Wigmore, A., Hunter, G., Pflügel, E., Denholm-Price, J. and Binelli, V. (2009) Using Automatic Speech Recognition to Dictate Mathematical Expressions: The Development of the "TalkMaths" Application at Kingston University. Journal of Computers in Mathematics and Science Teaching, 28, 177-189. http://www.editlib.org/p/30301
16. Windows Speech Recognition Engine (2014) Microsoft Windows 7 Professional Operating Systems.
17. Windows Speech Recognition (2014) http://msdn.microsoft.com/en-us/library/
18. Mathematics for Grade 1 (2011) First Semester. Ministry of Education, KSA.
19. Sohlberg, M.M., Ehlhardt, L. and Kennedy, M. (2005) Instructional Techniques in Cognitive Rehabilitation: A Preliminary Report. Seminars in Speech and Language, Theime Medical Publishers Inc., 26, 268-279. http://dx.doi.org/10.1055/s-2005-922105

CHAPTER 14

A Prototype of a Semantic Platform with a Speech Recognition System for Visual Impaired People

Jimmy Rosales-Huamaní[1], José Castillo-Sequera[2], Fabricio Puente-Mansilla[1], Gustavo Boza-Quispe[1]

[1]National University of Engineering, Lima, Peru

[2]Alcala University, Madrid, Spain

ABSTRACT

In the world, 10% of the world population suffer with some type of disability, however the fast technological development can originate some barriers that these people have to face if they want to access to technology. This

Citation: Rosales-Huamaní, J., Castillo-Sequera, J., Puente-Mansilla, F. and Boza-Quispe, G. (2015), A Prototype of a Semantic Platform with a Speech Recognition System for Visual Impaired People. Journal of Intelligent Learning Systems and Applications, 7, 87-92. doi: 10.4236/jilsa.2015.74008.

is particularly true in the case of visually impaired users, as they require special assistance when they use any computer system and also depend on the audio for navigation tasks. Therefore, this paper is focused on making a prototype of a semantic platform with web accessibility for blind people. We propose a method to interaction with user through voice commands, allowing the direct communication with the platform. The proposed platform will be implemented using Semantic Web tools, because we intend to facilitate the search and retrieval of information in a more efficient way and offer a personalized learning. Also, Google APIs (STT (Speech to Text) and TTS (Text to Speech)) and Raspberry Pi board will be integrated in a speech recognition module.

Keywords: Semantic Web, Ontology, ASR, Raspberry Pi

INTRODUCTION

In recent years the size of the World Wide Web (WWW) has grown dramatically; this has led to a considerable increase in the difficulty to find data about a particular issue, due to the ambiguity of terms used to make queries on the web.

The Semantic Web, also known as the Data Web and Web 3.0 [1] pretend to solve this problem creating a mechanism for the exchange information with certain meaning. To provide a website with a comprehensible meaning by computers, it is necessary to have a knowledge representation. The Semantic Web proposes the use of collections of information called ontologies in order to have a structured knowledge.

By other hand, people with disabilities are nearly 10% in the world; these people have to deal with many physical barriers and some new barriers have been added: Technology. These are causing the digital gap, also known as the digital divide or digital stratification [2] .

To be precise, in case of blind people, they require special help to work with any kind of computer system. Furthermore, these people needs appropriate tools to get relevant data from Internet.

From our point of view, in any case, the implementation of a web platform has to address certain problems like meaning understandable by computers, efficient retrieval of information and accessibility for everyone.

The World Wide Web Consortium (W3C) offers standards which are internationally accepted. They offer quantifiable rules, however, web developers often fail to implement them effectively. One of the reasons is that most of the available accessibility guidelines appear too costly [3] .

According to [4] , with the Semantic Web, there are now new opportunities to build flexible systems that will meet the needs of disabled students. Disability aware systems could be designed using Semantic Web technologies, leading to personalized environments that will enable disabled students to have relevant learning resources and to work independently, with little assistance from a tutor.

For these reasons, in this paper we make a prototype of a platform based on semantic web with speech recognition using natural language allowing blind students access to knowledge resources and learn independently of their tutor. The present work is divided as follow: in Section 2 we review related papers. The next section discusses the current problems. Afterwards, in Section 4 we present our proposal, in Section 5 we present the conceptual scheme of architecture and finally in Section 6 expected contribution is presented.

REVIEW OF LITERATURE

The state-of-art was based in papers related to ontology, Semantic Web and accessibility for disabled people. In this section, we review papers from 2010 to date.

In [3] was developed an ontology called CO to represent user interaction in its context and improve web accessibility for all people. In this work, four important concepts are identified: User context, physical context, environmental context and computational context.

In [5] was developed a model based on ontologies for integrating several web services and their delivery to users with reduced mobility. Under this proposal, people with disabilities are able to search on web for services.

In [6] was developed a prototype system based on an ontology for Internet information retrieval for autistic people through learning styles. In this paper, the autistic user expect to retrieve information with different characteristics, but this is difficult for autistic people, because of their lack of ability to process and retain information. In this work the aim is to find the desired result, based on a suitable set of keywords that are based on their memories of people with autism.

In [7] was proposed the use of the URC framework (The Universal Remote Console) in form of UCH- oriented Gateway (The Universal

Control Hub) and some services of Ontologies, such as ODP (Platform for dialogue based on Ontologies) to provide interactive services accessible to any TV architecture. This platform is called VITAL (Vital Assistance for the Elderly) and helps to elderly people to participate in dialogue.

In [4] was developed an ontology called ADOOLES (Abilities and Disabilities Ontology for Online Learning and Services) based on personalized online instruction for disabled students in higher education. This ontology was built on ADOLENA (Abilities and Disabilities Ontology for Enhancing Accessibility) that was developed by [8] .

In [9] , a middleware based on ontologies for personalize tourism to people with special needs was presented. Its function was to retrieve and classify information in places adapted for people with special needs. This was supported by PATRAC (Accesible Heritage) philosophy. Furthermore, they proposed a content manager based on ontologies divided in three designed modules. The content manager uses SOAP (Simple Object Access Protocol) web services.

Independently, in [10] was developed HIV (Heavyweight ontology Based Information Extraction for Visually impaired User) that provide a mechanism for highly precise information extraction using heavyweight ontology and built-in vocal command system for visually impaired internet users.

Finally, [11] presented the research program of the London Metropolitan University, which aims to use Semantic Web and mobile Internet for care of the disabled and elderly people using intelligent agents. The authors use as a conceptual background the International Classification of functionality, Disability and Health (ICF), it has been established as a standard for the classification of the various states of health. Where the core of the framework is a pilot whose ontological domain is disability.

CURRENT PROBLEMS OF WEB PLATFORMS FOR ACCESSIBILITY

A review of the literature found the following problems:

- A big part of e-learning environments are not yet accessible for all users, because there are many electronic barriers that prevent access to online resources, and it does not have access technical aids (such as the use of screen reader) [3] .

- The number of students with disabilities in UK higher education institutions increases every year. Delivering education online is becoming increasingly challenging as institutions encounter some disabilities requiring adjustments of learning environments. The law requires that people with disabilities be given equivalent learning experiences to their non-disabled peers through reasonable adjustments. Educational institutions have thus utilised assistive technologies to assist disabled students in their learning, but some of these technologies are incompatible with some learning environments, hence excluding some disabled students and resulting in a disability divide [4] .
- Disabled people represent an important part of our society, they have different needs based on the type of disability that they presented, and being the assistance provided to them important and the use of new technologies should accommodate their needs [11] .

PROTOTYPE OF SEMANTIC PLATFORM WITH SPEECH RECOGNITION SYSTEM

In order to achieve the prototype we consider the following steps:

1) Building of Ontology. For an easy and rapid extraction of information by the user, the knowledge about a particular subject or domain will be stored in an ontology. Such ontology contain terms and the relationships among these terms. Terms are often called classes, or concepts; these words are interchangeable. The relation- ships between these classes can be expressed by using a hierarchical structure: superclasses represent higher- level concepts and subclasses represent finer concepts, and the finer concepts have all the attributes and features that the higher concepts have. The ontology is designed in the language OWL (Ontology Web Language) that is most popular language for creating ontologies today [12] .

In addition for modelling the ontology we should follow the recommendations of Methontology that is a standard created by the Ontology Engineering Group of the Polytechnic University of Madrid (UPM), which comprises the following steps: Specification, conceptualization, acquiring knowledge, integration, implementa- tion, maintenance, evaluation, and documentation [13] .

2) Semantic Platform Implementation

The implementation of the Semantic Platform will be using Jena libraries API for Java that allow the management of ontologies in OWL code and support a reasoner engine.

According to [14] Jena is a library to develop applications based on RDF (Resource Definition Framework) and OWL documents. It is only used in application code as a collection of APIs, and there is no GUI of any kind. Also provides a framework to development Semantic Web applications using Java language.

Furthermore, the platform will be based on the Model-View-Controller scheme, which implement servlets to manage user queries. Such queries can be verified in an ontological editor using SPARQL (SPARQL Protocol and RDF Query Language) [15] , so as W3C recommend, SPARQL will be used to consult RDF or OWL documents.

3) Adaptation of Speech Recognition System to Semantic Platform.

Automatic speech recognition systems (ASR) compared to other human-machine interaction systems like keyboard, mouse, etc. provide better naturalness. Speech recognition seems so natural and simple for people but for machines is quite complicated. For this reason, a recognition of patterns is used, these patterns are a set of linguistic units as (words, syllables, sounds, shapes).

There are studies that use queries patterns using SPARQL [16] . We propose a mechanism to facilitate the interaction between the user and the platform through an interface that use natural language. We pretend to create a module that translates user queries in natural language to SPARQL queries. To solve this problem we will build a series of templates in SPARQL.

In our platform, a template consists of a SPARQL representation, which reflects the internal structure of the question from natural language. This module would be integrated into the server and also linked to the ASR system. A user with visual disabilities requires an accessible medium to interact with the platform. To achieve this, the following processes are required.

a) Voice-to-text. The process used for adapt the voice recognition system is the ASR (Automatic Speech Recognition). In [17] , we can see a considerable number ASR systems, some open source, other privative and even based in cloud services. In the last case, we focus specifically in API Google STT Service, because it is a cloud computing system and does not compromise the performance of the local computer. According to [18] , thanks to the processing in the cloud, the ASR can be used in devices that have no high-performance processor and avoid the use of complex algorithms. In [19] was presented a system using API Google STT that operate together with reduced board computer Raspberry Pi, with excellent results (85% - 90% accuracy). The advantage of using this Raspberry Pi is its small size that makes ideal to be embedded anywhere, without saturating the available space. By other hand, the low cost of equipment enables this massive distribution.

b) Text-to-Speech. To convert Text to Speech (TTS) we propose to use the cloud services of Google, using Google Translator, although is a less complex process compared with ASR. Other possibility could be run locally on your Raspberry Pi, obviously with a reduced quality of voice synthcsis.

CONCEPTUAL SCHEME OF ARCHITECTURE

The conceptual scheme is roughed out in Figure 1 and explained as follow.

1) Information Request Module (IRM).

This module allows the user to makes consult through the keyboard and computer screen, this information is sent to a KRM. Once information is processed, the requested are shown to the user in the Prototype Portal.

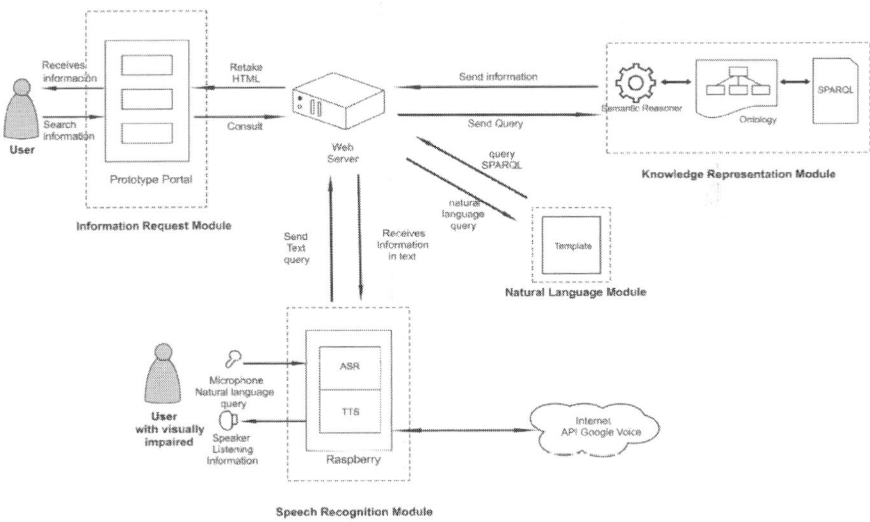

Figure 1. Conceptual scheme of architecture.

2) Knowledge Representation Module (KRM). The module consists of an ontology that contains all the con- cept models of study case, and is used to describe and represent a specific area of knowledge such as medicine, tourism, film, etc.

The ontology provides a way to encode knowledge and semantics such that machines can understand. Also, the ontological model contain logical rules. These rules depend on the selected domain, and it will need to be implemented as part of ontological model properties.

Depending on the source of the query, this module can interact with the other modules including IRM and NLM. In our prototype the SPARQL language will be used to extract different information from the ontology and answer the queries made by different modules.

3) Speech Recognition Module (SRM). This module allows to visually impaired people make queries in our Semantic Platform. For instance, the user ask for information in the microphone and such consult is converted to text in the ASR system. Then, this text is sent to the NLM to identify the appropriate template. After identifying the appropriate template, in KRM we make the SPARQL query to get the required information. This information is returned to the SRM in order to be converted to speech using TTS (Text-to-Speech). Finally, information is read for the user.

4) Natural Language Module (NLM). This module analyses and compare text queries come from SRM with certain patterns to create queries in SPARQL language and then it will be sent to KRM.

Although the process of formulating a natural language query and transform to SPARQL language is quite complex, it is possible to perform the query using query patterns [16] .

In [20] , they present a new approach based on a syntactic analysis of the questions to produce a SPARQL template that reflects the internal structure of the question.

With this in mind, we propose to use a series of templates associated with natural language. To give an illustration, in the query "Tell me the name of all transport to the city of Lima", template natural language query would be: "Tell me the name of all transport to the city of %PLACE%" where %PLACE% is a variable that the system recognize and is associated in the following SPARQL template:

```
SELECT?name WHERE
{
?transport table:name?name.
?transport table:transport_offered_destination?transport_offered_destination.
Filter(?transport_offered_destination = %PLACE%)
}
```

The system will replace the variable %PLACE% with Lima and send SPARQL query resultant to the KRM, where the information initially is requested, will be obtained, finally this information will be read by the SRM.

EXPECTED CONTRIBUTIONS AND FUTURE WORK

Actually, there are studies about the accessibility to internet for disabled people using tools of the Semantic Web. The reason of our proposal is the lack of works that use natural language to achieve the integration of semantics and ASR systems as a tool for people with visual disabilities.

The implementation must choose a particular domain and such ontology must contain all knowledge of this specific domain.

Once implemented the prototype of Semantic Platform with ASR system, the following benefits are expected:

- The integration of semantics and ASR system using natural language for assisting visually impaired people through the web.
- The developed platform architecture based on the prototype.
- The high accuracy with the use of the Raspberry Pi in ASR implementation.
- Generation of different templates SPARQL depending on the domain ontology for natural language queries.
- The expected SPARQL query templates will be quite similar to queries in the day-to-day language.
- As a complement and from the implemented prototype, a navigation support systems using voice commands, can be created to help people with visual disabilities, providing autonomy in its movement in an unfamiliar environment.
- The construction of a more flexible and personalized platform using tools of the Semantic Web.

As a future work, we expect to develop a prototype in the domain of tourism. The prototype will help people with visual disabilities to obtain information about several tourist attractions in Peru.

REFERENCES

1. Berners-Lee, T., Hendler, J., Lassila, O., et al. (2001) The Semantic Web. Scientific American, 284, 28-37.
2. Garcia-Crespo, A., Ruiz-Mezcua, B., Gonzalez-Carrasco, I., Lopez-Cuadrado, J., Hernandez, Z., Barahona, R. and Holnes de Toppin, L. (2014) Accessibility Services and Interactive Digital Television: An Opportunity to Reduce the Digital Gap. IEEE Revista Iberoamericana de Tecnologias del Aprendizaje, 9, 8-16.
3. Zakraoui, J. and Zagler, W. (2010) An Ontology for Representing Context in User Interaction for Enhancing Web Accessibility for All. http://pf-mh.uvt.rnu.tn/56/ [Citation Time(s):3]
4. Nganji, J.T., Brayshaw, M. and Tompsett, B. (2011) Ontology-Based E-Learning Personalization for Disabled Students in Higher Education. Innovation in Teaching and Learning in Information and Com-puter Sciences, 10, 1-11. [Citation Time(s):3]
5. Kehagias, D. and Tzovaras, D. (2010) An Ontology-Based Framework for Web Service Integration and Delivery to Mobility Impaired Users. In: Lytras, M., Ordonez De Pablos, P., Ziderman, A., Roulstone, A., Maurer, H. and Imber, J., Eds., Knowledge Management, Information Systems, E-Learning, and Sustainability Research, Springer Berlin Heidelberg, Berlin, 555-563.
6. Gupta, S. and Garg, D. (2011) Ontology Based Information Retrieval for Learning Styles of Autistic People. In: Mantri, A., Nandi, S., Kumar, G., and Kumar, S., Eds., High Performance Architecture and Grid Computing, Volume 169 of Communications in Computer and Information Science, Springer Berlin Heidelberg, Berlin, 293-298. http://dx.doi.org/10.1007/978-3-642-22577-2_40
7. Epelde, G., Valencia, X., Abascal, J., Diaz, U., Zinnikus, I. and Husodo-Schulz, C. (2011) Tv as a Human Interface for Ambient Intelligence Environments. 2011 IEEE International Conference on Multimedia and Expo (ICME), Barcelona, 11-15 July 2011, 1-6. http://dx.doi.org/10.1109/ICME.2011.6012186
8. Keet, C.M., Alberts, R., Gerber, A. and Chimamiwa, G. (2008) Enhancing Web Portals with Ontology-Based Data Access: The Case Study of South Africa's Accessibility Portal for People with Disabilities. OWLED, 432. http://ceur-ws.org/Vol-432/

9. Alonso, K., Aginako, N., Lozano, J. and Olaizola, I. (2012) Ontology Based Middleware for Ranking and Retrieving Information on Locations Adapted for People with Special Needs. In: Miesenberger, K., Karshmer, A., Penaz, P. and Zagler, W., Eds., Computers Helping People with Special Needs, Volume 7382 of Lecture Notes in Computer Science, Springer Berlin Heidelberg, Berlin, 351-354. http://dx.doi.org/10.1007/978-3-642-31522-0_53

10. Bukhari, A. and Kim, Y.-G. (2012) Ontology-Assisted Automatic Precise Information Extractor for Visually Impaired Inhabitants. Artificial Intelligence Review, 38, 9-24.

11. Vassilev, V., Ulman, M., Ouazzane, K., Kazemian, H., Aigbodi, M. and Boyd, R. (2013) Ontocarer: An Ontological Framework for Assistive Agents for the Disabled. The 3rd International Conference on Digital Information Processing and Communications (ICDIPC2013), Dubai, 30 January-1 February 2013, 404-416.

12. Yu, L. (2007) Introduction to the Semantic Web and Semantic Web Services. CRC Press, Boca Raton. http://dx.doi.org/10.1201/9781584889342

13. Fernández-López, M., Gómez-Pérez, A. and Juristo, N. (1997) Methontology: From Ontological Art towards Ontological Engineering. http://oa.upm.es/id/file/88930

14. Yu, L. (2011) A Developers Guide to the Semantic Web. Springer Science & Business Media, Berlin. http://dx.doi.org/10.1007/978-3-642-15970-1

15. Antoniou, G. and Van Harmelen, F. (2004) A Semantic Web Primer. MIT Press, Cambridge, USA.

16. Pradel, C., Haemmerl, O. and Hernandez, N. (2012) A Semantic Web Interface Using Patterns: The Swip System. In: Croitoru, M., Rudolph, S., Wilson, N., Howse, J. and Corby, O., Eds., Graph Structures for Knowledge Representation and Reasoning, Springer Berlin Heidelberg, Barcelona, 172-187. http://dx.doi.org/10.1007/978-3-642-29449-5_7

17. Duarte, T., Prikladnicki, R., Calefato, F. and Lanubile, F. (2014) Speech Recognition for Voice-Based Machine Translation. IEEE Software, 31, 26-31.

18. Stefanovic, M., Cetic, N., Kovacevic, M., Kovacevic, J. and Jankovic, M. (2012) Voice Control System with Advanced Recognition. 20th

Telecommunications Forum (TELFOR), Belgrade, 20-22 November 2012, 1601-1604. http://dx.doi.org/10.1109/TELFOR.2012.6419529

19. Naeem, A., Qadir, A. and Safdar, W. (2014) Voice Controlled Intelligent Wheelchair Using Raspberry Pi. International Journal of Technology and Research, 2, 65.

20. Unger, C., Bühman, L., Lehmann, J., Ngonga Ngomo, A.-C., Gerber, D. and Cimian, P. (2012) Template-Based Question Answering over RDF Data. Proceedings of the 21st International Confer-ence on World Wide Web, New York, 639-648.

SECTION 4: LANGUAGE UNDERSTANDING TECHNOLOGY

CHAPTER 15

English Sentence Recognition Based on HMM and Clustering

Xinguang Li[1], Jiahua Chen[1], Zhenjiang Li[2]

[1]Cisco School of Informatics, Guangdong University of Foreign Studies, Guangzhou, China

[2]School of Business Adminstrtion, South China University of Technology, Guangzhou, China

ABSTRACT

For English sentences with a large amount of feature data and complex pronunciation changes contrast to words, there are more problems existing in Hidden Markov Model (HMM), such as the computational complexity of the Viterbi algorithm and mixed Gaussian distribution probability. This

Citation: X. Li, J. Chen and Z. Li, "English Sentence Recognition Based on HMM and Clustering," American Journal of Computational Mathematics, Vol. 3 No. 1, 2013, pp. 37-42. doi: 10.4236/ajcm.2013.31005.

article explores the segment-mean algorithm for dimensionality reduction of speech feature parameters, the clustering cross-grouping algorithm and the HMM grouping algorithm, which are proposed for the implementation of the speaker-independent English sentence recognition system based on HMM and clustering. The experimental result shows that, compared with the single HMM, it improves not only the recognition rate but also the recognition speed of the system.

Keywords: English Sentence Recognition, HMM, Clustering

INTRODUCTION

The pauses between English words can simplify speech recognition. Because the endpoint detection of a word (i.e. detecting the starting point and the end point of the word) is relatively easy, and the Coarticulation effect between words can be reduced to the minimum. In addition, generally the word pronunciation is more serious, because there must have pauses between words which make less fluent reading. In view of the above reasons, many techniques can be used for the English word speech recognition system [1].

Compared with English word, more feature data and more complex changes in pronunciation make the English sentence speech recognition more difficult. Firstly, English sentence has a larger vocabulary and no obvious pause between words with pronunciation. That is to say, there is no clear boundary between sub-words. Secondly, every word pronunciation in English sentence is usually more natural, and associated language pronunciation is more casual than isolated word pronunciation, thus the coarticulation effect is more serious. Furthermore, affected by the context, in the process of English pronunciation, rhythm, intonation, stress and speed in English sentence may be different, even the same speaker at different times or in different environment, the prosodic features are different.

As a mainstream technology for large-vocabulary speaker-independent continuous speech recognition system, the Hidden Markov Model (HMM) [2-5] has achieved considerable success. Analyzing the short-term energy of speech signal and extracting the speech feature with a frame length, this paper takes Markov modeling on the whole sentence [6,7]. Model training uses a training set recorded by many speakers and the statistical theory is used to resolve the differences between the individual and the whole, so as to make the speaker independent single sentence Markov modeling robust. When recognizing speech, the system uses Viterbi algorithm to decode and find out the correct recognition result. Using Markov modeling on single sentence can describe the correlation of the words within each sentence. Under the condition of sufficient training speech, the speaker independent small statement English sentences modeling can be achieved with a high accuracy. However, HMM needs prior statistical knowledge of speech signal and has weak classification decision ability and other problems, including the computational complexity of the Viterbi algorithm and mixed Gaussian distribution probability. These shortcomings make it difficult to further improve the recognition performance of the single HMM [8].

Most of the literatures [9-14] in the field of speech recognition improve clustering algorithm within HMM and take them as the method of pattern classification, to optimize the model parameters estimation, but the effect for sentence recognition was not ideal. For English sentences with a large amount of data and complex pronunciation changes, the shortage of HMM is more apparent, making recognition time longer. In order to effectively improve the recognition efficiency, this paper, on the basis of the single HMM, attempts to integrate clustering algorithm with HMM and apply to the English sentence recognition. According to the characteristics of English sentences and the similarity between them, the English sentences data set is divided into several groups, each of which consists of some sentences with similar phonetic feature. So when recognize an English sentence, there is no need for all the sentences on Viterbi decoding, just to calculate the HMM parameters within the selected group which the input speech belongs to. In the case of appropriate clustering groups, the system will save a considerable mount of calculation, and the recognition performance can be greatly improved. This is not only to provide a new reference method for speech recognition in small device applications which meet the requirement of realtime, but also to lay the foundation of speech recognition for a new English sentence evaluation system.

WHOLE DESIGN PROCESS

As shown in **Figure 1**, first to pretreat the input speech signal, including pre-emphasis, frame processing, window adding and endpoint detection. Then extract the speech feature parameters MFCC and reduce the dimensionality of MFCC by segment-mean algorithm. The dynamic time warping (DTW) algorithm is followed to determine the speech feature clustering group K. Then calculate the HMM parameters within Group K and finally output the recognition results with post-processing.

CORE ALGORITHM

Segment-Mean Algorithm

As K-means clustering algorithm has the iterative characteristics with randomly selected sample point, coupled with the higher dimensionality of speech feature parameters, so the stability of clustering results is relatively poor. For this reason, this article explores the segment mean algorithm for dimensionality reduction of speech feature parameters, as shown in **Figure 2**.

Fragmenting the speech feature parameters into segments with the same dimension, the Segment-Mean algorithm consists of four steps:

1) Define the speech feature parameters as S (K,J), where K denotes the orders of the MFCC parameters; J denotes the number of fragmented frames. Assumes T is the number of frames before fragmented. Then fragment the speech feature parameters into N segments can be:

$$M(i) = S(K,J), J = \left[\frac{T}{N}(i-1)+1\right],\cdots,\left[\frac{T}{N}i\right] \tag{1}$$

M(i) represents the i-th segment of the fragmented speech feature parameters. The value of N is set to the statue number of the HMM.

2) After fragmenting the speech feature parameters into average segments, we continue fragment M(i) into M average segments (The value of M is set to the observation sequence number of the HMM). The calculations of child segments see the above formula.

3) The mean of each child segments is given by $\overline{M(i)}_k$, k = 1,2, …, M.

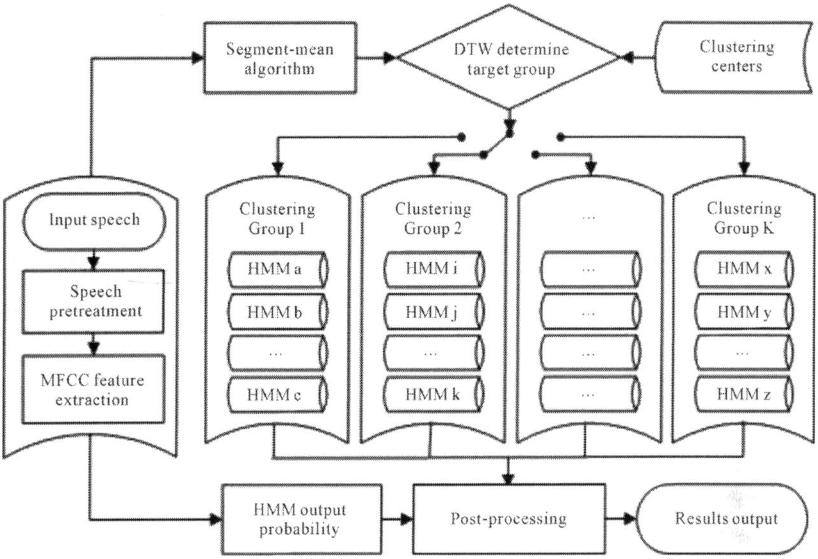

Figure 1. The frame diagram of speech recognition based on HMM and clustering.

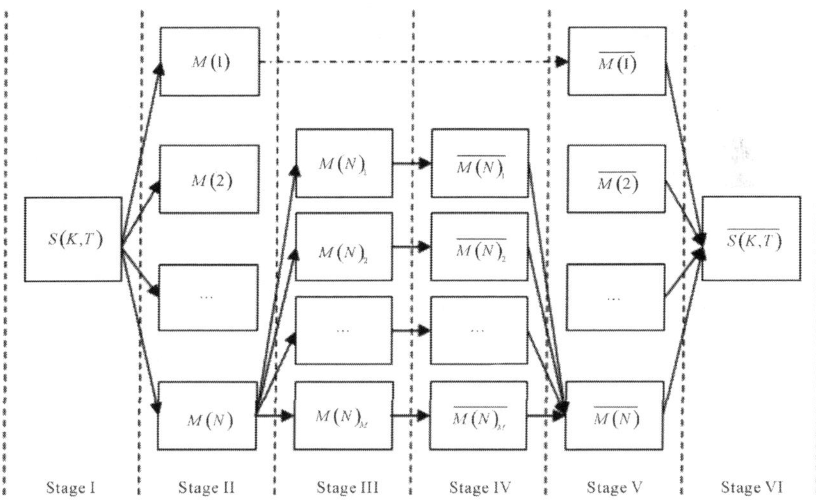

Figure 2. Segment-mean algorithm for dimensionality reduction of voice feature coefficients.

4) Merge all the mean of the child segments into a matrix. The matrix denotes the speech feature parameters output after

dimensionality reduction. It is defined as $\overline{S(K,T)}$. The size of $\overline{S(K,T)}$ is $K \times M \times N$.

The total numbers of parameters in **Figure 2** are shown in **Table 1**. The segment-mean algorithm turns the size of feature parameters matrix from T × K to K × M × N. That is to say the algorithm successfully removes the frame length T from the matrix. This means, the matrix (dimensionality reduction) keeps the same size after the segment-mean calculation. And the size of feature parameters matrix is determined for K (the orders of the speech feature parameters), N (size of the segment) and M (size of the child segment).This makes speech with different length can be structured as a matrix of the same size, which largely facilitates the implementation of speech feature clustering algorithm.

Clustering Cross-Grouping Algorithm

In order to further enhance the performance in the field of speech feature clustering, this paper presents a new secondary training method-clustering cross-grouping algorithm.

As shown in **Figure 3**, the clustering cross-grouping algorithm consists of three steps:

- Cluster the features of the training speech samples using K-means clustering algorithm.
- Calculate the distances between the training speech samples and the cluster centers using dynamic time warping (DTW) algorithm. For each sample, the minimum distance determines its target group.
- Check whether the target group contains the training sample. If included, the classification is correct; else the sentence will be added to the target group.

HMM Grouping Algorithm

In the recognition system based on single HMM, when using Viterbi algorithm to do decoding operations, all the model parameters must be involved in the computation. Assume the number of system vocabulary is n, then the number of HMM parameters is n. When recognizing a sentence, each output probability is calculated by Viterbi algorithm within n HMMs respectively. Because each isolated sentence has a unique HMM parameter with corresponding. We are able to have the sentences in the feature clustering groups mapped to the corresponding HMM parameters. Therefore we achieve the clustering grouping HMM model as **Figure 4** shown.

As the clustering cross-grouping algorithm is good in grouping performance, the number of the HMM parameters in the clustering group is always less than or equal to the number of system vocabulary. Also, the improved speech feature clustering model ensures a high grouping accuracy rate. Hence, this paper proposes to integrate the feature clustering model and HMM to form a hybrid model—English sentence recognition system based on clustering and HMM (as **Figure 1** shown).

EXPERIMENTAL RESULTS AND ANALYSIS

In order to verify the validity of the proposed model, the recognition rate and time on the single HMM and the hybrid model based on HMM and clustering were compared in speaker-independent English sentence recognition systems. The number of system vocabulary is 30. This experiment selects 30 different English sentences as standard sentences, 900 English sentences recorded by 30 individuals as training samples and 450 English sentences recorded by 15 individuals as test samples.

Table 1. The parameter table of voice feature coefficients processing segment-mean algorithm.

Stage	I	II	III	IV	V	VI
Size of matrix	$T \times K$	$\left(\frac{T}{N}\right) \times K$	$\left(\frac{T}{NM}\right) \times K$	$\left(\frac{T}{NM} \times \frac{1}{\frac{T}{NM}}\right) \times K$	$M \times K$	$(M \times N) \times K$
Number of parameters	$T \times K$	$T \times K$	$T \times K$	$K \times M \times N$	$K \times M \times N$	$K \times M \times N$

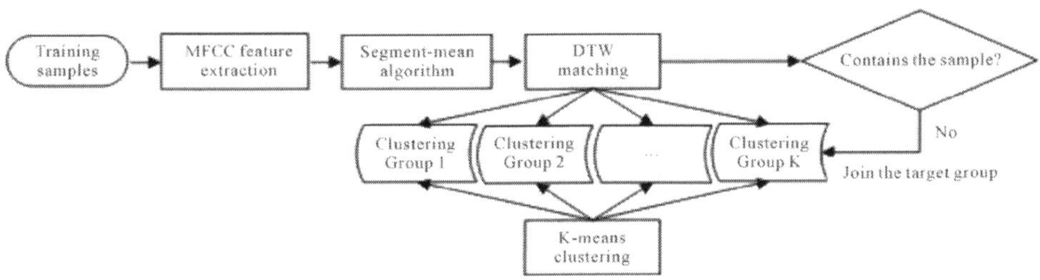

Figure 3. Clustering cross-grouping algorithm.

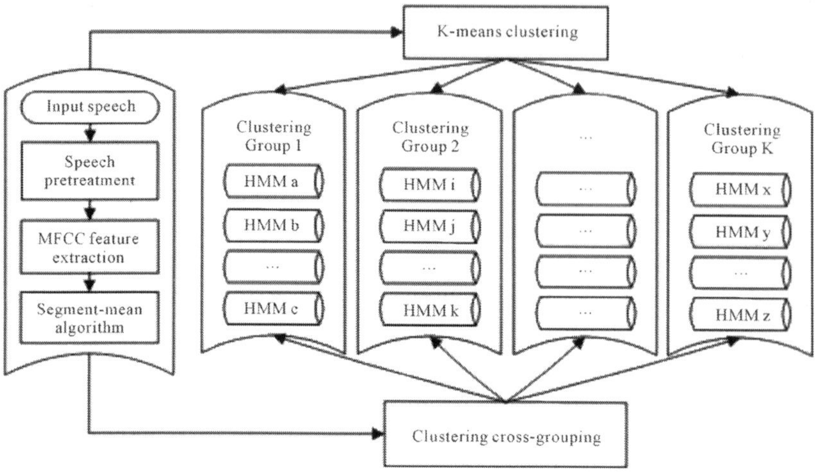

Figure 4. HMM grouping algorithm.

Take Sentence 1 "Can I have breakfast served in my room?" as an example to show the recognition rate and time in different recognition methods.

For example, comparing the sentences from Student 1, the system gives recognition results as shown in **Figure 5**.

No matter whether of the single model or the hybrid model the recognition results are correct, but the former total recognition time is 1.85 seconds, the latter total recognition time was 1.41 seconds, only 76.22% of the former. That is to say, the recognition time decreases, and the system efficiency is improved.

Compare the sentences from all the students (student 1 to 15), the results are show as **Table 2**. The experiments show that the recognition rate of the single HMM and the proposed model are both 100%; but the former average recognition time is 1.5753 seconds, the latter average recognition time of 1.2587 seconds, only 79.90% of the former, so as to improve the recognition efficiency.

Figure 5. The recognition result of sentence 1 from student 1.

Table 2. The recognition time table of sentence 1 (15 samples) in different recognition methods.

No. / Recognition time (s)	1	2	3	4	5	6	7	8	9	10	11	12	13	14	15
Single model	1.44	1.52	1.86	1.64	1.44	1.45	1.41	1.37	1.94	1.79	1.62	1.64	1.40	1.59	1.52
Hybrid model	1.23	1.25	1.30	1.25	1.26	1.24	1.26	1.26	1.31	1.29	1.25	1.24	1.22	1.29	1.23

Table 3. The overall recognition performance table in different methods.

Model / Item	Single model	Hybrid model
Average recognition rate	96.89%	99.78%
Average recognition time (s)	1.7687	1.2248

Table 3 is the overall recognition performance comparison in different recognition methods. The experimental results show that, compared with the English sentence recognition system based on single HMM, the average recognition rate of the English sentence recognition system based on HMM and clustering (the proposed model) increased by 2.89%, while the average recognition time accounted for only 69.25% of the former, improving the system efficiency.

CONCLUSION

On the basis of the English sentence recognition method and the traditional HMM speech recognition technology, an improved algorithm based on HMM and clustering is proposed for the implementation of the English sentence recognition system. The experimental results show that the improved system in accordance with the method proposed in this paper, not only improve the recognition rate of the system, but also reduce the amount of computation of the system (i.e., the recognition time), to achieve the goal of improving system performance. But how to determine the clustering groups to further improve the recognition efficiency and applied to more large-scale English sentence recognition is in need of further research.

ACKNOWLEDGEMENTS

Xinguang Li, Jiahua Chen, Zhenjiang Li (2011B031400003).

REFERENCES

1. M. Zhu, X. Wen, J. Huang and L. Zhou, "Computer Speech Technology," Revised Edition, Beijing University of Aeronautics and Astronautics Press, Beijing, 2002.
2. L. R. Rabiner, "A Tutorial on Hidden Markov Models and Selected Applications in Speech Recognition," Proceeding of the IEEE, Vol. 77, No. 2, 1989, pp. 257-286. doi:10.1109/5.18626
3. L. R. Rabiner and B. H. Juang, "Fundamentals of Speech Recognition," 1st Edition, Prentice Hall, Upper Saddle River, 1993.
4. Q. He and Y. He, "An Extension of MATLAB Programming," 1st Edition, Tsinghua University Press, Beijing, 2002.
5. J. Han, L. Zhang and T. Zheng, "Speech Signal Processing," 1st Edition, Tsinghua University Press, Beijing, 2004.
6. L. Lippmann, E. Martin and D. Paul, "Multi-Style Training for Robust Isolated-Word Speech Recognition," Proceedings of the 1987 IEEE International Conference on Acoustics, Speech and Signal Processing, Dallas, 6-9 April 1987, pp. 705-708.
7. L. R. Rabiner, J. G. Wilpon and F. K. Soong, "High Performance Connected Digit Recognition Using Hidden Markov Model," Proceedings of the 1988 IEEE International Conference on Acoustics, Speech and Signal Processing, New York, 11-14 April 1988, pp. 119-122.
8. Y. Bao, J. Zheng and X. Wu, "Speech Recognition Based on a Hybrid Model of Hidden Markov Models and the Genetic Algorithm Neural Network," Computer Engineering & Science, Vol. 33, No. 4, 2011, pp. 139-144. [Citation Time(s):1]
9. S. K. Bhatia, "Adaptive K-Means Clustering," Proceedings of the Seventeenth International Florida Artificial Intelligence Research Society Conference, Miami, 12-14 May 2004, pp. 695-699.
10. A. Likas, N. Vlassis and J. Verbeek, "The Global K-Means Clustering Algorithm," Pattern Recognition, Vol. 36, No. 2, 2003, pp. 451-461. doi:10.1016/S0031-3203(02)00060-2
11. T. Kanungo, D. M. Mount, N. S. Netanyahu, C. D. Piatko, R. Silverman and A. Y. Wu, "An Efficient K-Means Clustering Algorithms Analysis and Implementation," IEEE Transaction on Pattern Analysis and Machine Intelligence, Vol. 24, No. 7, 2002, pp. 881-892. doi:10.1109/TPAMI.2002.1017616

12. X. Ma, Y. Fu and J. Lu, "The Segmental Fuzzy c-Means Algorithm for Estimating Parameters of Continuous Density Hidden Markov Models," Acta Acustica, Vol. 22, No. 6, 1997, pp. 550-554.
13. L. Zhao, C. Zou and Z. Wu, "The Segmental Fuzzy Clustering Algorithm for Estimating Parameters of the VQHMM," Journal of Circuits and Systems, Vol. 7, No. 3, 2002, pp. 66-69.
14. H. Wang, L. Zhao and J. Pei, "Equilibrium Modified K-Means Clustering Method," Journal of Jilin University (Information Science Edition), Vol. 24, No. 2, 2006, pp. 172-176.

CHAPTER 16

A Comparative Study to Understanding about Poetics Based on Natural Language Processing

Lingyi Zhang[1], **Junhui Gao**[2]

[1] Wuxi No. 1 High School, Wuxi, China.

[2] American and European International Study Center, Wuxi, China

ABSTRACT

This paper tries to find out five poets' (Thomas Hardy, Wilde, Browning, Yeats, and Tagore) differences and similarities through analyzing their works on nineteenth Century by using natural language understanding technology and word vector model. Firstly, we collect enough poems from these five

Citation: Zhang, L. and Gao, J. (2017), A Comparative Study to Understanding about Poetics Based on Natural Language Processing. Open Journal of Modern Linguistics, 7, 229-237. doi: 10.4236/ojml.2017.75017.

poets, build five corpus respectively, and calculate their high-frequency words, by using Natural Language Processing method. Then, based on the word vector model, we calculate the word vectors of the five poets' high-frequency words, and combine the word vectors of each poet into one vector. Finally, we analyze the similarity between the combined word vectors by using the hierarchical clustering method. The result shows that the poems of Hardy, Browning, and Wilde are similar; the poems of Tagore and Yeats are relatively close—but the gap between the two is relatively large. In addition, we evaluate the stability of our approach by altering the word vector dimension, and try to analyze the results of clustering in a literary (poetic) perspective. Yeats and Tagore possessed a kind of mysticism poetics thought, while Hardy, Browning, and Wilde have the elements of realism combined with tragedy and comedy. The results are similar comparing to those we get from the word vector model.

Keywords: Poets, Natural Language Processing, Word Vector Model, Similarity, Cluster Analysis

INTRODUCTION

Deep Learning is a new field in machine learning, a learning method based on the representation of data. The concept is derived from the study of artificial neural networks. By combining low-level features to form a more abstract high- level representation of attributes, categories, or features, the aim is to discover the distribution of data. The earliest neural network in deep learning originated from the MCP artificial neuron model in 1943 (Bryant, 2016), which was used to simulate human neuronal responses by computers at that time. In 1958, Rosenblatt invented the perceptron algorithm that used MCP for machine learning (Rhys, 2017).

The deep learning in natural language began in 2006 when Hinton proposed the concept of Deep Belief Network (DBN) (Imagination Tech, 2017). Previously, the neural network was a complex one that was difficult to train, and only studied as a mathematical theory. In addition, Word vector model is the most common model used in natural language deep learning process. The core idea of this model is to symbolize the language into 1 and 0, a mode that is suitable for machine learning. Andrew L et al. used a probabilistic model of documents, which learns semantically focused word vectors, to learn the word representations to encode word meaning—semantics (Maas, Andrew, & Ng, 2011).

Mikolov et al. proposed two new model structures for computing continuous vector representations of words from very large data sets to measure the similarity between syntactic and semantic words, and the results are compared to the previously techniques based on different types of neural networks (Mikolov, Chen, Corrado, & Dean, 2013).

Attabi et al. studied the effectiveness of anchor models to solve multiple emotion recognition problems from speech, based on the FAU AIBO Emotion Corpus—a database of spontaneous children's speech. Compared with generative model such as the Gaussian Mixture Models, the anchor models improve significantly the performance of GMMs by 6.2 percent relative in such problems (Attabi & Dumouchel, 2013).

Sreeja et al. discussed the automatic recognition of emotions in English poems, which included Love, Sad, Anger, Hate, Fear, Surprise, Courage, Joy and Peace, by using the Vector Space model with a total of 348 poems of 163 poets mined from the web (Sreeja & Mahalakshmi, 2016).

Zhou Yingying et al. conducted experiments on the Chinese Quora—Zhihu— by using the topic2vec vector model in Chinese corpora. They found out that the convolutional neural network (CNN) with topic2vec gained an accuracy of 98.06% for long content texts, 93.27% for short time texts and an improvement comparing with other word embedding models (Zhou & Fan, 2016).

According to a series of previous study in deep learning of natural language, we can find that some have studied the syntax and semantics of text on the basis of word vector models. Some, based on the study of their predecessors, compared the efficiency of different models applied to the similar task. Others did detailed research such as using plenty of poems as corpora to carry out emotion recognition. Based on the study above, we will use the traditional word vector model for comparative poetics study.

MATERIALS AND METHOD

We will describe them from data, word vector calculations, and comparative approaches among poets in the following content.

Materials

Four of the five selected poets are from England, including Thomas Hardy, Wilde, Browning, and Yeats. The one left is Tagore, a poet from India. We selected a total of 257 poems from Thomas Hardy (Poemhunter, 2017), 96 poems from Oscar Wilde (Poemhunter, 2017), 63 poems from Browning (Blackcatpoems, 2017), nearly 400 poems from (Yeats, 1951 ; Blake, 2002), and 86 poems from Tagore (Tagore, 2011).

The main reason for selecting the five poems is to avoid the errors caused by all sorts of differences. Firstly, the origin version of poems of their works are all in English. In this way, we do not need to translate their works in which we get the second-hand poems containing the translation errors in order to get accuracy results from analysis. Secondly, the gaps between their living years are very small since nearly all of their works are produced in early nineteenth Century to mid twentieth Century, which was the golden years of the development of European poetry. Thus, the problems which may be caused by the differences between archaic words and modern words can be effectively avoid. For example, in old English, poets used "thou" in lieu of "you" to express you's nominative form and "thee" in lieu of "you" to express you's accusative form. The five poets who all gathered during nineteenth Century and twentieth Century almost eliminate the use of old English, although some old words may also appear in their poems rarely. In other words, we will not choose to compare Beowulf with Mark Twain's The Million Pound Note because they do not belong to different language systems at various times.

Word Vector Calculation

Although the research of natural language has already existed, traditional natural language study is a basic bottom-up study, from words, sentences, and paragraphs, and finally to the structures of text, but still can not let the computers understand the natural language well. One of the obstacles is the poor understanding of semantics. Before word2vec occurred, the research of semantic in NLP was mainly based on the understanding of latent semantic (LSA, Latent Semantic Analysis), and then its subsequent model (topic model) was introduced (Niketim, 2016).

Word2vec and topic models are completely different things. In the topic model, the basic granularity is still the word, and the topic is a probabilistic combination of words.

The semantics mined from the topic model of the article is at high level. In word2vec, however, the word "fundamental granularity" has a new expression, which is called the word vector (word embedding).

Before the occurrence of word vector, we often used the method called 1-of-N (or one-hot). In this representation, the great majority of elements is 0, and only one dimension is 1. This dimension represents the current word.

Suppose that we have five words in our table: King, Queen, Man, Woman, Child. If we want to represent 'Queen', we can express it in 1-of N, as shown in Table 1.

This simple method has two drawbacks. One is the curse of dimensionality. Another is a phenomenon called "lexical gap", namely the isolation between any two words, and is unable to judge a synonym like "microphone" and "Mike".

The new method of word representation is called Distributed Representation. This method in representing word uses the position of a real vector to represent a word such as [0.792, −0.177, −0.107, 0.109, −0.542, …], as shown in Table 2.

For each poet, we combine all the poems we collected, and construct the corpus by NLTK. Then, the corresponding word vectors are generated by Word2vec.

Natural Language Toolkit, referred to as NLTK, is a Natural Language Processing kit and a often used Python library in NLP, which was developed by Steven Bird and Edward Loper in the information science department at University of Pennsylvania (Baike, 2017).

Comparative Approaches among Poets

For each poet, we find the common high-frequency words of him and other poets, and assume that each high-frequency word is a 100 dimensional vector, and finally combine all the vectors into one corresponding to the high-frequency words.

Then, we calculate the distance between the five vectors by cosine method. The cosine similarity is derived by the cosine value of the angle between the two vectors in the vector space to measure the difference between the two individuals. The closer the cosine is to one, the more the angle is closer to zero degrees, namely the close resemblance between the two vectors. This is called "cosine similarity" (Yuhushangwei, 2016).

Table 1. Expression in 1-of-N.

0	1	0	0	0
King	Queen	Man	Woman	Child

Table 2. Distributed Representation.

	King	**Queen**	**Woman**	**Princess**	**...**
Royaling	0.99	0.99	0.02	0.98	...
Mascalining	0.99	0.05	0.01	0.02	...
Feminin	0.05	0.93	0.999	0.94	...
Age	0.7	0.6	0.5	0.1	...
...	...	...	...	...	...

After we get the distance between the five poets, the value is subtracted by 1, and we consider this value as the similarity between the five poets. Afterwards, we employ cluster analysis to analyze the relationship between the five poets.

The difference between clustering and classification is that the classes divided by clustering are unknown. Clustering is a process that classifies data into different classes or clusters, so the objects in the same closer have great similarity, while objects between different clusters have great diversity. From the point of view of statistics, clustering analysis is a way to simplify date through data modeling.

There are many kinds of clustering methods, and here we use hierarchical clustering. This method decomposes the given date set as a hierarchical level until reaching a certain condition. Concretely, it can be divided into two programs: condensed and split. Hierarchical agglomerative cluster is a bottom-up strategy. Firstly, take each object as a cluster, and then combine these clusters into bigger clusters until all the objects are in one cluster, or a certain condition is reached. The great majority of the hierarchical clustering method belongs to this class, and only the definitions of the similarity between clusters are different. Split level clustering is opposite to hierarchical agglomerative cluster, by using strategy of top-down. It will first put all the objects into one cluster, and then gradually subdivided them into smaller clusters until each object form a cluster, or a certain condition is reached.

RESULTS

We will show our results from three aspects: statistics of high-frequency word, similarity calculation, and cluster analysis.

Statistics of High-Frequency Word

The statistics of the high-frequency words of the five poets are shown in Table 3. This table is arranged from left to right, and from top to bottom. The word in the upper left corner has the highest number of occurrence, which is 1225; The word in the lower right corner has the minimum number of occurrence, which is 392.

Similarity Calculation

We set the word vector dimension to 100, then calculate the word vector, and finally compare the similarity between the five poets, as shown in Table 4.

Cluster Analysis

Based on Table 4, we use hierarchical clustering, and the results are shown in Figure 1.

Table 3. Public High-Frequency Words (first 20).

word	times	word	times	word	times	word	times
one	1225	come	715	know	530	shall	432
would	999	day	661	time	504	upon	420
like	941	life	623	king	480	never	416
said	821	man	584	old	442	night	399
heart	786	love	531	could	441	let	392

Table 4. Similarity between the Five Poets.

	browning	hardy	tagore	wilde	yeats
browning	1.00	0.79	0.22	0.81	0.26
hardy	0.79	1.00	0.54	0.78	0.54
tagore	0.22	0.54	1.00	0.34	0.61
wilde	0.81	0.78	0.34	1.00	0.40
yeats	0.26	0.54	0.61	0.40	1.00

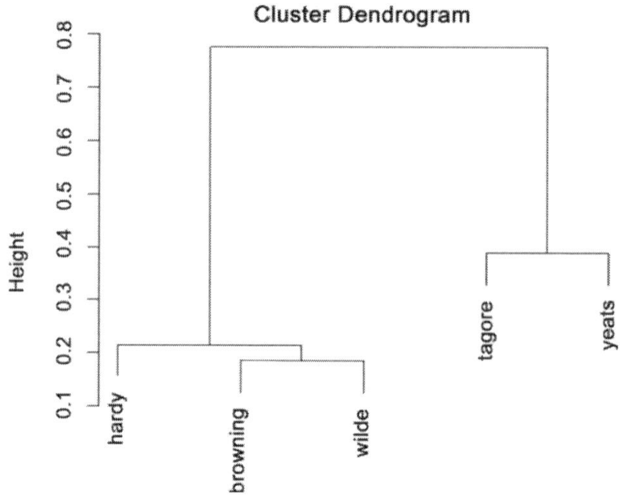

Figure 1. A Hierarchical Clustering Map of Five Poets by a 100 Dimensional Vector Model.

In Figure 1, the abscissa is five poets. The ordinate is the distance between those poets. The shorter the distance between the poets, the higher the similarity. From Table 1, Hardy, Browning, and Wilde are similar, with the difference of about 0.2, especially the latter two. Tagore and Yeats are close to each other, with the difference of about 0.4, not as close as the first three poets. However, the difference between the group of Hardy, Browning and Wilde and the group of Tagore and Yeats is large, with the value between 0.7 and 0.8 (the largest difference is 1).

DISCUSSION

As mentioned earlier, we talked about the definition of 100 dimensional computational vector of word, and obtained the results in Tables 1-4. In oder to test the stability of the results, we also use 80 dimension and 120 dimension to calculate the word vector, and the result we get from the calculation is very close to that of 100 dimension. Take 120 dimension as an example. The clustering result we obtain is shown in Figure 2. The results of Figure 1 and Figure 2 are very close to each other, indicating that our method is stable and reliable.

From a literary perspective, Tagore is a patriotic poet, and his works reveal his patriotism and the spirit of Democracy. Yeats showed the reverence to Aestheticism and Romanticism in his early years. After he experienced the nationalist political movement in Ireland in his forties, the style of his poetry gradually went close to realism.

Tagore and Yeats developed their friendship because of poetry. They shared many points of view in literature. First of all, Tagore and Yeats had direct contacts in life. In 1912, they met each other due to "Gitanjali". Yeats admired Tagore's talent very much, and helped Tagore publish this collection and made the preface of it. Second, both of them possessed a kind of mysticism poetics thought. Tagore's belief is a mixture of religious philosophy while Yeat's belief is derived from his natural disposition, which is personal philosophy. Third, although they are modern poets, they do not belong to Modernism since both of them criticize the modernist literature in their poems. Therefore, the results we obtained from literary appreciation are similar to those gained from the cluster analysis above (Wang, 2012).

Wilde is one of the representative poets of aestheticism, with fairy tales as the main characteristic. His poems are full of the elements of duality, which shows the simultaneism of aesthetics and tragedy. Wilde is good at describing the contradiction between characters and the cruel social background. His tragic beauty and death consciousness contain his understanding about life (Sun, 2012).

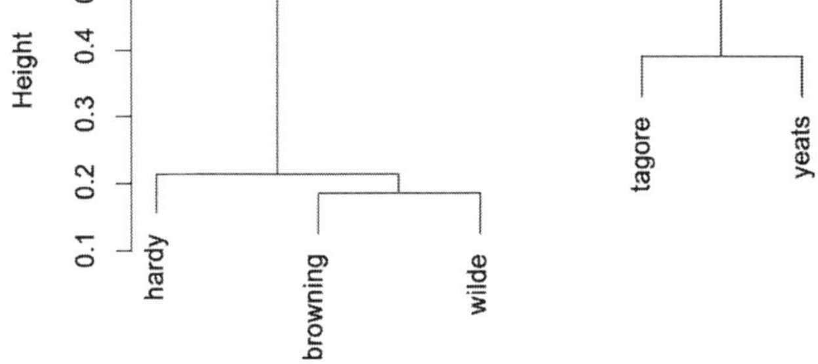

Figure 2. A Hierarchical Clustering Map of Five Poets by a 100 Dimensional Vector Model.

Likewise, the poems of Thomas Hardy also have tragic color, which is mostly the natural revelation of personal experience and emotion. Hardy believes that society is the root of pain; the personality of human beings leads to the suffering in the world; and the destiny is controlled by the universe. The analysis of these unique perspectives illustrates the ubiquitous tragedy and distress in his poems (Ma, 2009). Robert Browning is a British poet and a playwright. He creates a unique from of poetry, referred to as “dramatic monologue”, using a cinematic narrative technique-Montage-to restructure and integrate time and space. Browning loves to show the changes in characters’ psychological and story scenes through personal confession. Owning the color of the mixture of tragedy and comedy, His poems express the complexities of the characters and their attitudes of life. To sum up, although the styles of the three poets belong to different genres, all of them do well in depicting tragedies, and showing the irreconcilable contradictions between man and society (Zhang, 2007). Thus, the results we obtained from literature perspective are similar to those gained from the cluster analysis above.

The main contribution of our work is that this research is the first work to study different poets’ works by using the word vector model, which is pioneering and original. The drawback is that the number of the poets we used is limited. Also, the poet’s geographical distribution was not uniform enough since of the five poets, four of them came from England, and one left came from India. Finally, the dimensions we used are limited that we only employed 80, 100, and 120 the three dimensions to calculate their difference, but larger ones have not been used.

CONCLUSION

This paper uses vector model and hierarchical clustering in deep learning to investigate the similarities between the works of the five poets—Thomas Hardy, Oscar Wilde, Robert Browning, William Yeats, and Rabindranath Tagore—in the nineteenth Century. Our research contributes to the field which combines mathematical analysis and literary analysis together. High frequency words picked from the five poets are analyzed by the word vector model in 100 dimensions. The results show that the poems of Hardy, Browning, and Wilde are similar; the poems of Tagore and Yeats are relatively close. We also have employed other dimensions such as 80 and 120 to test the stability of our results, which have been proved reliable then. In addition, we have obtained the similar results by analyzing the works of the poets from a literary perspective which indicate their similarity in the interpretation of the tragedy, and the conflicts between men and the society.

REFERENCES

1. Attabi, Y., & Dumouchel, P. (2013). Anchor Models for Emotion Recognition from Speech. IEEE Transactions on Affective Computing, 4, 1-11. https://doi.org/10.1109/T-AFFC.2013.17
2. Baike (2017). Natural Language Toolkit. https://baike.baidu.com/item/NLTK/20403245?fr=aladdin
3. Blackcatpoems (2017). Robert Browning. http://www.blackcatpoems.com/b/robert_browning.html
4. Bryant, L. J. (2016). The History of Deep Learning. CSDN Blog. http://blog.csdn.net/u012177034/article/details/52252851
5. Imagination Tech (2017). The History and Problems of Deep Learning in Natural Language. http://www.sohu.com/a/161325083_468740
6. Ma, L. (2009). On the Topics of Tradedy, Love & Marriage, and Christianity in Thomas Hardy's Novels and Poetry. M. Thesis in Aesthetics, Tianjing Normal University, 8-11.
7. Maas, A. L., & Ng, A. Y. (2011). A Probabilistic Model for Semantic Word Vectors. 1-8.
8. Mikolov, T., Chen, K., Corrado, G., & Dean, J. (2013). Efficient Estimation of Word Representations in Vector Space. Computer Science, 1-12.
9. Niketim (2016). The Introduction of Word Vector. CSDN Blog. http://blog.csdn.net/u013362975/article/details/53319002
10. Poemhunter (2017). Oscar Wilde Poems. https://www.poemhunter.com/oscar-wilde
11. Poemhunter (2017). Thomas Hardy Poems. https://www.poemhunter.com/thomas-hardy
12. Rhys (2017). Rosenblatt's Perceptron Algorithm. http://blog.sina.com.cn/s/blog_166b82f8b0102xcu3.html
13. Sreeja, P. S., & Mahalakshmi, G. S. (2016). Comparison of Probabilistic Corpus Based Method and Vector Space Model for Emotion Recognition from Poems. Asian Journal of Information Technology, 15, 908-915.
14. Sun, C. W. (2012). Literature Review of Research on Wilde's Works in the Past Thirty Years (pp. 1-4). Shenyang: Liaoning University.
15. Tagore, R. (2011). Gitanjali. Annals of Neuroscience, 18, 66.

16. Wang, X. S. (2012). The Comparison of Tagore and Yeats' Poetic Thoughts (pp. 1-3). M.Sc. Thesis, Chongqing: Chongqing Southwest University.
17. Yeats, W. B. (1951). The Collected Poems of W.B. Yeats. Wordsworth Poetry Library, 1, 118-134.
18. Yuhushangwei (2016). The Calculation Method and Application of Cosine Similarity. http://blog.csdn.net/yuhushangwei/article/details/48541891
19. Zhang, W. (2007). On the Cinematic Narrative Feature of Robert Browning's Poetry (pp. 5-7). M.Sc. Thesis, Hangzhou: Zhejiang University.
20. Zhou Y. Y., & Fan, L. (2016). Deep Learning on Improved Word Embedding Model for Topic Classification. Computer Science and Application, 6, 629-637. https://doi.org/10.12677/CSA.2016.611077

CHAPTER 17

Semi-Supervised Learning of Statistical Models for Natural Language Understanding

Deyu Zhou[1] and Yulan He[2]

[1]School of Computer Science and Engineering, Key Laboratory of Computer Network and Information Integration, Ministry of Education, Southeast University, Nanjing 210096, China

[2]School of Engineering and Applied Science, Aston University, Birmingham B4 7ET, UK

ABSTRACT

Natural language understanding is to specify a computational model that maps sentences to their semantic mean representation. In this paper, we

Citation: Deyu Zhou, Yulan He, "Semi-Supervised Learning of Statistical Models for Natural Language Understanding", The Scientific World Journal, vol. 2014, Article ID 121650, 11 pages, 2014. https://doi.org/10.1155/2014/121650.

propose a novel framework to train the statistical models without using expensive fully annotated data. In particular, the input of our framework is a set of sentences labeled with abstract semantic annotations. These annotations encode the underlying embedded semantic structural relations without explicit word/semantic tag alignment. The proposed framework can automatically induce derivation rules that map sentences to their semantic meaning representations. The learning framework is applied on two statistical models, the conditional random fields (CRFs) and the hidden Markov support vector machines (HM-SVMs). Our experimental results on the DARPA communicator data show that both CRFs and HM-SVMs outperform the baseline approach, previously proposed hidden vector state (HVS) model which is also trained on abstract semantic annotations. In addition, the proposed framework shows superior performance than two other baseline approaches, a hybrid framework combining HVS and HM-SVMs and discriminative training of HVS, with a relative error reduction rate of about 25% and 15% being achieved in F-measure.

INTRODUCTION

Given a sentence such as "I want to fly from Denver to Chicago," its semantic meaning can be represented as FROMLOC(CITY(Denver)) TOLOC(CITY(Chicago)).

Natural language understanding can be considered as a mapping problem where the aim is to map a sentence to its semantic meaning representation (or abstract semantic annotation) as shown above. It is a *structured classification* task which predicts output labels (semantic tag or concept sequences) from input sentences where the output labels have rich internal structures.

Early approaches rely on hand-crafted semantic grammar rules to fill slots in semantic frames using word pattern and semantic tokens [1, 2]. Such rule-based approaches are typically domain-specific and often fragile. In contrast, statistical approaches are able to accommodate the variations found in real data and hence can in principle be more robust. They can be categorized into three types: generative approaches, discriminative approaches, and a hybrid of the two.

Generative approaches learn the joint probability model, (C, S), of input sentence S and its semantic tag sequence C, then compute $P(C \mid S)$ using Bayes' rule, and finally take the most probable semantic tag sequence C. The hidden Markov model (HMM), a generative model, has been predominantly employed in statistical semantic parsing. It models sequential dependencies by treating a semantic parse sequence as a Markov chain, which leads to an efficient dynamic programming formulation for inference and learning. Discriminative approaches directly model posterior probability $(C \mid S)$ and learn mappings from S to C. Conditional random fields (CRFs), as one representative example, define a conditional probability distribution over label sequence given an observation sequence, rather than a joint distribution over both label and observation sequences [3]. Another example is the hidden Markov support vector machines (HM-SVMs) [4] which combine the flexibility of kernel methods with the idea of HMMs to predict a label sequence given an input sequence.

Nevertheless, statistical models mentioned above require fully annotated corpora for training which are difficult to obtain in practical applications. It thus motivates the investigation of train statistical models on abstract semantic annotations without the use of expensive token-style annotations. This is a highly challenging problem because the derivation from each sentence to its abstract semantic annotation is not annotated in the training data and is considered hidden.

A hierarchical hidden state structure could be used to model embedded structural context in sentences, such as the hidden vector state (HVS) model [5], which learns a probabilistic pushdown automaton. However, it cannot incorporate a large number of correlated lexical or syntactic features in input sentences and cannot handle any arbitrary embedded relations since it only supports right-branching semantic structures.

In this paper, we propose a novel learning framework to train statistical models from unaligned data. Firstly, it generates semantic parses by computing expectations using initial model parameters. Secondly, parsing results are then filtered based on a measure describing the level of agreement with the sentence abstract semantic annotations. Thirdly, the filtered parsing results are fed into model learning. With the reestimated parameters, the learning of statistical models goes to the next iteration until no more improvements could be achieved. The proposed framework has two advantages: one is that only abstract semantic annotations are required for training without the explicit word/semantic tag alignment; and another is that the proposed learning framework can be easily extended for training any discriminative models on abstract semantic annotations.

We apply the proposed learning framework on two statistical models, CRFs and HM-SVMs. Experimental results on the DARPA communicator data show that the framework on both CRFs and HM-SVMs outperforms the baseline approach, the previously proposed HVS model. In addition, the proposed framework shows superior performance than two other approaches, a hybrid framework combining HVS and HM-SVMs and discriminative training of HVS, with a relative error reduction rate of about 25% and 15% being achieved in F-measure.

The rest of this paper is organized as follows. Section 2 gives a brief introduction of CRFs and HM-SVMs, followed by a review on the existing approaches for training semantic parsers on abstract annotations. The proposed framework is presented in Section 3. Experimental setup and results are discussed in Section 4. Finally, Section 5 concludes the paper.

RELATED WORK

In this section, we first briefly introduce CRFs and HM-SVMs. Then, we review the existing approaches for training semantic parsers on abstract semantic annotations.

Statistical Models

Given a set of training data $D = \{(S_i, C_i), i = 1, . . . , N\}$, to learn a function that assigns to a sequence of words $S = \{s^1 , s^2 ,...,s^T\}$, $si \in$ s, $i = 1, . . . , T$, a sequence of semantic concepts or tags$C = \{c^1 , c^2 ,...,c^T\}$, $ci \in$ c, $i = 1, . . . , T$, a common approach is to find a discriminant function $F : \mathrm{S} \times \mathrm{C} \rightarrow \mathrm{R}$ that assigns a score to every input $S \in \mathrm{S}$ and every semantic tag sequence $C \in \mathrm{C}$. In order to obtain a prediction $(S) \in \mathrm{C}$, the function is maximized with respect to $f(S) = \arg\max_{C \in C} F(S, C)$.

Conditional Random Fields (CRFs)

Linear-chain CRFs, as a discriminative probabilistic model over sequences of feature vectors and label sequences, have been widely used to model sequential data. This model is analogous to maximum entropy models for structured outputs. By making a firstorder Markov assumption on states, a linear-chain CRF defines a distribution over state sequence $C = \{c^1 , c^2 ,...,c^T\}$ given an input sequence $S = \{s^1 , s^2 ,...,s^T\}$ (T is the length of the sequence) as

$$p(C \mid S) = \frac{\Pi_t \Phi_t \left(c^{t-1}, c^t, S\right)}{Z(S)}, \qquad (1)$$

where the partition function $Z(S)$ is the normalization constant that makes the probability of all state sequences sum to one and is defined as $Z(S) = \Sigma_c \Pi_t \Phi_t(c^{t-1}, c^t, S)$.

By exploiting the Markov assumption, (S) can be calculated efficiently by variants of the standard dynamic programming algorithms used in HMM instead of summing over the exponentially many possible state sequences c. $\Phi(c^{t-1}, c^t, S)$ can be factorized as

$$\Phi\left(c^{t-1}, c^{t}, S\right) = \exp\left(\Sigma_k \theta_k f_k\left(c^{t-1}, c^{t}, S, t\right)\right), \quad (2)$$

where θ_k is the real weight for each feature function $fk(c^{t-1}, c^t, S, t)$. The feature functions describe some aspect of a transition from $c\ t{-}1$ to $c\ t$ as well as $c\ t$ and the global characteristics of S. For example, f_k may have value 1 when POS(s^{t-1}) = DT and POS(s^t) = NN, which means that the previous word s^{t-1} has the POS tag "DT" (determiner) and the current word $s\ t$ has the POS tag "NN" (noun, singular common). The final model parameters for CRFs are a set of real weights $\Theta = \{\theta_k\}$, one for each feature.

Hidden Markov Support Vector Machines (HM-SVMs)

For HM-SVMs [4], the function $F(S, C)$ is assumed to be linear in some combined feature representation of S and C; $F(S, C) := \langle w, \Phi(S, C)\rangle$.The parameters w are adjusted so that the true semantic tag sequence Ci scores higher than all other tag sequences$C \in \mathrm{C}_i := \mathrm{C}\backslash C_i$ with a large margin. To achieve the goal, the following optimization problem is solved:

$$\min_{\xi_i \in \mathbb{R}, w \in \mathcal{F}} \quad \mathrm{Cons}\sum_i \xi_i + \frac{1}{2}\|w\|^2$$

$$\text{s.t.} \qquad \langle w, \Phi(S, C_i)\rangle - \langle w, \Phi(S, C)\rangle \geq 1 - \xi_i,$$

$$\forall i = 1, \ldots N, \quad C \in \mathscr{C} \setminus C_i, \quad (3)$$

where ξ_i is nonnegative slack variables allowing one to increase the global margin by paying a local penalty on some outlying examples and Cons dictates the desired tradeoff between margin size and outliers. To solve (3), the dual of the equation is solved instead. The solution w can be written as

$$\widehat{w} = \sum_{i=1}^{N} \sum_{C \in \mathscr{C}} \alpha_i(C)\, \Phi(S_i, C), \quad (4)$$

where $\alpha_i(C)$ is the Lagrange multiplier of the constraint associated with example i and C_i.

Training Statistical Models from Lightly Annotated Data

Semantic parsing can be viewed as a pattern recognition problem and statistical decoding can be used to find the most likely semantic representation. The majority of statistical approaches to semantic parsing rely on fully annotated corpora. There have been some prior works on learning semantic parsers that map natural language sentences into a formal meaning representation such as first-order logic [6–10]. However these systems either require a hand-built, ambiguous combinatory categorical grammar template to learn a probabilistic semantic parser [11] or assume the existence of an unambiguous, context-free grammar of the target meaning representations [6, 7, 9, 12, 13]. Furthermore, they have only been studied in two relatively simple tasks, GEOQUERY [14] for US geography query and ROBOCUP (http://www.robocup.org/) where coaching instructions are given to soccer agents in a simulated soccer field.

He and Young [5] proposed the hidden vector state (HVS) model based on the hypothesis that a suitably constrained hierarchical model may be trainable without treebank data whilst simultaneously retaining sufficient ability to capture the hierarchical structure needs to robustly extract task domain semantics. Such a constrained hierarchical model can be conveniently implemented using the HVS model which extends the *flat-concept* HMM model by expanding each state to encode the stack of a pushdown automaton. This allows the model to efficiently encode hierarchical context, but because stack operations are highly constrained it avoids the tractability issues associated with full context-free stochastic models such as the hierarchical HMM. Such a model is trainable using only lightly annotated data and it offers considerable performance gains compared to the flat-concept model.

Conditional random fields (CRFs) have been extensively studied for sequence labeling. Most applications require the availability of fully annotated data, that is, an explicit alignment of sentence and word-level labels. There have been some attempts to train CRFs from a small set of labeled data and a large set of unlabeled data. In these approaches, a training objective is redefined to combine the conditional likelihood of labeled data and unlabeled data. Jiao et al. [15] extended the minimum entropy regularization framework to the structured prediction case so a training objective that combines unlabeled conditional entropy with labeled conditional likelihood is yielded. Mann and McCallum [16] augmented the traditional conditional likelihood objective function with an additional term that aims to minimize the predicted label entropy on unlabeled data.

Entropy regularization was employed for semisupervised learning. In [17], a training objective combining the conditional likelihood on labeled data and the mutual information on unlabeled data is proposed. It is based on the rate distortion theory in information theory. Mann and Mccallum [18] used labeled features instead of fully labeled instances to train linear-chain CRFs. Generalized expectation criteria are used to express a preference for parameter settings in which the model distribution on unlabeled data matches a target distribution. They tested their approach on the classified advertisements data set (CLASSIFIED) [19] consisting of classified advertisements for apartment rentals in the San Francisco Bay Area with 12 fields being labeled for each of the advertisements, including size, rent, neighborhood, and features. With only labeled features, their approach gave a mediocre result with 68.3% accuracy being achieved. With an additional inclusion of 100 labeled instances, the accuracy is increased to 80%. The DARPA communicator data used in our experiment appear to be more complex than the CLASSIFIED data since semantic annotations in the DARPA communicator data describe embedded structural context in sentences while semantic labels in the CLASSIFIED data do not represent any hierarchical relations.

THE PROPOSED FRAMEWORK

Given the training data $D = \{(S_1, A_1), \ldots, (S_N, A_N)\}$, where Ai is the abstract annotation for sentence S_i, the parameters Θ will be estimated through a maximum likelihood procedure. The log-likelihood of (Θ) with expectation over the abstract annotation is calculated as follows:

$$L(\Theta) = \sum_{i}^{N} \sum_{C_i^u} P(C_i^u \mid S_i) \log P(C_i^u \mid S_i), \tag{5}$$

where C^u_i is the unknown semantic tag sequence of the ith word sequence. To learn statistical models, we extended the use of expectation maximization (EM) algorithm to estimate model parameters. The EM algorithm [20] is widely employed in statistical models for parameter estimation when the model depends on unobserved latent variables. Given a set of observed data D, a set of unobserved latent data, or missing values D , the EM algorithm seeks to find the maximum likelihood estimation of the marginal likelihood

$$L(D \mid \theta) = \sum_{D^u} p(D, D^u, \theta) \tag{6}$$

by alternating between performing an *expectation* step and a *maximization* step.

- E-step: given the current estimate of the parameters, calculate the expected value for unobserved latent variables or data.
- M-step: find the parameter that maximizes this quantity. These parameter estimates are then used to determine the distribution of the latent variables in the next E-step.

We propose a learning framework based on EM to train statistical models from abstract semantic annotations as illustrated in Figure 1. The whole procedure works as follows. Given a set of sentences S = $\{S_i, i = 1, \ldots, N\}$ and their corresponding semantic annotations A = $\{A_i, i = 1, \ldots, N\}$, each annotation Ai is expanded to the flattened semantic tag sequence C_i at initialization step. Based on the flattened semantic tag sequences, the initial model parameters are estimated. After that, the semantic tag sequence Ci is generated for each sentence using the current model, $\mathcal{C} = \{C_i, i = 1, \ldots, N\}$. Then, $\mathcal{C}$ is filtered based on a score function which measures the agreement of the generated semantic tag sequences with the actual flattened semantic tag sequences. In the maximization step, model parameters are reestimated using the filtered $\mathcal{C}$. The iteration continues until convergence. The details of each step are discussed in Figure 1.

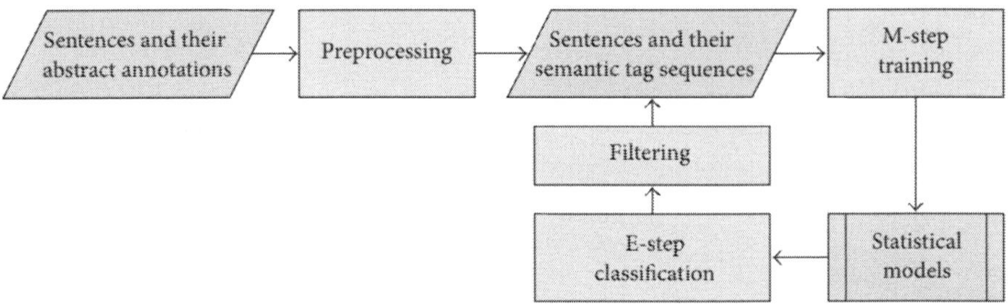

Figure 1: The proposed learning framework of training statistical models from abstract semantic annotations.

Preprocessing

Given a sentence labeled with an abstract semantic annotation as shown in Table 1, we first expand the annotation to the flattened semantic tag sequence as in Table 1(a). The provision of abstract annotations implies that the semantics encoded in each sentence need not be provided in expensive token style. Obviously, there are some input words such as articles, which have no specific semantic meanings. In order to cater for these irrelevant input words, a DUMMY tag is introduced in the preterminal position. Hence, the flattened semantic tag sequence is finally expanded to the semantic tag sequence as in Table 1(b).

Table 1: Abstract semantic annotation and its flattened semantic tag sequence.

Sentence	I want to return to Dallas on Thursday.
Annotation	RETURN (TOLOC (CITY (Dallas)) ON (DATE (Thursday)))
(a) Flattened semantic tag list:	
RETURN RETURN+TOLOC RETURN+TOLOC+CITY (Dallas) RETURN+ON RETURN+ON+DATE (Thursday)	
(b) Expanded semantic tag list:	
RETURN RETURN+DUMMY RETURN+TOLOC RETURN+TOLOC+DUMMY RETURN+TOLOC+CITY (Dallas)	
RETURN+ON RETURN+ON+DUMMY RETURN+ON+DATE (Thursday) RETURN+ON+DATE (Thursday)+DUMMY	

Expectation with Constraints

During the *expectation* step, that is, calculating the most likely semantic tag sequence given a sentence, we need to impose the following two constraints which are implied from abstract semantic annotations.

(1) Considering the calculated semantic tag sequence as a hidden state sequence, state transitions are only allowed if both current and next states are listed in the semantic annotation defined for the sentence.

(2) If a lexical item is attached to a preterminal tag of a flattened semantic tag, the semantic tag must appear bound to that lexical item in the training annotation.

To illustrate how these two constraints are applied, the sentence "I want to return on Thursday to Dallas" with its annotation "RETURN(TOLOC(CITY(Dallas)) ON(DATE(Thursday)))" is taken as an example. The transition from RETURN+TOLOC+CITY to RETURN is allowed since both states can be found in the semantic annotation and follows constraint 1. However, the transition from RETURN to FLIGHT is not allowed as it does not follow constraint 1 and FLIGHT is not listed in the semantic annotation. Also, for the lexical item Dallas in the training sentence, the only valid semantic tag is RETURN+TOLOC+CITY because to apply constraint 2 Dallas has to be bound with the preterminal tag CITY.

We further describe how these two constraints can be imposed into two different models, CRFs and HM-SVMs:

$$\alpha_t\left(c^t = c \mid S\right) = \sum_{c'} \alpha_{t-1}\left(c^{t-1} = c' \mid S\right) \exp \sum_k \theta_k f_k\left(c^{t-1} = c', c^t = c, S\right)$$

$$\beta_t\left(c^t = c \mid S\right) = \sum_{c'} \beta_{t+1}\left(c^{t+1} = c' \mid S\right) \exp \sum_k \theta_k f_k\left(c^{t+1} = c', c^t = c, S\right) \tag{7}$$

$$\alpha_t\left(c^t = c \mid S\right) = \begin{cases} 0, & \text{when } g\left(c^t, c, s^t\right) = 1, \\ \sum_{c'} \left\{ \alpha_{t-1}\left(c^{t-1} = c' \mid S\right) \times \exp \sum_k \theta_k f_k\left(c^{t-1} = c', c^t = c, S\right) \right\}, & \text{otherwise,} \end{cases}$$

$$\beta_t\left(c^t = c \mid S\right) = \begin{cases} 0, & \text{when } g\left(c^t, c, s^t\right) = 1, \\ \sum_{c'} \left\{ \beta_{t+1}\left(c^{t+1} = c' \mid S\right) \times \exp \sum_k \theta_k f_k\left(c^{t+1} = c', c^t = c, \mathbf{x}\right) \right\}, & \text{otherwise.} \end{cases} \tag{8}$$

Expectation in CRFs

The most probable labeling sequence in CRFs can be efficiently calculated using the Viterbi algorithm. Similar to the forward-backward procedure for HMM, the marginal probability of states at each position in the sequence can be computed as

$$P\left(c^t = c \mid S\right) = \frac{\alpha_t\left(c^t = c \mid S\right) \beta_t\left(c^t = c \mid S\right)}{Z(S)}, \tag{9}$$

where $Z(S) = \sum_c \alpha_t(c \mid S)$.

The forward values $\alpha(c^t = c \mid S)$ and backward values $\beta_t(c^t = c \mid S)$ are defined in iterative form as (7).

Given the training data $D = \{(S_1, C_1), \ldots, (S_N, C_N)\}$, the parameter Θ can be estimated through a maximum likelihood procedure. To calculate the log-likelihood of (Θ) with expectation over the abstract annotation as follows,

$$L(\Theta;\Theta^t) = \sum_i^N \sum_{C_i^u} P(C_i^u \mid S_i;\Theta^t) \log P(C_i^u \mid S_i;\Theta)$$

$$= \sum_i^N \sum_{C_i^u} P(C_i^u \mid S_i;\Theta^t) \sum_t \sum_k \theta_k f_k(c', c, S_i)$$

$$- \sum_i^k \log Z(S_i), \tag{10}$$

where C_i^u is the unknown semantic tag sequence of the ith word sequence and $Z(S_i) = \sum_c \exp(\sum_t \sum_k \theta_k f_k(c^{t-1}, c^t, S_i))$. It can be optimized using the same optimization method as in standard CRFs training.

To infer the word-level semantic tag sequences based on abstract annotations, (7) are modified as shown in (8), where (c^t, c, s^t) is defined as follows:

$$g(c^t, c, s^t) = \max \begin{cases} 1, & c \text{ is not in the allowable semantic tag list of } S, \\ 1, & c \text{ is not of class type and } s^t \text{ is of class type,} \\ 0, & \text{otherwise.} \end{cases} \tag{11}$$

Expectation in HM-SVM

To calculate the most likely semantic tag sequence C for each sentence S, $C =\hat{}\ \arg\max_{C\in C}(S, C)$, we can decompose the discriminant function $F : S \times C \rightarrow R$ into two components, $F(S, C) = F_1(S, C) + F_2(S, C)$, where

$$F_1(S,C) = \sum_{\sigma \in c, \tau \in c} \delta(\sigma,\tau) \sum_{l=1}^T [[c^{l-1} = \sigma \wedge c^l = \tau]],$$

$$F_2(S,C) = \sum_{\sigma \in c} \sum_{l=1}^T \gamma(s^l, \sigma) [[c^l = \sigma]]. \tag{12}$$

Here, (σ, τ) is considered as the coefficient for the transition from state (or semantic tag) σ to state τ while $\gamma(s^l, \sigma)$ can be treated as the coefficient for the emission of word s^l from state σ. They are defined as follows:

$$\delta(\sigma,\tau) = \sum_{i,\overline{C}} \alpha_i(\overline{C}) \sum_{m=1}^{|\overline{C}|} [[\overline{c}^{m-1} = \sigma \wedge \overline{c}^m = \tau]],$$

$$\gamma(s^l,\sigma) = \sum_{i,m}\sum_{C} [[c^m = \sigma]]\,\alpha_i(C)\,k(s^l, s_i^m), \tag{13}$$

where $k(s^l, s_i^m) = \langle \Psi(s^l), \Psi(s_i^m) \rangle$ describes the similarity of the input patterns Ψ between word $s\ l$ and word $s\ ^m{}_i$, the mth word in the training example i, and $\alpha_i(C)$ is a set of dual parameters or Lagrange multiplier of the constraint associated with example i and semantic tag sequence C as in (4). Using the results derived in (13), Viterbi decoding can be performed to generate the best semantic tag sequence.

To incorporate the constraints as defined in the abstract semantic annotations, the values of (σ, τ) and $\gamma(s_l, \sigma)$ are modified for each sentence:

$$\delta(\sigma,\tau) = \begin{cases} 0, & \text{when } g(\sigma,\tau) = 1, \\ \sum_{i,\overline{C}} \alpha_i(\overline{C}) \sum_{m} [[\overline{c}^{m-1} = \sigma \wedge \overline{c}^m = \tau]], & \\ & \text{otherwise,} \end{cases}$$

$$\gamma(s^l,\sigma) = \begin{cases} 0, & \text{when } h(\sigma, s^l) = 1, \\ \sum_{i,m}\sum_{C} [[c^m = \sigma]]\,\alpha_i(C)\,k(s^l, s_i^m), & \\ & \text{otherwise,} \end{cases} \tag{14}$$

where $g(\sigma, \tau)$ and $\mathrm{h}(\sigma, s^l)$ are defined as follows:

$$g(\sigma,\tau) = \begin{cases} 1, & \tau \text{ is not in the allowable semantic tag list,} \\ 0, & \text{otherwise,} \end{cases}$$

$$h(\sigma, s^l) = \begin{cases} 1, & \sigma \text{ is not of class type and } s^l \\ & \text{is of class type,} \\ 0, & \text{otherwise,} \end{cases} \tag{15}$$

where $g(\sigma, \tau)$ and $\mathrm{h}(\sigma, s^l)$ in fact encode the two constraints implied from abstract annotations.

Filtering

For each sentence, the semantic tag sequences generated in the expectation step are further processed based on a measure on the agreement of the semantic tag sequence $T = \{t_1, t_2, \ldots, _n\}$ with its corresponding abstract semantic annotation A. The score of T is defined as

$$\text{Score}(T) = 2 * \frac{S_{\text{recall}} * S_{\text{precision}}}{S_{\text{recall}} + S_{\text{precision}}}, \tag{16}$$

where $S_{\text{precision}} = N_r/n$, $S_{\text{Recall}} = N_r/p$. Here, Nr is the number of the semantic tags in T which also occur in A, n is the number of semantic tags in T, and p is the number of semantic tags in the flattened semantic tag sequence for A. The score is similar to the F-measure which is the harmonic mean of precision and recall. It essentially measures the agreement of the generated semantic tag sequence with the abstract semantic annotation. We filter out sentences with their score below certain predefined threshold and the remaining sentences together with their generated semantic tag sequences are fed into the next maximization step. In our experiments, we empirically set the threshold to 0.1.

Maximization

Given the filtered training examples from the filtering step, the parameters Θ are adjusted using the standard training algorithms.

For CRFs, the parameter Θ can be estimated through a maximum likelihood procedure. The model is traditionally trained by maximizing the conditional log-likelihood of the labeled sequences, which is defined as

$$L(\Theta) = \sum_{i=1}^{N} \log\left(P\left(C_i \mid S_i; \Theta\right)\right), \tag{17}$$

where N is the number of sequences.

The maximization can be achieved gradient ascent where the gradient of the likelihood is

$$\frac{\partial}{\partial \theta_k} = \sum_{i=1}^{N} \sum_{t} f_k\left(c_i^{t-1}, c_i^t, S_i, t\right) - \sum_{i=1}^{N} \sum_{S} p_\theta\left(C \mid S_i\right) \sum_{t} f_k\left(c^{t-1}, c^t, S_i, t\right). \tag{18}$$

For HM-SVMs, the parameters $\Theta = w$ are adjusted so that the true semantic tag sequence C_i scores higher than all the other tag sequences $C \in \mathrm{C} := \mathrm{C} \setminus C_i$ with a large margin. To achieve the goal, the optimization problem as stated in (3) is solved using an online learning approach as described in [4]. In short, it works as follows: a pattern sequence S_i is presented and the optimal semantic tag sequence $C_i = (S_i)$ is computed by employing Viterbi decoding. If C_i is correct, no update is performed. Otherwise, the weight vector w is updated based on the difference from the true semantic tag sequence $\Delta\Phi = \Phi(S_i, C_i) - \Phi(S_i, C_i)$.

EXPERIMENTAL RESULTS

Experiments have been conducted on the DARPA communicator data (http://www.bltek.com/spoken-dialog-systems/cu-communicator.html/) which were collected in 461 days. From these, 46 days were randomly selected for use as test set data and the remainders were used for training. After cleaning up the data, the training set consists of 12702 utterances while the test set contains 1178 utterances.

The abstract semantic annotations used for training only list a set of valid semantic tags and the dominance relationships between them without considering the actual realized semantic tag sequence or attempting to identify explicit word/concept pairs. Thus, it avoids the need for expensive treebank style annotations. For example, for the sentence "I wanna go from Denver to Orlando Florida on December tenth," the abstract annotation would be FROMLOC(CITY) TOLOC(CITY(STATE)) MONTH(DAY).

To evaluate the performance of the model, a reference frame structure was derived for every test set sentence consisting of slot/value pairs. An example of a reference frame is shown in Table 2.

Performance was then measured in terms of F-measure on slot/value pairs, which combines the precision (P) and recall (R) values with equal weight and is defined as $F = 2 * P * R/(P + R)$.

Table 2.

I wanna travel from Denver to San Diego on March sixth.	
Frame	AIR
Slots	FROMLOC · CITY = Denver
	TOLOC · CITY = San Diego
	MONTH = March
	DAY = sixth

We modified the open source of the CRF suite (http:// www.chokkan.org/ software/crfsuite/) and SVM[HMM] (http:// www.cs.cornell.edu/people/tj/svm light/svm hmm.html/) to implement our proposed learning framework. We employed two algorithms to estimate the parameters of CRFs, the stochastic gradient descent (SGD) iterative algorithm [21], and the limited-memory BFGS (L-BFGS) method [22]. For both algorithms, the regularization parameter was empirically set in the following experiments.

Overall Comparison

We first compare the time consumed in each iteration using HM-SVMs or CRFs as shown in Figure 2. The experiments were conducted on the Intel(R) Xeon(TM) model Linux server equipped with 3.00 Ghz processor and 4 GB RAM. It can be observed that, for CRFs, the time consumed in SGD is almost doubled compared to that in L-BFGS in each iteration. However, since SGD converges much faster than L-BFGS, the total time required for training is almost the same.

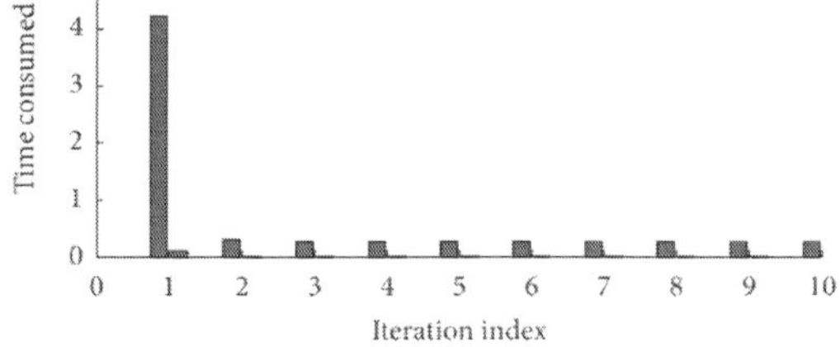

(a) CRFs with L-BFGS

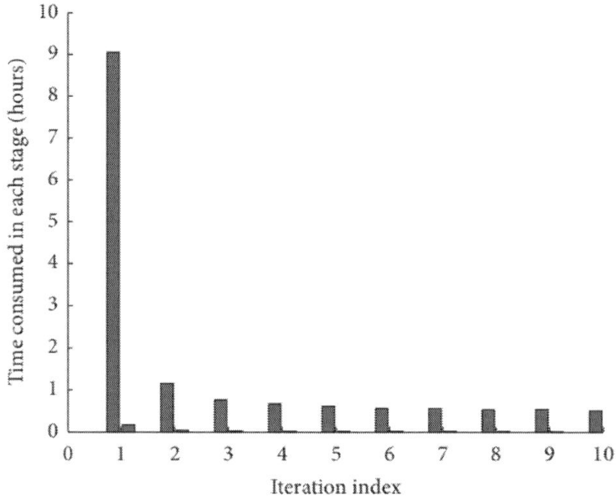

(b) CRFs with SGD

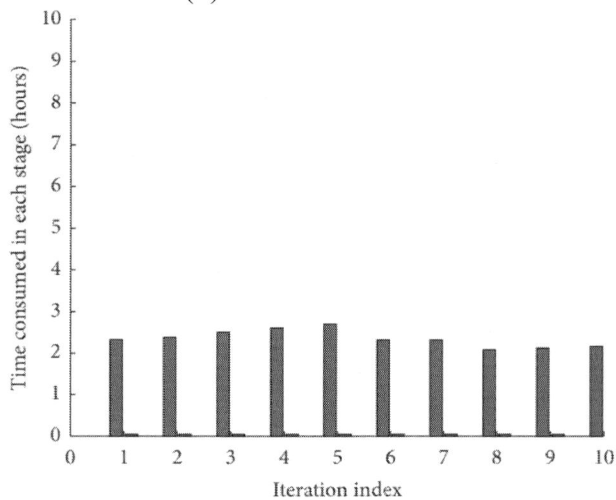

(c) HM-SVMs

Figure 2: Time consumed in each iteration by CRFs and HM-SVMs.

As SGD gives balanced precision and recall values, it should be preferred more than L-BFGS in our proposed learning procedure. On the other hand, as opposed to CRFs which consume much less time after iteration 1, HM-SVMs take almost the same run time for all the iterations. Nevertheless, the total run time until convergence is almost the same for CRFs and HM-SVMs. Figure 3 shows the performance of our proposed framework for CRFs and HM-SVMs at each iteration. At each word position, the feature set used for both statistical models consists of the current word and the current part-of-speech (POS) tag. It can be observed that both models achieve the best performance at iteration 8 with an F-measure of 92.95% and 93.18% being achieved using CRFs and HM-SVMs, respectively.

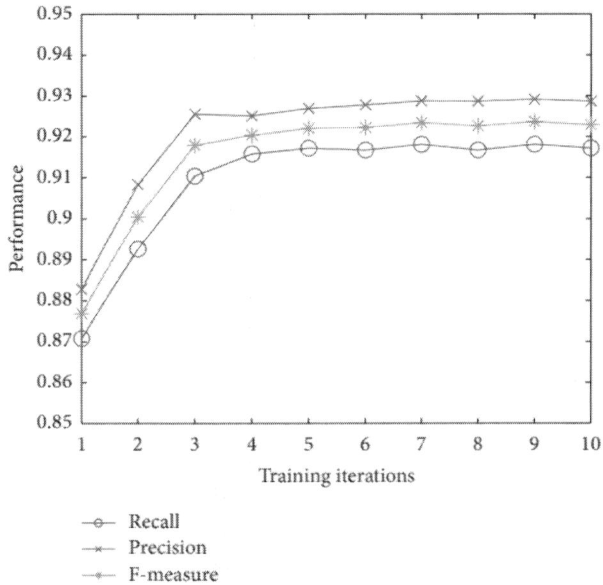

(a) CRFs with L-BFGS

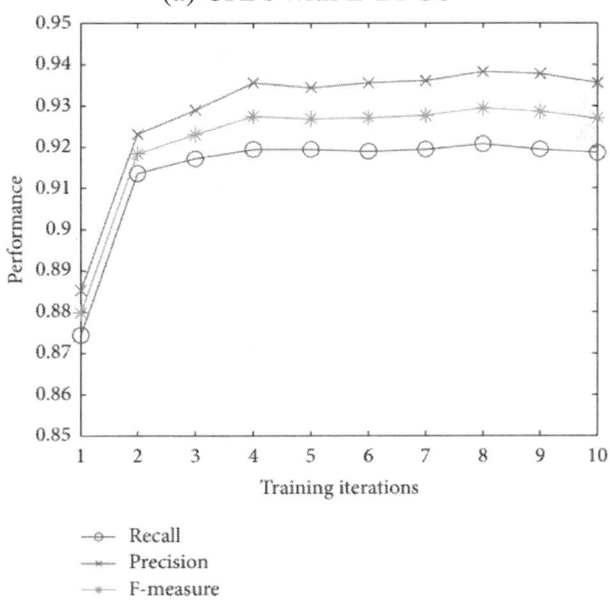

(b) CRFs with SGD

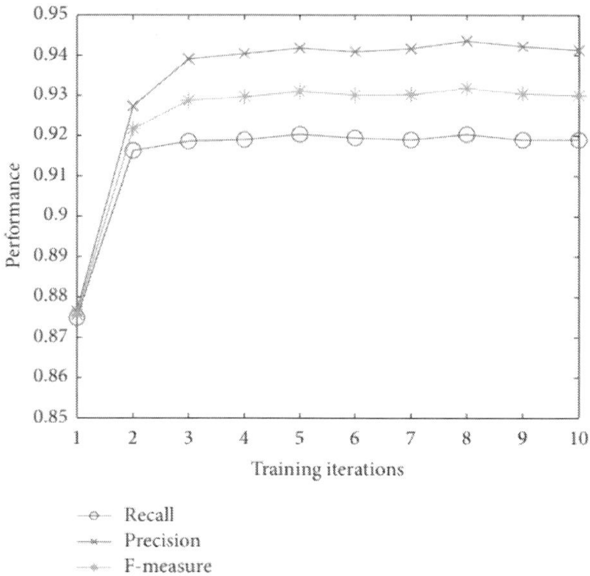

(c) HM-SVMs

Figure 3: Performance for CRFs and HM-SVMs at each iteration.

Results with Varied Features Set

We employed word features (such as current word, previous word, and next word) and POS features (such as current POS tag, previous one, and next one) for training. To explore the impact of the choices of features, we explored with feature sets comprised of words or POS tags occurring before or after the current word within some predefined window size.

Figure 4 shows the performance of our proposed approach with the window size varying between 0 and 3. Surprisingly, the model learned with feature set chosen by setting window size 0 gives the best overall performance. Varying window size between 1 and 3 only impacts the convergence rate and does not lead to any performance difference at the end of the learning procedure.

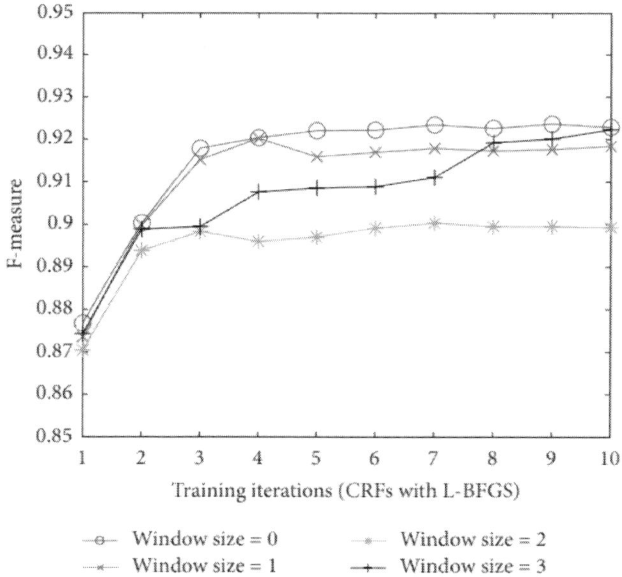

(a) CRFs with L-BFGS

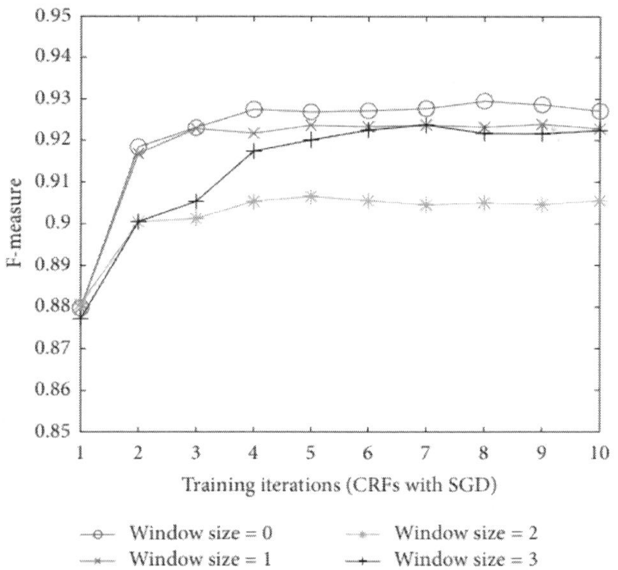

(b) CRFs with SGD

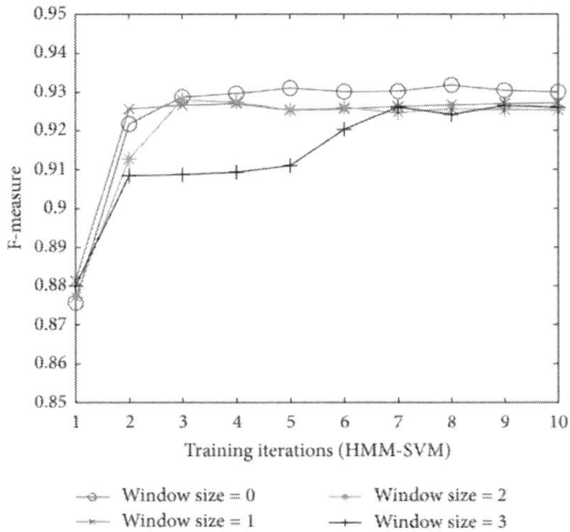

(c) HM-SVMs

Figure 4: Comparison of performance on models learned with feature sets chosen based on different window sizes.

Performance with or without Filtering Step

In a second set of experiments, we compare the performance with or without the *filtering* step as discussed in Section 3.3. Figure 5 shows that the *filtering* step is indeed crucial as it boosted the performance by nearly 4% for CRFs with L-BFGS and 3% for CRFs with SGD and HM-SVMs.

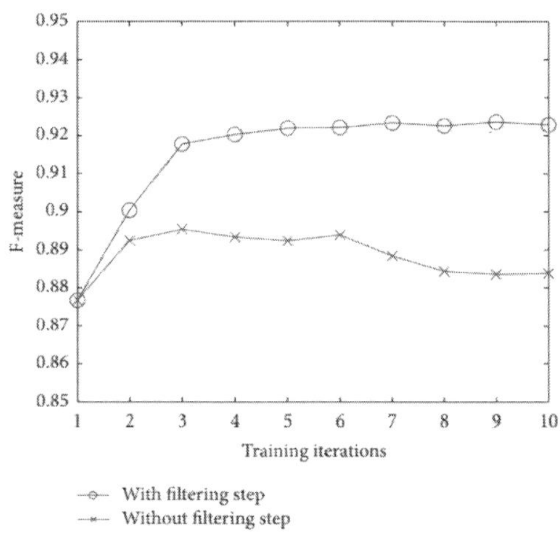

(a) CRFs with L-BFGS

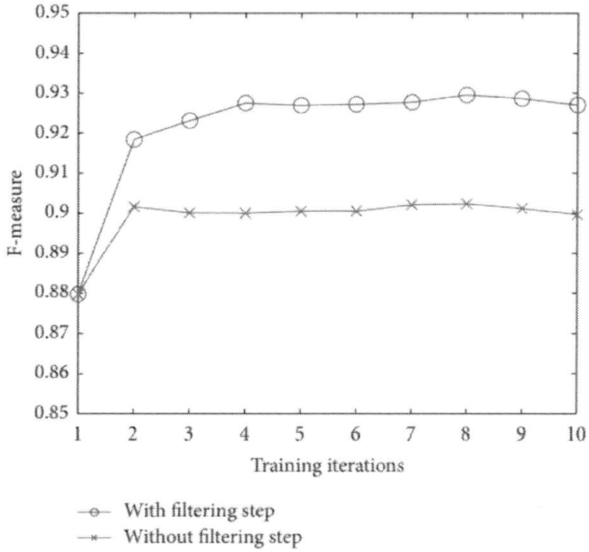

(b) CRFs with SGD

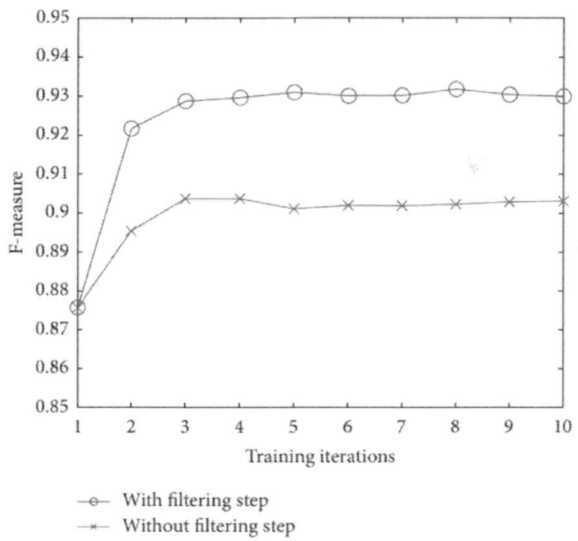

(c) HM-SVMs

Figure 5: Comparisons of performance with or without the *filtering* stage.

Comparison with Existing Approaches

We compare the performance of CRFs and HM-SVMs with HVS, all trained on abstract semantic annotations. While it is hard to incorporate arbitrary input features into HVS learning, both CRFs and HM-SVMs have the capability of dealing with overlapping features. Table 3 shows that they outperform HVS with a relative error reduction of 36.6% and 43.3% being achieved, respectively. In addition, the superior performance of HM-SVMs over CRFs shows the advantage of HM-SVMs on learning nonlinear discriminant functions via kernel functions.

Table 3: Performance comparison between the proposed framework and three other approaches (HF denotes the hybrid framework and DT denotes discriminative training the HVS model.

Measurement	**HVS**	**HF**	**DT**	**Proposed framework**	
				CRFs	HM-SVMs
Recall (%)	87.81	90.99	91.49	92.08	92.04
Precision (%)	88.13	90.25	91.87	93.83	94.36
F-measure (%)	87.97	90.62	91.68	92.95	93.18

We further compare our proposed learning approach with two other methods. One is a hybrid generative/discriminative framework (HF) [23] which combines HVS with HM-SVMs so as to allow the incorporation of arbitrary features as in CRFs. The other is a discriminative approach (DT) based on parse error measure to train the HVS model [24]. The generalized probabilistic descent (GPD) algorithm [25] was employed to adjust the HVS model to achieve the minimum parse error rate.

Table 3 shows that our proposed learning approach outperforms both HF and DT. Training statistical models on abstract annotations allows the calculation of conditional likelihood and hence results in direct optimization of the objective function to reduce the error rate of semantic labeling. On the contrary, the hybrid framework firstly uses the HVS parser to generate full annotations for training HM-SVMs. This process involves the optimization of two different objective functions (one for HVS and another for HM-SVMs). Although DT also uses an objective function which aims to reduce the semantic parsing error rate, it is in fact employed for supervised reranking where the input is the N-best parse results generated from the HVS model.

CONCLUSIONS

In this paper, we have proposed an effective learning approach which can train statistical models such CRFs and HM-SVMs without using the expensive treebank style annotation data. Instead, it trains the statistical models from only abstract annotations in a constrained way. Experimental results show that, using the proposed learning approach, both CRFs and HM-SVMs outperform the previously proposed HVS model on the DARPA communicator data. Furthermore, they also show superior performance than the two other methods: one is the hybrid framework (HF) combining both HVS and HM-SVMs, and the other is discriminative training (DT) of the HVS model, with a relative error reduction rate of about 25% and 15% being achieved when compared with HF and DT, respectively.

In future work, we will explore other score functions in *filtering* step to describe the precision of the parsing results. Also, we plan to apply the proposed framework in some other domains such as information extraction and opinion mining.

ACKNOWLEDGMENTS

The submitted paper is the extended version of the conference paper for CIKM 2011 with the title "A novel framework of training hidden Markov support vector machines from lightly-annotated data." The authors thank the anonymous reviewers for their insightful comments. This work was funded by the National Natural Science Foundation of China (61103077), Ph.D. Programs Foundation of Ministry of Education of China for Young Faculties (20100092120031), Scientific Research Foundation for the Returned Overseas Chinese Scholars, State Education Ministry, and the Fundamental Research Funds for the Central Universities (the Cultivation Program for Young Faculties of Southeast University).

REFERENCES

1. J. Dowding, R. Moore, F. Andry, and D. Moran, "Interleaving syntax and semantics in an efficient bottom-up parser," in *Proceedings of the 32th Annual Meeting of the Association for Computational Linguistics*, pp. 110–116, Las Cruces, NM, USA, 1994.
2. W. Ward and S. Issar, "Recent improvements in the cmu spoken language understanding system," in *Proceedings of the Workshop on Human Language Technology*, pp. 213–216, Plainsboro, NJ, USA, 1994.
3. J. D. Lafferty, A. McCallum, and F. C. N. Pereira, "Conditional random fields: probabilistic models for segmenting and labeling sequence data," in *Proceedings of the 18th International Conference on Machine Learning (ICML '11)*, pp. 282–289, 2001.
4. Y. Altun, I. Tsochantaridis, and T. Hofmann, "Hidden markov support vector machines," in *Proceedings of the International Conference in Machine Learning*, pp. 3–10, 2003.
5. Y. He and S. Young, "Semantic processing using the hidden vector state model," *Computer Speech and Language*, vol. 19, no. 1, pp. 85–106, 2005.
6. R. J. Kate and R. J. Mooney, "Using string-kernels for learning semantic parsers," in *Proceedings of the 21st International Conference on Computational Linguistics and the 44th Annual Meeting of the Association for Computational Linguistics (ACL '06)*, pp. 913–920, 2006.
7. Y. W. Wong and R. J. Mooney, "Learning synchronous grammars for semantic parsing with lambda calculus," in *Proceedings of the 45th Annual Meeting of the Association for Computational Linguistics (ACL '07)*, pp. 960–967, June 2007.
8. W. Lu, H. Ng, W. Lee, and L. Zettlemoyer, "A generative model for parsing natural language to meaning representations," in *Proceedings of the Conference on Empirical Methods in Natural Language Processing (EMNLP '08)*, pp. 783–792, Stroudsburg, PA, USA, October 2008.
9. R. Ge and R. Mooney, "Learning a compositional semantic parser using an existing syntactic parser," in *Proceedings of the 47th Annual Meeting of the ACL*, pp. 611–619, 2009.

10. M. Dinarelli, A. Moschitti, and G. Riccardi, "Discriminative reranking for spoken language understanding," *IEEE Transactions on Audio, Speech and Language Processing*, vol. 20, no. 2, pp. 526–539, 2012.
11. L. S. Zettlemoyer and C. Michael, "Learning to map sentences to logical form: structured classification with probabilistic categorial grammars," in *Proceedings of the 21st Conference on Uncertainty in Artificial Intelligence (UAI '05)*, pp. 658–666, July 2005.
12. A. Giordani and A. Moschitti, "Syntactic structural kernels for natural language interfaces to databases," in *Machine Learning and Knowledge Discovery in Databases*, W. Buntine, M. Grobelnik, D. Mladeni, and J. Shawe-Taylor, Eds., vol. 5781 of *Lecture Notes in Computer Science*, pp. 391–406, Springer, Berlin, Germany, 2009.
13. A. Giordani and A. Moschitti, "Translating questions to SQL queries with generative parsers discriminatively reranked," in *Proceedings of the 24th International Conference on Computational Linguistics*, pp. 401–410, 2012.
14. J. Zelle and R. Mooney, "Learning to parse database queries using inductive logic programming," in *Proceedings of the AAAI*, pp. 1050–1055, 1996.
15. F. Jiao, S. Wang, C.-H. Lee, R. Greiner, and D. Schuurmans, "Semi-supervised conditional random fields for improved sequence segmentation and labeling," in *Proceedings of the 21st International Conference on Computational Linguistics and 44th Annual Meeting of the Association for Computational Linguistics (COLING/ACL '06)*, pp. 209–216, July 2006.
16. G. S. Mann and A. McCallum, "Efficient computation of entropy gradient for semi-supervised conditional random fields," in *Proceedings of the Human Language Technology Conference of the North American Chapter of the Association for Computational Linguistics (HLT-NAACL '07)*, pp. 109–112, 2007.
17. Y. Wang, G. Haffari, S. Wang, and G. Mori, "A rate distortion approach for semi-supervised conditional random fields," in *Proceedings of the 23rd Annual Conference on Neural Information Processing Systems (NIPS '09)*, pp. 2008–2016, December 2009.
18. G. S. Mann and A. Mccallum, "Generalized expectation criteria for semi-supervised learning of conditional random fields," in *Proceedings of the 46th Annual Meeting of the Association for Computational Linguistics*, pp. 870–878, June 2008.

19. T. Grenager, D. Klein, and C. D. Manning, "Unsupervised learning of field segmentation models for information extraction," in *Proceedings of the 43rd Annual Meeting of the Association for Computational Linguistics (ACL '05)*, pp. 371–378, Ann Arbor, Mich, USA, June 2005.
20. J. A. Bilmes, "A gentle tutorial of the em algorithm and its application to parameter estimation for gaussian mixture and hidden markov models," in *Proceedings of the International Conference on Systems Integration*, 1997.
21. S. Shalev-Shwartz, Y. Singer, and N. Srebro, "Pegasos: primal estimated sub-gradient solver for svm," in *Proceedings of the 24th International Conference on Machine Learning (ICML '07)*, pp. 807–814, June 2007.
22. J. Nocedal, "Updating quasi-newton matrices with limited storage," *Mathematics of Computation*, vol. 35, no. 151, pp. 773–782, 1980.
23. D. Zhou and Y. He, "A hybrid generative/discriminative framework to train a semantic parser from an un-annotated corpus," in *Proceeding of the 22nd International Conference on Computational Linguistics (COLING '08)*, pp. 1113–1120, Manchester, UK, August 2008.
24. D. Zhou and Y. He, "Discriminative training of the hidden vector state model for semantic parsing," *IEEE Transactions on Knowledge and Data Engineering*, vol. 21, no. 1, pp. 66–77, 2009.
25. H. K. J. Kuo, E. Fosler-Lussier, H. Jiang, and C.-H. Lee, "Discriminative training of language models for speech recognition," in *Proceedings of the IEEE International Conference on Acustics, Speech, and Signal Processing (ICASSP '02)*, vol. 1, pp. 325–328, IEEE, Merano, Italy, May 2002.

CHAPTER 18

Linguistic Factors Influencing Speech Audiometric Assessment

Martine Coene,[1,2] Stefanie Krijger,[3] Matthias Meeuws,[2] Geert De Ceulaer,[2] and Paul J. Govaerts[1,2,3]

[1]Language and Hearing Center Amsterdam, Free University Amsterdam, Amsterdam, Netherlands

[2]The Eargroup, Antwerp, Belgium

[3]Department of Otorhinolaryngology, Ghent University, Ghent, Belgium

ABSTRACT

In speech audiometric testing, hearing performance is typically measured by calculating the number of correct repetitions of a speech stimulus. We investigate to what extent the repetition accuracy of Dutch speech stimuli

Citation: Martine Coene, Stefanie Krijger, Matthias Meeuws, Geert De Ceulaer, Paul J. Govaerts, "Linguistic Factors Influencing Speech Audiometric Assessment", BioMed Research International, vol. 2016, Article ID 7249848, 14 pages, 2016. https://doi.org/10.1155/2016/7249848.

presented against a background noise is influenced by nonauditory processes. We show that variation in verbal repetition accuracy is partially explained by morpholexical and syntactic features of the target language. Verbs, prepositions, conjunctions, determiners, and pronouns yield significantly lower correct repetitions than nouns, adjectives, or adverbs. The reduced repetition performance for verbs and function words is probably best explained by the similarities in the perceptual nature of verbal morphology and function words in Dutch. For sentences, an overall negative effect of syntactic complexity on speech repetition accuracy was found. The lowest number of correct repetitions was obtained with passive sentences, reflecting the cognitive cost of processing a noncanonical sentence structure. Taken together, these findings may have important implications for the audiological practice. In combination with hearing loss, linguistic complexity may increase the cognitive demands to process sentences in noise, leading to suboptimal functional hearing in day-to-day listening situations. Using test sentences with varying degrees of syntactic complexity may therefore provide useful information to measure functional hearing benefits.

INTRODUCTION

Noise is omnipresent in many aspects of daily life and is known to interfere with oral communication. This is the case in settings as diverse as schools, offices, public transportation, restaurants, and even home. For hearing individuals, understanding speech in such noisy listening conditions can be a serious challenge. In noisy surroundings, auditory perception and processing of speech are even more compromised for individuals with a hearing impairment. Although this so-called "cocktail party effect" has been known for many years [1, 2], it is not yet fully understood how the listener is able to tune in to a single voice in the presence of background noise.

Current models of speech perception take successful speech-in-noise understanding to result from the interaction between auditory, linguistic, and cognitive processing mechanisms: it requires the processing of acoustic signals at the level of the peripheral auditory system to combine with the top-down processing of these input signals at the higher level of the brain by using several components of human cognition, including linguistic knowledge [3, 4].

Recent research regarding functional hearing in daily life situations has investigated speech understanding in noise in several populations, with a special focus on children and elderly listeners with and without hearing impairment. In general, it has been shown that the perceptual accuracy of both children and adults decreases as the signal becomes noisier. The adverse effect of noise has been demonstrated for normal-hearing listeners as well as for listeners with hearing loss. The outcomes of studies targeting child populations indicate that small children require more advantageous signal-to-noise ratios (lower noise levels) than older children and adult listeners [5–7]. A mirror image of the developmental pattern in children is found in elderly adults, a problem to understand speech in noise typically progressing in ageing listeners [4, 8–10].

LINGUISTIC CUES TO SPEECH UNDERSTANDING

For both populations, a variety of factors are claimed to contribute to speech-in-noise understanding. Age, noise level, and cognitive performance of the listener all interact with hearing loss. As such, age-related perception difficulties have been related to a decline in cognitive abilities that play a critical role in speech processing in general, including (verbal) working memory and inhibitory control [11–13].

For a few decades already it has been clear that the speech signal itself may also have an important contribution to word and sentence understanding accuracy. When a speech sound in a sentence is deleted and replaced by a noise such as a cough, many listeners are able to restore this portion of missed information. This "auditory induction" ability has been considered a special linguistic application of a general ability to perform phonemic restoration of interrupted signals [14]. Several researchers have also focused on particular features of the linguistic system itself. At the phonosyntactic level, for instance, it has been shown that the articulation of vowels is highly influenced by the consonants by which these vowels are preceded or followed. If for whatever reason listeners have missed part of the incoming message, it may be recovered thanks to information coming from such coarticulation effects [15]. In addition, it has been shown that perception of auditory information is interacting with lexical knowledge as well: when auditory information is ambiguous, listeners have the tendency to make phonetic categorizations that lead to words rather than nonwords ("Ganong effect" [16]), a principle which is the driving force even behind erroneous phonemic replacements in speech audiometric assessment [17].

Some studies have focused more particularly on morphosyntactic features of the linguistic system of the target language [18, 19]. Syntactic complexity and presentation rate of the linguistic message play an important role in sentence understanding, with less accurate performance being associated with syntactically more complex sentences. The effect increases with an increasing speech rate, in the presence of hearing loss and age-related cognitive decline [20]. Further syntactic analysis shows that perception in noise becomes more difficult in sentences with a noncanonical word order and in sentences with complex verb argument structures [21, 22]. Furthermore, speech perception seems to be sensitive to the degree of syntactic complexity of the message. Center-embedded Subject Relative clauses ("the cat that chased the dog meowed"), for instance, yield better sentence repetition scores than sentences with higher syntactic complexity such as center-embedded Object Relative clauses ("the cat that the dog chased meowed") [20, 23].

AIM AND RESEARCH QUESTIONS

Building on insights from the literature, it becomes clear that both stimulus- and knowledge-driven processes are highly involved in speech understanding in noise [24, 25]. The exact contribution of auditory and linguistic processes is, however, still under discussion. The present study aims to increase our knowledge with respect to the role of syntactic features in speech-in-noise understanding. More particularly, we investigate how word identification accuracy in noise is influenced by lexical constraints such as the part of speech of the target word, on the one hand, and by syntactic constraints such as the structural complexity of the utterance serving as a natural linguistic context by which this word is surrounded, on the other hand. In addition, we examine the contribution of syntactic structure to the listening effort of the listener by measuring his/her reaction times in responding.

By analyzing verbal repetition scores in adult listeners for words that belong to different parts of speech and that are embedded in utterances with varying syntactic complexity and length, we will be able to better understand an important part of the nonauditory processes involved in speech understanding in noise. In what follows, we will try to answer the following research questions:

- Is verbal repetition accuracy influenced by the syntactic structure of the carrier sentence, the part of speech of the target word, the length of the carrier sentence, or a combination of these linguistic factors?
- Is listening effort determined by the syntactic complexity and/or the length of the sentence stimulus?

The answer to these questions will have immediate implications for the audiological practice. Standard speech audiometric test batteries make use of short meaningful sentences that are presented at a given intensity to determine the patient's hearing performance. If sentence materials are used for audiological testing, they need to be balanced in such a way that linguistic complexity contributes as little as possible to the variation in speech audiometric outcomes. If on the other hand no such effect is found, linguistic complexity can be safely "ignored" as a potential confounding factor for this type of audiometric testing.

In the remaining part of the article, we will first try to operationalize the concept of linguistic complexity in a relatively objective way and discuss some psycholinguistic evidence in favor of the role of syntactic and morpholexical cues to speech understanding (Sections 4 and 5). In Section 6 we will present in more detail the development of the test materials and the proposed analyses. Finally in Sections 7 and 8 we will present the results of these analyses and discuss the potential implications for the clinical practice. The general conclusions can be found in Section 9.

SYNTACTIC COMPLEXITY, COGNITIVE LOAD, AND SPEECH UNDERSTANDING

In (psycho)linguistic research, the construct of linguistic complexity has received a good deal of scholarly attention. Although the concept is often used as an index of language proficiency in second language learners, it is generally defined rather sloppily as "the range of forms that surface in language production and the degree of sophistication of such forms" [26]. Similarly, syntactic complexity has been related to the degree of cognitive effort required to produce or interpret particular utterances. Here, syntactic complexity is taken to be "for some reason more difficult, more complex, less entrenched, less frequent, less accessible or in any way cognitively more complex" [27].

More recently, several attempts have been made to operationalize this concept in an objective way [28–31]. Various measures have been proposed, ranging from using pure length (as in the number of syllables, words, or intonation units) of an utterance as a proxy for syntactic complexity to fully fledged in-depth analyses of syntactic tree structures [31]. Although the first approach has the advantage of being readily available, involving no additional structural analysis, it has been shown at many occasions that increased sentence length does not necessarily go hand in hand with increased syntactic complexity. As a matter of fact, the use of utterance length as a measure of linguistic complexity was challenged already a few decades ago, especially by generative approaches to syntax: "it is interesting to note that it is apparently not the length in words of the object that determines the naturalness of the transformation but, rather, in some sense, its complexity. Thus 'They brought all the leaders of the riot in' seems more natural than 'They brought the man I saw in'. The latter, though shorter, is more complex" [32, page 477].

Current linguistic research generally agrees upon the fact that utterances with the same number of words or syllables may differ in linguistic complexity resulting from underlying differences in the hierarchical nature of syntactic structure of its constituents. Within a formal framework, the richly articulated internal syntactic structure is captured by using a set of descriptive tools allowing a schematic representation of structural units by means of syntactic trees (see, e.g., [33]). Elementary trees of individual vocabulary items of a language may combine into phrases and sentences; that is, more complex structures are generated by combining syntactic building blocks in well-defined ways, forming so-called simple "canonical" sentences exhibiting the base word order for the particular language in question. Under particular conditions, it is possible to move one or more elements out of their base position into a designated position in the syntactic tree, deriving a sentence with a word order that is different from the canonical one.

Within such a framework, larger syntactic units are represented as nodes in the syntactic tree. Representing linguistic complexity by means of nodes within trees is not merely a formal construct that may be used to describe syntactic variation within a given language in a more systematic way. The way in which the syntactic tree is derived is taken to reflect a psychological entry to syntax, as the different operations underlying syntactic tree formation are representing the functioning of the human parser itself. Current formal syntactic theories are built around a minimalist principle [34] by which syntactic representations should be pure and simple, stripped of all features that are not relevant to the cognitive systems they provide input for. Similarly, syntactic derivations are considered to be subject to principles of economy involving the shortest possible route and the fewest possible steps [35].

Under such a view, linguistically complex structures are cognitively more demanding than their less complex counterparts. One way to quantify syntactic complexity is by counting the number of nodes by which a particular phrase or sentence is dominated, where more nodes indicate a higher degree of formal complexity [29, 36]. The number of syntactic nodes may be taken to reflect part of the computational resources required by the human brain to structure a sequence of words. Roll et al. [31] show that the total number of syntactic nodes in a sentence is a very robust measure of syntactic complexity that is able to account for differences in disfluency of spontaneous speech.

But most often processing difficulties are thought to be proportional to the cognitive cost that comes with syntactic movement [37]. Against this background, it follows rather naturally that utterances which contain a constituent that has been moved out of its base position will show a decreased processing accuracy as compared to utterances with a canonical word order. In order to process a new sentence, the listener needs to activate the syntactic structure; this requires sufficient memory resources. This memory constraint may explain why sentences with a canonical word order are relatively easy to process: for syntactic constituents that appear in their basic sentence-initial position, no memory load is associated with keeping in mind the expectation of them potentially occurring later on in the sentence [36, 38].

Under such a view, passive clauses—that is, structures in which the semantic theme argument (i.e., the participant of a situation upon whom an action is carried out) of the verb occupies the sentence-initial position—will be syntactically more complex than active ones due to a greater cognitive cost for maintaining the possibility of an agent argument (i.e., the participant that carries out the action in a situation) appearing in the clause until encountered after the verb. Compare in this respect (1a-b) from Dutch:

(a) Die hond bijt de man (active). That dog$_{\text{AGENT}}$ bites the man$_{\text{THEME}}$.

(b) De man wordt gebeten (door die hond) (passive). The man$_{\text{THEME}}$ is bitten (by that dog$_{\text{AGENT}}$).

Passive clauses such as (1b) are thought to be derived from the underlying canonical sentence of the type Subject$_{\text{AGENT}}$ Verb Object$_{\text{THEME}}$ by moving the theme into the sentenceinitial position, inserting an appropriate auxiliary (Du. worden) in front of the past participle and an optional by-phrase, the latter referring to the agent of the action expressed by the main verb.

The principle that cognitive costs are proportionally related to the complexity of syntactic movement has been invoked to explain more fine-grained differences in sentence processing between structures that are characterized by movement. As movement has a cognitive cost proportional to the length of the path, longer distance movements are taken to require additional computational resources resulting in reduced interpretation accuracy and longer reaction times [39].

This "shortest-movement" principle has been studied in more detail in the context of relative clauses exhibiting subject-extraction versus object-extraction: in spite of having the same length in words, movement of the relativized noun out of its original subject position of the embedded clause as in (2a) will be shorter and therefore less complex than similar movement out of the object position of the embedded clause (2b):

(a) De jongens die [~~de jongens~~ de oude man kusten], vertrokken gehaast (subj rel). The boys who the old man kissed, left in a hurry. The boys who kissed the old man, left in a hurry.

(b) De jongens die [de oude man kuste ~~de jongens~~], vertrokken gehaast (obj rel). The boys whom the old man kissed, left in a hurry.

If syntactic movement operations are indeed representative for the functioning of the human mind, speech processing of utterances with a longer movement path may be taken to require an additional cognitive effort as compared to utterances characterized by shorter movement. Previous studies have shown that this is indeed the case: when confronted with complex sentences, the comprehension accuracy of hearing impaired listeners drops significantly, due to the fact that extra cognitive load that comes with processing such complex speech is leaving insufficient resources for the comprehension process [40–42]. More recently, Wendt et al. [43] have investigated the extent to which linguistic complexity influences the duration of speech processing in combination with hearing impairment and/or noisy listening conditions in a more objective way by using an eye-tracking approach. More particularly, for participants with hearing impairment, longer processing durations were found for sentence structures with a higher level of linguistic complexity. In noise conditions, the processing durations for complex sentences were linked to cognitive factors such as working memory capacity.

THE ROLE OF OPEN VERSUS CLOSED WORD CLASSES IN SENTENCE UNDERSTANDING

In addition to measures related to syntactic structure, morpholexical features of linguistic units have been shown to influence speech understanding. In the literature, evidence is presented that listeners use their (implicit) knowledge regarding differences between word classes to come to sentence understanding. Current linguistic theories generally take grammatical classes of words (e.g., nouns, verbs, prepositions, and pronouns) to fall into two main groups depending on the context-dependent character of their semantic content: (i) words that do not possess meaningful content by themselves but are mainly used to express a grammatical relationship with other words in the sentence are taken to represent a closed class of function words (e.g., *pronouns* or *prepositions*), whereas (ii) words that have an autosemantic content allowing for independent lexical meanings are members of an open class of lexical words (e.g., *nouns* or *verbs*).

There is empirical evidence that the open versus closed class distinction has a reflection in sentence understanding. More particularly, the role of open/closed class words in the processing of spoken sentences has been related to differences in sentence-level prosodic structure: whereas open class words mostly contain at least one stressed syllable, closed class words are most often realized by means of a weak syllable [44]. From an acoustic point of view, the distinction between both classes can often be derived from the presence of full versus reduced vowels. In English, such phonological differences between closed and open word classes are robust and consistent [45, 46]. The human mind has been shown to exploit this phonological information when processing speech, especially with respect to identifying lexical unit boundaries in spoken sentences [47].

A number of studies have investigated whether the phonological differences between closed and open class words trigger differences in auditory processing. The results mainly indicate that open class words have a speech perception advantage over closed class words, probably due to the fact that the presence of a full vowel makes the former stand out more prominently in running speech. It has been shown, for instance, that listeners who are asked to detect a portion of a sentence that was replaced by a noise burst will have less difficulties in doing so when the noise replaces an open class word [48]. Yet other studies have come to rather opposite findings showing that the lexical access process is more complex for open class words than for closed class items [49]. Based on syntactic grounds, similar conclusions have been reached arguing that closed class words mainly encode syntactic information and are therefore subject to relatively little contextual variation making them easier to process [50].

In the next section we will describe how a set of test sentences has been generated and coded in such a way that it is possible to investigate the potential contribution of morpholexical and syntactic features to the identification of words in spoken sentences.

MATERIALS AND METHOD

Materials

We used the *Linguistically Controlled Sentences for Dutch* (LiCoS), a sentence repetition task consisting of 12 lists of 30 Dutch sentences each containing 2 target words. In this task, sentence repetition accuracy is expressed in terms of the number of correctly repeated target words per sentence (0, 1, or 2). All sentences have been generated in such a way that their semantic predictability is low: they contain no fixed expressions, nor do the two keywords within one sentence belong to the same semantic field (e.g., *de* ***schoenmaker*** *danst niet vaak met zijn* ***verloofde***, "the shoemaker does not dance often with his fiancée"). Lexical frequency was controlled for by selecting the key words out of the 5000 most frequent words of modern spoken Dutch. Taken together, the 360 test sentences are a representative set of the phonological, lexical, and grammatical variation found in modern spoken Dutch. Half of the test materials have been recorded by a male speaker of Dutch, the other half by a female speaker carefully balancing for the speaker's gender over the different types of sentences.

The linguistic parameters taken into account involve (i) the syntactic structure of the sentences (*SynStr)*, identifying different types of sentences with varying levels of syntactic complexity; (ii) the *part of speech* of the first and second target word in each sentence (*PoS1, PoS2)*, representing 2 major word classes (in agreement with current linguistic approaches, these word classes are representing both open and closed class parts of speech (open: nouns, verbs, adjectives, and adverbs; closed: pronouns, prepositions, determiners, and conjunctions)); (iii) the *length of the sentence* (*SentLen*) expressed in terms of the total number of syllables of the verbal stimulus.

The complete test set may be considered to be a representative sample of the variation of linguistic complexity taking the *Corpus of Modern Spoken Dutch* (Corpus Gesproken Nederlands [51]) as a reference. It therefore contains syntactically "simple" main clauses next to clauses with "medium" complexity (e.g., Passives) and "fully complex" structures (e.g., subject and Object Relative clauses). Variation with respect to the length of the sentence within one syntactic type is limited to 2 syllables per sentence. In a similar vein, all sentence lists were balanced with respect to the length of the key words, each list having a representative proportion of mono-, bi-, tri-, and quadrisyllabic words.

For this study, we have selected a subset of sentences with a length of 11 to 12 syllables equally divided over 6 syntactic types of different complexity. An overview of the syntactic types of the test sentences and of the part of speech of the target words with relevant examples is given in Tables 1 and 2, respectively.

Table 1: Inventory of the syntactic types of the test sentences.

SynStr	# syllables	Examples
Topic Verb Subject	11	*Over het algemeen ben jij nogal speels.* Generally (speaking) you are quite playful.
	12	*Tegen de avond zou het kunnen regenen.* By tonight it might be raining.
Passive	11	*Deze acteur wordt door de pers geprezen.* This actor is praised by the press.
	12	*Toetsen worden door de ouders ondertekend.* Written tests shall be signed by the parents
Coordination	11	*Hij gaat naar het zwembad en zij naar de stad.* He is going to the swimming pool and she (is going) into town
	12	*We vonden het erg leuk en bleven dus langer.* We liked it very much and therefore stayed longer
Subordination	11	*Hij dacht niet dat jij die tafel zou kopen.* He didn't think that you would buy that table
	12	*Ze had geluk dat die windhoos haar net mistte.* She was lucky that the tornado just missed her.

Subject Relatives	11	*De meubels die in de schuur staan, mogen weg.* The furniture that is in the barn can be thrown away.
	12	*De schilder die zonet hier was, is nu weg.* The painter who was just here, has left now.
Object Relatives	11	Ze kent geen burger die altijd zijn plicht doet. She doesn't know a citizen who always does his duty.
	12	*De fles die op tafel stond, gooide hij omver.* He threw away the bottle that was on the table.

Table 2: Inventory of the part of speech of the target words within the sentences.

Class	PoS	Examples			
Open	Adjective	*Groot*, "great"	*Moeilijk*, "difficult"	*Aanwezig*, "present"	Plaatselijke, "local"
	Adverb	*Al*, "already"	*Even*, "a while"	*Donderdag*, "thursday"	
	Noun	*Vrouw*, "woman"	*Zusje*, "little sister"	*Zakenman*, "businessman"	*Belastingen*, "taxes"
	Verb	*Kent*, "knows"	*Wijzen*, "point"	*Bevallen*, "given birth"	
Closed	Preposition	*Met*, "with"	*Tegen*, "against"		
	Pronoun	*Ze*, "she"	*Ervan*, "thereof"	*Iedereen*, "all"	
	Determiner	*Die*, "that"			

Method

All sentences were presented in a stationary speech noise of −5 dB SNR with the speech noise component fixed at 65 dB SPL. Speech noise was created by spectrally shaping white noise to match the long-term average spectrum of the complete set of sentences. Finally, processing speed was measured in terms of the reaction time of the listener in repeating each individual sentence.

The speech repetition task was performed in one of the quiet rooms of the MediaLab at Free University Amsterdam. In agreement with the local ethical procedures (Ethical Approval EC02.14b), all participants were given oral and written information regarding the goals and procedure of the test and gave their written consent to participate in this study. Prior to the sentence repetition task, the hearing performance of all participants was tested through pure-tone audiometry (500 Hz, 1000 Hz, 2000 Hz, and 4000 Hz). Only participants with hearing thresholds <30 dBHL at all tested frequencies were included. They were given the instruction to repeat as much as they could of each sentence. No additional information was given with respect to which words in the sentence served as target words to measure verbal repetition accuracy.

The sentences were inserted in A§E 2012® audiometric assessment software [52] and presented in free field with the loudspeakers set at 1-meter distance of the listener. All correct and erroneous repetitions of target words were scored directly in the A§E 2012 software program (Figure 1) by the test administrator, a native speaker of Dutch coming from the same (dialectal) region of the participants. Within sentences, target words were only flagged as being correctly repeated if all phonemes were fully pronounced, including grammatical morphemes such as person and tense or plural markers combining with the nominal or verbal item; for example, repetition of the sentence *de ananas wil**de** ze niet opeten*, "she didn't want to eat the pineapple" (target words underlined), as *de ananas wil ze niet opeten*, "she doesn't want to eat the pineapple," yielded a score of 1. In modern spoken Dutch, standard pronunciation often involves the deletion of word final *-n*, regardless of the morphological status of the syllable and lexical category to which it belongs (*mole(n)*, "mill," *goude(n)*, "golden," and *tege(n)*, "against"). Therefore, in nouns with *-en* plural marking, the omission of the entire plural morpheme has been scored as incorrect (*belasting* instead of *belastingen*) whereas the omission of the *mere -n* ending has been flagged as correct (*belastinge* instead of *belastingen*).

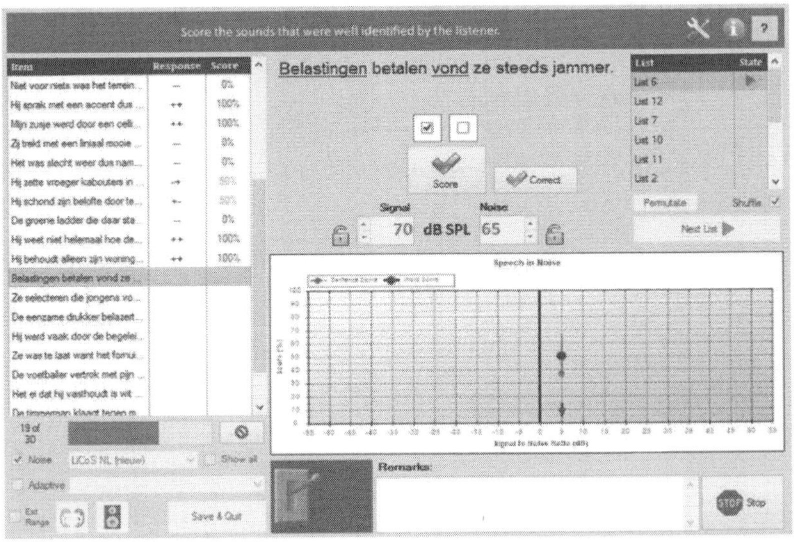

Figure 1: Screen shot of the LiCoS sentence repetition task implemented in A§E 2012 software while presenting the test sentence *belastingen betalen vond ze steeds jammer*, "she always disliked paying taxes." Sentence repetition scoring is based on the two target words *belastingen* and *vond* (underlined) and may each be flagged when repeated correctly.

Participants

30 normal-hearing Dutch speaking adults were included in this study, involving 8 males and 22 females within the age range of 19–57 years (average age in years = 27.2; SD = 9.89). None of the participants had any experience with speech audiometric testing or sentence repetition tasks. Audiometric data are given in Table 3.

Table 3: Participant data.

Participant	Gender	Age	PTA AS	PTA AD
1	Female	56	21.25	17.5
2	Male	22	1.25	5
3	Male	35	8.75	5
4	Female	21	23.75	18.75
5	Female	22	13.75	8.75
6	Female	22	18.75	10

7	Male	21	11.25	10
8	Male	22	13.75	5
9	Female	20	10	6.25
10	Female	19	13.75	10
11	Female	29	10	6.25
12	Female	23	13.75	15
13	Female	19	16.25	13.75
14	Female	22	7.5	5
15	Female	26	7.5	8.75
16	Female	24	27.5	21.25
17	Female	42	27.5	26.25
18	Female	23	12.5	12.5
19	Female	57	17.5	16.25
20	Male	30	12.5	11.25
21	Male	33	28.75	25
22	Male	23	13.75	8.75
23	Female	23	11.25	12.5
24	Female	25	7.5	3.75
25	Female	24	10	10
26	Female	22	10	6.25
27	Female	23	16.25	13.75
28	Female	22	13.75	11.25
29	Male	24	12.5	13.75
30	Female	42	15	15

RESULTS

Syntactic Structure and Sentence Length

Table 4 presents the means with standard deviations of the percentage of correct repetitions per sentence based on 30 listeners. A repeated measures ANOVA was run using the syntactic structure and the length of the test sentences as within-subjects variables. The results show a significant main effect for both linguistic variables. Firstly, the proportion of correct repetitions revealed to be significantly affected by the syntactic structure of the carrier sentence, (5, 67.97) = 4.92, $p < .007$, and $\eta^2 = .145$, representing a small effect. A post hoc analysis showed that listeners obtain significantly lower repetition scores with Passives compared to Topic V Subj structures ($F(1,29) = 26.15, p < .001$). Taking Topic V Subj structures as a baseline, all other comparisons between syntactic structures were not significant. Figure 2(a) depicts the 95% CI of the repetition scores for the different syntactic structures under analysis.

Table 4: Means and standard deviations of the percentage of correct scores for verbal repetition based on syntactic structure and length of the test sentences.

	Mean	**SD**
Syntactic structure		
Topic V Subj	70.04	(11.86)
Passives	62.92	(10.05)
Subordinated	69.51	(8.61)
Coordinated	69.77	(9.25)
Subject Relatives	78.00	(7.32)
Object Relatives	64.13	(8.84)
Sentence length		
11 syllables	71.43	(9.49)
12 syllables	65.43	(9.52)
Syntactic structure sentence length		
Topic V Subj		
11 syllables	76.08	(10.06)
12 syllables	64.00	(10.46)
Passives		
11 syllables	65.94	(8.62)
12 syllables	59.90	(10.60)
Subordinated		
11 syllables	72.86	(8.05)
12 syllables	66.17	(7.93)
Coordinated		
11 syllables	73.33	(9.07)
12 syllables	66.20	(8.09)
Subject Relatives		
11 syllables	72.92	(16.44)
12 syllables	69.76	(12.54)
Object Relatives		

11 syllables	61.67	(24.33)
12 syllables	70.95	(15.46)

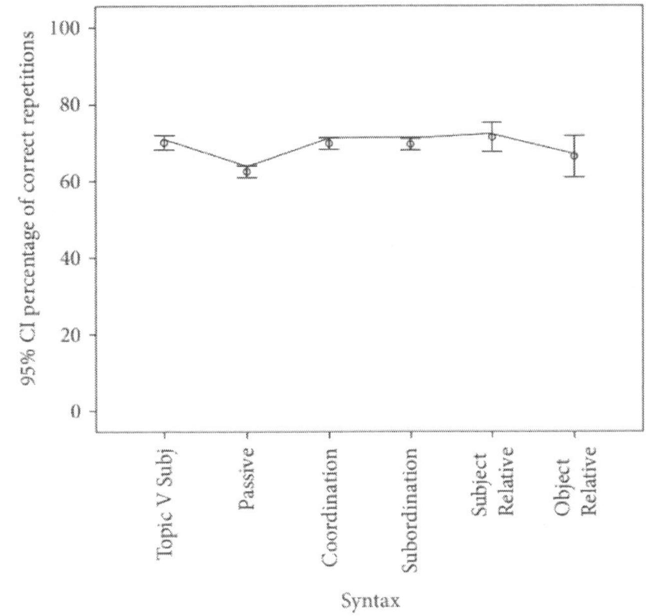

(a)

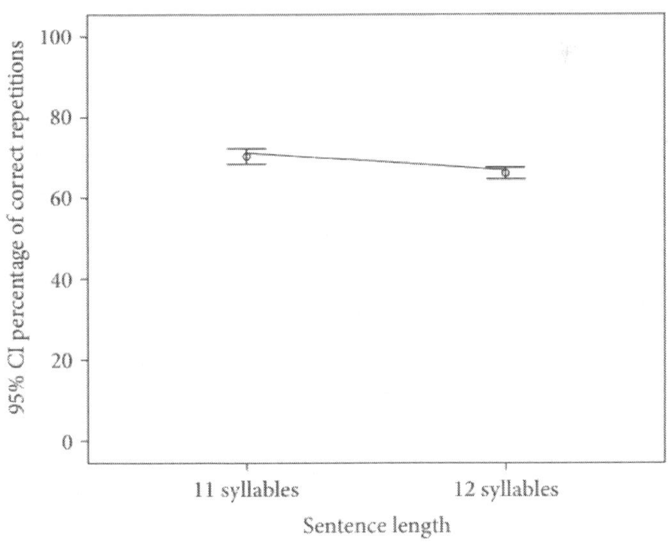

(b)

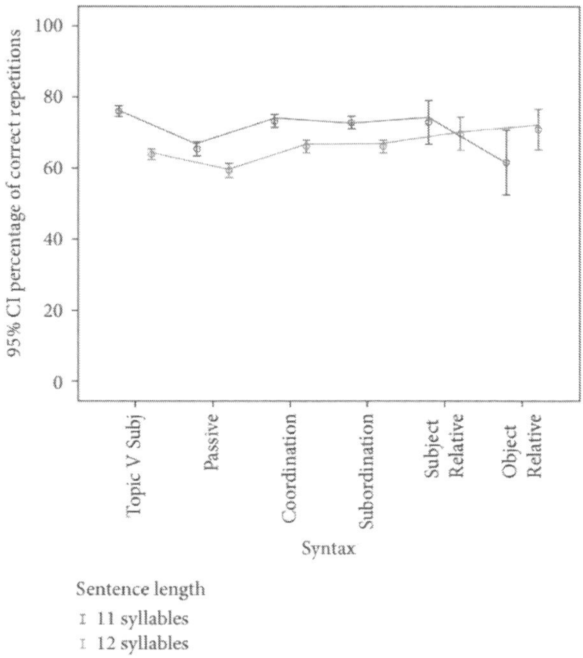

(c)

Figure 2: Mean percentage of correct verbal repetition scores with 95% confidence intervals. (a) Comparison based on syntactic structure. (b) Comparison based on sentence length in syllables. (c) Comparison based on the interaction between syntactic structure and sentence length in syllables.

Secondly, a significant main effect of sentence length was also found, with lower correct verbal repetitions for sentences of 12 syllables of length as compared to sentences of 11 syllables, $F(1, 29) = 11.49$, $p < .002$, and $\eta^2 = .284$, representing a medium effect (see Figure 2(b)).

Finally, the effect of the interaction between both linguistic variables was tested. The results of this analysis indicate that sentence length is interacting significantly with the syntactic structure of the sentence used as a verbal stimulus ((4, 116) = 6.24, $p < .002$, and $\eta^2 = .177$). As can be observed in Figure 2(c), the number of correct repetitions decreases with the increasing length of the sentence, except for Object Relatives. A post hoc analysis of within-subject contrasts for the interaction between syntactic structure and sentence length showed significant effects for all syntactic types ($F(1, 29)$, Passives = 5.96, $p = .021$; Subordinates = 5.40, $p = .027$; Coordinates = 4.57, $p = .041$; Subject Relatives = 6.65, $p = .015$; Object Relatives = 14.77, $p = .001$).

Part of Speech and Sentence Length

Table 5 presents the means with standard deviation of the percentage of correct repetitions per key word based on 30 listeners for open versus closed word classes.

Table 5: Means with standard deviations of the percentage of correct scores for verbal repetition based on the part of speech of the key words and the length of the test sentences.

	Mean	**SD**
Part of speech		
Open	64.08	(7.71)
Closed	69.33	(15.84)
Sentence length		
11 syllables	72.28	(14.83)
12 syllables	66.20	(13.45)
Part of speech sentence length		
Open		
11 syllables	65.17	(7.51)
12 syllables	63.00	(7.88)
Closed		
11 syllables	64.67	(10.08)
12 syllables	74.00	(19.05)
Open word classes: part of speech sentence length		
Adjectives		
11 syllables	75.28	(11.88)
12 syllables	67.67	(5.17)
Adverbs		
11 syllables	78.79	(15.53)
12 syllables	62.99	(8.22)
Nouns		
11 syllables	71.23	(5.80)
12 syllables	67.33	(5.17)
Verbs		
11 syllables	67.78	(8.88)
12 syllables	62.99	(8.22)

First, a repeated measures ANOVA was run using the open/closed word class distinction and the length of the test sentences as within-subjects variables. The results show that the percentage of correct verbal repetitions is significantly affected by the type of part of speech (open/closed) of the key words, $F(1, 29) = 4.55$, $p = .042$, and $\eta^2 = .136$, and by the length of the sentence, $F(1, 29) = 7.6$, $p < .01$, and $\eta^2 = .208$, as well as by the interaction between both of the variables, $F(1, 29) = 19.8$, $p = .001$, and $\eta^2 = .406$.

As can be read from the descriptive statistics in Table 5 and Figure 3, in sentences that are 11 syllables long, higher repetition scores are obtained for adjectives, adverbs, and nouns than for function words. In sentences that are 12 syllables long, a reverse effect occurs, the percentage of correct repetitions for adjectives, adverbs, and nouns being situated within the lower bound of the 95% CI for function words. For the category of verbs, however, the number of correct repetitions is low, regardless of the length of the sentences in which they occur.

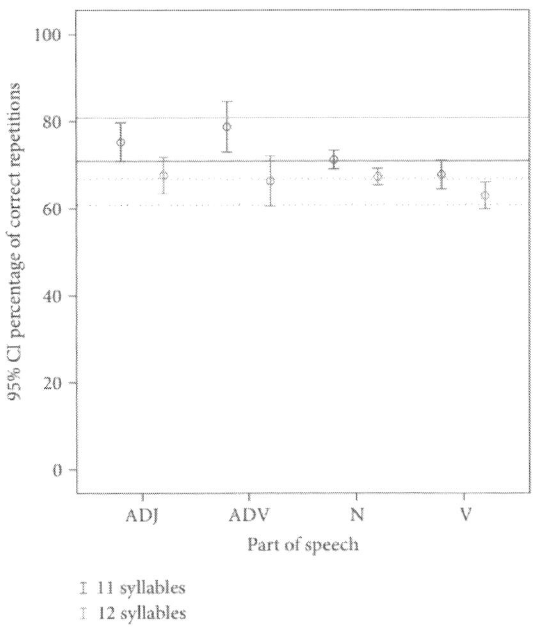

Figure 3: Mean percentage of correct verbal repetition scores with 95% confidence intervals. Comparison based on the part of speech of the key words for lexical categories. ADJ = adjectives, ADV = adverbs, N = nouns, and V = verbs. The dotted and full horizontal lines represent, respectively, the lower and upper bound of the 95% CI for function words (blue lines = 11 syllables; green lines = 12 syllables).

Ease of Listening

Table 6 presents the means with standard deviations of the reaction times in milliseconds in repeating each sentence type based on 30 listeners. A repeated measures ANOVA was run using the syntactic structure and the length have a significant main effect on the reaction times of the listeners ($F(5, 102) = 2.67$, $p = .043$, and $\eta 2 = .084$ for syntax; $F(1, 29) = 10.2$, $p = .003$, and $\eta^2 = .260$ for sentence length) and that there is a significant interaction effect between both linguistic variables ($F(5, 145) = 3.49$, $p = .005$, and $\eta^2 = .108$); see Figure 4.

Table 6: Means with standard deviation of the reaction times in repeating the test sentences in milliseconds based on syntactic structure and length of the test sentences.

	Mean	**SD**
Syntactic structure		
Topic V Subj	8140	(1036)
Passives	8555	(1322)
Subordinated	8555	(975)
Coordinated	8771	(1082)
Subject Relatives	8560	(1638)
Object Relatives	8783	(1426)
Sentence length		
11 syllables	8412	(1095)
12 syllables	8665	(1186)
*Syntactic structure * sentence length*		
Topic V Subj		
11 syllables	8112	(1148)
12 syllables	8168	(928)
Passives		
11 syllables	8584	(1319)
12 syllables	8527	(1347)
Subordinated		
11 syllables	8432	(878)
12 syllables	8678	(1064)
Coordinated		
11 syllables	8652	(972)

12 syllables	8889	(1187)
Subject Relatives		
11 syllables	7931	(980)
12 syllables	9189	(1919)
Object Relatives		
11 syllables	9629	(1629)
12 syllables	8936	(1197)

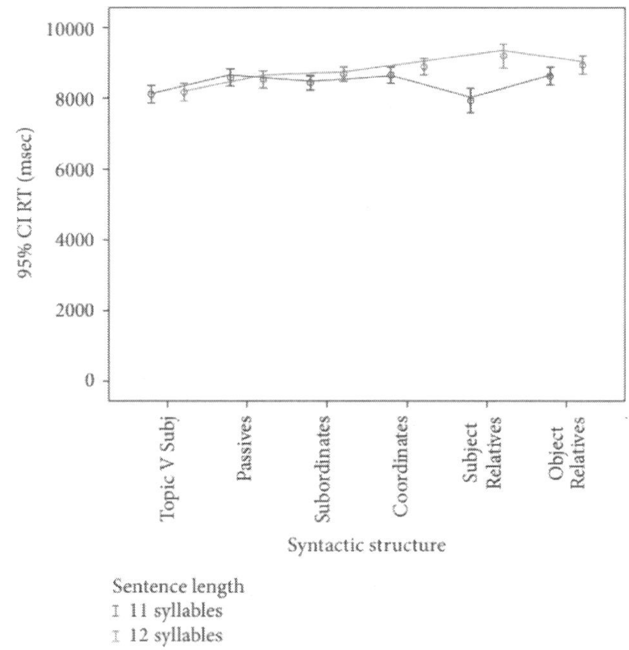

Figure 4: Mean reaction times in repeating the test sentences in milliseconds with 95% confidence intervals. Comparison based on the interaction between syntactic structure and sentence length in syllables.

Post hoc analyses of within-subject contrasts show that Topic Verb Subject sentences require significantly lower reaction times as compared to all other syntactic structures (Passives ($F(1, 29) = 7.68, p = .01$), Subordinates ($F(1, 29) = 5.83, p = .022$), Coordinates ($F(1, 29) = 15.18, p = .001$), Subject Relatives ($F(1, 29) = 4.26, p = .048$), and Object Relatives ($F(1, 29) = 8.46$, $p = .007$)). At the interaction level, no effect of sentence length on reaction times was found for Topic V Subj, Passives, Subordinates, Coordinates, and Object Relatives. Only Subject Relatives revealed to be highly sensitive to sentence length, yielding significantly smaller reaction times for test samples that were 11 syllables long ($F(1, 29) = 7254$, $p = .012$).

DISCUSSION

Our results indicate that language grammar at least partially shapes auditory processing: when confronted with speech stimuli with high linguistic complexity such as passive clauses or Object Relatives, many listeners have difficulties in reconstructing meaningful sentences out of the perceived words. This language-driven aspect of auditory processing becomes noticeable at both the level of accuracy and speed of verbal repetition: while the highest percentage of correct repetition scores is obtained with the sentences that have low syntactic complexity within the test set (Topic Verb Subject structures), the structures with highest syntactic complexity (Object Relative clauses) take most time to be processed. Although syntactic structure has a significant effect on speech perception by its own, it becomes even more pronounced in combination with an increased sentence length. This interaction effect is remarkable given that the difference in length exhibited by the set of test sentences is just 1 syllable. The fact that longer sentences yield significantly lower repetition scores in case of Passives as compared to Topic Verb Subject sentences may be related to the cognitive cost associated with the increased length of the movement path associated with the former structure.

However, our analysis did not reveal any perceptual disadvantage for Subject Relative clauses. If it is indeed the case that the human mind prefers syntactic structures that involve shorter movement over structures with longer—and therefore cognitively more costly—movement paths, this finding is rather unexpected. Relative clauses being generally considered one of the most complex structures in natural language, one would expect them to be associated with a very low repetition accuracy. Yet relative clauses also differ from the other syntactic structures under investigation in that they are typically F(ocus)-marked constructions of which the relativized head noun is standing out in speech (e.g., *de SOKKEN die ze kwijt was, zijn weer terecht*, "the SOCKS that she had lost have been found again," versus *ze was haar sokken VERLOREN maar ze zijn weer terecht*, "she had LOST her socks but they have been found again"). According to well-known theories of focus and syntax-prosody interface [53, 54], an F-marked constituent in syntax is interpreted as new or contrastive information in the context. Experimental studies of auditory processing indicate that language users are sensitive to such focused speech materials: not only do words bearing high stress appear to be easier to process during sentence comprehension, they also direct the listener's attention to important elements in the sentence and enable him to make predictions of upcoming accent locations in the entire sentence. These predictions are taken to facilitate sentence understanding [55]. Although our study does not provide direct evidence to claim that focus-marking influences sentence repetition accuracy, the data analyzed here are certainly compatible with current insights regarding the role of multiple components of language in human speech processing. In artificial intelligence approaches to automated speech recognition, for instance, besides expert knowledge regarding the phonetics, phonotactics, and lexicon of spoken language, syntactic and pragmatic features are typically integrated in the design of particular models and algorithms in view of enhancing speech recognition accuracy [56].

To evaluate the single contribution of syntactic structure to speech repetition accuracy, we may compare the two types of relative clauses within our data set. Subject and Object Relative clauses are taken to show similar focus-marking on the head noun; this implies that differences in repetition accuracy may be taken to result from differences in syntactic complexity between the two categories. This is precisely what comes out of the data analysis, Object Relatives exhibiting significantly lower repetition scores than Subject Relatives. Our results are in line with a vast body of literature showing a rather robust asymmetry in the comprehension of Subject versus Object Relatives, the latter being more difficult to understand and involving longer processing times. For the sake of completeness, we would like to point out that, besides syntactic complexity, other factors may influence the accuracy and processing difficulty of different types of relative clauses as well. Animacy, frequency, or internal make-up of the relativized antecedent may influence relative clause understanding, up to the point where Object Relatives will yield better repetition scores than Subject Relatives. In controlled experiments, for instance, it has been demonstrated that placing an inanimate entity in sentential subject position and an animate entity in the Object Relative clause greatly reduces the difficulty normally associated with Object Relative clauses [57].

As for the effect of the different parts of speech of the key words on verbal repetition accuracy, the reduced performance of listeners with verbs as target words is striking. Contrary to adjectives, adverbs, and nouns, repetition accuracy on verbs is as low as that on closed word classes such as prepositions, conjunctions, determiners, and pronouns. We believe that this may be related to the fact that repetitions of verbs have been flagged as correct if and only if they contained the verbal lexeme carrying all its grammatical morphemes (including tense and person/number agreement with the subject). Dutch verbal inflection being characterized by the frequent use of morphemes with low perceptual salience, repetition mistakes often consisted in the omission of such tense or plural markers. Compare in this respect, for instance, the unstressed syllables and nonsyllabic consonants as -de marking past tense on verbs like irriteerde, "irritated$_{\text{PAST.SG}}$," to the determiner de, "the." In this sense, the perceptual nature of verbal morphemes is not different from that of function words and may therefore explain the observed similarities in repetition performance for both classes of words.

In some cases the omission of these grammatical markers on the verb may even have led to sentences that are wellformed in Dutch (e.g., het vest dat ik van je zus leen is blauw, "the jacket that I am borrowing$_{\text{1.SG.PRES}}$ from your sister is blue," instead of het vest dat ik van je zus leende is blauw, "the jacket that I borrowed$_{\text{1.SG.PAST}}$ from your sister is blue"). The observed similarity in perceptual difficulty between bound and unbound grammatical morphemes is a characteristic that Dutch shares with other Germanic languages such as English. In Romance languages such as Italian, verbal inflections are typically vocalic in nature (e.g., Maria canta$_{\text{PRES.3.SG.}}$, "Mary sings") and are therefore expected to trigger less repetition errors. Psycholinguistic research presents experimental evidence in support of the claim that vowels are indeed more perceptually salient than consonants [58]. In atypically developing children, this perceptual factor of morphology has been taken to account for differences in verbal production accuracy: due to the fact that English verb endings are perceptually less salient than their Italian counterparts, Englishspeaking children with specific language impairment have a harder time acquiring verbal morphology than their Italianspeaking peers [59]. Whether similar perceptual properties of morphemes may be invoked to explain the reduced repetition accuracy of verbs in Dutch speech audiometric testing contexts should be further investigated in a contrastive setting including speech stimuli and native listeners of both types of languages.

Finally, by measuring the reaction times that listeners need to repeat each of the test sentences, we intended to shed some light on the potential differences in listening effort associated with the understanding of sentences with different linguistic complexity. In this respect, our study offers some interesting outcomes: for speech understanding in noise, earlier studies were able to find increased reaction times at particular measuring points during sentence processing indicating an increase in local processing costs triggered by syntactic complexity [21]. Our data show that an effect of syntactic complexity on reaction times also exists at the level of the entire sentence. Prolonged reaction times with relative clauses as compared to Topic Verb Subject sentences may be taken to reflect increased processing times associated with increasing syntactic complexity. Interestingly, longer Object Relative clauses do not need more time to be processed than shorter ones; bearing in mind that they triggered more repetition errors than other syntactic structures, this seems to indicate that whereas pragmatic salience may have a beneficial influence on listening effort, it does not necessarily favor perceptive accuracy.

For the present study, only young hearing participants were recruited. For hearing impaired listeners, and even more so in the case of elderly individuals, the increased reaction times that are associated with understanding syntactically complex sentences such as Object Relatives may be expected to be even more pronounced as more cognitive effort is needed to fill in missing parts of the auditory information leaving less resources to process syntax. A recent study using an eye-tracking paradigm points in this direction: when confronted with linguistically complex sentences, the eye fixations of hearing impaired listeners toward a target picture which matches the acoustically presented sentence are significantly longer than in normal-hearing listeners. Even at high levels of speech intelligibility hearing impaired patients are shown to spend more time processing sentences [43].

Taken together, these findings may have important implications for the clinical practice. Firstly, they illustrate that perceptual accuracy measured in terms of correct verbal repetitions may well represent just one aspect of functional hearing. In spite of good levels of speech intelligibility, the cognitive demands imposed by particular linguistic contexts in combination with hearing loss may lead to suboptimal functional hearing in day-to-day adverse listening situations. In this respect, the duration of sentence processing may reflect the contribution of nonauditory factors to the "ease of language understanding" in the sense of Rönnberg et al. [60].

Secondly, our findings confirm other similar analyses indicating that the choice of test materials used to measure speech perception performance has an important effect on the outcomes [61]. In case speech materials with low linguistic complexity are used, the observed hearing performance accuracy may indicate a considerable benefit obtained from a hearing aid or a cochlear implant while the subjective evaluation by the patient is dissatisfactory

[62]. In a recent study [63], it was shown that self-assessment of the ability to perform in particular listening situations significantly correlated with speech perception measured by means of a sentence repetition task while no such correlation was found with phoneme discrimination [63]. If linguistic factors indeed make an important contribution to subjective hearing benefits, the use of test sentences with varying degrees of syntactic complexity may provide useful information with respect to the functional hearing of the patient.

CONCLUSION

In current speech audiometric test settings, the hearing performance of patients is typically measured by calculating the number of correct repetitions of a speech stimulus. In this study we have investigated if sentence repetition in noise is influenced by morpholexical constraints such as the part of speech of the target word, on the one hand, and by syntactic constraints such as the structural complexity of the utterance serving as a natural linguistic context by which this word is surrounded, on the other hand. The outcomes of our study showed that variation in verbal repetition accuracy is at least partially influenced by the linguistic make-up of the sentence: at the lexical level, we found that repetition scores are significantly lower with verbs than with nouns, adjectives, or adverbs but similar to prepositions, conjunctions, determiners, and pronouns. The reduced repetition performance for verbs and function words is probably best explained by the similarities in the perceptual nature of verbal morphology and function words in the Dutch language.

At the level of syntax, six categories of structures were compared exhibiting different structural complexity according to the length of the movement path of one or more constituents in the sentence. An overall effect of syntactic structure on speech repetition accuracy was found. The lowest number of correct repetitions was obtained with passive sentences, reflecting the cognitive cost of processing a complex structure in which the semantic object of the verb has been moved out of its base position. The fact that no perceptual disadvantage was found for relative clauses is unexpected but probably best explained by the fact that relativized nouns are generally focus-marked items and are therefore perceptually standing out in the sentence. When such pragmatic factors are controlled for, the negative effect of syntactic complexity becomes noticeable again: worse repetition scores are obtained with syntactically more complex Object Relative clauses as compared to less complex Subject Relative clauses.

Finally, by measuring reaction times in repeating each test sentence, we were able to show that processing speed is dependent upon the same syntactic features. In this respect, similar reaction times with Object Relative clauses as compared to less complex sentence types indicate that whereas pragmatic salience may favor listening effort, perceptive accuracy seems to be mainly determined by syntactic complexity.

Taken together, our findings may have important implications for the audiological practice. Nonauditory factors such as lexical and syntactic features of the target language system may increase the cognitive demands to process sentences in noise. In combination with hearing loss, this may lead to suboptimal functional hearing in day-to-day listening situations even for patients with good speech discrimination outcomes. In this sense, the use of test sentences with varying degrees of syntactic complexity may provide useful information to subjective benefits of particular hearing devices for the patient.

Funding

The research has received funding from the Netherlands Organisation for Scientific Research, within the NWO Alfa Meerwaarde funding scheme (Martine Coene), a Ph.D. fellowship of the Research Foundation Flanders, FWO Vlaanderen, Belgium (Stefanie Krijger), and the European Union's Seventh Framework Program for Research, Technological Development and Demonstration under FP7-PEOPLE-2012-IAPP project "Hearing Minds," Grant Agreement no. 324401 (Paul J. Govaerts).

ACKNOWLEDGMENTS

The authors wish to thank Renske Berkmoes for her help in collecting the data from Dutch native listeners as part of a M.A. research project, jointly supervised at VU Amsterdam by Martine Coene and Paul J. Govaerts.

REFERENCES

1. E. C. Cherry, "Some experiments on the recognition of speech, with one and with two ears," *The Journal of the Acoustical Society of America*, vol. 25, no. 5, pp. 975–979, 1953.
2. E. C. Cherry and W. K. Taylor, "Some further experiments upon the recognition of speech, with one and with two ears," *The Journal of the Acoustical Society of America*, vol. 26, no. 4, pp. 554–559, 1954.
3. C. Smits and J. M. Festen, "The interpretation of speech reception threshold data in normal-hearing and hearing-impaired listeners: steady-state noise," *Journal of the Acoustical Society of America*, vol. 130, no. 5, pp. 2987–2998, 2011.
4. D. R. Moore, M. Edmondson-Jones, P. Dawes et al., "Relation between speech-in-noise threshold, hearing loss and cognition from 40–69 years of age," *PLoS ONE*, vol. 9, no. 9, Article ID e107720, 2014.
5. J. S. Bradley and H. Sato, "The intelligibility of speech in elementary school classrooms," *Journal of the Acoustical Society of America*, vol. 123, no. 4, pp. 2078–2086, 2008.
6. M. Fallon, S. E. Trehub, and B. A. Schneider, "Children's perception of speech in multitalker babble," *Journal of the Acoustical Society of America*, vol. 108, no. 6, pp. 3023–3029, 2000.
7. A. Stuart, G. D. Givens, L. J. Walker, and S. Elangovan, "Auditory temporal resolution in normal-hearing preschool children revealed by word recognition in continuous and interrupted noise," *The Journal of the Acoustical Society of America*, vol. 119, no. 4, pp. 1946–1949, 2006.
8. S. Kortlang, M. Mauermann, and S. D. Ewert, "Suprathreshold auditory processing deficits in noise: effects of hearing loss and age," *Hearing Research*, vol. 331, pp. 27–40, 2016.
9. T. Schoof and S. Rosen, "The role of auditory and cognitive factors in understanding speech in noise by normal-hearing older listeners," *Frontiers in Aging Neuroscience*, vol. 6, article 307, 2014.
10. S. L. Smith and M. K. Pichora-Fuller, "Associations between speech understanding and auditory and visual tests of verbal working memory: effects of linguistic complexity, task, age, and hearing loss," *Frontiers in Psychology*, vol. 6, article 1394, 2015.
11. M. A. Akeroyd, "Are individual differences in speech reception related to individual differences in cognitive ability? A survey of twenty

experimental studies with normal and hearing-impaired adults," *International Journal of Audiology*, vol. 47, supplement 2, pp. S53–S71, 2008.

12. P. A. Tun, V. A. Williams, B. J. Small, and E. R. Hafter, "The effects of aging on auditory processing and cognition," *American Journal of Audiology*, vol. 21, no. 2, pp. 344–350, 2012.
13. J. Besser, *The connected ear. Influences of cognitive and auditory-temporal processing on speech understanding in adverse conditions [Ph.D. thesis]*, Vrije Universiteit Amsterdam, Amsterdam, Netherlands, 2015.
14. R. M. Warren, C. J. Obusek, and J. M. Ackroff, "Auditory induction: perceptual synthesis of absent sounds," *Science*, vol. 176, no. 4039, pp. 1149–1151, 1972.
15. A. M. Liberman, F. S. Cooper, D. P. Shankweiler, and M. Studdert-Kennedy, "Perception of the speech code," *Psychological Review*, vol. 74, no. 6, pp. 431–461, 1967.
16. W. F. Ganong, "Phonetic categorization in auditory word perception," *Journal of Experimental Psychology: Human Perception and Performance*, vol. 6, no. 1, pp. 110–125, 1980.
17. M. Coene, A. van der Lee, and P. J. Govaerts, "Spoken word recognition errors in speech audiometry: a measure of hearing performance?" *BioMed Research International*, vol. 2015, Article ID 932519, 8 pages, 2015.
18. W. O. Olsen, D. J. Van Tasell, and C. E. Speaks, "Phoneme and word recognition for words in isolation and in sentences," *Ear and Hearing*, vol. 18, no. 3, pp. 175–188, 1997.
19. J. Benichov, L. C. Cox, P. A. Tun, and A. Wingfield, "Word recognition within a linguistic context: effects of age, hearing acuity, verbal ability, and cognitive function," *Ear and Hearing*, vol. 33, no. 2, pp. 250–256, 2012.
20. A. Wingfield, S. L. McCoy, J. E. Peelle, P. A. Tun, and L. C. Cox, "Effects of adult aging and hearing loss on comprehension of rapid speech varying in syntactic complexity," *Journal of the American Academy of Audiology*, vol. 17, no. 7, pp. 487–497, 2006.
21. R. Carroll and E. Ruigendijk, "The effects of syntactic complexity on processing sentences in noise," *Journal of Psycholinguistic Research*, vol. 42, no. 2, pp. 139–159, 2013.

22. V. Uslar, E. Ruigendijk, C. Hamann, T. Brand, and B. Kollmeier, "How does linguistic complexity influence intelligibility in a German audiometric sentence intelligibility test?" *International Journal of Audiology*, vol. 50, no. 9, pp. 621–631, 2011.
23. F. Volpato and M. Vernice, "The production of relative clauses by Italian cochlear-implanted and hearing children," *Lingua*, vol. 139, pp. 39–67, 2014.
24. E. L. J. George, J. M. Festen, and T. Houtgast, "Factors affecting masking release for speech in modulated noise for normal-hearing and hearing-impaired listeners," *Journal of the Acoustical Society of America*, vol. 120, no. 4, pp. 2295–2311, 2006.
25. E. B. Goldstein, *Sensation and Perception*, Wadsworth-Thomson, Pacific Grove, Calif, USA, 2002.
26. L. Ortega, "Syntactic complexity measures and their relationship to L2 proficiency: a research synthesis of college-level L2 writing," *Applied Linguistics*, vol. 24, no. 4, pp. 492–518, 2003.
27. B. Mondorf, "Support for more-support," in *Determinants of Grammatical Variation in English*, G. Rohdenburg and B. Mondorf, Eds., pp. 251–304, 2003.
28. M. Chen and K. Zechner, "Computing and evaluating syntactic complexity features for automated scoring of spontaneous non-native speech," in *Proceedings of the 49th Annual Meeting of the Association for Computational Linguistics*, pp. 722–731, Portland, Ore, USA, June 2011.
29. F. Ferreira, "Effects of length and syntactic complexity on initiation times for prepared utterances," *Journal of Memory and Language*, vol. 30, no. 2, pp. 210–233, 1991.
30. B. M. Szmrecsanyi, "On operationalizing syntactic complexity," *JADT 2004: 7es Journées Internationales d'Analyse Statistique des Données Textuelles*, pp. 1031–1038, 2004.
31. M. Roll, J. Frid, and M. Horne, "Measuring syntactic complexity in spontaneous spoken Swedish," *Language and Speech*, vol. 50, no. 2, pp. 227–245, 2007.
32. N. Chomsky, *The Logical Structure of Linguistic Theory*, Chicago University Press, Chicago, Ill, USA, 1975.
33. A. Carnie, *Modern Syntax: A Coursebook*, Cambridge University Press, Cambridge, UK, 2011.

34. N. Chomsky, *The Minimalist Program*, MIT Press, Cambridge, Mass, USA, 1995.
35. C. J. W. Zwart, "'Shortest steps' vs. 'fewest steps'," in *Minimal Ideas. Syntactic Studies in the Minimalist Framework*, W. Abraham, S. D. Epstein, H. Thrainsson, and C. J. W. Zwart, Eds., pp. 239–261, John Benjamins, Amsterdam, Netherlands, 1996.
36. J. Hawkins, *A Performance Theory of Order and Constituency*, Cambridge University Press, Cambridge, UK, 1994.
37. M. P. Marcus, *Theory of Syntactic Recognition for Natural Languages*, MIT Press, Boston, Mass, USA, 1980.
38. E. Gibson, "Linguistic complexity: locality of syntactic dependencies," *Cognition*, vol. 68, no. 1, pp. 1–76, 1998.
39. G. Fanselow, R. Kliegl, and M. Schlesewksy, "Processing difficulty and principles of grammar," in *Constraints on Language: Aging, Grammar and Memory*, S. Kemper and R. Kliegl, Eds., pp. 170–200, Springer, Berlin, Germany, 1999.
40. M. K. Pichora-Fuller, "Cognitive aging and auditory information processing," *International Journal of Audiology*, vol. 42, no. 2, pp. 26–32, 2003.
41. P. A. Tun, S. McCoy, and A. Wingfield, "Aging, hearing acuity, and the attentional costs of effortful listening," *Psychology and Aging*, vol. 24, no. 3, pp. 761–766, 2009.
42. A. Wingfield, P. A. Tun, and S. L. McCoy, "Hearing loss in older adulthood: what it is and how it interacts with cognitive performance," *Current Directions in Psychological Science*, vol. 14, no. 3, pp. 144–148, 2005.
43. D. Wendt, B. Kollmeier, and T. Brand, "How hearing impairment affects sentence comprehension: using eye fixations to investigate the duration of speech processing," *Trends in Hearing*, vol. 19, pp. 1–18, 2015.
44. A. Cutler, "Phonological cues to open- and closed class words," *Journal of Psycholinguistic Research*, vol. 22, no. 2, pp. 109–130, 1993.
45. A. Cutler and D. M. Carter, "The predominance of strong initial syllables in the English vocabulary," *Computer Speech and Language*, vol. 2, no. 3-4, pp. 133–142, 1987.
46. A. Waibel, *Prosody and Speech Recognition*, Pitman, London, UK, 1988.

47. A. Cutler and D. G. Norris, "The role of strong syllables in segmentation for lexical access," *Journal of Experimental Psychology: Human Perception and Performance*, vol. 14, no. 1, pp. 113–121, 1988.
48. A. Salasoo and D. B. Pisoni, "Perception of open and closed class words in fluent speech," in *Research on Speech Perception*, Progress Report 7, pp. 187–195, University of Indiana, 1981.
49. A. Cutler and S. Butterfield, "Rhythmic cues to speech segmentation: evidence from juncture misperception," *Journal of Memory and Language*, vol. 31, no. 2, pp. 218–236, 1992.
50. M. F. Garrett, "Words and sentence perception," in *Handbook of Sensory Physiology, Vol VIII: Perception*, R. Held, H. J. Leibowitz, and H. L. Teuber, Eds., pp. 611–625, Springer, Berlin, Germany, 1978.
51. N. Oostdijk, "Het Corpus Gesproken Nederlands: veelzijdig onderzoeksinstrumentvooro.a.taalkundigentaalenspraaktechnologisch onderzoek," *Link*, vol. 14, no. 1, pp. 3–6, 2003.
52. K. Daemers, M. Yperman, C. De Beukelaer, G. De Saegher, G. De Ceulaer, and P. J. Govaerts, "Normative data of the A§E® discrimination and identification tests in preverbal children," *Cochlear Implants International*, vol. 7, no. 2, pp. 107–116, 2006.
53. E. Selkirk, *Phonology and Syntax: The Relation between Sound and Structure*, MIT Press, Cambridge, Mass, USA, 1984.
54. E. Selkirk, "Sentence prosody: intonation, stress, and phrasing," in *Handbook of Phonological Theory*, J. Goldsmith, Ed., pp. 550–569, Basil Blackwell, Oxford, UK, 1995.
55. A. Cutler and D. J. Foss, "On the role of sentence stress in sentence processing," *Language and Speech*, vol. 20, no. 1, pp. 1–10, 1977.
56. M. A. Anusuya and S. A. Katty, "Speech recognition by machine. A review," *International Journal of Computer Science and Information Security*, vol. 6, no. 3, pp. 181–205, 2009.
57. M. J. Traxler, R. K. Morris, and R. E. Seely, "Processing subject and object relative clauses: evidence from eye movements," *Journal of Memory and Language*, vol. 47, no. 1, pp. 69–90, 2002.
58. L. B. Leonard, K. K. McGregor, and G. D. Allen, "Grammatical morphology and speech perception in children with specific language impairment," *Journal of Speech and Hearing Research*, vol. 35, no. 5, pp. 1076–1085, 1992.

59. L. B. Leonard, "Language learnability and specific language impairment in children," *Applied Psycholinguistics*, vol. 10, no. 2, pp. 179–202, 1989.

60. J. Rönnberg, T. Lunner, A. Zekveld et al., "The Ease of Language Understanding (ELU) model: theoretical, empirical, and clinical advances," *Frontiers in Systems Neuroscience*, vol. 7, article 31, 2013.

61. V. N. Uslar, R. Carroll, M. Hanke et al., "Development and evaluation of a linguistically and audiologically controlled sentence intelligibility test," *Journal of the Acoustical Society of America*, vol. 134, no. 4, pp. 3039–3056, 2013.

62. G. H. Saunders, T. H. Chisolm, and H. B. Abrams, "Measuring hearing aid outcomes-not as easy as it seems," *Journal of Rehabilitation Research & Development*, vol. 42, no. 4, pp. 157–168, 2005.

63. A. Heinrich, H. Henshaw, and M. A. Ferguson, "The relationship of speech intelligibility with hearing sensitivity, cognition, and perceived hearing difficulties varies for different speech perception tests," *Frontiers in Psychology*, vol. 6, article 782, 2015.

Index

O

P

Q

R

S

T

V

W